SPECTERS OF LIBERATION

✣

SUNY Series in Radical Social and Political Theory

Roger S. Gottlieb, Editor

SPECTERS OF LIBERATION

GREAT REFUSALS IN THE NEW WORLD ORDER

⚜

MARTIN J. BECK MATUŠTÍK

STATE UNIVERSITY OF NEW YORK PRESS

Cover: The Dismantling of the Berlin Wall. An East Berliner pounds years of frustration into the concrete of the Berlin Wall, on the day after the Wall fell, on November 9, 1989. © David Turnley, Detroit Free Press, Blackstar.

Published by
State University of New York Press, Albany

© 1998 State University of New York

For information, address State University of New York Press,
State University Plaza, Albany, N.Y. 12246

Production by M. R. Mulholland
Marketing by Hannah J. Hazen

Library of Congress Cataloging-in-Publication Data

Matuštík, Martin Joseph Beck, 1957–
    Specters of liberation : great refusals in the new world order /
Martin J. Beck Matuštík.
        p.   cm. — (SUNY series in radical social and political
theory)
    Includes bibliographical references (p.   ) and index.
    ISBN 0-7914-3691-8 (HC : acid free). — ISBN 0-7914-3692-6 (PB :
acid free)
    1. Postmodernism—Social aspects. 2. Democracy. 3. Radicalism.
I. Title. II. Series.
HM73.M385 1997
300'.1—dc21   97-17277
                                                                        CIP

10 9 8 7 6 5 4 3 2 1

In memory of my mother, Magdalena,
who refused hopelessness against overwhelming odds

✤

CONTENTS

PREFACE

October 11, 1992 brings to an end the 500th year of the Old World Order, sometimes called the Colombian era of world history, or the Vasco de Gama era, depending on which adventurers bent on plunder got there first. Or "the 500-year Reich," to borrow the title of a commemorative volume that compares the methods and ideologies of the Nazis with those of the European invaders who subjugated most of the world [Höffer et al., eds., *Das Fünfhundert-jährige Reich*]. The major theme of this Old World Order was a confrontation between the conquerors and the conquered on a global scale. It has taken various forms, and been given different names: imperialism, neocolonialism, the North-South conflict, core versus periphery, G-7 (the 7 leading state capitalist industrial societies) and their satellites versus the rest. Or, more simply, Europe's conquest of the world.

—Noam Chomsky, *Year 501*

✤ ✤ ✤

The Enemy is the common denominator of all doing and undoing. And the Enemy is not identical with actual communism or actual capitalism—he is, in both cases, the real spectre of liberation.

—Herbert Marcuse, *One-Dimensional Man*

✤ ✤ ✤

Dissent and Democracy as Specters of Liberation

I am often asked how I, who was once an anti-Communist political dissenter in my native Czechoslovakia, have become a critic of real existing democracies. The Communist authorities admonished me in 1977: "put up or shut up!" I fled into exile. Later I was given another patriotic advice, now in order to put in place the arrogance of an ungrateful U.S. immigrant: "love it or leave it!" After 1989, in the New World Order (NWO), 'It' (as in, 'Coke is It') tends to encompass both sides of the deposed Iron Curtain. I face at once an existential and theoretical difficulty. This study offers an installment on a response I would like to elaborate not alone but with others who are troubled in similar existentially material situations.

The NWO is both a mere rhetorical imaginary and a frightening historical prospect. It begins minimally with 1492 and the Columbian conquest of the so-

called New World. The Nazi Holocaust, the Cold War period, and finally the post-Communist nightmare of this century are being followed by a global conquest in the name of liberal democracy, just as in the Columbian era the robbery of gold and lands was accomplished under the name of the Cross. The rhetoric projects this internationalization of the liberal credo *as a gospel and eschaton of justice and liberty realized. Yet the 500-year commemorations (1992) of* La Conquista *are instructive not for the parades but the refusals of the imagined and threatened* ordo. *Unmasking this period as the 'Five Hundred Year Empire,' various groups refuse its real economic immiseration, political oppression, cultural marginalization, and racial and ethnic cleansing. The advice "love it, or leave it" had genocidal consequences for entire populations colonized by White Euro-Americans. The oppressed found neither the chance to love 'It' nor the option to leave 'It': if they were not gassed or maimed, they were enslaved, used up, converted, assimilated.*

The resisting survivors in various communities begin to frame another response: "we are here, we love it, we stay, therefore we leave 'It'!" The two axes of their great exodus/refusals are, one, dissent from the established order, its canons and formal promises, and, two, struggle for radical, multicultural, and socioeconomic democracy. I hope that these pages resonate with and contribute to this poem of the oppressed—with their hope of at long last finding a 'home' in a changed world.

✦✦✦

Two related trends in recent sociopolitical theory are of particular significance. The first trend brings the concerns of some critical (e.g., Gould, Ingram, Kellner, Marsh, Outlaw, Postone) and postmodern (e.g., Butler, Cornell, Derrida, Jameson, Jaggar, Martin, Young) social theorists closer than expected. Without unhelpful divisions or tendentious labeling and without blurring their methodological differences, it is fair to say that thinkers in both groups share suspicions of the viability and justice of the projected NWO. The second trend splits some critical and postmodern theorists into those who emphasize the formal and those who emphasize the substantive in their approaches. Without blurring methodological differences, some in each group tend towards either politically liberal (e.g., Habermas, Rawls, and Rorty) or politically and economically radical (e.g., Ingram, Laclau, Marsh, Martin, Mouffe, and Young) democracy. My interest lies in searching for democracy, viewed as a communicative, inclusively participatory form of life, not in academic polemics between the received binary divisions that pit critical against postmodern social theorists; in discerning positions, not in judging authors; in dialogue on the sociopolitical options for the present age, not in protecting schools for their own sake.

This study draws on critical and postmodern social theorists alike and is inspired by the persistence of the Marcusean Great Refusal. This persistent passion reflects, however, my groping, and I apologize for any incomplete or one-sided treatment of people's theoretical positions or lives. If my story is sound, then the new either/or—either economically neoliberal and politically liberal or politico-economically radical democracy—takes on much greater social significance than established borders between the modern and postmodern. If this is so, then forms of transgression and critical agency can, maybe ought to, enter into an alliance against the rhetoric and realities of the NWO. The issue is no longer whether or not to seek one revolutionary agency of Refusal. *We* must ask how multiple refusals may enhance chances for a more just world. Social analysis and allied struggles for justice (critical post/modern theory and practice) draw on multidimensional resources. There is time for clowning and refusal, performance and determinate action, singular transgressions and agencies in coalitions and solidarity, play and revolution. Their joint venture (a multidialectic) conserves subversive hope for justice, indeed, raises specters of liberation.

A study like this one would be silly if it claimed to be exhaustive. It need not posit closed totality behind either the deployed rhetoric of the NWO (a drive for unidimensionality) or behind its great refusals (one hegemonic struggle against oppressive hegemonies). Even without a grand or self-transparent totalizer, refusals—transgression and agency, dissent and democracy—can raise specters of liberation. Hope could learn to be soberly self-critical of any romantically idealist and lyrically revolutionary reason. Yet even a psychoanalytically sober hope need not relapse into tired cynicism. Hope could act like an obstinate revolutionary—dissenting from an unimaginatively positivist and conformistically materialist reality. Alert to its subjected and disciplined and abject histories, to its unconscious and tragic underside, hope need not inscribe its desire for recognition and justice with proselytizing fanaticism. This hope stands against the naïve idealism of a radical neoconservative revolutionary and the disciplinary materialism of a neoliberal conservative. This hope acts disjunctively—refusing that calculated cynicism which gave us efficient death camps, right- and left-wing terror, ethnic and racial and gender cleansing, and a multinational colonization of labor and resources. If these are historically contingent forms of ways individuals and communities become subjected and abjected and disciplined, these forms cannot be the original sins of identity, language, or the human social condition. That insight, shared by a new generation of critical post/modern social theorists as well as by dissenting individuals and resisting communities, also belongs to the great refusals of the NWO today. On its margins, hope raises specters of liberation.

What's the 'Existential' Got To Do With It?
Or: Why Am I Such a Theoretical Fossil?

I lay my cards on the table, even if I cannot play the full deck here. Perhaps my disclosure can delay the departure of an incredulous reader a bit longer. And getting delayed in a good conversation, maybe the reader will recognize having followed somewhat similar paths even if with different means, or, better, will claim to have already made some of my arguments.

If at the beginning was abjection and fall, then identity formation, linguistic interaction, and social institutions are human's original sin. All recognition is thus always already misrecognition. If racial hatred and patriarchy and unjustly uneven development of individuals and social groups are all variously inscribed into the very presocialized human drives, then the NWO is our best option to keep them at bay: it satisfies the useless want of recognition. Let me assume that the need for recognition is not a useless passion and that siblinghood need not become social terror. While humans may not make very good gods—we know that from mythologies of divinities and church histories—there is nothing in human history or biology that limits our finite possibilities by our historically disastrous forms of life. If distributions of finitude and scarcity are contingent, then the death struggle for recognition is a derivative performance rather than a defining aspect of human needs. Abjection, reification, disciplinary society appear all but counterintuitively justified as foundational or quasi-transcendental reality principles of identity formation, linguistic interaction, and institutions. The need for mutual recognition cannot be posited as always already a failed reality of who we are, a prosthetic god.

Actual dissent and resistance by individuals and communities may not but recognize first the need for mutual recognition as an existentially material need. The sociology which projects abject or disciplinary socialization into human drives cannot critically explain how one in fact refuses the established order at all. Against the historically socialized performance principle of the NWO (contingent reality principle) existential performativity clarifies the very possibility of dissent and resistance as well as the need and possibility of mutual recognition. The 'existential' need not, indeed cannot be ascertained at the expense of what is social, historical, and communicative about human existence; yet existential performativity and socially constructed freedom need not disregard the psychoanalytic dimensions of socialization. I will explain by existential performativity that in virtue of which both one-day-old infants and adults individualized via socialization—in varied degrees—may socially bond with and yet resist the other (whether lovingly or out of a desire for liberation). Existential performativity marks that dimension of refusals without which hope and emancipation are not imaginable. What cannot be imagined, thought, and invented, has no historical instantiation either. The attempt to introduce radical democratic recognition and justice into existence would then be a useless passion, hence a terror, too. But I have imbibed too much in Central European tragic irony and humor to be able to take such a seriously posturing conclusion seriously. And that is my deck of cards, viz., why after all these years I am still so 'existential' in my critical theorizing.

Book-Movements

I examine in nine chapters some possible resources of refusal today:

1. The need for recognition expresses not only group claims to ethical authenticity or liberal claims to moral autonomy. Today's need enlivens complex struggles for cultural and political, social and economic, antiracist and antipatriarchal forms of life. What is foreshadowed in this chapter becomes increasingly explicit in what follows in chapters six, eight, and nine.
2. The possibility of struggles on behalf of a fully just recognition assumes an existence of individuals capable of dissent. This competence is safeguarded neither by traditions nor by formal procedures alone, otherwise one could not legitimately dissent from either of them.
3. Dissensus makes little political sense as a nominalist transgression of all normative or universal concerns. Democracy for our times calls for a revolutionary multicultural enlightenment. Many a thinker and activist jointly unmask the identity- and capital-logic of the NWO. This task invites a new political coalition among critical and postmodern social theorists.
4. This collaborative venture in critical post/modern social theory solicits radical critique and democracy. Radical critical theorists can join with radical deconstructionists to raise the specters of a world that would be free. These specters, in turn, empower a consistent deconstruction and invigorate a critical social theory without apologies.
5. A multicultural enlightenment refuses Eurocentric models of critique and democracy: a critical theory of radical democracy is performed from the body and social margins, thereby sustaining hope given for the sake of those without hope. The body performativity complements the formal-pragmatic performativity of speech. Thus, a generalized postconventional ethics becomes a more concrete and radical asymmetrical reciprocity.
6. Communities formed in resistance, in order to curb regressions to a nationalism of conquest and cleansing, learn how to safeguard ongo-

ing existential competence for democratic dissent. They welcome hybrid identities and difference; and they strive for broad coalitional politics and even solidary bonds with struggles for justice other than their own local solidarity.

7. Pure transgression without critical agency can become empty; agency incapable of meeting the need for dissent may collapse into the status quo. Existential and sociopolitical refusals are more dialectical. Body-politics can keep procedural democracy in check against oppressive, racist, and patriarchal consensus. And democratic agency empowers singular acts of dissent to join in the ethics and politics of difference and broader coalitions.

8. The aesthetics of dissenting and democratic existence gives rise to complex sociopolitical aesthetics of resistance and, in turn, to different forms of self-limiting existential and democratic revolutions. The question of violence and nonviolence should be viewed in relation to the radical democratic means and aims of disobedient and revolutionary dissent.

9. To end with a call for existential democracy is not an embarrassing relapse to an apolitical inwardness or a decisionist—left or right—fascism. One finds democratic refigurations of existential categories in early twentieth-century attempts to join critical social and existential theory. Such refigurations were central to the East European dissent that led to the revolutions of 1989. They gain ascendancy in recent critical race and gender theory and in sociopolitical and economic critiques of neocolonialism. Liberation theory and praxis recapture dissent and democracy as the two axes of great refusals in the NWO. Refusals invent and bring into actuality democracy as anticolonial coalition and postcolonial solidarity.

Note on Style

I heard recently a professional philosopher at a cocktail party lambast those who mix theoretical arguments with political and autobiographical narratives as bad taste and bad philosophy to boot. If unexamined life is still not worth living, then the above is a prescription for living such a life or for philosophizing that has nothing to contribute to living. I decline the offer to bifurcate myself in that fashion, joining a large company of bad philosophers in bad taste to converse with. Let the dead bury the dead! This book speaks explicitly in two voices, which are visually demarcated; this book therefore shifts gears between a theoretical and a political and even personal style. I found it fitting to let both coexist in their respective desires for recognition. In addition, various voices interrupt one another in the text in order to escape academic and market pressures as well as attempts to subdue them by the mastering author or an overzealous book reviewer, both of whom live under these same pressures. Finally, since I do not believe in *sui generis* geniuses or authorial stars, I seek coalitions and hope for solidarity of multiple voices that address my own.

'Black' and 'White' are used as names, not as essences or adjectives describing an actual color of one's skin. *We* and *us* indicate concrete rather than generalized scope.

ACKNOWLEDGMENTS

I am influenced by people close to me, as well as by people I remember with-out having known them personally. My grandfather from my mother's side, Natan Beck, was a legend to me, narrated in bits and pieces of memory by his two children (my mother Magdalena and my uncle Ernest), my father Radislav, my older brother Pavel, and the family friends who remember Natan as a skillful and sought-out physician in the small Slovak village of Myjava. It is said that his immediate family was saved from an imminent transport to Auschwitz by a local Slovak guardsman, responsible for rounding up Jews, because Natan cared for his seriously ill wife. I was told stories about my mother's family's struggle to evade transports, about their hiding in a horse stall with help from a Slovak Christian family, and about Grandpa's desperate plan for family suicide whose success was prevented by his daughter, my mother, who overheard her parents' conversation. I learned about the time they spent in the mountains with the Slo-vak National Uprising (Natan then directed hospitals on resistance territory), and later with the Red Army, and about being perhaps the only Jewish family to return to Myjava in 1945. The original family house, where Natan practiced medicine, stands next to the City Hall in the central part of town, boasting fresh paint and the business logo of its new owners (the house built by Natan is still known in town as 'Beckov'). Its ownership has been twice expropriated (in the Nazi era, while the Becks were forced out of Myjava, the title was transferred to a non-Jewish Czech family; in the Communist era the house served first as dis-trict Party headquarters, then as a kindergarten complex), and lost to the family again in the post-Communist restitutions after 1989 (for a small payment to the state the title was returned to the descendants of the family who first acquired the house in the Nazi period, and who sold it to a new business venture). Through these narratives I discovered later that Natan's family came to Myjava in the nineteenth century (his grandfather, my great-great grandfather, Nátan Adam Beck, moved there in June 1871, and his father, Jakub Beck, was born in Myjava in 1872), and that those who died before the transports from Myjava to Auschwitz began are buried at the town's old, relatively preserved Jewish ceme-tery. Natan was one of ten siblings, and I know now that of the nine living adults, his sisters Olga (with husband and four-year-old son), Frida, and Man-cika (with their families), and his brother Béla's wife, Viera (with daughter), all perished in Auschwitz. Fani Löwingerová (mother of Helena Pressburgerová, Natan's first wife, and my grandmother) and her cousin Matyáš Löwinger, met the same end. Blanka Löwingerová, an Auschwitz survivor and a distant rela-

tive, took me in 1997 to Galanta's Jewish cemetery to the grave of Max Mordechai Pressburger (husband of Fani and my great grandfather). The house in Galanta, where the Pressburgers lived, no longer exists—on its lot stands a supermarket; the Communists raized the synagogue that stood next door and erected a sídlište (mass housing project). With Natan's two surviving brothers, Béla Beck and Ervín Veselý, and his first-born sister and an Auschwitz survivor, Etelka Becková, who in 1947 moved to Israel and later to Australia. I never had any direct contact. Only in 1997 was I able to establish the first contact with my relatives who emigrated from Czechoslovakia between 1946–48 and with their families. After I posted a message on the Net, someone who knew Etelka Becková contacted her living descendants in Sydney. 'Out of the silence' of my mother's generation arrived a letter dated August 29, 1997: "My name is Gary Binetter." Gary, born in Sydney one year after me, is a grandson of Etelka and my second cousin.

Having been brought up without knowing my mother's parents in a secular household and during the reign of the Communists who continued the anti-Semitic attitudes of the previous era, I knew next to nothing of my Jewish matrilineage. Assimilated Czech and Slovak, I became fully aware of my genealogy only after 1989, although my clues date back to my youth: a year before the Prague Spring of 1968, my mother, perhaps anticipating Alexander Dubček's socialism with a human face, recovered her family's Jewish name as her pen name (the family Beck masked its origins from the Nazis under a Lutheran pseudonym "Veselý/á" = Happy, and that's how my grandparents are buried in Myjava). I still call my uncle Ernest and cousins Ivo and Vlado, the first two living in the Czech Republic, Veselý. My book harkens to that name's dangerous memory. At this very late time when the present Slovak-state propaganda and its new official school textbook of Slovak history play down, indeed deny, that between 1939–45 the clero-fascist Slovak state zealously followed Hitler in the methodical Holocaust of all its Jews, setting this personal record in public is no longer a private matter. The personal becomes thus theoretically relevant and political, and the theoretically relevant and political is likewise personal.

I have been gifted by the genuine friendship of thinkers who make my work in the U.S. academy more humane and meaningful: Alison Brown, Richard Dienst, Diane Gruber, David Ingram, Kathleen League, James L. Marsh, Bill Martin, Gail Presbey, Ramsey Eric Ramsey, George Trey, Merold Westphal, Iris M. Young—to name a few. Among those who in addition contributed in some fashion to this work, I mention Linda Martín Alcoff, Petr Brabec, Pat Burke, Pinar Fatma Canevi, Segun Gbadegesin, Craig Hanks, Burt Hopkins, Gürol Irzik, Ferda Keskin, Doug Kellner, Charles Mills, Lucius Outlaw, Bill Rehg, Hugo Rodríguez, Marilou Sena, Calvin O. Schrag, and, in Purdue's past monthly gatherings, Lewis R. Gordon, Leonard Harris, Bill McBride, and Charlene Seigfried. I learned much from Purdue's graduate students, among these Heidi Bostic, Damian Konkolly, Tim Martell, Nick Meriwhether, Natalija

Mićunović, Bill Pamerleau, Jeff Paris, Stephen Pluháček, Senem Saner, Tom Spademan, Raj Thiruvengadam, Bill Wilkerson, as well as Michael R. Hames-Garcia, a visiting graduate student from Cornell University. Frank Cunningham and Tom Jeannot were the two of three manuscript readers for SUNY who disclosed their identity, and so I can thank them for very thorough and helpful comments. Kathleen League did a superb philosophically nuanced copyediting of the manuscript, and Stephen Pluháček and Jeff Paris prepared an excellent book index. Clay Morgan, the former senior editor for SUNY Press, and Roger Gottlieb, my SUNY series editor, were most supportive at all stages of the book production.

Writing this book would not have been possible without a junior research leave (fall 1994)—a semester free from teaching duties—which continues to be generously granted by my department's head, Rod Bertolet, and the School of Liberal Arts of Purdue University, to untenured faculty. I have benefited from two consecutive Fulbright lectureship awards for the Czech Republic (January–December 1995): as a visiting assistant professor of philosophy at Charles University and a guest at Ivan Havel's Center for Theoretical Study. During this time I enjoyed many stimulating conversations and the Blue Monday seminars with Zdeněk Pinc, chair of the philosophy department at Charles University. I cherished an intensely rich intellectual environment and Thursday seminars at I. Havel's Center. Weekly evenings at the Havel family restaurant were a gift since philosophers, journalists, and politicians from Prague and abroad gather there. Exchanges with Václav Bělohradský, Doug Dix, Egon Gál, Hana Havelková, Pavel Kouba, Josef Moural, Karel Novotný, Martin Palouš, Miroslav Petříček, Josef Velek, and other faculty and students in Prague, Brno, and Bratislava mark the pages of this book project.

In the preface to his Fanon, Lewis Gordon highlights our panel on Fanon and Marcuse in Los Angeles and our activities in Prague. He attended a three-hour panel discussion in Czech of my Postnational Identity at Carolinum, Charles University, Prague, April 13, 1994 (sponsored by I. Havel with Z. Pinc and Ivan Chvatík), witnessed my professional homecoming after an eighteen-year exile, and, in spite of linguistic barriers, comprehended the significance of this event for me and the other Czechs. The only other non-Slavic person present at this session was Patricia Huntington, who has been my closest friend, intellectual companion, and loving feminist partner for over ten years. Rush Limbaugh's 'feminazis' are not part of my life experience, nor do I share the academy's fear of their imminent invasion. Patricia is responsible for bringing me to Guatemala in 1994 despite my phobia of the military there, and a fear of closely watched borders dating to my life behind the Iron Curtain. The same visit brought the plight of Chiapas, Mexico to the pages of this study. I owe Patricia gratitude for those eye-opening experiences, for joining me in 1997 on a trip to my Jewish family past and to Auschwitz, as well as for what I have learned from our conversations about gender studies. At a deep level my authorship is indebted to this constant learning and our companionship; however, I bear responsibility for my authoring. Prague's Charles University is to date the only institution that, in 1995, employed both of us without forcing us to commute while we navigate teaching and life together. This gift from 'poetic justice' was offered by the same place that forced my exile in 1977 and occasioned my immigration to the U.S. Z. Pinc and I. Havel were most generous in going out of their way to support my tenure process in the U.S. academy at a crucial stage.

Empowered by love and the earnestness of others, I dream of the best of all possible worlds: liberated existence in which broader coalitions, solidary bonds, unoppressive communities, and intimate relationships spring up all around. Such hope suffuses these pages.

✦✦✦

Presentations of unpublished chapters. Chapters 1 and 4–9 are published for the first time. I would like to acknowledge the following conferences and institutions for allowing me to present my work and learn from open discussion with professional and general publics:

Chapter 1: International Philosophers for the Prevention of Nuclear Omnicide (American Philosophical Association, New York, December 28, 1995); Philosophy Departments at American University (Washington, D.C., March 5, 1996), Villanova University (Conference, "The Academy and Race," March 9, 1996), and Howard University (Washington, D.C., March 11, 1996); and Annual Critical Theory Conference (Prague, May 25, 1996).

Chapter 2 (after being rewritten): The Søren Kierkegaard Research Centre, University of Copenhagen (Denmark, November 19, 1995).

Chapter 3 (after being rewritten): Philosophy Department, Seattle University (January, 1994).

Chapter 4: discussions of Derrida's *Spectres de Marx*—Society for Phenomenology and Existential Philosophy (panel with two other commentaries by Simon Critchley and Rebecca Comay, Seattle, October 1, 1994); International Institute of Intercultural Studies, Kafka Society (in Czech; Prague, April 27, 1995); Annual Critical Theory Conference (Prague, May 14, 1995); Philosophy Department at Boğaziçi University (Istanbul, May 6, 1997) and French Studies Department at Brown University (Providence, September 22, 1997); discussions of books by Ingram and Marsh—Society for Phenomenology and Existential Philosophy (Chicago, October 13, 1995); and Radical Philosophy Association (American Philosophical Association, New York, December 29, 1995).

Chapters 5 and 6: Annual Critical Theory Conference (Prague, April 12, 1994).

Chapter 7: International Institute of Intercultural Studies, Masaryk University (in Czech; Brno, April 6, 1995); Ivan Havel's Center for Theoretical Study (in Czech; Prague, April 13, 1995); Philosophy Department at Boğaziçi University (Istanbul, July 4, 1995); and the Blue Monday seminar, Charles University (in Czech; Prague, December 4, 1995).

Chapters 5 and 9: the Black Caucus, panel with Lewis Gordon on "Existential Perspectives On Nationalism, Race, and Resistance" (American Philosophical Association, Los Angeles, April 1, 1994); and the Cultural Studies Collective (Purdue University, April 28, 1994).

Previously published material. Two longer essays and a short statement authored by me were rewritten for this book. I wish to acknowledge the following publishers for permission to reprint lengthy quoted material from copyrighted texts of which I was the author:

In chapter 2, from "Kierkegaard's Radical Existential Praxis, or Why the Individual Defies Liberal, Communitarian, and Existential Categories," in *Kierkegaard in Post/Modernity*, co-edited by Martin J. Matuštík and Merold Westphal, 239–64. Copyright 1995 by Indiana University Press, Bloomington.

In chapter 3, from "Derrida and Habermas on the Aporia of the Politics of Identity and Difference: Towards Radical Democratic Multiculturalism," *Constellations: An International Journal of Critical and Democratic Theory* 1, no. 3 (January 1995): 383–98. Copyright 1995 by Blackwell Publishers, London. (Czech translation by Stanislav Polášek: *Filosofický časopis* [August 1995], 633–52.)

In chapter 4, from "From 'Theoretical Cleansing' to Basic Philosophical Rights: A Manifesto," *The American Philosophical Association Proceedings* 67, no. 6 (June 1994): 72–73. Copyright 1994 by the American Philosophical Association.

1

THE NEED FOR RECOGNITION

They have pulled down our forests, cut down our branches, burnt our trunks, but they could not kill our roots.

—The Nahua Banner, Zócalo, Mexico City, Columbus Day 1992

✢✢✢

[T]he construction of the false universality . . . infected key concepts and strategies of the analyses and practices of liberalism and Marxism. . . . The new society must be won in the struggle to realize it. The excursion through "difference" involves, potentially, more than a concern on the part of women, peoples of Amer-Indian, African, Hispanic, Asian descents, gays, etc., to tell our own stories and in doing so, to re-affirm ourselves. The important point is *why* the histories and cultures—the modalities of being, the life-worlds—are meaningful and important, *why* they have an integrity worth preserving and struggling for while subjecting them to progressive refinement.

—Lucius T. Outlaw, *On Race and Philosophy*

✢✢✢

"[W]e decided to hold on to separate cultural identities. But we broke the bond between genes and culture, broke it forever. We want there to be no chance of racism again. But we don't want the melting pot where everybody ends up with thin gruel. We want diversity, for strangeness breeds richness." "It's so . . . invented. Artificial. Are there black Irishmen and black Jews and black Italians and black Chinese?"

—Marge Piercy, *Woman on the Edge of Time*

✢✢✢

To Habermas's credit, he has brought existential concerns once again within the legitimate reach of his formal critical and democratic social theory. At the time when I located existential interests in his innovative readings of Kierkegaard, critical theorists did not accentuate this as a major aspect of Habermas's opus. A widely circulated view prevails that Habermas jettisons the methodology of existential phenomenology in the process of adopting the full linguistic-communication turn. Habermas's existential leanings can be, however, traced to his dissertation. Recently he has introduced "ethical-existential discourse" into an architectonic of the linguistic-communication turn. And nowadays, seeking links between autonomy (liberal-moral claims to universal individual rights) and authenticity (communitarian-ethical claims to specific rights of individuals within marginalized groups), or between formal pragmatics and existential philosophy, is a favored undertaking.[1]

It is timely to gain from these novel interchanges between existential and critical social theory. Among the key innovations, three important contributions by Habermas's theory stand out. He situates existential categories within an intersubjectivist notion of identity formation. Such categories are expanded through the linguistic-communication turn of philosophical methodology. And they are projected within the regulative ideals of a communication community and a radically democratic republic.[2]

A novel opening for rejoining existential philosophies of liberation to the ongoing liberal-communitarian debates surfaced, first, with Taylor's "Politics of Recognition" and Habermas's rejoinder, and, second, with Taylor's *Ethics of Authenticity*, Honneth's *Struggle for Recognition*, and Habermas's discourse-theoretical view of moral autonomy. Third, I begin to show how the possibility of dissent marks a distinct existential dimension (with regard to the relations among humans and their finite material resources) of group claims and liberal politics. I will argue for needing to recognize this dimension within local groups and universal procedures alike. New efforts at linking authenticity and autonomy still seem inadequate to articulate this dimension of the need for recognition.[3]

1. A Discourse-Theoretical Dimension of Recognition

Between Taylor's social ethics (communitarian emphasis) and Habermas's procedural justice (liberal emphasis), there lurks a margin of difference. And this accounts for their two methodological paths to multicultural democracy. On a closer study this disjunction between their communitarian and liberal emphases becomes less significant than their agreements that the monological character of classical liberal individualism is inadequate for an adequate democratic theory. Their communitarian-liberal debate reaches, I hold, a consensus—albeit minimal—on what both do and do not want. With this minimal consensus, democratic theory benefits from Taylor's agreements with Habermas that self-relation is co-original with one's communicative competence. It gains from placing Habermas's discursive autonomy and procedural justice in the context of Taylor's view of ethical authenticity as a group claim to contextual justice. Of interest in this context is Walzer's definition of the difference between "Liberalism 1" and "Liberalism 2." A Liberal 1 employs formal procedures of universal justice. A Liberal 2 adds the criteria of difference which mark contextual justice. The more robust considerations of Liberal 2 provide correctives to the thin Liberal 1. Taylor believes that such correctives get going on the procedural basis provided by "Liberalism 1." Habermas finds "Liberalism 1" likewise wanting. Yet instead of settling with Taylor on *two* principles operating a dialogic tandem between "1" and "2," he reforms "Liberalism 1" by a *single* discourse principle. Habermas disagrees with *any* liberalism insofar as it relies on possessive individualism—its monologicality. Procedural justice is formally liberal; as communicative it needs no ethical correctives. It is at home in the collective identity- and will-formation of discourse ethics. Such features of Habermas's position indicate that to view the Habermas-Taylor exchanges as a genre of the liberal-communitarian debate pure and simple is unhelpful. (E.g., liberals hold out for individual rights and communitarians for the good). Rather, the respective positions of Habermas and Taylor represent two versions of concretion—at times couched by them in existential terms—overcoming classical and modern individualist "Liberalism 1." Taylor's communitarian "Liberalism 2" produces a supplement to "Liberalism 1." Habermas revises *any* liberalism via dialogues of recognition.[4]

My purpose is not to blur their distinct contextualist and procedural views of justice. I wish to show in this first round how Taylor and Habermas share a discourse-theoretical perspective on identity formation, morality and ethics, and politics. My key consists in their agreement on the communicative core of selfhood. Their exchanges on multicultural democracy bring their liberal-communitarian debate and the communicative ethics controversy to a closure.

First, both hold an intersubjectivist notion of identity-formation. Taylor's own critique of the monological derivations of self-identity is not unique. It shares much with Habermas's discursive reading of Kant and Hegel. Says Taylor, "there is no such thing as inward generation, monologically understood. In order to understand the close connection between identity and recognition, we have to take into account a crucial feature of the human condition that has been rendered almost invisible by the overwhelmingly monological bent of mainstream modern philosophy."[5] Taylor parallels Habermas in a recourse to Mead's social psychology of self- and language-formation. Taylor relies on Wittgenstein's critique of a private language:

People do not acquire the languages needed for self-definition on their own. Rather, we are introduced to them through interaction with others who matter to us—what George Herbert Mead called "significant others." The genesis of the human mind is in this sense not monological, not something each person accomplishes on his or her own, but dialogical.[6]

In sum, Taylor and Habermas agree that there are no unsocialized selves with private words for I or Self. Such words and our competence for recognizing and communicating them to ourselves and others are generated in one's individualization through socialization. This process accounts for a discursive basis of self-relation and social recognition. The very notion of the communicatively competent self cannot emerge without a discourse-theoretical perspective.

Secondly, Taylor and Habermas agree that the linguistic-communications turn in philosophical methodology forms now the starting point for practical discourse. This turn remains decisive for Taylor, unlike for MacIntyre, even if both privilege a communitarian legitimation of claims. Such legitimation might seem incompatible with Habermas's procedural methodology. However, Taylor retrieves all dominant goods from a post-Hegelian angle. He concedes to a critical modernist that in complex pluralist societies *we* can appropriate ethical self-understanding and communal life (*Sittlichkeit*) only via reflectively available historical contexts. Good is not found as a positive given. Ethical goods *for us* are repeated by historical consciousness. What is received historically must be critically sorted out. Modern critics must do this in order to reach a moral point of view (*Moralität*).[7]

Taylor insists on an anthropological or ontological priority of the good over the right. Can this communitarian emphasis be at all consistent with that postmetaphysical thinking which emphasizes a priority of moral autonomy over uncritical ontology? Habermas begins performatively—with communicative competencies of speakers and hearers individualized through socialization—and not by defining first the ontological or anthropological sources of the self. The pragmatics of human evolution teaches humans to rely on communicative competence, performatively justifying all claims, and not on sedimented traditions. All anthropological and ontological categories undergo "linguistification": contents inherited from culture pass through social evolution. Existentially speaking, contents are not necessarily discarded but return to *us* through repetition. Unquestioned authorities, those holdovers of kings, are deposed by the popular sovereignty of discursive problematization. The turn to language, or "linguistification," must hold itself self-critically, not as a new monarch. Dialogue provides a sole medium of appeal for the discursive legitimation of claims. Taylor's turn to language cannot but assume this linguistification of the good. The reflective retrieval of goods admits a discursively performed genealogy, namely, critical ontology or existential anthropology.[8]

A critical repetition of received goods may be said to employ concrete genealogy. I give a qualified yes to this critically genealogical aspect of an otherwise communitarian methodology: even a post-Hegelian priority of the good ("Liberalism 2") cannot bypass a linguistification. Habermas articulates this insight formally under procedural morality. For Taylor, discursively available goods provide a concrete corrective to the procedural priority of individual rights. Dominant goods, and not procedures, define the self. In a complex world, goods become human sources in a critical and existential, i.e., postmetaphysical, manner. This performative concretization of ethical life dramatizes goods on a stage which Taylor cannot but share with Habermas. Within the linguistified public space, Taylor's goods are never dominant lords, but rather modern existential dramas of new epiphanic languages.[9]

Thirdly, communicative competence completes itself in democratic politics. Taylor and Habermas defend the politics of recognition. Habermas requires a complex but single principle of justice. His procedural principle does not define practical discourse and communicative competence on a metalevel—as if from above or below. Justice is neither a metaphysical nor a transcendental nor a metaprinciple. Justice defines the formal procedures of a concrete communication community and, when viewed politically, of a radically democratic republic.

Taylor argues that Habermas's generalized *procedural justice* could benefit from a complement and a corrective by concrete *differential justice*. As I further elaborate in chapters six and nine, this argument presents a variation of Benhabib's distinction between the generalized and the concrete other as well as the critical gender and race theories, such as Young's, Outlaw's, or West's. Taylor wants us to attend differentially to the concrete others, viz., identity needs of certain groups. This proffers that politics of recognition by which *authentic* needs and rights of concrete others are recognized. Minorities are often assimilated by successful and dominant majorities. An oversight and marginalization of minority positions can occur. Universal rights insufficiently recognize these concrete minority needs.[10]

Habermas has come to learn a great deal from gender and race theorists (I say this even though in the following chapters I am critical of what Habermas did not learn). He acknowledges dangers of homogenization and imperialism vis-à-vis marginalized group rights. Such dangers come from any hegemonic, however otherwise legitimate, consensus on global human rights. He implicitly admits as much to his critics: there might have been such an oversight in his prior, proceduralist, evaluation of the U.N.-sponsored and consensually justified allied intervention in the Persian Gulf War. Procedural justice can be parochially partial to *our* national interests, though these are cloaked by the veneer of cosmopolitan, democratic universalism.

> *Eurocentrism and the hegemony of Western culture* are in the last analysis catchwords for a struggle for recognition on the international level. The Gulf War made us aware of this. Under the shadow of a colonial history that is still vivid in people's minds, the allied intervention was regarded by religiously motivated masses and secularized intellectuals alike as a failure to respect identity and autonomy of the Arabic-Islamic world. The historical relationship between the Occident and the Orient, and especially the relationship of the First to the former Third World, continues to bear the marks of a denial of recognition.[11]

I do not find Taylor ambiguous on the discursive basis of the politics of recognition. He depicts recognition from an intersubjective, not a possessively individualistic, standpoint. Habermas's suspicion of Taylor's communitarian advocacy of collective minority rights would benefit from beginning with this mutual agreement: Taylor employs a proceduralist basis exactly when he raises ethical claims to group rights. Procedural justice is in no way devalued by this differential justice. From an opposite side, Taylor's critique of "Liberalism 1" only gains by meeting in Habermas's discourse model an ally, not a foe of multicultural democracy. The discourse model of democracy is better fit to collaborate with differential justice than "Liberalism 1." On this point there remains little to separate Habermas from Taylor. Communicative competencies, when institutionalized in democratic procedures, allow for advocacy on behalf of minority rights. Differential justice is not necessarily some principle over, above, or against procedural justice. Cogent reasons for collective rights can be heard precisely when communicative competencies are employed within communicative democracy.[12]

On all three points, I conclude in this first round that there is less ground for fundamental disagreements between Taylor and Habermas than assumed by the received communitarian-liberal debate. Minimally, disagreements should not be sought in what both do or do not want but in how they go about it. Both strive for a degree of critical and concrete multicultural justice found in neither "Liberalism 1" nor uncritically communitarian traditionalism. Within their shared discourse-theoretical view of selfhood, practical philosophy, and politics, one meets two versions of making "Liberalism 1" concrete and critical in multicultural societies.

Rounds two and three pass beyond the communitarian-liberal debate: what counts as a sufficiently critical practical discourse? What counts as a concretely critical justice both in the group claims to authenticity and in the liberal notions of moral autonomy and procedural politics? What admits dissent both from consensual and ethically or group-anchored forms of recognition?

2. The Need for Authenticity or Autonomy?

How do collectives—struggling for identity and group rights—negotiate their regional claims to ethical authenticity in relation to one another? (Do not conflicting local narratives achieve only a highly contested validity?) How does anyone's universal point of view recognize the generalized claims to moral autonomy in relation to multicultural differences? (Does not proceduralism achieve only a highly formal universal validity?) Posing these questions together: how should one recognize communicative competence—whether under the rubric of authenticity or of autonomy—in existing? The sum question aims at critical justice in its local (individual and group) and universal (autonomous and political) dimensions.

It appears that starting with *authentic* group rights would make one more receptive to local needs than beginning with universal procedures. On this reading, Taylor is the one who elaborates the more concrete sources of selfhood. His communicative version of authenticity can no longer be identified with a nonrational, antisocial, decisionist freedom of a certain existential*ist* or classical liberal individualism. This authenticity may not be identified with one's monological being in the world—a being first safeguarded at an acommunicative outer border of fallen sociality and then delivered to a nationalist destiny. Authenticity must emerge within a critically valued sociality. Taylor expands a communicative selfhood into the politics of recognizing specific identities and multicultural differences. A critical politics of identity and difference relies on the dialogically available sources of selfhood. Authenticity stands for claims by marginalized collectives, not by a solitary self or a heroic nation. Need for authenticity encodes an intersubjective, ethical, and democratic claim to a wholesome form of life of various peoples struggling for justice within multicultural society.[13]

Commencing with *autonomy* and formal justice evinces a strong relativization of strictly communitarian legitimations. On this reading, one must negotiate the debate between Hegelian and Kantian views. Habermas expands a post-Hegelian, communicatively competent category of autonomy into a procedural politics of democratic recognition. As a Kantian, he emphasizes individual rights, albeit safeguarded in democratic procedures and institutions. As a Hegelian, he defines autonomy by the reciprocal recognition of communicative competencies. Yet claims to autonomy cannot safeguard an uncritical preservation of any cultural species as such.[14]

Beginning from these two starting points, Taylor emerges as someone who stresses authenticity, self-realization, and the *eudaimonistic* sources of the self. And Habermas comes to be regarded as someone who privileges moral autonomy and procedural self-determination. This is the crossroad reached by the received view of their communitarian-liberal debate. Yet this contrast now seems a bit simplistic. Both thinkers root communicative competence and justice in degrees of concretion found neither among "Liberals 1" nor among classically oriented, premodern, or uncritical communitarians. Authenticity, freed up from the individualistic and narcissistic culture of authenticity, invites a social complement in postconventional group ethics. This postconventional ethic (*Sittlichkeit*) of authenticity calls for a multicultural form of life well suited for our modern, and perhaps postmodern, cultures.[15]

Why not adopt a more dialectical reading of the ethic of authentic self-realization and the morality of autonomous self-determination as found, e.g., more recently in Honneth and Willett? For Honneth, autonomy and authenticity represent two orientations toward shared intersubjective expectations. If groups violate autonomy (moral liberalism), they harm shared intersubjectivity. Still, some deviations from generalized moral norms may be essential (read: ethically authentic) to individual or group self-realization. Life-forms are not always and in all senses conformable to general normative expectations. An ethical perspective on self-esteem (an intersubjective recognition of talents, contributions, one's worthiness) might legitimate an authentic priority of concrete individuals or groups over certain established or dominant figures of autonomy or self-respect (an intersubjective and contextual recognition of a set of moral rights). Significantly, deviations from generalized moral norms can be validated communicatively. They are at times *ethically* essential to our vulnerable and feeling selves. And this ethics complements the primordial material needs, which Willett finds to be crucial to one's tactile sense of social and individualized integrity, and which Honneth identifies as essential to nurturing bodily confidence. Recognizing needs for tactile sociality and bodily integrity, just as recognizing multicultural ethical needs, is necessary for sustaining individual or group identity in difference.[16]

Honneth builds from recognizing the need for confident bodily integrity to recognizing the need for ethical self-esteem and moral self-respect; he sees these needs as three distinct intersubjective dimensions of social recognition. Willett on the other hand stipulates the need for tactile sociality at all three levels. For her, there is a degree of a/symmetry from day one of human lives. She draws on the cutting-edge child development research into "correspondences between infant and adult, between face and face." Even if these correspondences cannot be given direct discursive formulae of something humans share in common, she explains, there is a sense of tactile bonding, e.g., between the mother, who touches or sings to the infant, and the infant, who displays mood-responses to particular tones and touches. Babies are not self-aware, developed, intentional, and existential selves. Yet they exhibit from day one both "a spirited expression of preferences" and "a dislike for what the adult is doing," i.e., both relationality and "spirited resistance." In my rejoinder, then, any recognition of the need for ethical self-realization and moral autonomy of adults, and any politics of identity-in-difference, will require harnessing this primordial existentially social situation of the one-day-old. This is so because even as a self-choosing existential individual an adult carries within oneself this tactile and vulnerable layer of social self-in-another. Willett's "tactile sociality" marks an onto-genetically primordial dimension in infant and adult forms of social recognition. Inspired by this articulation, I redefine and employ throughout the 'existential' as a locus of spirited (tactile) a/symmetrical correspondences of refusal-in-relation to others; this locus becomes an adult site for communicatively competent—social yet dissenting—individuals.[17]

Now Taylor's ethics calls, first, for substantive ties to others and, second, to "*other* issues of significance beyond self-choice."[18] A communicative reading of authenticity already disproves monologism, decisionism, or a quasi-mystical, culturally laden recourse to myths of the folk. Yet Taylor, unlike Honneth, does not think that in modernity one can reconcile self-determining autonomy with self-realizing authenticity. He, thus, needs to retrieve various sources of the self *eudaimonistically*. He yokes the narcissistic culture of authenticity with a *phronetic* horizon of group-authenticity, not with an existential repetition of this horizon. This narcissistic culture, he holds, emerges *ex nihilo*, in an illusion of being wholly self-created. It is the culture of "Liberals 1" or of voluntarist existentia*lists*. Both types engender fragmentary and subjectivist individualities. Taylor's transcendental critique of this culture meets Habermas's pragmatic-communicative critique of it only half way:

> [A]uthenticity can't be defended in ways that collapse horizons of significance. . . . Horizons are given. . . . I can define my identity only against the background of things that matter. . . . Authenticity is not the enemy of demands that emanate from beyond the self; it supposes such demands.[19]

If one can affirm a shared ground with Habermas and Honneth, it cannot lie in Taylor's stress on self-transcendence beyond human tasks. This 'beyond' bespeaks an emphatically metaphysical aim which is not easily harnessed into the linguistification of uncritical claims to transcendence. I propose to join instead these positions in the discourse-theoretic and existential demand assumed by authenticity: "the need for recognition." And for Taylor authenticity qualitatively conditions one's links to others. These links are facilitated through an ethical recognition, not in a privacy of asocial existence. The competence for authenticity presupposes the communicative self and vice versa. Taylor, thus, reformulates atomistic claims to authenticity: in 'the *ethics* of *authenticity*' both terms mean something inherently social.[20]

Taylor is not unique in revising the methodologically subject-centered treatment of authenticity. I reiterate: to Habermas's credit, he retrieved issues of existential self-realization for his communications-theoretic framework. That he does not get very excited about reintroducing methods of existential and social phenomenology within this framework is a moot point. Others have shown how abandoning that authenticity which can be traced to a Cartesian strand of phenomenology or to Heidegger's overcoming of Cartesianism cannot disqualify a critical social theory conceived of as dialectical phenomenology.[21]

Taylor's ethics of authenticity and "individualism as a moral principle" engender the politics of difference. Anchored in a phenomenology of culture, race, and gender, this politics can only further enhance the still merely formal frame of discourse ethics:

[T]he ideal of authenticity incorporates some notions of society, or at least of how people ought to live together. Authenticity is a facet of modern individualism, and it is a feature of all forms of individualism that they don't just emphasize the freedom of the individual but also propose models of society.[22]

Taylor raises to himself a question which should also concern Habermas: "we have to ask what is involved in truly recognizing difference." Multicultural society, based on equal recognition of differences, concretizes formal proceduralism. The ethics of authenticity solicits a "substantive agreement" on what constitutes recognition. "Recognizing difference, like self-choosing, enforces a horizon of significance, in this case a shared one." This shared context does not require a homogenization of complexity into some premodern *polis* or modern instrumental melting pot or postmodern pastiche. Multicultural democracy calls for a concrete, embodied, and participatory politics of recognition. "The demands of recognizing difference themselves take us beyond procedural justice."[23]

It is less interesting to contrast Habermas and Taylor following Habermas's outline:

> On closer examination, however, Taylor's reading [of the democratic constitutional state, for which Michael Walzer provides the terms Liberalism 1 and Liberalism 2] attacks the [liberal] principles themselves and calls into question the individualistic core of the modern conception of freedom.[24]

I say this with confidence since Taylor rejects only the subjectivist individualism of the culture of authenticity. And he defends another individualism, viz., the one armed with a pragmatic-social sense of the moral principle. The more interesting matter for a comparative reading is, then, the issue that the very same rejection and defense are true for Habermas.

Habermas's objections to Taylor are also raised against Habermas's communications theory: i.e., that it tilts towards collectivist criteria. Discourse ethics waters down—so some Kantian, Aristotelian, and existential critics of it argue—the individual core of moral autonomy or *phronesis* or self-choice. I do not find Taylor's communicatively tailored authenticity to be any more or less individualistic than Habermas's communicatively grasped autonomy. Both build upon a post-Hegelian integration of self-realization and self-determination. They espouse intersubjectivist views of identity, morality, and the politics of recognition.[25]

The contrast between Taylor's category of authenticity and Habermas's of autonomy must lie, then, in how they reform the modern individualist, viz., the "Liberal 1." This, rather than arguments for the primacy of authenticity or autonomy, explains better their selective emphases. Again, the proper measure of contrast between them are not the now familiar rounds of the communitarian-liberal debate but rather two versions of concretely critical justice.[26]

Taylor appeals to individualism as a moral principle. The 'moral' differs here from procedural principles. Taylor's principle is really no principle at all but an ethical form of life. Ethical life-forms gather shared contexts of meaning and value. The individual character of Taylor's communitarianism consists, however, not primarily in a neo-Hegelian demand that we anchor the Kantian moral subject in concrete ethical life. Rather, Taylor's defense of the ethics, as opposed to the culture, of authenticity harbors a sort of group-claims-based individualism. This ethics, just as in Outlaw's elaboration of Du Bois's claim on behalf of the conservation of races, pertains to recognizing authentic claims of specific community, culture, or group. Taylor argues that the ethics of authenticity gives us more than a society of fragmented individual atoms. This 'more' projects functional equivalents to a community of shared meaning and value. The politics of recognition emerging from the latter grounds democracy in the ethically authenticated sociality. Ethical democracy becomes authenticated via political recognition of different, multicultural groups. Taylor's self-realizing, authentic individual (in a pragmatically social expansion of individualism) bespeaks its communal equivalents in group self-realization. Such equivalents secure one's communicative competence in shared forms of life. Moral individualism is expressive of this intersubjective (not subjectivist) ethics. This concrete justice, says Taylor, allows democracy to recognize specific differences politically.[27]

Habermas anchors individualism in communicative competencies to raise, accept, or reject validity claims. These are shared by socialized individuals. Even if historically traditional forms of socialization have become fragmented, anomie does not rob humans of communicative competence. They have now nothing but a recourse to this competence. Insofar as their competencies are intersubjectively shared—define the very communicative sense of moral autonomy—Habermas puts "Liberalism 1" aside. Morality in discourse ethics is a group and not a monologically individualist competence. For this reason, Habermas rejects the minimalist view of rights of "a truncated Liberalism 1" but does not adopt a new "model that introduces a notion of collective rights that is alien to the system." He democratizes the actualization of private and civil rights in public policies. If basic rights are not only formally universalized but contain the need of their differentiated democratic realization, then one does not need Taylor's added quasi-principle of collective rights, Habermas concludes.[28]

What about the objection some raise against Habermas or Honneth and which the former raises to Taylor: is a group perspective superimposed over the individual capacity to judge? Taylor holds out for ethical individualism within "Liberalism 2" and Habermas for moral individualism in discourse ethics. Both recognize the need for shared intersubjective grounds in order to socially integrate the morally autonomous and the ethically authenticated individuals.

To sum up, Habermas's moral individualism of rights enshrines a procedural principle of social integration, and it differs from Taylor's individualism as a moral principle. The latter's individualism requires a shared lifeworld. This is significant for evaluating what constitutes a genuine politics of recognizing cultural, gender, or racialized differences. So to blur Taylor's ethical, group-claims-based individualism with Habermas's moral principle as such is misleading. Yet to characterize Taylor's position as does Habermas, namely as a retreat from individual freedom and rights, is also unhelpful. Learning from the nuanced models of bodily, ethical, and moral levels of social recognition (as in Honneth and Willett), we fare better by differentiating in Habermas and Taylor two views of how to reform liberalism, two communicative individualisms, and two dimensions of social integration. In concluding round two of this discussion, I put aside disagreements on whether or not in genuine multicultural democracy only procedural morality possesses the status of moral principle. Habermas agrees at the end of the day that ethics permeates morality. This position preserves a modicum of hope in recognizing the need for a productive complementarity between these two validity domains of communicative ethics: ethical authenticity (the need for an intersubjective recognition of self-esteem in personal and group identities, in turn building from recognizing the need for bodily integrity and tactile sociality) and moral autonomy (the need for an intersubjective recognition of self-respect and a determinate set of rights). If spirited resistance marks a distinct dimension (distinct from correspondences between adults and infants) within tactile relations of one-day olds to their social world, should not dissent mark a distinct dimension in ethical and moral recognition?

3. An Existential Politics of Recognition

Habermas's "ethical neutrality of law and politics" in the constitutional state is problematized by multigendered, multiracial, and generally multicultural dimensions of democracy. These dimensions become apparent when one scrutinizes the strict analytic separation of ethics and morality. The permeation of procedural justice by ethical justice surfaces socially and discursively, not, therefore, because communitarian theoreticians thought this out. The degrees and variable nature of this separation pertain to one's primordial experience of bodily integrity and tactile sociality and to the ethical needs for recognition as persons and groups; they also comprise the concrete, i.e., lived contents of discourse ethics.[29]

Let me assume an agreement with Habermas and disagreement with Taylor: in this case no other practical principle besides the formal-pragmatics of discourse ethics is needed. But, then, I consent to agree only if Habermas concedes to continue debating the permeable borders between ethics and morality, the particular and the universal. The razor-edge borders hold analytically for the benefit of traditional theory. Is not critical theory more concrete? Practical discourse concerned with multigendered, multiracial, and multicultural dimensions of democracy places this split on the table. Formal justice is still learning how to live with concrete multicultural justice, so one could argue after reading critical race and gender theorists such as Outlaw or Willett. Honneth's dialectical model of recognition drives home that the latter justice learns how to defend authentic group claims in complex cultures with the aid of the former.[30]

Someone might still wonder, is there any difference in positions between Taylor and Habermas? Maybe this is not the most pressing topic to decide for a new generation of critically traditional and critically post/modern theorists. Here is an urgent issue: neither a politics of authentic group difference nor a politics of procedural recognition may be fully competent to sustain various communities of meaning and value where distortions due to racism, patriarchy, and the lack of economic democracy are to greater or lesser degrees involved. This suspicion about sorely lacking sufficient critical competencies indicates the dangers of imperial oversights in certain communitarianism and liberalism alike.[31]

Critical theorists doubt that even a socially situated authenticity could make its projected modern ethics a reliable basis for public criticism. Would moral agency evaluating the available goods fare better? Note Outlaw's suspicion: "Neither the full nature and extent of our oppression, nor our historical-cultural being as African and African-descended peoples, has been comprehended adequately by the concepts and logics involved in Marxian and liberal analyses and programs for the projects of modernity in societies in Europe and Euro-America." Many a race and gender theorist suspect proceduralism of requiring valuative criteria that are too strong. A high price is being paid for formal autonomy and its consensual procedures: racially or gender-blind laws uphold civic, state, and international constitutions. These procedures exhibit crippling blindspots. Life-forms are not insular vis-à-vis one another. Democratic states, even when entering into international leagues, can be hegemonically partial in their purported neutrality vis-à-vis gender, race, or particular life-forms. Do not the projects of authenticity and autonomy under our present discussion fail in equal senses the critical test they require *qua* cornerstones of radical multicultural democracy?[32]

My core question turns now not on whether to opt for authenticity or for autonomy in the two communicative ways under discussion. I have already settled (with Habermas, Honneth, and Taylor) on needing to recognize a collaboration of both. But how can life-forms resist uncritical insularity or domination by problematic racialized, gender, and class constructs—whether these are deployed systemically or through ongoing attitudes? How can dominant or ascendant group identities sustain authentic (i.e., sober) coexistence with genuine difference? Which group claims are legitimate? When does liberating one life–form oppress others?

✠ ✠ ✠

Answers might be less ambiguous in Taylor's examples of the French Quebecois rights within the dominant Anglo culture of Canada.[33] Answers are not so obvious concerning struggles by native American cultures or in the Yugoslav and post-Soviet quagmires. Ascending groups tend to collapse the politics of dif-

ference for which their group claims were invoked in the first place. If French Canada did split off from English Canada, would it allow authentic group-rights to native Canadian Americans? Consider Chechnya or Afghan group-claims against previous Russian imperialism: these are hardly disputable, but East European post-1989 liberation is shot through with problematic anti-Roma, anti-Vietnamese, and generally anti-Black homogenizations of social identities. Finally, what about the relations among race and gender and class? Do some collective claims (e.g., by gay men) take preference in cases of complex struggles (e.g., by women)? Forms of life do not carry markers for adding or subtracting identity and difference in politically recognizable, relevant, and normative ways. Taylor's and even Honneth's liberal-communitarian defense of group claims is underdetermined to address these queries from within its ethics of authenticity.

✦✦✦

The marginalized voice has an urgent need to limit harmful consensual assimilations of group differences. But a high price is paid for setting such limits via emphatic communitarian models. Habermas would question uncriticizable fundamentalist forms of life. Can they easily immigrate into international life with pluralistic and complex modern societies? Minimally, projects of open society could check and balance various, often competing claims to group difference. *We* do not get open societies from a form of life (*Sittlichkeit*) as such.[34]

My questioning of Habermas comes thus from an opposite angle: how can even the pluralistic and tolerant constitutional state and the procedurally based international law sustain a justly pluralist coexistence of different forms of life? Is not there a danger that consensual procedures lead to a top down cultural or other imperialism? It matters little whether or not openness is something by which only the modern Euro-American culture gifted the globe (this dubious claim is the *locus classicus* of the missionary complex of the West inscribed now in the secular Eurocentric export of liberal democracy) or something emerging in various forms and in different cultures and at different times. In either case, radical openness and honesty can live only in those life-forms which allow for their critical sobriety vis-à-vis others. The Eurocentric exceptionalist attitude fails any concrete sobriety test, however much it toasts universalism. When Euro-American civilizations no longer listen to voices of difference within or without established institutional structures, then racist, patriarchal, or socioeconomic imperialism arrives through the back door of even highly developed proceduralism. As systematic yet personally anchored attitudes, these lifeworld distortions infect our rational conversations *from within*.

✦✦✦

*The membership of the Security Council of the U.N. encodes its general-
ized other as a generalized arrogance of dominant civilizations. Can the council
represent either ethical authenticity or moral autonomy for all concerned? It is
doubtful that its present liberal definition of justice would remain the same
should all concerned (e.g., the Mayans from Chiapas) be heard. I cannot avert a
suspicion that these voices of difference, when heard at our conferences on critical and democratic theory or in our journals and political institutions, would
affect also our well-cherished and established liberal (in fact emphatically communitarian?) consensus.*[35]

✤✤✤

It cannot hurt to examine the *material content* of the ethics of authenticity: what claims and whose group warrant a just difference within universal justice? It would do no harm if proceduralists were to interrogate
the *lived form* or the attitudes one deploys via moral autonomy and formal justice: how do existential and political economies affect *our* universality? How can *we* resist trends to homogeneity and imperial hegemonies of consensual procedures? Communitarianism and liberalism in
the two communicative versions under discussion represent an advance.
Yet they seem insufficient to carry out this dual, existentially material
hermeneutics of suspicion on their own. In avoiding badly circular rea-
soning—from a group ethic of authenticity to moral autonomy, or in
reverse—*an existentially material view of the need for recognition aims to provide a missing key.* I articulate this key throughout in various specters of
liberation. I mean by it the concrete historical manifestations of the
human need to undo all unjust distribution of scarcity and to invent the
coalitional and even solidary bonds of recognition for emancipatory practices of radical existential and multicultural democracy.[36]
    But what can an existential perspective add to ethical authenticity
(i.e., the need of self-esteem of individuals and groups) and moral autonomy (i.e., the need for self-respect)? If one is to hold onto existential categories as even fruitful for critical social theory and practice, these cannot
be identifiable with the possessive and psychoanalytically naïve individualism of "Liberal 1." Neither can they seek legitimation by uncritical and
equally psychoanalytically naïve communitarians. These two restrictions
ward off the extremes of positing unsituated, unmotivated self-choice
and a decisionist political existential*ism*—whether left- or right-wing.
Such methodological restrictions and psychoanalytical sobriety about
identity formation of individuals and groups do not yet exhaust the existential attitude—its irony—as such.[37]

✤✤✤

My elaboration of a critical social theory of recognition learns from East Central European political humor, which is imbued with an existentially material and psychoanalytical sense of the tragic. And because this sense of the tragic (e.g., in Žižek's narrations of "Eastern Europe's Republics of Gilead," the rape of the nations is carried out in the name of the Nation-Thing) is a form of humorous warding off, one acquires a sense of sobriety. Had Central Europeans lost their capacity to laugh—in the midst of the conquering armies and gas chambers—they would have perished a long time ago. Some call this communicative competence for irony and humor a mark of the Slavic Soul, but this trait is rather distinctive of Jewish stories and Romany songs in that part of the world—take your pick of folk myths. One feature is common to them all, tragic humor can neither befriend cynicism nor can it confuse the historical shapes of human abjection with an ontologically psychic structure of being human. To be able to laugh, one cannot be simply a dupe of history or innate instincts. That's why I speak of an existentially material and psychoanalytical sense of the tragic. Kundera's Book of Laughter and Forgetting *distinguishes between the tired grins of the tragic hero and the lighthearted smirks of the romantic, each with their pernicious underside only badly mimicking a liberating laughter. Kundera indirectly indicates how to forget those grins and smirks, how to laugh for liberation. With Jaroslav Hašek, Bohumil Hrabal, Franz Kafka, or Václav Havel, one may discover that when you and I laugh, we already resist stupidity or naked aggression. Laughter is most insubordinate since its outburst cannot be contained, indeed, it can be as contagious as fire.*

In an example that I remember, street and poster humor kept the Soviet invaders of Czechoslovakia in 1968 on their toes for several months. After that self-defensive carnival, Prague became a sad, humorless city under a spell until the velvet days of 1989, which brought the capacity for unselfish joy back. And with joyous irony breaking out from under the silence created by the bloody suppression of the student march on November 17, 1989, hated power crumbled as if in a historical instant. In the 1970s, Havel's "Power of the Powerless" tried to remember irony (we forget those empowering moments so quickly, we get preoccupied with the new Thing, badly serious, so readily!). This dangerous memory leads to a greengrocer's Velvet Revolution from below: when the totalitarian Thing one day ceased to cast its oppressive and repressive spell, the greengrocer no longer felt compelled to display the silly Party commercials in the shop window. (Such an existentially material freedom to become insubordinate even while powerless in totality would have an equivalent in the act of the ordinary "Television Man" if he or she turned off the TV—and its democratic marketing of stupidity—even for a day and maybe a week and maybe for a very long time. Imagine the worldwide panic: "This is CNN"—and nobody is/will be watching![38])

Revolutions often begin with such ironical protests when the world-order-Thing is no longer It (again, as in "Coke is IT"). I.e., it is neither neurotically enjoyable nor nostalgically sought-out as a purportedly stolen/promised Heaven *(one never had IT/will never have IT). And thus comes a day when the known IT becomes a tragically comic (simply stupid, i.e., laughable) reality known to all as a denuded emperor. Facing this crisis, one may either poorly imitate laughter and get despondent with the demons and drunk with the angels. Or one may laughingly lighten up one's historical finitude in order to rise against human injustices which are the tragedy that matters and that is to be overcome. And at the same time one learns to sober up in order to strip the despondent and drunk desires, which support the false sense of existing, of their illusion. Laughters that wake up liberation specters do not fuel the need for recognition as do some nightmarish ghosts of abject and useless passion; emancipatory laughter invents an active "hope now." Such tragically comic satisfaction of the need for recognition wards off with laughter the hell of self and others, both found jointly in a fraternity-terror.*³⁹

✤ ✤ ✤

Reaching a critical standpoint, it does not suffice to translate existential self-choice either into the goods held by a "Liberal 2" or formal procedures. Otherwise the job of having a critical standpoint vis-à-vis individual or group claims could be settled best by *eudaimonistic* authenticity or by moral autonomy or by a communitarian-liberal debate. My existential approach points to a dimension needed for sustaining both ethical authenticity and moral autonomy. This dimension holds a key to the public discourse on those traditions which *we* wish to keep and those *we* want to transform or jettison. The sought-for existential dimension of recognition inheres in concrete humans. These are embodied, social, and linguistic actors. The key to the thick existential dimension of recognition must be operative on the primordial bodily level of tactile sociality as much as in the distance one is able to take vis-à-vis problematized group identities and skewed normative procedures. In each case, we must theorize the communicative competence for recognition and refusal: a tactile social ability to demand recognition of others (e.g., by smiling) or resist bodily violation (e.g., by refusal to smile back or by crying); an ethical social competence for solidary relations and resistance to their violation from within or without; and a moral competence to take yes and no positions on criticizable validity claims in speech. The 'existential', as I define it, is the mode enabling both bonding and resistance on all three theorized levels of tactile, ethical, and moral individualization through socialization.⁴⁰

Thinkers from Kierkegaard to Nietzsche, Freud, and Marx, from Sartre and Beauvoir to Marcuse and Fanon, agree: one is individualized in socialization. They all are good Hegelians to contest Hegel—and today Gadamer, Mead, or Wittgenstein—on this hermeneutic point. Here one must not contest Taylor and Habermas or Honneth either. The challenge lies in viewing existential categories in light of the agreements: the discourse-theoretical method (section 1 above) and the practical complementarity of authenticity and autonomy (section 2 above). How is one to link existence with the contents of claims to authenticity and with the form of procedurally raising claims? Which claims to difference are ethically authentic? How does existence affect raising and evaluating validity claims? Is there an internal connection of existence (as a distinct critical dimension) with communicative competencies, and does this link affect ethical self-realization and moral self-determination?[41]

A Preliminary Sketch: Excursus on Two Sets of Aporias within the Need for Recognition

I limit myself to two sets of aporias facing complex democracies. One, the economic exploitation of scarcity distorts both the communitarian and the liberal versions of the nation-state. Two, the politics of racism, patriarchy, heterosexism, in combined varieties, supplement this exploitation. And they accomplish this equally in regional and global political cultures.

Enjoying one's specific difference. There is an authenticity claimed by groups: which community or whose justice counts as legitimate difference? *Any* communitarian angle gives *per definitionem* an answer partial to the scope of its solidarity. Regional claims to difference can conflict with other struggles—both within and outside this original difference. However otherwise universal, a group-based solidarity can become merely provincial. The communitarian basis for justice seems too weak to resist the global exploitation of material scarcity. The nation-state promises rights both in political and economic terms and, thereby, mobilizes groups for anti-imperial liberation struggles. And this nation-state is poorly equipped to secure universal justice since it postpones equality for the benefit of its ascending national *nomenklatura*. An enjoyment of "the national Thing . . . a kind of *'particular Absolute' resisting universalization,"* in Žižek's Lacanian purview, frustrates equality promised in the process of mobilizing group-solidarity. Lest all strive for universal recognition of all by all (this would mean radical political as well as economic democracy) one group authenticity can emerge as inauthentic for another group. Nationalism becomes a cover for the provincialism of a new *nomenklatura* writ in large letters. Historical National Socialism is the nemesis of any provincial pseudo-universalism. Neither can represent an ethically authentic claim to difference.[42]

Not only Soviets but also liberal claims to universal democracy are criticized for lacking true universalism. Marginalized groups suspect that universal justice is for politically and economically dominant groups. These groups hegemonize all procedures. Because today there are no other than national states, liberal democracy emerges within nation-states. Critics of liberalism decry its politically and economically oppressive, culturally homogenizing, and patriarchally and racially assimilative character. Since, as Young warns against emphatic Hegelianism (such as Honneth's, Taylor's, or even Benhabib's), groups are multidimensional; justice as the politics of difference, voicing the complex existentially material needs of the marginalized, alone can enhance struggles for greater political and economic democracy.[43]

It would seem that in its most optimistic moments the nation-state promises all groups that they will enjoy a high degree of democratic recognition, politics, and economy. This promise of modern national movements of liberation fuels the attractiveness of both its communitarian and liberal revolutions. And this same promise occasions ongoing legitimation and motivation crises of the established "Nation-Thing"— whether in state socialism or late capitalism. *We* come to hate the strange ways others fashion their enjoyment, yet *we* hate the Other in the other (their enjoyment) because we hate it in ourselves—never having owned this Thing in the first place; thus Žižek explains the depth-roots of ethnocentrism, anti-Semitism, and racism. This tension between specters of liberation (promise) and their theft (the aporia of nationalism as an "impossible desire")[44] problematizes all tendentiously local partialities in group authenticity and the imperial partialities in consensual aims.

In sum, a liberal-communitarian recognition of identity and difference needs sociopolitical and economic—embodied, radically democratic, and existentially sober—dimensions of multicultural recognition. What is decisive for the political economy of struggles for recognition is a twofold need: an overcoming of an uncritically communitarian grasp of the politics of identity and difference, yet also of the uncritically liberal split between tactile and discursive sociality, between esteem and legitimacy.

Enjoying one's universal significance. Balibar speaks of nationalisms within nationalism: these mark racist and patriarchal partialities in the universal claims to authenticity and autonomy. Partialities affect the ethical projects of authenticity—whether individualistic or communitarian. Partialities also affect the projects of universal justice—whether in moral autonomy or procedural politics. In both, such partialities represent racist and patriarchal distortions of claims to authenticity and autonomy. Motivated interests in distorted social identities affect equally regional and global lifeworlds *from within*. By agreeing with Balibar that racism and sexism are certain supplements to economic exploitation and to nationalism in general, I do not assign them a role of ethical or moral superstructure. Racist and patriarchal interests—whether intentionally ideological or not—pertain to the body, hence to one's material existence. Because racism and patriarchy distort communicative competencies with their own logic and just as pervasively as does the lifeworld exploitation of concrete labor, they are not yet overcome by a critique of political economy.[45]

Habermas addresses the colonization of the lifeworld *from without*: the culprits here are the functionalist subsystems, that is, the hegemonic demands of efficient markets and administrative power. With this focus, Habermas is situated better than Taylor to articulate requirements for global justice in complex multicultural democracy. Yet Taylor's, Honneth's, or Benhabib's concerns with social ethics place them more concretely than Habermas within the struggles against cultural imperialism. Taking the two positions together, effective critique must address the distortions affecting lifeworlds also *from within*. This 'within' pertains to local communities and universal procedures. Such distortions affect lived labor as much as they do social identities. I focus here on the second area of issues, on social identities: neither the communitarian-liberal multiculturalism nor the formal-liberal democracy under discussion block racist and patriarchal distortions to the projects of self-realization and self-determination. An antiracist, antipatriarchal, existentially concrete politics of identity and difference is to provide a missing key to filling this gap *within* the lifeworld.[46]

How can one detect cases of someone authentically and autonomously adopting classist and bigotry-laden social identities? Because contents of traditions are not equally suitable to concrete recognition, critical traditionalists eschew empty, decisionist, or outrightly uncritical claims to some originary authenticity. Any fruitful notion of authenticity will result from a performative achievement of recognition, understood in all its existential dimensions (socially tactile, ethical, and normatively discursive). Existentially anchored critical post/modern theorists and activists commence pragmatically and phenomenologically—in the present age. They begin in its ontic domains with various situations of human struggles for justice. They can thus oppose exploitative, racist, and patriarchal sociality, seeking instead sober local solidarity and just global democracy. Whether in Sartre's sketch of anti-Semites with faces of liberal democrats, or in Fanon's unmasking the fact of Blackness invading the White masks of universalism, or in Marcuse's exposure of one-dimensional needs legitimated by late capitalism and state socialism, or in Young's and Bartky's descriptions of justice distorted by patriarchy, or in Cruikshank's narration of the gay and lesbian struggles, I detect those instrinsic limits of communitarian and liberal standpoints which an existentially material key can offset. One needs to recognize these as western articulations of the limits within western communitarian-liberal debates, and one needs to complement them with a multiculturally democratic conversation of civilizations.[47]

An existentially material hermeneutics of suspicion provides the following key: it teaches that in order to relate to oneself and others critically, one must be competent to exercise a certain distance—what Kierkegaard meant by repetition and Du Bois by double consciousness—from inherited traditions and one's motives. Communitarians need this distancing in order to inhabit traditions soberly. Liberals need it in order to inhabit procedures critically. Neither traditions nor procedures teach a sober distancing; they assume it—from the levels of tactile sociality to ethical, moral, political, legal, and economic struggles for recognition. Without explaining, each in turn presumes that individuals in local or political cultures possess a critical relation to the past, present, and future motives. Sartre, even while ambivalent towards psychoanalytic explanations of how social and individual neuroses distort responsible freedom, judged the motives of the sham-democrat to be just as dangerous to the Jews and the Blacks as those of the overt anti-Semite or a clansman.[48]

Many a gender and race theorist persistently point out that the formal-pragmatic structure of validity claims in discourse ethics, while necessary and indeed welcome, is insufficient to perform (in the body) and institutionalize (in concrete justice) the existentially material (tactile as well as discursive) dimensions of democracy. To burden democratic theory with *their* persistence does not burden it with legislating authenticity. First of all, even if we still keep the notion of authenticity, it is no longer to hold to a depth essence to be discovered or legislated. Habermas agrees here that radical democratic socialism, too, must be (re)conceived as a concretely lived—hence existentially material—project. Secondly, I reject the fear of burdensome existential requirements: it is a blackmail that misconstrues an existentially material sense of justice. The fear of a moralizing legislation from on high, even when legitimate, is not a valid counter to such requirements. Democratic theory needs to recognize that humans bring bodies, attitudes, and motives into discursive debates on their traditions. The fact that racist, patriarchal, and homophobic attitudes seriously affect existing lifeworlds and liberal procedures (e.g., court rooms and juries and judges) *from within* (i.e., not as a functionalist rationality *from without* where Habermas locates the remaining problems of colonization) suggests that reaching a universal communicative recognition and competence is incomplete without actively critical dissent from these attitudes. Mere absence of overtly bigoted claims does not safeguard liberal theory and practice from distortions of democratic procedures by the bad faith of attitudinally and systematically deployed bigotry (e.g., through patriarchal and racialized distortions of tactile sociality). My rejoinder articulates certain existential dimensions supporting the above mentioned persistent gender and race correctives. In this coalitional and solidary persistence—in hegemonic articulations to ongoing democratic struggles—such correctives can hopefully affect how critical theorists (in line with the received frames of the liberal-communitarian debate or not) come to theorize the need for recognition.[49]

Conclusions

There is a possibility that even with clear formal procedures *we* arrive at nothing more than unjust, racist, homophobic, and patriarchal consensus. This negative instance portends more than an empirical objection to failures of which a discourse theory *qua* theory of democracy could somehow hold itself innocent. The compartmentalizing, some might say Kantian, strategy of defending the discourse model no longer seems very productive. If genuine democracy is what the age of democracy really proclaims as its prize and want, then democratic actuality requires that *we* dissent from anything less than striving for communicatively competent, responsible, and just forms of life. One must refuse deploying uncritical theory and undemocratic practice. *We* need to inhabit in existence, and embody in the political economy of its institutions, antiracist, antipatriarchal, and anti-imperial critiques of reason and society.

An existential politics of dissenting difference differs from just any uncritical group or individual narration of difference. My rejoinder addresses equally certain liberal forms and certain communitarian narrations. Claims to authentic group difference, just as formal procedures, ought to pass an existential sobriety check. The check—as an expression of possible dissent—is always situated within a radically democratic project. Dissent cannot make exceptions to democratic justice in a wholly alien sense just as one cannot slip out of one's bodily sociality with others.

While agreeing with Habermas's procedural correctives to Taylor, I make my rejoinder to both as well as to Honneth or Benhabib: procedural and communitarian claims can benefit from considering justice in an existential politics of difference. A collaborative dialogue between existential dissent and the complex variety of communitarian-liberal positions ought to affect how one theorizes reciprocal recognition. This dialogue, when imaginatively enlarged, holds relevance for applying the full dimension of communicative recognition to political and regional cultures, to consensual procedures and multicultural democracy, and to law and international relations. Needing to recognize individuals-in-resisting communities, one must admit that dissent is possible from specific (regional) and generalized (political) cultures alike.

I hold that full recognition requires an *existentially material key* in order to unlock the socially tactile as well as discursive loci of possible refusals, and thereby engender a genuinely critical social theory of liberation. The question not asked in this chapter is, how are dissenting individuals possible as socially embodied, ethically related to concrete others, and radically and multiculturally democratic? How are, then, dissent and refusal possible from within both local or regional and political or global cultures? Such questioning is variously raised within the new directions pursued among some critically traditional as well as critically post/modern social (gender and race) theorists. They share a pursuit of the concrete or singular universals *within* the ongoing struggles—as an existentially multicultural and democratic project.[50]

2

Dissenting Individuals

There is a specter roaming around Eastern Europe, in the West they call it dissent.

—Václav Havel, *The Power of the Powerless*

✤✤✤

[S]ocial analysis can learn incomparably more from the individual experience than Hegel conceded, while conversely the large historical categories, after all that has meanwhile been perpetrated with their help, are no longer above suspicion of fraud. . . . In face of the totalitarian unison with which the eradication of difference is proclaimed as a purpose in itself, even part of the social force of liberation may have temporarily withdrawn to the individual sphere. If critical theory lingers there, it is not only with a bad conscience.

—Theodor W. Adorno, *Minima Moralia*

✤✤✤

Tolerance is first and foremost for the sake of the heretics—the historical road towards *humanitas* appears as heresy: target of persecution by the powers that be. Heresy by itself, however, is not token of truth.

—Herbert Marcuse, "Repressive Tolerance"

✤✤✤

[T]he real *leap* consists in introducing invention into existence.

—Frantz Fanon, *Black Skin, White Masks*

✤✤✤

There is a received view of the Kierkegaardian individual who dissents from Hegel's nation-state presumably on a private platform of an antisocial, apolitical, solipsistic, if not possessive individualism. This received wisdom ignores that existential individuals dissent from an atomistic, instrumentally rationalist individualism in modern politics and economy. To this received oversight has been added a new tune celebrating another Kierkegaard. He is regarded by some as a prophet of radical transgressions who writes under the erasure of all normative agency. His attack on reified modern rationality and on the self-owning, let me venture masculinist, notions of autonomy is to give evidence for a wholesale abandonment of ethicopolitical universals. Yet existential dissent jests where modernists expect unreasonably much from critical rationality and autonomous self-determination and is earnest where postmoderns sidestep the difficulty of life into a transgressive gesture about the undecidability of self-choice. This rebel unmasks oversights in the former's foundationalist, absolutist reason and the latter's jargon of textuality and abstract death of the self/author since each type prescinds from existing. Existential dissent thus delivers troubles to both poles of post/modernity.[1]

Existential subject-positions of dissent help me to reconsider with more honesty limits and motives informing critical theory-formation and practice. Kierkegaard's existential dissent points to a step to be taken beyond the divide between post/modern views which pass one another as ships in the night. I characterize such a step as existential praxis: How is one to act with contextualized communicative reason and relational agency yet allow for that individualized dissent which cares to be ethicopolitically responsible? I argue against three category mistakes: dissenting existential individuals are hardly communitarians, or possessive liberals, or antinormative proto-postmodernists. Rather, existential refusals inform critical theory and praxis, thereby empowering democracy-to-come. Existential individuals need not withdraw from the ethicopolitical when they embody radically egalitarian and multicultural singular universals.

1. Who Are the Dissenting Existential Individuals?

There are statements in Kierkegaard's 1846 critique of the age which slam the brakes on the internationalist call to a proletarian union issued two years later in Marx's *Communist Manifesto*. Kierkegaard is suspicious of the idea that "the age will be saved by the idea of sociality, of association." While the early Marx and Kierkegaard are preoccupied with the demise of the human individual (not unlike later Adorno and Marcuse), the latter argues that the leveling of the individual by the herd mentality of the age cannot be resisted directly through social union. "[N]ot until the single individual has established an ethical stance despite the whole world, not until then can there be any question of genuinely uniting." There are valid defenses of the progressive role played by the nation-state whether in 1848 or in a postcolonial opposition to western hegemony. Kierkegaard, just as Fanon, remains as much critical of nationalism as he is of the revolutionaries who attack the philistine bourgeoisie only through quantitative equality. Kierkegaard restates this most emphatically: "'The individual' is the category through which . . . this age, all history, the human race as a whole, must pass."[2]

Does one's refusal turn one into a possessive individualist, or a communitarian yearning for substantive sources of the self, or, on the flip side, an ally of postmodern suspensions of all normativity? Ironically, Kierkegaard has been hired to legitimate all three angles yet jests about these three responses to the crises of modernity while preserving earnestness about individual responsibility. How is that dissident possible who is neither a disencumbered moral agent, nor an effect of prevalent conventions, nor a beholder of nominal gestures bereft of liberating projects, concrete coalitional bonds, or even more intimate communal solidarity? Since Kierkegaard prompts us to rethink these ontologically and ethicopolitically problematic areas, critical theorists and activists may linger here, Adorno concedes in the epigraph above, without bad faith.

Westphal demonstrates that a classical liberal reading of Kierkegaard's category of the individual is a mistake. Had Kierkegaard wanted to return from Hegel's ethical totality of the rational state to premoral contract relations among atomistic individuals *qua* property owners, he would have exchanged holistic "dialectical individualism" for "compositional individualism." We would have to place Kierkegaard within the early stage of Hegel's argument and classify him as a possessive individualist sublated in Hegel's ethical totality. But Kierkegaard begins with Hegel's ethical challenge to liberal atomism, he begins with Hegel's holistic sublation of both the market and moral liberal. Kierkegaard's concern with the individual commences where Hegel's ends—in the rational ideal of the nation-state.[3]

If the nominalistic or possessive-individualist ontology of existential revolt is insupportable (contrary to the received view of existential philosophy from Kierkegaard to Sartre and Beauvoir), one must commence with a rich self whose singularly universal and radically egalitarian freedom is relational, historically situated, multiculturally polyvalent, and linguistic. If every I-individual is always already embedded in a cultural we-universal, then existential dissent from a social whole itself is holistic, never atomistic. Lest *we* deify the nation-state or a collective *dasein*, the existential individual must dissent from Hegel, Heidegger, the Nazi political existentialists, and Stalinists alike. Ethical life is not necessarily granted by a socialization into a cultural whole—not without reflecting on the multifarious cultural, sociopolitical, and economic need for radically democratic recognition. Dissent defines how individuals may adopt critical self-relations to themselves, thus, always to a whole in which they already descriptively begin.[4]

A famous case study of dissent is found in Johannes de Silentio's treatment of the Hegelian view of language and community. Language harnesses the ethical-universal. The individual is that subject-position in language which cannot be directly sayable or mediated by the universal. An existential dissident acts through silences or gaps in propositional speech.[5]

This silence cannot warrant the fanatic clash of fundamentalist monocultural individuals or civilizations, each speaking with certainties. De Silentio's defense of the knight of faith dissents from fundamentalism as well as attacks Cartesian apodictic agency and conventional cultural ethics (*Sittlichkeit*). That the single individual is higher than the universal does not prove a private self-ownership which knows no fear and trembling. And that Abraham cannot speak about his ordeal with Isaac and Sarah does not mean that anything goes. Depicting the individual in possessive or in purely anarchistic terms misses the target. To revel in textual undecidabilities of *Fear and Trembling* would mean to make a virtue out of one's aesthetic self-relation to fear and trembling, or to retreat into the resignation of pure textuality which stoically checks out from any embodied risk of having to fear and tremble. Heroic transgressions of the present age are not the credible dissent that de Silentio has in mind when he calls us back to inhabit the universal in fear and trembling. His earnest jest is that he speaks of agency in terms not clearly recognizable in our liberal-communitarian and post/modern debates. The jest is that one is to act responsibly towards others in the world even when neither self-transparency nor conventions (Abraham's patriarchy with the promise to father the human race) secure action. De Silentio's earnestness about the death of the self-possessive agent becomes sociopolitical in Anti-Climacus's critical praxis within the closed civilization of Christendom. Not offering anyone some blind faith in the total transgression of the ethical-universal, instead he rouses us to dissent from the established nation-states, buttressed orthodoxies, and powers that be.[6]

Fear and trembling embody a jesting spirit of seriousness. They occur for the one who chooses herself as a responsible actor in the world. This activist performer relies neither on dominant cultural models nor on one's will to be or not to be a self-sufficient agent as the criteria for moral action. The jest shows that wilful agency is in trouble; the earnestness plays a joke on jokers who mistook the jargon of agency-in-trouble for the pathos of living in it.[7]

Fine, dissenters need not be libertarians or possessive individualists. Still, is not their transgressive positionality (a teleological suspension of the ethical) plagued by decisionism? Can they sustain their claims otherwise than by arbitrarily asserting a resolve, by narrating *the* good life, by doing nothing at all? How is dissent possible, and ethically or politically meaningful?

What Kierkegaard teaches so well is that radical self-choice can be identified neither with willfulness, nor with communitarian givens of values, nor with value skepticism. Even granted an undecidability about the value sources of good and bad, self-choice stands for an act prior to having a value dilemma. Concretely situated individuals are socialized members of a polity; in reverse, to become a dissenting individual, it is insufficient to be individuated via socialization in a fixed civilization alone. I choose myself not *in abstracto* but as I already am. I do not choose this or that tradition, this or that value-sphere, but myself as capable of responsible, honest, hermeneutically reflexive choosing within what or where I already am socialized. Self-choice defines this performative possibility of dissent—it is qualitative, and it modifies how I embody choices. Self-choice, however, never directly justifies what I choose.[8]

Radical self-choice is, to place Nietzsche in reverse, prior to good and evil. This shows why existential dissent defies and baffles concerns of a liber(tarian)al individualist, existential*ist* voluntarist, communitarian monoculturalist, or postmodern cultural pastiche-activist alike. From the existential perspective that I articulate here, the possessive or voluntarist individualist confuses aesthetic choices of value domains with one's "choosing to will." The communitarian conflates civilizational value spheres or *eudaimonistic* domains of the good with existential sources of the self. The Web-surfing postmodernist mis/reads the death of the author, the end of the book, as if these meant that one has no responsibility to author one's performing self and living text.[9]

All three stylized types seem overly preoccupied with indeterminacies of modernity. The individualist, Kierkegaard's aesthete, gets paralyzed by the dizzy freedom of possibilities: if anything goes, nothing matters. The communitarian decries this modern virtueless situation: MacIntyre lectures Kierkegaard about the existentialist and emotivist maleducation of the young, while C. Taylor retrieves enduring forms of the good that would define our path. The postmodernist celebrates an ethical undecidability of what to choose. In place of becoming Kierkegaard's *Dear Reader*, harnessing the task of self-choosing, this one jettisons the receptive partner of dissenting transgressions, i.e., ethicopolitical, democratic agency.[10]

Radical self-choice, being an offspring neither of cultural nor *eudaimonistic* value-spheres, need not become lost in signifiers. Choice of oneself as this existing individual locates the chooser in a subject-positionality which Climacus calls truth. This subject does not retreat into navel-gazing (self-possession apart from the social) but ventures into an uncertainty of the "chasmic abyss." Charges of subjectivism and decisionism overlook the difference between choices pertaining to validity and those pertaining to identity claims. The charges would apply also to existential dissent if the category of self-choice directly determined validity claims (e.g., positive claims to the good life or of the moral right). This is not so since both the charges against and the celebrations of existential antinormativism represent category mistakes.[11]

How are existential questions related to ethical and moral ones? What is the rationale for the distinction between radical self-choice, on the one hand, and the value spheres of ethical or cultural life (*eudaimonia* and *Sittlichkeit*) and procedural morality (*Moralität*) or politics, on the other? Does not the distinction between an existential 'how' (I embody choices) and the validity domains of 'what' (I choose) dodge the problem of decisionism? It would be a vicious dodge if one could not envision the importance of dissent for ethical or cultural and civilizational, and moral or sociopolitical, universals. I claim that subject-positions of radical refusals circumscribe indirectly something very important for normative social theory and practices.

If ethical totality is to reside in every singular individual, then Kierkegaard's performative holism is ontologically neither derivable from Hegel's nation-state, nor from Kant's moral rigorism, nor from Habermas's formal procedural justice. Rather each presupposes this holism as its concrete beginnings. The existential individual (always already individualized via socialization) marks the most concrete yet the most ideal vanishing point of conceivable dissenting difference (non-identity). The horizon of possible dissent cannot but assume that each individual may embody a *sui generis* species-being. Therein—not in formally liberal, libertarian, or assimilative communitarian categories—lies the vanishing point of radically existential, multicultural, and egalitarian sociality, which I imagine in this study as well as seek in life. A dissenting act interlocks each individual with the human race, together as singular universals. A fragmentation between emphatically disencumbered and embedded claims evaporates. Existential dissent, speaking in terms of critical social ontology, is a relational performative.[12]

Existential ethics dislodges possessive decisionism and uncritical communitarian or civilizational *ethos*. Procedures and traditions admit of direct communication. Radical self-choice is not directly sayable through universalizing aims of language. (It is the suspension of the ethical-universal in fear and trembling that places individuals *and* communities in the chasmic abyss of distancing from any positivism of values or any traditionally received views.) It constitutes a modal condition of the possibility that one can hermeneutically and critically reflect on (dissent from) the normative ideals of the good and right at all. Kierkegaard's unsayable venture—becoming positioned as individuals—defies emphatic liberal, communitarian, and postmodern categories. It dissents from a cocksure, hypermasculinist subject of instrumental modernity and conventional guides to the good life. To wit, nowhere do I meet the death of my responsible agency. Self-choice presupposes hermeneutical and critical distance from given social norms. Yet this cannot justify private or authoritarian exceptions from ethical value-domains and achieved moral validity. Self-choice is the condition of the possibility that I can think normatively, act morally, and dissent from local groups as well as within public spheres.

2. Radical Existential Praxis as a Dimension of Dissent

One striking attempt at rethinking the category of the individual occurs in 1929 when the young Marcuse adopts Kierkegaard's activist critique of Christendom as an example of critical theory rooted in concrete philosophy. Kierkegaard's pamphlets against Danish Christendom and his street activism serve as models of social theory anchored in an individually embodied praxis. In Marcuse's early view, existential and socioeconomic critiques are not opposed: to be existentially concrete is not to dodge the social whole. They are two necessarily complementary forms of a materially concrete philosophy. The mature Marcuse rejects the German political existentialism because it abstracts from historical concretion and, thereby, plays into the hands of the Nazi nationalists. Yet in the 1960s, Marcuse calls for a new sensibility and radical subjectivity. He attempts to integrate existential dissent and subaltern resources of revolt into the activist notion of great refusals. In addition to Marcuse's Great Refusal and other efforts at an existentially rooted critical social theory, there have until recently transpired readings of the philosophy of existence mostly under what I label as ideal-typical category mistakes.[13]

Lessons from the shipwrecked voyages of the category of the individual can be drawn from the following questions: How do dissenting individuals affect procedural and contextual justice? How do they affect claims to moral autonomy as well as to ethically authentic forms of life? If the dissenting individual is the vanishing point of the teleological suspension of an ethical-universal, what would it mean to translate this singular position (without a dodge) into the same ethical-sociopolitical-universal? I shall discuss two translation efforts, even as I find each incomplete without the other: Habermas's (in relation to C. Taylor) and Derrida's. The first expands the preceding chapter, the second continues in the next two chapters. I intend, with Marcuse's help (particularly in chapters five, seven, and nine), to complete such efforts.

The Category of the Individual in Communicative Ethics

In his recent returns to Kierkegaard, Habermas accomplishes two innovations. One, he harnesses the category of the individual into what he calls postmetaphysical thinking, thereby depicting existential positions under the rubric of the performative claim to identity. In the latter term, he finds an opening for translating the Kierkegaardian verticality or inwardness into the horizontal or the publicly available linguistic forum of communication. Two, Habermas adopts a Kierkegaardian self-reflexive attitude in order to evaluate those cultures or civilizations that clash or become problematic. His originality lies in translating the existential either/or, typical for radical self-choice, into public debates on choices of vital elements in inherited traditions.[14]

But in both ways of translating the dissenting individual back into the universal, I argue, Habermas collapses existential categories into local narratives about the good life. He coins a mixed category of existential-communitarian discourse which he, then, to his satisfaction subsumes under the normative questions of moral autonomy. I agree that this latter subsumption of ethical goods under moral rights is made for otherwise cogent procedural reasons. Yet, I disagree, the former association of radical self-choice with the communitarian questions of the good life entails a category mistake. Habermas overlooks that an earnestly jesting individual resists those cultural narratives and homogenizing or assimilationist universalisms whose motives distort the truly egalitarian, liberation promises of identity and difference, theory and practice.

Habermas's first innovation is facilitated by Kierkegaard's depiction of "self-relation as a relating-to-oneself, wherein I relate myself at the same time to an antecedent Other on whom this relation depends." This "Other," unlike in German idealism or existential phenomenology, is no longer a transcendental, absolute, apodictic ego cogito "qua the subject of the original act of self-positing." The "performative attitude of the subject who chooses himself" is situated in life histories of other individuals. There are no private selves apart from the historical and linguistic facticity of relating in one's self-relation to others. I am responsible for the self which I posit in my identity claim and present to others. How can this be? Habermas provides the transcription of Kierkegaard's self-and-other relation into communicative ethics: responsibility (either to drift or to become a self) is awakened in the ego by its self-relation related to an alter. Ego's responsible yes and no attitude to the claims raised by the alter in dialogue is marked by the doubly reflexive contingency of dialogic reciprocity among responsible speakers. Habermas takes Kierkegaard's postsecular or "vertical axis" of self-relation before the wholly Other and tips it "into the horizontal axis of interhuman communication." In place of this wholly Other, the horizontal axis functions as the idealized speech condition which allows ego and alter, each, to maintain their performative continuity. This is no longer a traditionalist or uncritically ontological continuity. The performative attitude in communication itself allows for ethical self-understanding of what it takes to be a speaker and hearer. Habermas projects the condition of felicitous speech-acts into the generalized other—the regulative ideal of communicating community. The ideal assumes neither fixed communities nor free-floating selves. Neither ego nor alter relies on "the possessive individualism" or on a descriptively narrative "reconstructive appropriation of [his or her] life history." Each in relation to others authenticates and negotiates the performative "guarantee" to a continuity of ethical reconstructions. "The self of an ethical self-understanding is dependent upon recognition by addressees because it generates itself as a response to the demands of an other in the first place."[15]

In his second innovation, Habermas translates the Kierkegaardian self-reflexive attitude toward tradition into deliberative democracy and law. He corrects what he views to be the normative deficits of Kierkegaard's position. While formal pragmatics allows Habermas to bring the dissenting individual back into the linguistic universal, democratic theory and law reveal the sociopolitical import of this publicly anchored existential attitude. It is obvious that this latter move is aimed at offsetting the voluntarist character of some existential*ist* versions of the either/or. (If the self-choosing individual lives in deliberative democracy, it is the public debate, not the subjectivist facticity of value-choices, which serves as the normative guide for valid action.) It is, however, less obvious that Habermas appeals to Kierkegaard in order to prevent rooting deliberative democracy in performatively abstract ontologies, nationalist doctrines, or uncritical traditionalisms. This appeal is possible because dissenting individuals already know that no social convention and no civilization disposes with innocent origins. They are earnestly responsible, they jestingly defy the expectations of possessive individualism, group *ethos*, and the ethics of pure anarchy alike. Radical democracy can save antiessentialist and multicultural aspirations of identity and difference in concrete egalitarian, viz., existentially material terms.[16]

Kierkegaard, seemingly anticipating S. Huntington's public policy for the twenty-first century, warns that what follows the death of the instrumental modernist subject and of meaningful cultural signifiers need not be the end of ideology and history but a more acute leveling of clashing civlizations. *We* know this as 'ethnic cleansing'—whether under the rubric of cultural identity and difference politics or that of falsely equalizing, assimilationist universalism. As Tolić recently put it, the modernist grand narratives deposed by Gulag and Auschwitz give way to the postmodern wars of local as well as civilizational narratives symbolized by Sarajevo or Jerusalem. Eurocentric metanarratives dissipate into the New World Dis/Order of nationalisms and fundamentalisms—with no clear and distinct exit. Kirmmse finds Kierkegaard's warning reconcilable with the liberal political agenda of the revolutionary age of 1848. Yet Kierkegaard's individuals approximate Marcuse's radical subjectivities, not lukewarm liberals in western establishments. Dissenters may not get high on becoming cultural-social levelers or conservative cynics. The cultural undecidability of clashing civilizations grants no alibi, whereby *we* irresponsibly buttress *our* traditions while becoming multiculturally strategic in foreign affairs.[17]

Habermas turns to Kierkegaard's critique of the nation-state and Christendom in order to confront the latter-day nationalists and fundamentalists. Transposed into communicative ethics, existential self-choice enters into earnest public debates on the future of *our* traditions. Habermas invents his Kierkegaard-inspired political ethics in a 1987 paper given in Copenhagen. There he exposes the German historians who revise Germany's responsibility for its Nazi past. This innovation has become even more timely in the post-1989 remaking of the world order.[18]

✦ ✦ ✦

Consider the debate about the Czechoslovak Velvet Revolution. Whereas Habermas shares with Havel the view that guilt cannot be apportioned to groups, there is ample room for negotiating our present relationship to the past and, thus, to our choices for the future by which we define who we are and want to be. Some people in the post-Communist countries (Michnik brands them ironically the 'clean hands') are disaffected with the velvet character of the change. Given that former Communists not only sit on stolen monies but, as the Communists-cum-capitalists, have legitimated their old market monopolies in unabashed apologies for the capital-logic, some charge Havel's humanism with being at best the failure of a naïve intellectual and at worst a conspiracy that secured for the past regime the punishment-free transfer of power. The tragic irony of the charges is that the amorality of the market stands under this accusation along with the former state-socialist orthodoxy. This is what Fraser labels, paraphrasing Lyotard, the 'postsocialist condition'. Without recognizing the lack of genuine democracy in the present markets as much as in the past regime (both promised to give everyone socially equal chances), what guarantee is there that a bloody change or more severe purges (lustrace) of the old structures would have dealt a decisive blow to totalitarianism? The call for a strong hand discloses the revolutionary impatience of those whom Michnik characterizes as the anti-Communists with the faces of Bolsheviks: they dream that a collectively assignable guilt can grant all a clean slate. I agree that an intermediate position should exist between a meekness vis-à-vis the Stalinist past and an authoritarian or fascist reaction to it. Will not the failure to find such a middle way lead to collapsing responsible self-choice into antidemocratic leveling? Can't one meet this confusion in its most cynical form within some extreme right-left or black-red nationalist coalitions in the Russian Federation or in the division of Bosnia's territory among Croats and Serbs? To secure the possibility of forging democratic structures where there were none, I would take any day Havel's or Michnik's existential irony of disciplinary power (their 'nonpolitical politics' rather unpopular now in the East) over joining the nationalists or the black-shirt skinheads. That the former nomenklatura *wears the coat of the free market or the colors of nation-states should strip all illusions about its having* any *innocent origins. Democracy with a human face was impossible in Stalinist regimes and proscribed after the reform socialism of Prague Spring (1968); it is impossible under and proscribed by market and power imperatives. Faith in 'capitalism with a human face' is a postsocialist relic if not an antidemocratic misnomer.*[19]

✢ ✢ ✢

Countries still learn to live in the void of existential self-choice by facing the difficulty of beginnings. This learning is crucial for ongoing openness to others, even though authenticity cannot be legislated for individuals or civilizations and even though anything learned by either can contribute also to regress into new uncritical narratives of innocent, difficulty-free beginnings. Dissenting individuals and groups need democratic publics. In a civic forum, whereby received traditions become self-reflexively available in practical discourse, Habermas argues that self-choice takes on an incisively normative character. In place of nationalist worship of symbols and flags, citizens ought to come together in constitutional patriotism, under more sober procedures of a linguistified sacred. In dialogue cultural and economic needs can be politically recognized. To decide what claims are normative, we appeal to the deliberative competence of actors and accept as legitimate what can be recognized by all concerned. In complex societies this process requires existentially material (concretely embodied and economic) and multicultural (multiracial and multigender) democracy.

Now I contend that in the process of his two innovative translations of dissensus into communicative democracy and law, Habermas has lost some important aspects of the critical role played by refusing individuals. Radical existential praxis cannot be given over to public policy choices alone. Policies may not take for granted that citizens *have become* capable of responsible self-choice in the first place. Deliberative democracy and law assume *having at hand* "unleashed individual liberties"[20]—viz., communicatively competent dissenting individuals.

In dissent one must learn to inhabit the ethical-universal (this curbs individualist atomism) and yet not be commensurable with it (this checks the Hegelian holism or any uncritical *ethos* or essentializing identity). Inscribing dissent in this dual movement, I can show how it recognizes individual and coalitional claims (liberal moral and political concerns) as well as solidary claims emerging in struggles (communitarian ethical concerns for authentic group needs). Dissent safeguards procedural democracy *and* groups against universalist or regional homogenizations, and the fragmentation of antiessentialist struggles.

In responsible citizenship lies the heart of Havel's term 'existential revolution' as he expands a greengrocer's refusal of oppression into democratic action. Such democratized existential categories can provide a check and balance on totalitarian drives that might emerge from individuals, groups, or civilizations when these pick some value-domain of the universal or of the specifically good and try to make others commensurate with it. In forging a coalition with Habermas's communicative model of democracy, I hold that by admitting dissent we draw a key distinction between communitarian (cultural) and existential dimensions of self-choice.[21]

The Category of the Individual and Communitarian-Liberal Debates

Taylor, in holding with Hegel that the 'I' and the 'we' are co-original, raises two issues: as discussed in the previous chapter, like Habermas, he undertakes the linguistic-communication turn in philosophical methodology, and yet he finds in Kierkegaard a modernist resource for new, subtler languages of "personal resonance." Taylor seeks a personally indexed entry to traditional sources of the self in order to sustain modern individuals under the experiential and ecological demands of the age. First, then, he defines personal identity by a competence to answer for oneself within the discursive space of questions. One needs moral orientation since modernity is no longer reducible to a dominant identity-frame. He lists among key moral sources of modernity theism, Enlightenment rationality, and romantic expressivism. Searching for identity can be meaningful only "in the interchange of speakers." He concurs with Habermas that identity is linguistic. The linguistification of inwardness marks the "original position of identity-formation." "The full definition of someone's identity . . . usually involves not only his stand on moral and spiritual matters but also some reference to a defining community."[22]

Secondly, Taylor explores the personally indexed access to mythology, metaphysics, and theology. He insists that *we* cannot return to a classicist world view or retreat to a culture of subjectivism. Turning inward while decentering the subject are two moments of the same nonsubjectivist and nonobjectivist need for self-affirming recognition. "[T]he turn inward may take us beyond the self as usually understood, to a fragmentation of experience which calls our ordinary notions of identity into question . . . or beyond that to a new kind of unity, a new way of inhabiting time." He argues that reflexivity and acts of creative self-transformation accompany the plurality of our experiences. The poet becomes "the bringer of epiphanies." Taylor proposes that "[d]ecentering is not the alternative to inwardness; it is its complement." The reflexive turn "intensifies our sense of inwardness." This interior intensification does not promote brooding in subjectivism, just as post/modern decentering need not imply that one must fall into objectivism: "The modernist multilevelled consciousness is . . . frequently 'decentered': aware of living on a transpersonal rhythm which is mutually irreducible in relation to the personal. But for all that it remains inward; and is the first only through being the second."[23]

Taylor retrieves Kierkegaard's, Dostoyevsky's, and Nietzsche's dynamic transformations of inwardness. These thinkers effuse with a modernist creative imagination, whereby I can transform what I interpret and affirm; and my relation to the world and others is changed in my self-relation. The difference between a MacIntyre, longing for the golden age of an Aristotelian *polis*, and a Kierkegaard, choosing to be a self within a critical self-relation to tradition, is that if I am the latter, "[a]ll the elements in my life may be the same, but they are now transfigured because chosen in the light of the infinite. . . . Through choice we attain self-love, self-affirmation." Through this self-choice, I attain a transformed posture toward myself and tradition. Where Kierkegaard projects self-affirmation before the vertical other, Nietzsche's yes to the world is a self-overcoming. Yet both are speaking and acting within a tradition. Therein they articulate and perform a discourse of transfiguration, "a vision which doesn't alter any of its contents but the meaning of the whole."[24]

Poets bespeak these traditional sources—divine, worldly, aesthetic. Poets do not offer a "regression . . . to a new age of faith." They cannot raise positivist or fundamentalist claims, but rather performative, "invocative uses of language; those whereby we bring something about or make something present by what we say." At this point, Taylor does not seek a formal moral point of view but a concrete ethic of the good in a mode of invocative, epiphanic language.[25]

Given his partial yes to Habermas, by a new language of "personal resonance," Taylor *ought to* mean that life-form in which posttraditional individuals inhabit communicative spaces of existential questioning. True, he envisions a concrete narrative identity which has the quality of an "epiphany," a "moral source," a new language that would "make crucial human goods alive for us again." Yet he reads this disclosive language in communitarian (Hegelian and Aristotelian), not existential (Kierkegaardian, Beauvoirean, Marcusean) terms. A communitarian retreat conflicts with the call for radical self-choice, unless one interprets the latter through the former in fixed social identities, that is, nonexistentially. Rather than working from within a category of the self-reflexive individual, Taylor attaches his narrative to the authority of a *Sittlichkeit*. Because he seeks a normative priority of the 'We' to the 'I'—and not merely a descriptive priority of a hermeneutical *we* to the particular 'I'— he reduces the language of inwardness or self-choice to *eudaimonistic* ethics. In order to enter modes of personal resonance that the possibility of dissent demands of individuals *and* groups, Taylor should effect his return to local narratives via existential reflexivity, not in the positive security of their givenness.[26]

With Hegel, Taylor retrieves the value sources of identity within a postconventional, modern ethic. Yet, Taylor argues that the role of philosophy is not merely to elucidate the moral point of view but to orient us to viable projects of the good life. Habermas notes that Taylor, unlike his communitarian kin, MacIntyre, is neither a metaphysician nor an anti-modernist. Taylor, he says, is a Catholic skeptic who seeks the whole of morality in larger ethical meanings. Taylor is a genealogist of morals who nonetheless directs his neoexistentialist skepticism to constitutive, substantive goods.[27]

Habermas asks Taylor: Can modern identity be defended in an ethic of the substantive good and still with postmetaphysical means? He answers no to Taylor's affirmative answer. Let us keep in mind that Habermas agrees with Kierkegaard's articulation of the identity-crises of the present age. He *should not* have implicated Kierkegaard in Taylor's position. Yet neither Taylor nor Habermas distinguish the category of the existential individual from the communitarian questions of the good or even from theological dogmatics. Both set autonomy (moral right) and authenticity (read as an ethical question of the good) against one another. A third dimension—dissenting existential individuals—vanishes from cultural narratives and liberal democracy. It is this concrete mediating possibility of democratic dissent that I wish to recover.

Taylor reasons in a neo-Hegelian fashion: authenticity is intelligible only as a group-ethical achievement. He orients modern identity not on the basis of self-choice but rather via objective sources of the good which are to constitute our identity. And he wants to find a substantive ethic of authentic personal resonances that could include all these goods. Habermas reasons in a neo-Kantian manner: he celebrates the plurality of gods and demons—the many goods of modernity—on the basis of moral legitimation or autonomous self-determination. But both thinkers, in their two opposing emphases on a group ethic of authenticity and formal moral autonomy, engage in reductionism that waters down the category of existential, qualitative identity. I showed that Taylor assimilates the dissenting individuals into universal goods. And Habermas assimilates them, as if they were always already part and parcel of *eudaimonistic* or civilizational value-choices of the good, under the procedural moral right.[28]

Taylor and Habermas find in Kierkegaard a resource for articulating modern identity. Both view Kierkegaard under what Habermas labels, by means of a communitarian-neoexistentialist category, *ethical-existential discourse*. In transcribing active performatives into clinical or valuative questions of the good life, both thinkers, for opposing reasons, assimilate or essentially fix the possibility of dissent. Taylor brings Kierkegaard under the ethical fold of *eudaimonia* by extending the existential sources of the self into new social ethics. Habermas educates possessive individualists by inviting them to a procedural forum. Yet the performative-existential attitude of dissenters challenges the very communitarian-liberal framework of the debate.[29]

Diverging from the Habermas-Taylor debate, I object to each for shared reasons. I think that it is a mistake to render the category of radical self-choice under the questions of the good or bad life. Possible dissent marks a mode of existence, whereby I relate self-reflexively to my tradition, groups, and choose myself as someone capable of good or bad faith in the first place. If this is true, then one can neither domesticate dissent by a fixed prior or future communitarian solidarity (Taylor) nor subordinate it along with other questions about the good (ethical life-projects) under the right, procedural morality, and law (Habermas). The term "ethical-existential"—if it stands for *eudaimonia* or fixed social *ethos*—is a Kierkegaardian misnomer.[30]

Taylor wants substantive democracy; Habermas envisions deliberative democracy. Taylor affirms the dominant shared ethical goods as sources of the self but not the possibility of dissent. Habermas's normative procedures take advantage of dissent only to bind it hand-and-foot by public morality or law. Neither elucidates possibilities of existential-democratic dissent from local or civilizational narratives of *the* good and from partial political cultures of nation-states.

I tend to agree with Habermas's misgivings that genuine democracy can be built on the basis of the overlapping substantive sources of the good. Is not democracy which is anchored in a national vision of the good but a convex mirror of wanting some objectively positivist domain of *eudaimonia* whereby an aesthete can secure self-choice before he or she ventures any choice? Do not both the essentializing communitarian and the bootstrapping neoexistentialist starting points, not unlike nominalist transgressivity, begin with arbitrary sources of solidarity or wilfulness, thus begging the question whether one can begin *that way* in the first place? To avoid the essentializing-homogenizing as well as bootstrapping-voluntarist approaches to the self, I distinguish the existential-performative from the communitarian categories, and an existential ethics from an ethic of substantive group authenticity or civilizational value-projects.[31]

It is interesting that Habermas gets quite near this distinction when he unleashes on the communitarian Taylor the negating Adorno and the deconstructive Derrida. The personal resonance sought for by Taylor lies in the epiphanic value-domain of art; but aesthetics cannot provide the substantive utopia of the good. Adorno teaches us that there is no full-proof aesthetic substitute for religious epiphany or premodern substantive unity. Likewise for Derrida, modern art is bereft of the positive good and the true and, hence, cannot be the normative source of morality. Should new or post/enlightenment thinkers and activists choose an aesthetic way or an aesthetic critique? One cannot privilege aesthetic over practical and theoretical rationality in order to win over the lost positivity of the good. Adorno's praxis of theorizing discloses but a negative epiphany of fragmented memory and damaged life (a materially negative utopia or an aesthetic critique). And this 'negative' cannot replace the disenchanted, materially, religiously, or metaphysically fixed utopias. Even Marcuse's affirmative cultural, political, and economic appeals to the aesthetic dimension are never nostalgic glances to a golden age. A utopian imaginary is to invent at best sources for social critique and liberation praxis. Taylor seems unsatisfied with aesthetics as a source of such revolutionary refusals. But an aesthetic way alone lacks the critical, to be sure for Habermas nonquietist, force of a valid claim.[32]

The Category of the Individual in Post/Modernity

Derrida opts for the transgressive Kierkegaard, that is, for the politics of the impossible. While I am critical of that 'Derrida 1' whose transgressions find home mainly in the mainstream North American academic receptions of deconstruction, I affirm the 'Derrida 2' whose dissent *can* empower the marginalized agency of the oppressed. I am in no fashion undecidable on this issue of which of the *two Derridas* can help us build coalitions against the neocolonial discourses of power. I opt for the latter, along with radical existential praxis, as a direction that admits politically relevant coalitions of critical post/modern social theorists.

In Derrida's Kierkegaardian "hope, fear, and trembling," one meets the crisis of European (read: modern) identity as such. Derrida abandons the ethical-universal idea of 'Europe'. Yet some readings of his transgression do not allow one to return there even in the limited sense conceded by Adorno's negatively apprehended material utopia or Marcuse's affirmative refusals. In the anti-Enlightenment readings of 'Derrida 1', all dialectical links with the ethical-universal vanish. I question whether or not Derrida's insistence on remaining in the moment of "imminence, [which is] at once a chance and a danger," must situate him on the other side and even against Habermas's defense of critical Enlightenment.[33]

I read 'Derrida 2' as serving an intensified, radicalized promise of the Enlightenment—the satisfaction of the existentially material needs for recognition. Both Derrida and Habermas are confronting nationalism, xenophobia, and racism; each envisions some form of radical multicultural democracy as a corrective to intra- as well inter-civilizational clashes. True, Habermas translates Kierkegaard's fear and trembling into a normative public debate about our disastrous traditions, whereas Derrida translates this same urgency into a gesture that is to resist any procedural coaptation. Does one have to view Habermas's and Derrida's failures to encounter one another at the end of the day as a proof that notions of dissenting individuals are philosophically and politically useless since they cannot be harnessed into democratic procedures where alone dissensus is morally, sociopolitically, and legally relevant? There is no normative argument *in Derrida*, nor in the politically retrograde uses of him, that prevents me from bringing his transgression and Habermas's democratic agency into mutual collaboration. If my ambition is not to make Habermas and Derrida reconcile *their* differences, still my argument points to such a missing positionality between liberals and communitarians as well as within post/modernity. Finding this missing link by earnest jesting with certain modernity and postmodernity is not a dodge of the issue between singular and universal perspectives. Rather, it offers a genuine alternative to the parameters in which these debates are now structured.[34]

If Derrida's critique of nationalism and racism were not to be normative in either the liberal or communitarian or discourse-ethical senses, how is one to communicate its political import? Derrida operates with a conceptually broad sense of the political. He calls for overcoming the binary opposition between Eurocentrism and anti-Eurocentrism and for adopting the posture that disrupts all capital headings, whether in their power-centers or in their economic capital-logic. He attacks the homogenizing logic of the proper name (i.e., capital as a cultural heading and as private property) in order to re-vision, not reject, the promise of egalitarian recognition. Does not this reading of Derrida's Kierkegaardian particularized interventions decenter assimilative universalism for the sake of an intensified political economy of recognition? How else can *we* grasp Derrida's hope for, fear and trembling about, multiculturalism free of ethnic, racial, gender or economic cleansing? What else can receptivity to refugees without destroying their alterity mean? Can *we* in good faith bracket Derrida's deconstructive Marx from his deconstructive Kierkegaard? Can *we* bracket Marx from Kierkegaard, and vice versa?[35]

The particularized element of Derrida's critique of Eurocentric rationality lies in adopting the transgressive method first originated by de Silentio against Hegel's ethical totality. If Derrida were arguing for a pluralized collage of diverse headings, he would be a postmodern liberal (e.g., in an edifying conversation of the West). If transgressions proffered just another, albeit anti-Eurocentrically postmodern, communitarian locus (Derrida's Paris over Aquinas's), one could only abstractly fantasize, not truly trespass Hegel's ethical-universal. Derrida's other of the heading differs from many other headings and from the hypermasculinist logic of the head. He attacks the capital-head as the root western metaphor of power and of money. The other of cultural and economic domination is the netherside of the heading. Derrida intimates this in a perpetually transgressive gesture that keeps the promise of democracy open, never settling its context, not even consensually closing it as a substantive regulative ideal.

In his well-argued defense of Derridean politics, Caputo depicts how deconstructive transgressions operate shuttles between the universal (deconstructible laws) and the singular (undeconstructible justice). This politics is not, Caputo insists, an an-archic retreat to a total deconstruction. The deconstructionist, just as de Silentio's Abraham, keeps one foot in the political sphere of democratic institutions. With the other foot one transgresses the laws of this sphere—for the sake of justice. The transgressive gesture "moves within the space of two impossibles," i.e., "the failed universal and the inaccessible singular." "[T]hat twofold impossibility constitutes the condition of its possibility."[36]

Is not there a sense in which Kierkegaard's individual defies that version of 'Derrida 1' whose operative categories, for all their conceptual expansion of the political, do not show us how (at times forbid us) to link the hope, fear, and trembling of transgressions to democratic dissent? 'Derrida 1', unlike Marx and unlike Kierkegaard in his authorship and attack on the established order, does not return to take a critical stance within the ethical-universal. When this 'Derrida 1' does come back, then it is not to be silent or remain in gaps but to claim every transgression as already a proto-normative condition of the impossible ethical-universal.

Let us say we hold, like Caputo, Kierkegaardian sympathies with Derrida's project and read the deconstructive transgressions of the ethical-universal as radical existential acts. There are questions that will not go away, especially if raised by voices from the colonized existentially material margins. Is Abrahamic silence a positive meaning of radical transgression; or do such gestures invite us to an *undecidable* postmodern epoch? Do they lure us to retreat into a premodern if not antimodern

Denken? Unsayable transgressions and undecidable gestures could then mean that the facticity of dissenting individuals *must* be mis/read in all search for normative validity? But is not *this* undecidability, *this* 'must' a dodge? In mis/reading texts, must not self-misreading matter to radical existential praxis? What if the celebrated impossibility turns culturally, politically, economically neocolonial? What if the notion of textual undecidability becomes existential and socioeconomic undecidability, thereby blocking the needed agency of personal and social recognition? What if this blockage conveniently prevents any unmasking of the ideological role that notions such as impossibility and undecidability might play in the neocolonial discourse? What then becomes of their celebrated radicality? My preferred version of 'Derrida 2', read here along with a certain Kierkegaard and Marx, disrupts any donkey who is stuck with these seemingly undecidable stacks of hay. A decisive either/or shows refusing individuals to be the loci of dissent from the oppressive ethical-universal. Such dissent occurs in the social concretion of domination. In existing, it transpires prior, yet in relation, to normative questions as the lived condition of *their* possibility.

Without dissent becoming embodied, how can one discern between, e.g., MacIntyre's antimodern and Derrida's postmodern Paris, or between S. Huntington's ethnocentrically 'invidious' multiculturalism and multicultural refusals in the NWO? Objections usually raised to Kierkegaard's antinormative posture apply better to any reified talk of transgressions, impossible or double binds, undecidable gestures, as well as to 'ludic' multiculturalism. The reified version of 'Derrida 1', of fear and trembling, disallows one from articulating any dialectical link of radical self-choice to the moral and sociopolitical universals. The marginalized deserve concrete historical hope. Their fear and trembling are existentially material, viz., real. *Their* transgressions target faces of oppression. I find nothing in Derrida's moves to prevent me (normatively or by coercion) from unmasking that jargon of textual transgressions which in our age acquiesces (on behalf of the underprivileged) to the impossibility of cultural and social change. Short of babbling abstractly of transgressions within texts, I am prompted to embrace, e.g., Fanon's existential leap. It invents and embodies refusals of racially motivated impossibilities such as the constructed facticity of inferior Blackness.[37]

That Kierkegaard's Abraham cannot speak is not *positively normative* for his obligations to the community. The unsayable pertains to his individual positionality which is in throngs of fear and trembling. The possibility of dissent can be *negatively normative* in deliberative democracy. Kierkegaard curbs uncritical demands that individuals conform to a skewed social whole. Only if a silence of hidden inwardness were positively normative, could a heroic being or a quietist resignation or claims to authoritarian exception be conflated with existential dissent. Judging from the appeals to fear and trembling in the curbing of a totalitarian established order, this conflation would be a false conclusion about the extent of radical existential praxis.[38]

Marcuse anticipates the dialectic of democratic dissent in his category of two-dimensionality: the radical subject is to be immersed in struggles of local communities *and* positioned in refusal of their homogenizing demands, responsible to democratic politics *and* reflectively opposed to one-dimensional political or procedural cultures. Nominalist transgressivity is missing the requisite existentially material key to unlock the need and struggles for recognition. One may invert Hegel's holistic mediation of individuals into a communitarian nation-state yet retain in a concrete dialectic the holistic dissenting possibilities (the singular individual) with the holistic democratic agencies (the singular universal). The 'Derrida 1' of transgressive textuality and the Habermas of procedural morality and law, both tend to misplace dissensus.[39] Refusals are neither wholly alien to democracy nor normatively explained away by its form. Dissent marks a critical link in Marcuse's radically democratic two-dimensionality. This alone accounts for the communicative competence for resistance against established claims to ethical authenticity and moral autonomy alike. Dissenting individuals harness this existentially communicative competence in empowering social agencies of democratic change.

3. Crossing the Divide between Critical and Postmodern Social Theory

Someone can object: I show how dissenters earnestly jest with the post/modern binary and how they ironize the yearning for community, but the joke is on them. How can the category of dissenting individual help critical social theory move beyond essentializing universalism and xenophobic particularism? What kind of democratic politics is realistic with radical existential praxis? What can rethinking these categories do that other views cannot?

One instance where the double movement of dissent and democracy played a key role, and where the failure to develop their linkage partly accounts for new forms of nationalist and fundamentalist hatred, is the development of post-1989 Europe. Existential ethics was best articulated in the dissenting communities of individuals who, not wholly unlike in Los Angeles of the April 1992 rebellion and far from tenured radicals, functioned as so many disruptive positionalities on the urban outskirts of totalitarian regimes. The normative moment enters in when dissenting individuals are to be translated into new democratic structures. The need for democratic dissent is given by the historically specific lack of transitional civil societies that could forge new institutions while taking some stock of the past damage. Both gaps require ongoing curbs on desires to define the present by a strong hand. To focus on a pure culturally transgressive moment feeds into quietist defeatism (so typical of reactions to political or economic setbacks) and into elitism (which reinforces the antiegalitarian desire for a strong authority). These two regressions lead to an eclipse of democratic institutions. An ethic of anarchy is a welcome tool against a totally administered society. Yet if left without the democratic agency of change, it can support reactionary trends in these historical conditions. One must not abstract from concrete material history into grand conceptual schemes alone, even where these are no longer metaphilosophies of history but textual or conceptual deconstructions.

It is possible to thematize the double positionality of dissent and democracy in a less historically linear and more dialectical manner. There is a need for singular and social agency in moments of dissent; and one may require dissenting correctives during the 'normal' times of democratic institutionalization. This is true for theory and practice alike. Dissidents were not merely some theoreticians of the postmodern ethics of anarchy. They were not pure anarchists (i.e., transgressors bereft of agency) either.

✤ ✤ ✤

Let's have "Charta 77" serve as an example. It was issued in 1977 as a dissenting act against the repressive post-1968 normalization by Gustav Husák's Czechoslovak government. At the time the act was ridiculed as a politically ineffective gesture of arrogant and self-serving intellectuals by the officials as well as by some dissidents. The Manifesto, inspired by Lévinas and Patočka alike, interpreted dissensus in terms of the individual and social responsibility that humans and citizens are called to bear toward others. Citizenship and a courage to act at the time of shared need were brought together. This was a call for human rights: the group placed concrete demands upon the government, appealed to international charters, and articulated a normative argument that the legitimacy of governments originates in democratic deliberation of its citizens. This existentially and historically grasped, and democratically developed, dissident responsibility formed the key basis for other theoretical documents issued by "Charta 77" since 1977—pertaining to the need for recognition in cultural, sociopolitical, and economic terms—leading up to the pathbreaking events of November 1989.[40]

The changes after 1989 raised new questions about what to do with the transgressive moment when it comes to a functioning democracy. Should powerless dissidents become the powerful? Should the greengrocer's revolt give way to professional politics? The question has not lost its interest even with Václav Havel's second Czech presidency and Václav Klaus's second term as the Czech prime minister. The question remains on the agenda in the democratic dissent against Slobodan Milošević's Party of the State—waged daily in peaceful street marches as well as by the 'information guerillas' from the Beograd radio station B-92. The most theoretically and practically innovative dissent appears in the moments when transgression and agency, each grasped in individual and social settings, collaborate to bring about liberation. There is a place for transgressions. They meet needs left unsatisfied by democratic institutions. To wit: nationalism, racism, and fundamentalism exercise a strong appeal for individual and group identities in transition; this appeal blocks the path to socially egalitarian and democratic deliberations. The problem of both transgression and agency is that world civilization lacks those types of citizens who are ready to relate transgressively towards their own traditions for the sake of satisfying the coalitional and even solidary need for recognition across multiple old and new divisions. Settling for the multiculturally divided (globally) and conservatively secured (domestically) civilizational spheres of influence is a recipe for a global civil clash among the multiple Republics of Gilead. We need to invent those institutions of popular sovereignty within which locally flexible yet globally responsible governments could replace fortresses of nation-states while wielding real counterweights to the flexibly global piracy by multinationals.[41]

Conclusions

What can be done short of developing competencies to dissent and act democratically? Many are hardened by the national or religious intransigencies of regional hatreds or by the NWO politics. The advantages of a group ethic of authenticity or of formal moral autonomy and procedurally democratic law hardly offset such lagging competencies. The competence to dissent marks, *negatively*, an ability to refuse oppressive communities; and it empowers, *positively*, democratic change. Both dissent and democratic agency must act in sync to retain the said competencies. This *both* is not a Hegelian both/and. The two retain an either/or logic, projecting dissenting individuals into multiculturally polycentric singular universals (i.e., one's critical individualization through socialization). Assimilation and fragmentation—neither goes well with this notion of concrete (egalitarian and multicultural) democracy. Dissent marks the most radical point of difference, opening paths to polities of diversity and confluence. These self-corrective loci of openness may prevent the homogenization of universalizing democratic procedures and the xenophobic reaction of regions. Existential individuals dissent both from disencumbered individuals of instrumental modernity and uncritical cultural ideals. They defy postmodern sensibilities, arriving in earnest jest after post/modern existential and social undecidability. As existentially material, the need for recognition must admit the possibility of dissent. Dissent and democracy, dialectically understood, open historically concrete, critical post/modern social theorists to a new multicultural enlightenment. From here may emerge broad coalitions and even new solidarities of our times. There remains hope.[42]

3

MULTICULTURAL ENLIGHTENMENT

Europe is dying in Sarajevo.

—Demonstration poster

✣✣✣

What could be more European, after all, then our tradition of senseless nationalist warfare.

—Michael Ignatieff, *Blood and Belonging*

✣✣✣

I could not resist pointing out somewhere in my dissertation that it was a defect on the part of Socrates to disregard the whole and only to consider numerically the individuals. What a Hegelian fool I was! It is precisely this that powerfully demonstrates what a great ethicist Socrates was.

—Søren Kierkegaard, *Journals and Papers* (1850)

✣✣✣

A paradoxical community is emerging, made up of foreigners who are reconciled with themselves to the extent that they recognize themselves as foreigners. The multinational society would thus be the consequence of an extreme individualism, but conscious of its discontents and limits, knowing only indomitable people ready-to-help-themselves in their weakness, a weakness whose other name is our radical strangeness.

—Julia Kristeva, *Strangers to Ourselves*

✣✣✣

A conservative cultural and identity politics for all domestic law and order and a neoliberal veneer of multiculturalism for foreign markets and policy—this is Samuel Huntington's sure, if perhaps unintended, prescription for *enhancing* the clash of civilizations in the NWO:

The Founding Fathers [of the U.S.] saw diversity as a reality and as a problem: hence the national motto, *e pluribus unum.* . . . The American multiculturalists . . . wish to create a country of many civilizations, which is to say a country not belonging to any civilization and lacking a cultural core. . . . A multicivilizational United States will not be the United States; it will be the United Nations. . . . Rejection . . . of Western civilization means the end of the United States of America as we have known it. It also means effectively the end of Western civilization. If the United States is de-Westernized, the West is reduced to Europe and a few lightly populated overseas European settler countries. Without the United States the West becomes a minuscule and declining part of the world's population on a small and inconsequential peninsula at the extremity of the Eurasian land mass. . . . The futures of the United States and of the West depend upon Americans reaffirming their commitment to Western civilization. Domestically this means rejecting the divisive siren calls of multiculturalism. Internationally it means rejecting the elusive and illusory calls to identify the United States with Asia.[1]

A heretical thought occurred to me that reversing this policy advice (admired by the likes of Henry A. Kissinger and Zbigniew Brzezinski, who praise it on the back bookcover) would be a step forward. Why not take these so-feared outcomes of a multicultural world—across national and civilizational borders—as good news about 'Europe', as *our* active imaginary, invention, policy? What if a multicivilizational league were the desired aim of perpetual peace?

The events of 1989 inspired Derrida and Habermas to reflect with urgency on the cultural identity of Europe and its exported promise of the modern idea of universal democracy. Derrida's sense of "imminence" permeates his questioning in "hope, fear, and trembling" about Europe emerging into new forms of violence, xenophobia, racism, anti-Semitism, and religious as well as secular fanaticism. Habermas, writing with the same urgency, depicts the present-day nationalist strife as a regression to the spring of the nations of 1848. He notes, however, that national political consciousness "presupposes an appropriation . . . of cultural traditions." Fragmented peoples become further exploited by political and other manipulations of their ongoing identity crises—"simultaneously mobilizing and isolating them as individuals." Derrida and Habermas agree that by promoting cultural identities against the difference of those designated as others, each side of the binary can entrench hatred.[2]

To find alternatives we must explain how neither the politics of identity nor that of difference alone successfully empower liberating coalitions or even closer solidarities. Each sort of politics leads at times to a demise of liberating gains on both sides of the Atlantic, both in the relation of the West to nonwestern cultures, as well as among the latter. How does the promise of multicultural and democratic society become colonized by that Grand Inquisitor of political correctness who inhabits now the Eurocentric as well as anti-Eurocentric clashes of civilizations in social and identity crises? A path to an overcoming of the impasse lies in meeting the real growing need for recognition within and among cultures and civilizations. Neither the politics of identity nor that of difference alone yet complete this task. To wit, the said overcoming cannot eliminate the ethical and sociopolitical aporia of identity and difference. I propose to join Habermas's fallibilist self-limitation of the western Enlightenment project (its revolutionary promise of social equality) with Derrida's multicultural-democratic intensification of this same project (refusing identity-logic in culture and capital-logic in the economy).

I distinguish Habermas's and Derrida's critiques of the present. Habermas curbs hatred by the procedural institutionalization of postnational identity; Derrida unmasks the joint logic of Eurocentrism and anti-Eurocentrism by attacking the ideas of a dominant center (the capital city) and techno-culture (the capital-logic). Considering their imagined encounter, the next generation might learn to forge coalitions among new *critical post/modern social theorists and activists.*

1. Habermas's Procedural Enlightenment

To say that Habermas delimits the Enlightenment promise of equality does not mean that he gives up its emancipatory project. In place of a material utopia, he envisions the regulative ideal of procedural justice. He shifts from material (Hegelian-Marxist) concerns to a more formal (Kantian) and pragmatist (Mead's) reading of democratic aspirations (Rousseau's and Marx's). This bespeaks a certain degree of theoretical sobriety and activist self-restraint by someone who grew up in post-Nazi Germany, next to the Iron Curtain, and today is face to face with the rise of neo-Nazi and nationalist hate groups on both sides of the old Cold War frontier. Habermas counsels democracy at home and globally to safeguard theory and practice against the rightwing fascist and left-revolutionary terror. This theoretical asceticism, which emerges in the wake of violence and both secular and religious fanaticism, limits a Habermasian critical theorist to the politics of the possible.

To recognize individual and cultural identities as immune to hate, Habermas argues, first, for an intersubjectivist anchor of all identity-formation; second, for a postnational political culture; and third, for a permanent democratic revolution. I will clarify these notions next.

Intersubjectivist Identity-Formation

As I have shown already, Habermas notes that the rise of reflective self-relation to one's place in a tradition and culture fosters those types of identities that are more fitted to deliberative democracy than to an emphatically nationalist politics of identity or difference. And he agrees with an existential insight that the notion of collective guilt (e.g., for the Nazi or Stalinist past) is difficult to sustain. Yet he could admit, e.g., that peoples of the Americas bear collective responsibility for their valuation or future choice of the heroic White-European Columbian narrative. Multicultural debates are about this civilizationally narrative either/or, whereby self-choosing individuals and groups engage in public discourses about their received traditions.[3]

The critically hermeneutical attitude does not preserve a self severed from cultural and social life. Habermas begins with an individualization which occurs always already through socialization. I learn to relate to self first in relation to others. The emergence of self-reflective identity is facilitated by discovering performatively constructed natures of all identities and cultural traditions. The received *and* performative character of traditions need not contravene each other theoretically and certainly does not disvalue the need for democratic struggles for recognition. If no civilizational origins are innocent, the issue for ethical existence becomes inscribed into self-realization. Ethical life is not defined by the given identity-constructions but in performing my relation to them. It goes without saying that one's repeated self-choice, the *how*, impacts one's embodied life, the *what*, and yet that some material conditions (i.e., what Fraser sets off from cultural recognition under the rubric of economic redistribution) are more suitable than others to meet this task. The existentially material task shifts for Habermas from an individual self-choice to public consciousness. The public fora perform every personal either/or vis-à-vis problematized traditions, not as one's private affairs. Habermas's innovation, discussed in the previous chapter, is to have formulated a sociopolitical context in which a relentless critique of individual histories may be integrated into a public need to recognize life-preserving value-orientations of cultures. In a distancing from traditions, *we* inhabit types of culture and personality competent, both democratically and multiculturally, to recognize ethical claims to authenticity and moral claims to autonomy. This social evolution curbs communitarian-nationalist authorities of the conventional 'We' by *our* ongoing critically hermeneutical attitude.[4]

Habermas's invention implies the need for a modern existentially material key, whereby a reflexive self-realization could resist undemocratic ego- and ethnocentrism of groups and civilizations yet allow for their multiculturally polycentric self-determination. An existentially material critique of traditionalist nationalism procures the mediating condition of the possibility for meeting the complex need for cultural recognition as well as procedural and distributive justice (i.e., the public reflexivity of cultural, moral, social, and legal norms). Neither Habermas, nor other thinkers, such as Taylor, Honneth, or Fraser, draw this last normative conclusion. Habermas introduces the Kierkegaardian either/or into democratic deliberations. Yet even in his work on law, he incorporates the notion of existential self-choice merely descriptively: this shows how the rise of existential reflexivity precedes an emergence of reflexive norm-orientation in such political domains as a moral self-determination via human and civic rights and an ethical self-realization via group sovereignty. But this move itself does not thematize the nature of the relation between the first and the second type of reflexivity. Interestingly, even with this oversight, Habermas recognizes the necessity of complementing deliberative social democracy with recognizing postnational personality and political culture.[5]

Postnational Political Culture and
Permanent Democratic Revolution

Habermas agrees with Hobsbawm's performative insight that nationalism constructs modern nations. Indeed, I do not hesitate to render it as an existential-performative insight insofar as Habermas wields a Kierkegaardian defense of the communicative individual against the demands for her conforming to the nation-state. One expects that postnational political culture should be more than a glove that descriptively fits a democratic hand of Habermas's model of recognition. Yet the descriptive, minimalist reading is the case. Habermas's moral, legal, and democratic theory requires a personality competent to dissent, deliberate, and sustain reflexively now decentered cultures. His theory, however, nowhere accounts for the conditions of this and its own possibility. Habermas assumes that *we* have ready-at-hand dissenting and communicative competencies and self-reflexive cultures. He notes, to his satisfaction, two leftover queries: how to integrate complex modern societies and how to legitimate moral, social, and legal norms?[6]

The notions of postnational political culture and permanent democratic revolution represent two complementary aspects of Habermas's answer to the problems of social integration and legitimation. The pragmatic side of these problems is how to resist nationalist and fundamentalist hatred that colonizes the politics of identity and difference. The theoretical side is how to transform the republican tradition of civic humanism and the classical liberal-individualist view of society. Habermas objects that the republican view mistakenly identifies nationhood with statehood, thereby identifying the democratic republic with the communitarian self-organization of particular peoples. He objects further that possessive individualism overlooks the source of moral self-determination which lies not in so many negatively delimited atomic liberties but in publicly conducted practical discourse. The republican (or communitarian) tradition proffers strong ethical reasons for a politics of identity. It helps little when it comes to the phenomena of Sarajevo. The liberal (atomistic) view stresses political differences. It fails to secure sources of normative bonding in complex modern societies. In his ingenious move, Habermas reformulates Enlightenment universalism as a radical multicultural democracy.

Habermas aims at a critically theoretical refiguring of Rousseau and Kant. He refrains from formulating a new metaphysics of history or a positive *telos* towards material justice. Further, he discerns the locus of human rights and popular sovereignty neither in nature nor in a substantive utopia. Such a locus resides in the performative mode of exercising fair political procedures. A radical democratic republic is, then, rooted neither in a religious or nationalist recognition of traditions, nor in a material vision of a completed revolutionary redistribution of wealth. And it is anchored neither in the nostalgia for the past nor in the romantic longing projected onto a future. The now permanent revolutionary project immigrates into the heart of deliberative democracy; its blood and heartbeat lie in institutionalized procedural justice. There remains nothing more to which *we* can appeal but *our* fair discourse and deliberative politics.

Habermas believes that a decentered model of personal, cultural, and political interaction safeguards the democratic promise of 1789 in a multiculturally universal way. His is, however, a largely formal model, shot through with theoretical asceticism and activist self-restraint. Since a formal universalism does not seem to be substantively legitimated, Habermas is convinced that procedural justice admits, to wit requires, a radical multicultural democracy. He concludes that a procedural rendition of the Enlightenment's dual promise of democratic freedom and equality can avoid the dominating and the fragmentary clashes of the politics of identity and difference.

2. Derrida's Deconstructive Enlightenment

Derrida does not give up the Enlightenment project of human rights and deliberative democracy. He intensifies their promise, first, in his hope, fear, and trembling that the spell of the dominant center can be resisted and, second, in his critique of techno-capital.

On the first count, Derrida implores that one's resistance to nationalist or fundamentalist hatred must be exercised on the level of personal and cultural identity-formation and cannot be relegated to public social policy choices alone. If this is true, then Habermas translated a Kierkegaardian either/or into moral and legal discourses precociously. Hence, a more thorough critique of any failed politics for recognition in both the politics of identity and difference must be thematized. On the second count, Derrida's critique of the danger posed by new economic colonizations of the post-1989 world seems more materially concrete than Habermas's formal theory of procedural justice. If this can be demonstrated, then critical social theory will need to integrate a Kierkegaardian hope, fear, and trembling with this untimely meditation on Marx.

Critique of Closed or Imperial Identity- and Culture-Formations

Derrida's reflections on identity-formation, his urgency about the proper name, have to do with an intimation that forming personal or cultural identity secures both a breath of promise and the locus of fanaticism. There is no identity without culture or tradition but also no single and innocent origin of culture or tradition. Derrida seems to discredit S. Huntington's conclusions drawn from their otherwise shared critique of equating modernization with western imperialist universalization: "Monogenealogy would always be a mystification in the history of culture." To inhabit personal-cultural identity is to be gathered at home and in difference with oneself in identity. This is an aporia for the politics of identity and difference; how are we to express a fidelity to a culture or, should we want to leave our traditions behind, how are we to recognize the need for recognition counter-culturally? Univocal (anti-)Eurocentric civilizational correctness cannot begin to take cognizance of this aporia without reinscribing the binary of hate into identity-formation depicted as a proper name. If we are to circumvent wars of religions or of nationalisms (they *enjoy* the same symptoms, the same particular and universal neuroses), we must inhabit a polycentric multicultural world by subverting the identity-logic of the proper name.[7]

Derrida attacks the proper name of 'Europe', the idea of Europe as the captain, headman, warrior, man, or more politically, the capital city and money-capital. The other of Europe might not be some other heading. It is "the other of the heading": viz., an identity and difference disobeying the form, sign, logics of headings, antiheadings, beheadings. This other of dominant cultures would allow for personal or group identity without giving it another proper name, something to be owned, mastered. Derrida depicts the events of 1989 as an earthquake which stirs up the "repetitive memory" of culture as a universal opening to ever possible change of the heading and, at the same time, the monster of the 'new', of some "new order." The task is to become suspicious both of the memory that wants to master the opening—confuse it with the phallus—and of the forgetfulness of an old-new world order. Identity which is at home in the other of the heading remains nonexclusive and yet responsible to such openings.[8]

From Derrida's angle, the problem for all politics of identity and difference lies in human striving for the head, the capital, the advanced point, the phallus. We will not get much help from a counterprogram that would reinscribe this same striving, e.g., into its anti-Columbian narrative. Derrida judges that the discourses of identity and difference have exhausted their possibilities. Here he overstates the case since the post-1989 Derrida argues for a critical intensification of the ideas of 1789, not their abandonment. If this were not so, there would be no aporia of inhabiting identity in difference. Aporetic 'double binds' in overcoming the binaries of hatred consist in repeating and breaking, continuing and opposing, remembering and letting go of identity. Those coming from western traditions cannot overcome Eurocentrism without becoming responsible for its history and without recognizing—retrieving/inventing—from history the dangerous memory of identities without closure.[9]

✦ ✦ ✦

Günther Grass spoke on this issue in his controversial lecture in Frankfurt shortly before German unification: the unique moral justification for the unified nation-state of Germany after 1989 is that Germans would remember Auschwitz together. We pay a high price for forgetting the past and not recognizing the NWO as quite old among civilizational and cultural hate-faults.

✦ ✦ ✦

Derrida thinks that transgressing the traditional borders and the proper names of identity must not portend that crisis which needs a resolution. Identity-crises occasion a dying away to a universal regulative claim that given sufficient time and space the ideal community could bring about some final solution. Derrida points out that, in principle, such a closure in an unmitigated universality or in the all-too-naïve celebrations of 1989 as the end of history is neither desirable nor sustainable. Unlike S. Huntington, he counsels that one can resist the binaries of hatred when names cease to function as the loci of property ownership and become at once a heightened memory of limit and a radical opening of identity.[10]

We would be unjust to Derrida if we overlooked how, perhaps paradoxically so, critically modern is his postmodern transgression of the universalist ideals of justice. Derrida moves away from trashing the Enlightenment project in a 'ludic' postmodern frenzy when he does not join the bandwagon of those among his followers who brand any mark of pathos about the ethicopolitical as a spirit of seriousness. There is great deal of pathos in Derrida's insistence that cultural identity "cannot and must not be dispersed into a myriad of provinces, into a multiplicity of self-enclosed idioms or petty little nationalisms, each one jealous and untranslatable." Nationalist homogenization within states (and their concomitant fragmentation), when codified into civilizational global spheres of power-influence, represents a dead-end of any democratic coexistence—anywhere. This outcome convexly mirrors some strands of academic postmodernism and uncritical celebrations of identity or difference. Yet Derrida warns against "centralizing authority" of the "hegemonic center," be it cultural value spheres of modernity, salable power-consensus, or transnational profit. A postmodern age might be offended by Derrida's earnestness. In the midst of jesting, Derrida insists that one ought not to flee the double aporia of dispersion and monopoly, since this experience gives rise to that pathos whereby one is delivered into the other of the heading. "I will even venture to say that ethics, politics, and responsibility, *if there are any*, will only ever have begun with the experience and experiment of the aporia." Echoing perhaps Havel's nonpolitical politics, Derrida articulates this locus of action in radically decentered identity as "neither political nor apolitical but . . . 'quasi-political'." A non- or quasi-political action risks "the possibility of the impossible."[11]

With a fallibilist politics of the possible, Habermas resists perverting dialogic reciprocity. Derrida's politics of the impossible takes its stance within the aporia of identity and difference. He helps us to find pathways between a politics of cultural domination (bankrupt or imperial westernizing modernism) and that of civilizational homogenization and nationalist fragmentation (misconceived postmodern politics of identity and difference). Derrida finds the modern West inscribing its imperial cultural domination into the "national ego," thereby ascribing a pseudo-cosmopolitan privilege to its particular 'we'. "Nationalism and cosmopolitanism have always gotten along well together." Both options flee the aporia of identity-in-difference. If *we* could show that it were possible to recognize the ethnicity of idioms, their multiplied borders, margins, or movements, without forging a new dominant center, perhaps there would be a way to address both a European civil strife and the North American multicultural debates better than by monoculturally asserting our western 'head(ing)s'.[12]

Unlike Habermas, Derrida does not put much hope in "the univocity of democratic discussion." He charges that Habermas's theory of communicative action employs a model of language that tends to exclude other linguistic models. This is a strong but too general objection. It may not get the inquiry far beyond Derrida's antagonism to Habermas. Leaving their dispute aside, I find that the difference does not consist in what they desire after 1989 but how they go about it. They stand much closer on what they do not want. They expose nationalist hatred and defend basic human and civil rights of minorities and immigrants. Both expose certain forms of inter- or transnationalism as imperial. And they promote multicultural democratic spaces—regionally and globally—of equally distributed recognition.[13]

Rather than viewing Habermas and Derrida as using distinct grammars, I view Derrida as bringing into the fallibilist politics of the possible a corrective to any regulative ideal of discursive closure. Instead of translating a Kierkegaardian self-choice into something to be settled by public social-policy debates about traditions or national identities (Habermas's move), Derrida maintains the logic of nonidentity (i.e., dissenting more strongly from any totalitarian consensus). Whereas Habermas's fallibilism presents a possibility of many headings in dialogic reciprocity, Derrida's politics of the impossible allows for an other of the heading. The former is a self-reforming model of rationality that opposes exclusionary practices inscribed into western canon. The latter shows that in the same breath as one hopes for justice, one must fear and tremble lest even fallibilist uses of the canon remain deceptive. Derrida's intensification and at the same time transgression of an Enlightenment promise of recognition, equality, and freedom marks sobriety not found within the confines of Habermas's fallibilist rendition of the same promise.

Specters of a Multiculturally Democratic Critique of Political Economy

There is a second instance in which Derrida's critique of the present age appears to be more concrete than Habermas's. Derrida attacks the notion of the proper name not only from the side of identity-formation or the need for ethical recognition. He unmasks the property owner who wants to master the name. As he embarks upon this rereading Marx's critique of private property, Derrida, perhaps somewhat naïvely, gestures that only after 1989 is he free to read Marx without interference from certain leftist dogmatism. To be sure, in the Frankfurt School of Social Criticism Marx was used to critique the Nazis and the Soviets with the same left hand long before the French discovered either Heideigger's politics or the Gulag. It would be fair to note that Derrida's return to Marx is a rather unpopular move after 1989 when many leftists experience a certain melancholy about social revolutionary projects. Habermas defines his own work in terms of Merleau-Ponty's designation of non-Communist leftism and is viewed, at least by liberals or leftists, to have abandoned the core of Marx's critique of capital. Derrida brings untimely meditations on techno-capital to East Central Europe—where sympathizers of postmodern Nietzscheanism seem caught by surprise. He raises Marx's specters against those on left and right who dream of banishing the word 'capital' from conversation.[14]

Derrida stylizes himself as someone who has never bowed down to "a certain Marxist intimidation" and who can, therefore, launch a new dissensus from the techno-capital exploitation of the events of 1989. "Is not this responsibility incumbent upon *us?*" he implores. Indeed, to some of his postmodern cronies, Derrida's ethicopolitical pathos might resound with an embarrassing lapse into the spirit of seriousness:

> Just as it is necessary to analyze and earnestly address—and this is the whole problem of ethico-political responsibility—the disparities between law, ethics, and politics, or between the unconditional idea of law . . . , between the structurally universalist pretension of these regulative ideas and the essence of European origin of this idea of law (etc.), is it not also necessary to resist with vigilance the neo-capitalist exploitation of the breakdown of an anti-capitalist dogmatism in those states that had incorporated it?[15]

The word 'capital' enters into our conversation with a double imminence. Derrida's *la capitale* refers to the *polis*, its heading marks struggles for recognition (e.g., in new power-centers of communication networks). Its double, *le capital*, binds modern culture to money. Derrida's urgency lies in his twofold critique of capital as the dominant cultural center of power and as the logic of artificial scarcity. One must notice the parallel between Derrida's attack on the double heading of modernity and Habermas's critique of the distortive effect of systemic functionalist imperatives (i.e., administrative power and money) on the lifeworld (i.e., personal and cultural identity). Judged from an existentially material theorizing, splitting off the need for recognition from the one for redistribution would achieve only a reified theoretical and practical purity. (We could get, e.g., S. Huntington's world order with Euro-American global economic hegemony intact in spite of its seemingly multicultural foreign relations.) A concretely critical post/modern social theorizing no longer rests satisfied with either abstraction or reductionism, either a dual-systems theory (cultural recognition and lifeworld vs. economic redistribution and systems of money and power) or a unified-systems theory (aligning all needs or struggles under one type). Derrida, like Habermas, exhibits passion for a life freed from political-cultural domination *and* material exploitation. The difference between them, then, cannot lie in what they want but in how concretely they pursue it.[16]

3. Critical Post/Modern Social Theorists and Activists:
For New Political Coalitions

New political coalitions among critical post/modern social theorists and activists could do worse than learning from an imagined encounter between Derrida and Habermas, especially while facing the possibilities of the NWO created according to S. Huntington's or some such advice. Habermas, unlike Marx, no longer envisions the possibility of a modern economy without market exchange and of modern politics without state administration. The material systems of power and money (surplus distribution) become problematic only when they encroach upon the symbolic reproduction of the lifeworld (cultural recognition). Cautioning against an all-out revolution that would deliver us to a system-free lifeworld, Habermas lowers our romantic expectations. Yet he does not fall into an activist quietism or despair. He considers the move to a permanent democratic revolution (whereby deliberative democracy rooted in procedural justice and legal institutions continues to resist all colonizing attempts by systems of economy and state) to be a sobering innovation in critical social theory. For all its aspirations to universalism, Habermas's theory responds to quite regional experiences: the Nazi terror of his youth, the Stalinist terror next door, and the present pan-Euro-American politics of identity and difference distorted by racial and national hatred. One would wish that Habermas viewed this local character of his own self-limiting theorizing as a strength rather than a hindrance to universalist projects of emancipation. Habermas vouches an unequivocal commitment to this project, something on which Derrida needlessly fudges. Yet Derrida's material urgency, likewise self-limiting and local, about global safeguards for justice opens up a more concrete critique of the post-1989 age than found in formal proceduralism alone.

Habermas's fallibilism blocks all metaphysical aspirations to guarantee the Enlightenment promise. Derrida, in his 'hope, fear, and trembling', intensifies this same promise. He resists absolutizations of personal and cultural identity, and he attacks the logic of techno-capital. In the first place, Derrida searches for counterhegemonic languages of translation that would avoid both the nationalist politics of difference and the assimilationist politics of identity. By focusing exclusively on the formal and universalist character of public deliberations, Habermas bypasses— within struggles for recognition—the need to resist the totalizing logic on the level of identity and consensus-formation. Once again, Habermas's dialogic reciprocity allows for the plurality of headings, but Derrida argues for that mode of communication which would let itself be decentered by the other of the heading. This 'other' procures that opening to feminist, multicultural, multiracial, indeed, queer concerns which Habermas's model, for all its genuine receptivity to other headings, is not ready to receive on *their own* terms. Habermas's approach postpones the mastery of the proper name. The name (viz., final truth) is (in principle if not in flesh) mastered in the regulative ideal of an infinite communication community. Derrida gives up the possibility, desire, usefulness of codifying such a mastery even in a regulative ideal.[17]

Regarding this first encounter between Derrida and Habermas, I submit that a path to radical multicultural democracy requires both contributions: Habermas articulates the procedural conditions of the possibility of communicative ethics. Derrida adopts an intensification/transgression of received emancipatory projects in an ongoing resistance to a totalizing closure of the liberation ideal itself. Derrida admits the politics of the impossible; Habermas limits himself to the possibility of dialogic reciprocity. Neither seems self-sufficient. Derrida's other of the heading, apart from being pinned down in ethicopolitical validity-domains, remains like the gesture of de Silentio's Abraham—incommunicable to Sara, Isaac, and the larger community. Habermas's dialogic reciprocity secures its regulative ideal from any fear and trembling. While secured from the need to resist absolutizing its own symbolic and communicative structures of the lifeworld, the very regulative ideal (it houses all generations in an idealized temporal communicative interaction among human beings, not among Olympian gods) is susceptible, in principle, to becoming but another dominant center of power.[18]

In the second place, Derrida, not unlike Havel, exhibits a certain degree of courage, a pathos that today one would expect more from Frankfurt than from Paris or Prague: after the events of 1989, Derrida attacks the right-wing attempts to dogmatize the economic reforms in East Central Europe. I do not chastise Habermas for his theoretical asceticism and activist self-restraint. One can appreciate a posture of someone who has lived through or next to rightist and leftist terror. In many instances, his position vis-à-vis modern economy and the state is much more congenial and realistic than Derrida's in addressing the aspirations of the transitional societies of the East. One who is emerging from a life behind the Iron Curtain will be literally inoculated to any mention of Marx—Marxism, Marxdom, Marxian, to any suggestion of leftist catechizing, just as Europeans became allergic to 'Christianity' or 'religion' after the Thirty Year War of Religions. That Habermas speaks of revolutionary projects in formal-procedural terms, not with the militancy evinced by the Shining Path, perhaps meets the occasion of this local context.[19]

Still, Derrida's return to Marx's critique of the market gospel expresses something honest, regardless of what celebratory or deprecatory views of Derrida's work one holds. He approaches Marx's *Capital* from a critical post/modern angle. This grants his gesture the credibility of someone who has neither been a Marxist believer nor a dissident. Derrida argues that the events of 1989 present the age with a "double duty" of unmasking both the "totalitarian dogmatism that, under the pretense of putting an end to capital, destroyed democracy" and the "religion of capital," an emerging new dogma. With such words, a stronger receptivity of East Central Europeans to a post-Heideggerian Derrida rather than to a post-Marxist Habermas is not the worst situation. Its irony is worth critical exploration.[20]

What Derrida means by democracy can be grasped from other duties that he names. There is the need for "hospitality" that integrates foreigners yet recognizes their "alterity." Further, westerners have a duty to remember the European as well as non-European genealogies of democracy; but they must remember that democracy is not a fixed regulative idea with a fixed future. "[A] democracy . . . must have the structure of a promise—*and thus the memory of that which carries the future, the to-come, here and now.*" This democracy calls for a politics that recognizes multicultural identity-in-difference and yet is bound in broad coalitions against nationalism, xenophobia, racism, and exploitation. The new coalitional politics of identity and difference would have to respect different forms of faith and thought. (I hope for the same coalition to emerge among the new generation of critical post/modern social theorists and activists who find their own polemic *passé*.) This respect need not abdicate the radical emancipatory project. Respect intensifies the promise by learning to read the transgressions of the Enlightenment as "the Enlightenment of this time"—I call it *multicultural enlightenment*. And Derrida does not claim that anything goes. He articulates the "duty" of responsibility: one ought to live with tensions between speech and action, aware of the aporia of identity and difference; in democracy one learns to respect irresponsibility and dissent for the sake of democracy.[21]

Habermas translates the emancipatory project into a democratic revolution which goes on permanently within the institutions of procedural justice. Derrida means by revolution the memory of democracy to come. Habermas delimits critical theory and practice to the tasks of possible justice. He sets aside Marx's vision of a material form of life beyond capital markets and bureaucracies. Yet he refuses the conservative vision of the status quo. His is a normative, radical democratic project of multicultural recognition and procedural social justice. Derrida intensifies the emancipatory hope in his material critique of what is going on in today's NWO. By joining a post/modern Marxian hope with a Kierkegaardian fear and trembling, he stands a double guard against NWO cynicism and revolutionary fanaticism. One may agree with Habermas's self-limiting normative formalism: critical social theory cannot deliver humans to final justice, it cannot console for death. One may agree with Derrida's critical transgressions and honest material concretion: without rooting a critical praxis of social theorizing in the material memory (a text) of a promise, one has lost both the revolutionary impetus and the existential vantage point from which to grapple with the present age at all.

Conclusions

I have not sought a confrontation between modernism and post-modernism. I have found instead an opening for a mutual enlightenment between Derrida's and Habermas's proposals for a radical democracy. In his critique of identity- and capital-logic, Derrida intimates more than a new politics of recognizing identity and difference. He envisions a new way of thinking about these topics. The novelty here is not identified with something wholly other than the emancipatory promise of democracy, nor is it the dubious NWO multi/monoculturalism of S. Huntington (namely, conservative identity politics at home and total fragmentation and dispersion for the rest of the world, and both without socioeconomic justice). The surprising discovery is to find out how modernist in emancipatory intent Derrida's postmodern transgression of universalism is. He argues for a radical multicultural democracy, for hospitality to foreigners, and for sociopolitical responsibility to curb market dogmatism. I deem as largely unhelpful most of what Derrida and Habermas have said about one another's views. Much more helpful is instead how each refigures post/modernity into a multicultural enlightenment for the present age.[22]

Habermas's case for intersubjectivist identity-formation, postnational political culture, and democratic revolution leads to procedural justice. His answer to the aporia of the politics of identity and difference, of which the nationalist enjoyment of mis/recognition and forms of material exploitation are core examples, lies in a radical democratic republic: this is neither a communitarian togetherness, nor an atomistic herd of individuals, nor a fixed material utopia, but a regulative ideal that governs formal procedures. Habermas believes that the reflexivity of traditions (ethical self-choice) must be sustained by public debates. Yet Derrida shows that even the most fallibilist model of identity, culture, and politics might be insufficiently critical insofar as it capitalizes on its own heading. One gets from Derrida's call for the other of the heading not something necessarily alien to Habermas's concerns but rather a dose of what I call an existentially material concretion. With fear and trembling, Derrida wants to resist all absolutizations of identity-formation—whether in regional cultures (nationalism) or political cultures (the possibility of a totalitarian consensus). In hope, he intensifies the emancipatory promise over and against too easy, too timely, settlement with the twofold capital-logic.

What emerges from this encounter is neither a rejection of Derrida or Habermas, nor a simple recipe for eclecticism. Perhaps, *we* receive an invitation to renew critical social theory with the existential pathos and material concretion of the young Marcuse. If this may be so, the task will be to pass beyond an unfruitful, largely academic, post/modern polemics at loggerheads with itself. Other journeys already raise new concerns of ethical dissent, moral agency, performative identity, and radical democracy. I cannot know what shape political coalitions among critical post/modern social theorists and activists will take. One has learned already that not to make steps in concrete hope, fear, and trembling is to evade the task. Assuming its challenge in this fashion raises new specters of deconstructive and critical theory.[23]

4

SPECTERS OF DECONSTRUCTION
AND CRITICAL THEORY

Neoliberalism offers a new world doctrine: surrender and indifference as sole forms of inclusion, death and forgetfulness as a single future for the excluded. . . . Stupidity and arrogance made to govern the nations of the world. Crime and impunity as the principal law. Robbery and corruption as the main industry. Assassination as the source of legitimacy. Lie as the supreme god. Jail and grave for those who will not be accomplices. The International of death. Permanent war. That is neoliberalism.

—"Comunicados," *Marcos*, La Realidad, April 4, 1996

✤✤✤

Over the last few years many Negroes have felt that their most troublesome adversary was not the obvious bigot of the Ku Klux Klan or the John Birch Society, but the white liberal who is more devoted to "order" than to justice, who prefers tranquility to equality.

—Martin Luther King, Jr.,
Where Do We Go from Here: Chaos or Community?

✤✤✤

Just as 20th-century Americans had trouble imagining how their pre-Civil War ancestors could have stomached slavery, so we at the end of the 21st century have trouble imagining how our great-grandparents could have legally permitted a C.E.O. to get 20 times more than her lowest-paid employees.

—Richard Rorty, "Fraternity Reigns"

✤✤✤

It was part of women's long revolution. When we were breaking all the old hierarchies. Finally there was that one thing we had to give up too, the only power we ever had, in return for no more power for anyone. The original production: the power to give birth. Cause as long as we were biologically enchained, we'd never be equal. And males never would be humanized to be loving and tender. So we all became mothers. Every child has three. To break the nuclear bonding.

—Marge Piercy, *Woman On The Edge Of Time*

✦ ✦ ✦

Our present age declares the spirit and the letter of Marx dead. Derrida endorses the core revolutionary demand of Marx's *Communist Manifesto*: to unmask the political economy of the NWO and gather a 'new International' among the oppressed. The dispossessed need not apologize for "a consistent deconstruction" which joins with a consistent critical social theory to become responsible and revolutionary. This stance brings Marx's coalitional and solidary call undiluted into our tired 'post-socialist condition'.[1] Enter the offense of Marx's specters today:

If we have no business with the construction of the future or with organizing it for all time there can still be no doubt about the task confronting us at present: the *ruthless criticism of the existing order,* ruthless in that it will shrink neither from its own discoveries nor from the conflict with the powers that be.

And Marx follows this by defining "critical philosophy" for the present age as

the self-clarification of struggles and wishes of the age. This is a task for the world and for us. It can succeed only as the product of united efforts.[2]

Will the textual activists in established and post-Communist democracies proudly proclaim with Derrida that deconstruction has been always already practiced in the spirit of a Marx? Or will they become ironized by this untimely disclosure of the Marxist heart of Derrida's authorship? Such an either/or query raises the specters of deconstruction which haunt primarily certain practices in deconstruction. They haunt a "Holy Alliance"[3] against Critical Theory. This Marxian specter haunts deconstruction regardless of whether or not one accepts Derrida's reading of Marx into deconstruction's intellectual and revolutionary biography as *bona fide* genuine. (Do *we* need to figure out whether or not *Derrida* or his gesture is earnest?)[4]

Will critical social theorists in established or post-Communist democracies now proudly proclaim that their ties to Marx go further than

Derrida's, that Critical Theory has been always already engaged in a sophisticated elaboration of Marx? Or will they find Derrida too late in coming, thus doubly *passé* in the post-Marxist age? This either/or query raises specters which haunt primarily certain practices in critical social theory. Derrida returns to Marx in Paris at the time when one rarely hears about Marx from Frankfurt. He devotes time to Marx in such improbable places as Moscow, Prague, Manhattan, and Irvine. At the regular gatherings of critical social theorists, appealing to Marx seems now as little popular (as much out of place and step) as it would be in most of post-1989 Europe, indeed in the NWO.[5] Does this mean that some followers of the left-liberal discourse on democracy and law are more honest in facing the complex constellations of the present age than are Derrida's delayed, fashionably unfashionable returns to Marx's revolutionary texts? Or is there a double irony? One meets a Marxist exposure of the Stalinist and the Nazi Heideggerian ghosts in Frankfurt quite some time before Parisians acknowledge Gulag along with Auschwitz. Yet a divorce of democratic critique and politics from material critique and economic democracy (albeit a *procedurally liberal*, legally fair divorce) plays into the hands of the *neoliberal* markets and power rhetoric. Should not this divorce be embarrassing given the untimely affirmation of the Marxist heart of deconstruction?

Let us say that a critical theorist adopts some variation of Habermas's distinction between the validity of liberal democratic norms (a discourse ideal of procedural justice) and the facticity of neoliberal markets and bureaucracies (the real existing justice). Could not one argue that without a *ruthless* critique of the NWO, even a valid liberal political ideality will be too weak to curb the neoliberal facticity of markets and power-bureaucracy? In its gallant oversight of material life, the lawful state and its well-intended liberal procedural norms can become part and parcel of neoliberal facts. And between facts and norms, there rises a specter which haunts critical social theory in ways that cannot be disposed of in an overdrawn polemic among modernists and postmodernists. The irony of this specter haunts the very core of what is meant by radical critique and radical democracy.[6] The specter pursues critical social theory regardless of whether or not one accepts Derrida's historical and theoretical links to Marx as *bona fide* more genuinely radical than those of orthodox or revisionist Marxists. (Do *we* need to figure out now whether or not *Derrida* or his 'reading' of Marx is original?)[7]

It is uninteresting to side with either Derrida or Habermas, or even against both. There looms another urgency. Derrida, just as Kierkegaard's de Silentio, opens his book on Marx with an Exordium. This is not a matter of some scholarly exercise but an invitation to "a heterodidactics between life and death," learning to live in fear and trembling, or what

Derrida means by learning to live more justly. The urgency lies in a decisive "instant" of ethicopolitical responsibility:[8] either to apologize for the
neoliberal status quo or to radically examine and democratically engage
it without apologies. The above sets of either/or raise material specters of
a certain Kierkegaard and Marx: one learns about life and death by existing and striving for liberation. I will join Derrida's incontinent ingression
into neoliberal facticity with Habermas's critical theory of popular democratic sovereignty. In the process, I maintain that dissent and democracy
are embedded in the concrete historical struggles for liberation.

1. The Persistence of Revolutionary Passion

Copenhagen admirers of Kierkegaard's aesthetic irony were
ironized and offended when they discovered his commitment to an existential self-transformation. The same might come to be true about some
readers of Derrida's untimely Marxian critique of the so-called Communist, post-Communist, and western democratic societies. In three regards
Derrida's Marx conjures up also specters of Kierkegaard. First, there is
the specter of the book; second, there figures the specter of enlightenment; and third, one faces the specter of revolution. In the book on Marx,
Derrida never mentions Kierkegaard by name. I take the liberty of reading Kierkegaard together with Marx in the hope of producing a better
grasp of just what specters haunt *us* today.[9]

The Book

What are the ends of *the Marx-book*, its *specters and ghosts?* Either
Derrida's fidelity to Marxist critique lies at the core of what the practitioners of deconstruction were doing all along, or Derrida's point of view
for his work as a Marxist author becomes now an offense for some forms
of such practice. The book either appears among the postmodern reading
public as praise (deconstruction just as critical social theory has always
already been a form of radical social praxis) or it portends the ghostly
grin of embarrassment (there has never been such praxis among deconstructionists just as such praxis has been smuggled out from Marxism).
The book either domesticates or radicalizes Marx's offense; it either signifies an aestheticizing (read: existentially self-evading) method of rotat-
ing crops or it embodies transformative praxis. The ends of *the book*, even
insofar as it is an aesthetic medium, lie in an open-endedness of the existential either/or. Its ends are not the messianism of a doctrine or some
realized eschatology. The specters of the book (aesthetics existentially
understood) provide historical occasions for radical self-choice.[10]

Derrida claims to have concealed deconstruction's Marxist heart
because prior to 1989 he resisted being a hostage to some Marxist intimi-

dation, messianic dogma, or a Party line.[11] This reminds me of Kierkegaard who, like Nietzsche, masked the offense of his authorship up to a point out of his respect for the reader's own authoring. The masked ends of pseudonymous authorship are not dogmatic but existential. They become existential when I, instead of becoming enamored by the variety of masks, grow capable of encountering myself, the other as other. Can Derrida's book be taken to legitimate one's undecidability on whether or not to engage in radical self- and social critique? Can his Marx relegate critical social theory and praxis to the problematic spirit of seriousness? At the instant when the religious establishment mistook Kierkegaard to be in praise of its practices, his writing (no longer cloaked by a pseudonym) became an attack on Christendom. Whether or not the reader should find Derrida's book undecidable or in a double bind on the questions of responsible praxis (even if one may legitimately employ categories of undecidability and double bind as the aesthetic media and occasions for self-choice) is not something on which I can voluntaristically decide here. Following or rejecting Derrida's authorship (is it genuine or is it a ruse?) is not the most interesting or decisive issue when it comes to a choice of myself as responsible for my existence. Even when *reading* 'Derrida 1' (authorship) as undecidable, must I not engage in self-reading, authoring, and deciding how to act on 'Derrida 2' (his critique of imperialism)? Staking out my agency on behalf of *authorship* as my sole given, could deliver me only to voluntarism, decisionism, or messianism. Is there this danger in responsible *authoring* with 'Derrida 2'?[12]

In his interview with Eribon, Derrida holds up the Marx-book as an ill-timed political act of insurrection.[13] Right on! Let us welcome Derrida's book as a self-authoring occasion for one's existential engagement and a Gramscian counterhegemonic strike against the NWO![14] Preferences for the undecidability of its authorship do not rise to a decisive occasion. Such meretriciously aesthetic preferences transform Derrida's decisive Marx into an offending spectacle for our age. The untimely urgency[15] to author and act responsibly[16] haunts any too timely admiration of the authorship's passive undecidability. The earnestness of the critical occasion haunts certain playful textual undecidabilities of the authoring. The Marx-book, insofar as *we* accept it as an act of refusal, raises a decisive question of my or *our* engagement. It raises that Marxian specter whose Kierkegaardian either/or haunts any abstract, ghostly deconstruction.[17]

A New Enlightenment

There is the specter of a new enlightenment which emboldens a radicalized critique of the present age. Both Kierkegaard and Derrida are suspicious of the neo-evangelical preaching of the good news[18] that the present age has culminated in the end of human history. Derrida objects to Fukuyama and the contemporary neoliberal establishment: "certain people dare to neo-evangelize in the name of the ideal of a liberal democracy which has finally realized itself as the ideal of human history."[19] Derrida traces this new gospel about "the end of history and the last man"[20] from 1989 back to the discussions about the end of ideology found already in the 1950s and in Kojève's Paris lectures on Hegel's *Phenomenology*. A realized eschatology or messianism of ends marks the post-Hegelian apocalyptic philosophy of history. As a deconstructive Kierkegaardian of sorts, Derrida suspects all such dogmatic uses of Hegel.[21]

This confrontation with Fukuyama's Hegel has its prototype in Kierkegaard's political treatise, "The Present Age."[22] Writing in 1846, only two years before Marx issued his *Manifesto*, Kierkegaard adopts the vantage point of the prior revolutionary age of 1789. From this historical angle, he attacks the nationalist conservatives (the Hegelian-Christian orthodoxy) and nationalist liberals (liberal establishment cooled off to the radical commitments of the revolutionary 1789). A century before Adorno's enlightenment critique of the culture industry in modernity and before Marcuse's critique of one-dimensional society, Kierkegaard describes the present age of leveling. The ostensible good news of modern times are enlightenment and political freedoms, but the facts are individual choices manipulated by the power of the press, markets, pseudoeducation, and the religious order. The paraded good news is the publicness of discourse; the reality disposes with a phantom of public opinion. The letter of the age says it is for liberal democracy and yet its spirit promotes the crowd, stifling the individual.

Echoing Kierkegaard's nineteenth century, Derrida finds Fukuyama's post-1989 celebration of the liberal democratic end of history at best premature and at worst wrong-headed. There is a massive body of material "evidence"[23] of human suffering and oppression: "never in the history of the earth and of humanity have violence, inequality, exclusion, famine, and thus economic oppression affected so many human beings." Note that Derrida's evidence intensifies rather than rejects the critical hope of the modern Enlightenment. He shows as wrong those who smirk at the promise of liberation. This promise is not among the master narratives of a modernist seriousness which *we* have somehow outgrown in our postmodern condition:

> Instead of singing the advent of the liberal democratic ideal and the capitalist market in the euphoria of the end of history, instead of celebrating the "end of ideologies" and the end of the grand emancipatory discourses, we should never neglect this macroscopic evidence, made up of innumerable singular sites of suffering: no

degree of progress allows one to ignore that never before, in absolute figures, never have so many men, women, and children been enslaved, starved, or exterminated on the earth.[24]

Derrida's evidence against neoliberal markets and the powers that be is not a politically preliberal or antidemocratic nostalgia for some classical golden age of a high culture. He has an egalitarian concern for the common human lot. Neither political liberalism nor conservatively communitarian monoculturalism can meet this concern. Derrida does not limit his analyses to Foucauldian micropractices. He expands any care for a singular suffering to macroscopic evidence. He parts company with Lyotard's dismissal of grand emancipatory discourses and Rorty's ambiguous uses of liberal irony. Yet Derrida does not seek blueprints for a substantive messianic utopia. He renews the liberal promise of the political Enlightenment in a radicalized sociopolitical and economic critique of the neoliberal age. Such a renewal he names a "new Enlightenment."[25] This naming marks an anti-imperial task of caring for the single one. The supporting evidence is inscribed on the bodies of sufferers. The ethicopolitical, historically concrete "task" is to forge new coalitions against all faces of oppression.[26]

Revolution

I began by discussing an either/or occasioned by any reading, writing, and authoring of books, and a book on Marx's specters in particular. The present age challenges any such authoring by radicalizing the spirit of an enlightenment critique. This authoring and critique, taken together, raise the specter of a revolution against neoliberal establishments.[27] And this revolution solicits a "new International" among the suffering and the oppressed.[28] Should not the liberal political theory and practice as well as the postmodern and critical social theory and practice benefit from such discontents of neoliberal markets and imperial politics?

We might be just as taken aback by Kierkegaard's loose affinity with the Communist struggle as by Derrida's explicit advocacy of an International after the fall of the so-called Marxist regimes. In his reflections on the national revolutions of 1848, Kierkegaard positions himself vis-à-vis Marx's specters roaming through Europe: "the communists here at home and in other places fight for human rights. Good, so do I. Precisely for that reason I fight with all my might against the tyranny of the [human] fear."[29] Note that neither Kierkegaard nor Derrida were disciples of Marx, whether at first or at second hand. No matter that their corpus lacks a systematic Marxist analysis. In the nineteenth century, just as today, some social revolutions turn radically conservative, some destructively nationalist, some glibly neoliberal. While now certain postmodern and critical social theorists shy away from Marx, is there not some credibility in social revolutionary, emancipatory claims made by faithful nonbelievers? Derrida's rallying cry builds from material evidence. He begins with a phenomenology of enslaved, starved, and exterminated bodies. In the often cited "telegram of ten words," he names this evidence the ten "plagues" of the NWO. Here is Derrida's *Top Ten* list: unemployment; homelessness among both internal and external exiles from democratic participation; merciless economic warfare among the nation-states; the insurmountable legitimation-difficulties of free markets, state interventions, and national protectionism; the growth of external debt that cripples the material well-being of a large part of the world; the military-industrial complex governing scientific research projects and production; proliferation of nuclear arms; "inter-ethnic wars (were there ever others?) . . . guided by an *archaic* phantasm and concept, by a primitive *conceptual phantasm* of community, the Nation-state, sovereignty, borders, blood and soil"; the world power of "the phantom-states" such as "the mafia and the drug consortium"; and "the present state of international law and its institutions" which, while purporting to be universal, "remain largely dominated . . . by particular Nation-states."[30] The bodies of singular evidence can be ignored at the peril of becoming ideological about the end of ideology as well as about the civilizational spheres of protected influence. Derrida finds no virtue in shedding the globally local narrative of liberation. Singular facts support a concrete universal-Shakespearean claim: something smells rotten in neoliberal democracy. "The 'new International' . . . is a link of affinity, of suffering and hope, a still discreet, almost secret link, as it was around 1848, but more and more visible—we have more than one sign of it."[31]

One can grasp what haunts *us* by describing this International as a care for historically concrete individuals and their social liberation. A new International would foster postnational and antidogmatic affinity among singular dissenters dispersed within existing oppressive conditions.[32] These sites of affinity-in-dissensus are effects of oppression, yet they affect individual and social care for one's existence. Derrida admits as much. He calls for "a new type of intellectual" and activist who meets challenges and "new responsibilities" of "new tele-technologies" and of "the transformations of the public space."[33] If sporadic singular transgressions of power and immiseration are to gather into an International, then dispersed struggles need to forge an "untimely link," joining in new forms of *the singular universal.*[34]

This term, *the singular universal*, marks Sartre's Marxian rendition of Kierkegaard. So the envisioned nonhomogenizing coalitions and solidary bonds among diverse single individuals and plural social movements are not so 'new' as Derrida's new International would imply. Keeping in mind Derrida's delimitations on any such International, read this Kierkegaard: "It is very doubtful . . . that the age will be saved by the idea of sociality, of association." Note at the same time that Kierkegaard's care for singularity never replaces one's responsibility for universal liberation: "Not until the single individual has established an ethical stance despite the whole world, not until then can there be any question of genuinely uniting." Concerns for singularity within solidarity, complementing Marx's emphasis on revolutionary sociality, are prefigured in Kierkegaard and run through Sartre, Beauvoir, Fanon, Marcuse, Havel, West, and other attempts to preserve existential singularity dialectically within sociality.[35]

"Times are out of joint,"[36] repeatedly invokes Derrida, after the manner of Hamlet. Derrida hopes that a temporal affinity without the common idea of association, without a definite revolutionary agency, is possible. An affinity can exist as a union in "disjoint"—

> without status, without title, and without name, barely public even if it is not clandestine, without contract, "*out of joint*," without coordination, without party, without country, without national community (International before, across, and beyond any national determination), without co-citizenship, without common belonging to a class.[37]

This International emerges not because dissenters are effects of systemic limits and oppression but insofar as they are social agents. Dissenting agency never functions apart from social sites. I argued that an existential perspective on what is meant by singular transgressions intervenes in postmodern and critical social theory. Transgressions transformed into dissensus are what inform agencies of social change. Singular concerns, if they are to embody a materially concrete "link of affinity," must translate solidarities of "friendship" into action. Derrida, again, concedes as much: dissent and revolution need a "practical or effective organization."[38]

Which Derrida? What Specters?

Approaching Derrida's text deconstructively, there lurks a tension between the two ends of the book, enlightenment, and revolution. At one end there pivots a distinct (albeit temporary and hesitant) anti-institutional position. A new International forms "the friendship of an alliance *without institution*." At the other end one finds a bold affirmation that deconstruction must be revolutionary. This practical task is required by any "consistent deconstruction."[39]

Again, at one end is Derrida's opposition to all humanism (existential or Hegelian-Marxist) and to any dogmatic *messianism* of the previous workers' internationals. He questions the viability of relying on the revolutionary agency, such as "the dictatorship of the proletariat." (Did we really need to wait for Derrida to teach us "that there is *more than one*" "spirit of Marx or of Marxism" and of humanism?)[40] At another end Derrida insists that, after the debacle of real existing socialisms and in the wake of the neoliberal market revivals, we must try to deliver concretely on the promise of liberation. Deconstruction incarnates "a certain emancipatory and *messianic* affirmation" with an urgency of the revolutionary 1968. This end of *Spectres* echoes *An Essay on Liberation*. And Derrida's "hope, fear, and trembling" are curiously at odds not only with Heidegger's quietist historicity but also with nonexistential, i.e., abstractly post/structuralist, practices in textual antihumanism. This renewed Marcusean confrontation with Heidegger raises Marx's specter in the very heart of deconstruction.[41]

Thinking constructively with Derrida, I want to affirm his as well as the young Marcuse's urgency.[42] It arises in both thinkers from Marx's material incarnation of a certain Heidegger (we know now that there is more than one). Marx and Kierkegaard confront Hegel's conceptual dialectic with real life; they transform historicity into a historical critique of the age; they make texts concrete through transformative praxis. The young Marcuse followed their lead in approaching Heidegger in this way. And one could reinvent such a Marcusean move for approaching Derrida. A more Marcusean Derrida already turns any deconstructive scholasticism on its feet: *Spectres* may now read nicely as a text for the new young left-Derrideans:

> And a promise must promise to be kept, that is, not to remain "spiritual" or "abstract," but to produce events, new effective forms of action, practice, organization, and so forth. To break with the "party form" or with some form of the State or the International does not mean to jettison every form of practical or effective organization.[43]

The tension I ascribe to Derrida appears because of a ghostly presence of a certain abstract (anti-Marcusean) Heidegger. This ghost inhabits a *quietist third way* between materialism and idealism; this ghost eschews an existentially material way of rooting thought in *ontic* human existence. The fate of a philosophy about existence, if severed from existing, becomes ghostly—bereft of people and institutions with a human face. Must not a consistent deconstruction, to avoid the above fate, admit human flesh and face? How else could one form global coalitions and even solidarities which would care for the single one and yet form a social union of sorts? How to heed Derrida's warning that the book, enlightenment, and revolution do not remain spiritual, without producing events, effective action, practice, organization? How to meet his claim: "deconstruction has never opposed institution as such," but sought out a "performative alliance" between memory of or fidelity to our past (a Marxian heritage) and the heterogeneity of the new or risky (a Kierkegaardian moment)?[44]

2. Revolution Without Institution?

Even if Derrida's deconstructive Marx-*Manifesto* for our times is untimely (read: unwelcome), what should one make of the demand for affinities "*without organization*, without party, without nation, without the State, without property (the 'communism' that we will later nickname the new International)"? What is to be done (with this demand)?[45]

Habermasian Interrogations

Habermas—even before Derrida, or the postmodern Gramscian theorists of interminable hegemonic struggles for radical democracy, Laclau and Mouffe—to a greater degree abandons the singular standpoint of class analysis. Yet, unlike these thinkers, Habermas retains a form of the concrete dialectics. Postmodern social theories gain much and lose little from Habermas's discursive employment of this dialectics. Learning to live more justly means being just also to Habermas. He is that social theorist who has worked hard on institutional construction, while others have spent time on institutional deconstruction. What precludes their theoretical affinity? To recast my earlier comments on the book, enlightenment, and revolution: First, Habermas articulates social equivalents to the singular acts of self-choice. Second, enlightenment critique, by acknowledging its pragmatic presuppositions, empowers one's responsible deliberation. Third, a discursively formed popular sovereignty admits multiple institutional organizations and sustains their openness to a revolutionary democratic permanence.

Authoring and editing an ethical life. I showed how Habermas takes advantage of Kierkegaard's question of radical self-choice in order to think with Hegel's social ethics against Hegel's emphatic institutionalism. Acts of dissensus are always already embedded in a form of life. One cannot dissent out of nowhere. One acts for reasons, e.g., when the received civilizational conventions become problematic. Habermas reiterates in different contexts that neither a Kierkegaardian existential individual nor a rebelling adolescent in crisis are akin to Robinson Crusoe. A dialectical and relational view of the individual links dissensus to traditions. Even singular refusals project, pragmatically speaking, another social form of life.[46]

The question about who one is or wants to be marks the horizon of dissent whereby one assesses the limits of received traditions. The singular acts of refusal and revolution cannot be thought otherwise than dialectically, that is, as social unities of negating dissent and positive agency. An undialectical affinity of dispersed transgressions signifies no solace from dogmatic universalisms. An undialectical individualism is not immune to begetting false wholes in the form of nominal certainties and local wars of fundamentalism—microsegments of great civilizational clashes.

✤ ✤ ✤

Communities engage in an either/or choice when they edit their problematic traditions. During 1992, the indigenous North and Latin American demonstrations against five hundred years of European conquest represent a dialectic of reading and authoring. Here occurs a dissensus within and yet away from received traditions. Five hundred years of resistance mark more than a loose affinity: there are the traditions of the Great Books, and there are responsible agents evaluating these traditions. Individuals take stock of troubled history and work for social change within their communities. Their resistance—recognized both in democratic and uncivil forms—authors, edits, and reconfigures the very notion of Canonical Texts.[47]

✤ ✤ ✤

Normative critique and a new enlightenment. Derrida invokes "a spirit of the Enlightenment," "the name of a new Enlightenment for the century to come." A consistent deconstruction is "a radical critique," "an interminable self-critique," "a radical and interminable, endless (both theoretical and practical . . .) critique." He reads a subversive Marx into enlightenment: the point of critical theory and praxis has not changed, it remains "an ideal of democracy and liberation." A deconstructive enlightenment does not apologize for the project of democracy as a revolutionary project of liberation. There is no exit! A critical spirit of Marx, so suggests Derrida, lives in our past, haunts our present, and visits in apparitions from the century to come. It is too bad that an inconsistent deconstruction loses the critical modernist heart. On this insight Derrida and Habermas share more than a slim affinity. Why insist that they continue a polemic? Moreover, Habermas formulates the pragmatic presuppositions of a consistent deconstructive critique. Must one accuse him of being dogmatic in the same way we find accused the ghosts of Stalin, now exorcised by Derrida (long after Sartre)? I think not. To wit: Habermas seems less interested in retrieving Marx than is Derrida.[48]

Thinking dialectically, one need not be offended by calling one's presuppositions of consistency fallibly normative. They are at best pragmatic presuppositions; they are invoked in living languages during a process of consistent deconstruction for which Derrida recruits us now. This normativity cannot be a party dogma or a practico-inert institution. Derrida—imploring one to live in hope, fear, and trembling, consistently and critically, in one but not another spirit of Marx—invokes the normative criteria operative in acts of this deconstruction. Normativity means thus the following: what walks like a duck might not be a duck. Not everyone dressed up like a deconstructionist, or writing like one, practices Derrida's consistent, Marxist deconstruction.

Dialectical thinking transforms dissenters into social agents. In the situations when humans are denied existence in a text or as a text, celebrating their textualities offers no solace in struggles for justice. What good is gesturing favorably to textualities without noticing a suffering exister? I plead for consistent textuality and deconstruction with a human face! Transgressors can learn to employ responsible action, emancipatory movements can learn to embody agencies of social change. Deconstruction for deconstruction's sake all but exhibits navel-gazing symptoms.[49] Derrida seems to invoke specters of liberation at the heart of deconstruction. If this appeal is normative in the flesh and blood of liberation struggles, should it not be performatively obligatory in the flesh and blood of a consistent deconstructionist?

✤✤✤

Frederick Douglass was a North American slave who neither was in a text nor was allowed to write one himself. His genealogy began in anonymous origins. Although probably born of a White father who was his master, Douglass had no parental name and no certainty of his birth day. Today's celebrations of the death of agency—a sort of immaculate conception for textual radicalism— would provide no way out for Douglass. As a slave, he was always already a book and agency under erasure avant la lettre. A ruthless critique of North American slavery and its colonizing Christianity prompted Douglass to learn how to read and write. He became an agent with a human face, a living text "written by himself." Douglass's radical linguistic revolt, taught to other slaves, raised specters of liberation in the Americas.[50]

✤✤✤

Revolution as popular sovereignty. That responsible agents exhibit the capacity to raise and defend claims leads Habermas to focus on public discourse as the locus of popular sovereignty. In recognizing another's singularity, one recognizes her agency. Together, as agents, we come not only to perform interminable critique but likewise to embody new institutional forms of life. Institutional agencies, thus conceived, constitute sites of perpetual democratic revolutions. These political institutions need not be built from above. They emerge from within civil society—as an expression of the egalitarian sovereignty of free citizens. Habermas finds this sovereignty best expressed in the ongoing transformations of law and in the democratic formation of our common will. Enter the dialectic of facticity (concrete lives of participants in democratic institutions) and validity (procedural justice is the minimal condition for sustaining popular sovereignty). Institutions and laws are contingent and indeterminate—deconstructible—forms of our actual performance. Yet in act, the presuppositions of our procedures cannot be deconstructed validly without falling into active contradiction with those very presuppositions.[51]

Habermas takes one step beyond Derrida: he names what would be the viable institutional models of popular sovereignty. One will score no interesting points against Habermas by criticizing him for doing *this*. Instead Derrida could help in expanding a bit more on what he himself means by an International. Derrida leaves the instituting moment of this alliance fuzzy. Why remain mystical or mystifying? If the loose affinity cannot empower a concrete agency of social change, then the singular transgressions remain aloof, blind, ineffective. Blind they are because the nominal gestures do not carry preinterpreted flags for our just and effective political allegiances. Without a critical social theory and praxis, affinities can bear ill consequences. Derrida's International transforms an affinity into action or it is really nothing at all. Affinities and actions robbed of responsible agencies are empty, thus dangerous. Aloof, blind, ineffective are revolutions without egalitarian and free procedures. Aloof, blind, ineffective is any institutionalized democracy without responsible and popular competencies for dissent.[52]

✦ ✦ ✦

Partido Constitucional Revolutionario, the proper name for a lived contradiction—a Party equated with the monopoly of the State, the Mexican ruling Party, PRI. It institutionalized social revolution by stealing it from its people: from Hidalgo's Independence cry in Dolores on September 16, 1810, from Zapata's uprising of 1910, from the elections of August 21, 1994. This co-optation of revolutions is a sport of professional politics, from the French Revolution to Stalinism to the eclipse of radical student demands in Paris of May 1968, Prague and Beijing in 1989, or Beograd in 1996. That PRI names a contradiction does not legitimate Derrida's reluctant anti-institutionalism. Killing an institutional 'proper' cannot suffice to change things for the Mexican people. The unprecedented victory of Cuauhtemoc Cárdenas in the 1997 mayoral elections in Mexico City occasions another beginning. Possibilities for a new alliance become apparent if one projects that which does not exist in Mexico. That missing possibility is neither neoliberalism (imperatives of money and power elites) nor intertextual revolutions without institutions. The envisioned path lies in radically democratic institutions. 'Marcos' and the Zapatista Movement (EZLN) announced in January 1994 from Chiapas a new revolution. This one, not desiring a simple takeover of power, makes itself, its war and peace, its rebellion and democratic disappearance, responsible to the indigenous civil society. This revolution inscribes into its very means and ends an institutional compact, a promise of perpetual peace, against a future take-over of its revolution.

✦✦✦

3. Draft from the Margins

Guarding against unnecessary academic contentions, I would like to take part in a coalitional dialogue between the Derridean materially concrete revolutionary passion and the Habermasian procedurally concrete institutions to house such a passion. In going into this debate, my presuppositions for a fruitful coalition are that I would settle for timely doses of both. I would like to do so without the weaknesses in each. The latter shows up when passions and procedures, each, become unduly influenced by the hegemonic dominant centers rather than by inclusive concerns of all affected who launch hegemonic struggles for liberation.

A Dialectic of the Concrete

To experience/author from the margins, one may not shy away from a spirit of class analysis. Such shyness strikes as premature those who live within the outskirts of dominant groups. Transforming the Marxian and Kierkegaardian dialectics (of authoring the book, enlightenment, and revolution) requires a recasting informed by concrete material struggles. Many books/voices are still excluded from history; an intensified enlightenment critique and a revolutionary passion are incomplete without reading/hearing the silenced ones of civil society.

✦✦✦

Uncivil rebellions. Civil disobedience presupposes the existence of democratic institutions, disputed texts, audible voices. Those who have none of these endure uncivil silence. They have no institutions to which they can appeal. This silence breaks out into an uncivil disobedience—giving birth to new institutions of civil society. The Mayan Communities of Population in Resistance (CPR) had their living texts burnt by the Guatemalan army: by scorched-earth policies, bombardments of villages, relocations into concentration camps, flights into the mountains. CPRs emerged in September 1990 from eleven years of struggle in the Sierra region of northern Guatemala, followed in 1991 by the CPRs in Ixcán and Petén. CPRs broke the silence of nonexistence, requesting recognition as unarmed civilians in a struggle for survival.

✛ ✛ ✛

Derrida's passion for the singular one harbors emphatic antihumanism and anti-institutionalism. This has always struck me as odd. In jettisoning the *ontic* specters of Kierkegaard and Marx, one does not do well to follow Heidegger's mandarin relation to existentially material life. Must we keep voices of the marginalized hostage to a hegemonic (western, White Man's) critique of western logocentrism? Neither Douglass nor the Mayan CPRs benefit much from having themselves robbed of their individual and institutional agencies. Their silences suffered both the logocentrisms and the phonocentrisms of the masters. Empowering human agency at the margins cannot mean the same as unmasking its inhumanism within the dominant centers. I celebrate Derrida's unmasking of the present unjust state of international law and, for this reason, disagree with exchanging an agency with a human face for an intertextuality without one. That a consistent deconstruction must not get lost in abstract historicity, conceptual revolution, or anonymous textuality is clear from its own *ontic-performative* care.

Marginal books, or of spirits and ghosts of liberation? Derrida spoke on "The Ends of Man" at a New York philosophical convention held during the revolutionary 1968. Here he urged us to link political, economic, and philosophical social struggles. "Democracy must be the form of the political organization of the society in which the members of this convention live." This demand requires that "1. The Philosophical national identity come to terms with a non-identity. . . . 2. The philosophers here do not identify with the official political policy of their country." Indeed, already in 1968 he calls for a democratic—philosophical and political—international. And he notes at the outset a concrete draft coming from the 1968 margins: "these were also the weeks when the Vietnam peace talks began and when Martin Luther King was assassinated. A little later, while I was typing this text, for the first time in history, the universities of Paris were invaded at the request of a rector by the forces of social order, then reoccupied by the students in the upheaval." Ironically the 1968 marginalia do not disrupt Derrida's conference text. "Because of its indetermination or its complexity, this political and historical horizon would call for interminable analysis. It is not to be undertaken here. I simply felt obliged to note and date the incertitude and anxiety in which I prepared this paper."[53]

✣ ✣ ✣

There is a new specter haunting the academy on both sides of the Atlantic, the specter of those concerned with race, gender, and class as legitimate issues of philosophical importance. This is the specter of marginal voices acting as gadflies to the mainstream. There are those who long for that procedural purity which effectively relegates such specters and their concerns to the dirty margins of the nonphilosophical. That is how some edit books, fields, schools, people.

In 1977, when I was a nineteen-year-old freshman at Charles University, the Prague guardians of philosophical correctness *(PC) were going to throw me out for reading Jan Patočka. They advised me then that Patočka was infiltrating the academy with a subversive political agenda. They requested that, if I wished to study, I had to make public statements distancing myself from his thought. In 1977, he was interrogated after he issued with Václav Havel the Manifesto for human rights, "Charta 77," and he suffered a kind of Socratic death (dying of a brain hemorrhage after being interrogated at the secret police station) on March 13 of that year. Patočka's underground Flying University was nurtured on the basis of broad philosophical rights and solidarity among theoretically diverse intellectuals, and provided a model of collaboration that later manifested itself in the revolution of November 1989.*

This autobiographical example evokes a dangerous memory. One reads nowadays in the papers written by undergraduates some thoughts held before them by the Cold-War guardians of purity: namely, that we need to return to the pure western tradition because paying attention to race in examining our received texts is just hatred of that tradition; because the feminist theorists are just feminazis bent on hating dead White Men; and because Blacks and women are just taking jobs from White males. While this is a naïvely obvious way in which undergraduates nursed on TV, and some on sophisticated-appearing studies such as S. Huntington's Clash of Civilizations, *voice their biases, one hears from many a graduate student a serious worry that the cultural climate for getting hired as a feminist or as a race or class theorist in the academy is inhospitable if not subliminally hostile. It is not uncommon that newly hired specialists in these areas must constantly try to prove themselves as thinkers to their departments even after they have gotten through the hiring committees during the interviews. When I encounter in print or in the university hallway the professionally posturing claims about race, feminist, or class theorists—"she or he is just a nonphilosopher" or "what they do is nonphilosophy"—I can't help but see the shadows and hear the echoes of those Prague totalitarians from 1977. The academic culture of resentment—even the celebrated, yet historically and geographically peculiar North American invention of splitting Analytic from Continental philosophy—also contributes to new hatreds. Isn't it time to get out of that western philosophical Cave of the unholy Cold-War alliance between the Stalinist and McCarthy heritages? (Are we climbing out from the ditch yet? Are we but lingering? Are we lashing out? Are we having a backlash?)*

Can the zeal for the purity of thought escape becoming a professional cover for forms of theoretical cleansing in the hallways of the academy? If diverse philosophers are incapable of cooperation at home, what can they contribute internationally other than an academic mirror image of Sarajevo's sniper alleys? Affirmative action on behalf of a race, gender, class of the marginalized includes (not excludes) certain books as legitimate in philosophical conversation. I maintain that in reality, PC is what the mainstream censors and editors of marginal books practiced long before they hijacked and unleashed this very concept onto the marginalized: in short, they practiced theoretical racism, a nationalism of conquest and patriarchy—all masked by the language of objectivity and institutional legitimacy. Basic consensus and political coalitions against this skewed situation could emerge on substantive and procedural issues: no individual or group may pursue philosophical correctness by theoretically cleansing another. Any such consensus, if it is to move beyond abstract individualism, must keep in mind the asymmetrical positionality of power in the material center and at the margins. Hence the PC scare emanates from the posture that has and uses its power to engage in cleansing. PC symbolizes power with an intent to exclude, to theoretically cleanse (under the appearance of objectivity, legitimacy, and democratic voting) a professional meeting; the hiring, tenure, or promotion process; the publication or peer review process; forms of association; and discourse. A marginalized group is not in a position— symbolically, structurally, materially—from which it may marginalize others. Affirmative justice recognizes and redresses, differentially, this unequal dialectic of concrete beginnings.[54]

✦✦✦

On ghosts one waits without expecting liberation, and some, like the ghosts of Stalin and Hitler, must be warned off perpetually. Even a non-quietist, messianic waiting requires creative work. The ashes of Auschwitz, the used-up bodies of Gulag, the atomic bombings of Hiroshima and Nagasaki, the genocide of the Americas, these keep the dangerous memory of damaged existence. Recalling such specters, liberation for humans in the flesh must be a historical, existential, material reality or it is nothing to write home about. Why can't *we* adopt Derrida's book on Marx in its spirit—but not a ghost—of insurrection? As an either/or path in Marx's spirit, this option intervenes in postmodern and critical social theory alike. Namely, the book's *other heading* lies in responsible authoring and calls for an intensified multicultural enlightenment. This *other* raises revolutionary specters, not ghosts of Marx.

Imagining concrete democracy. Some might object from another side of this dialectic of the concrete: Habermas defends the formal presuppositions of democratic institutions but disregards their relation to socioeconomic justice. Could the institutions of popular sovereignty come to mimic a moribund Institutional Revolutionary Party? Even with all the cogent formal-pragmatic apparatus on behalf of communicative reason, could Derrida's *ten plagues* become Habermas's nemesis? In order to check the neoliberal drive to profit and imperial power, what path might *our* political liberals take truthfully, rightly, and sincerely if not by linking a permanent democratic revolution with the material struggles at the margins of existing laws and institutions?

✦✦✦

The January 1994 cry from the Lacandón jungle, Chiapas, "basta ya!" "enough already!" introduces a decidable agency for a post-1989 coalition. 'Marcos' carries the title of Subcommander. 'Marcos' stands for more than a singular site of transgression, for more than an invisible affinity among those in struggle. Zapatistas, like the CPRs, were invisible for many years. Their dissent is made responsible to the democratic agencies of change. These are represented by the civil society of the indigenous. A dialectic between revolution and institution became obvious at the historic National Democratic Convention (the New Aguascalientes, Mexico, August 6–9, 1994). The convention call was issued by an uncivil, belligerent revolutionary force (EZLN). The gathering consisted of six thousand democratically elected civilian delegates from all states of Mexico with twenty delegates from the EZLN. The convention took place on rebel territory because the insurrection allowed for the gathering in the first place. Yet the rebels made themselves responsible to the elected convention body. Witness this transgression for the sake of forging the broad democratic agencies: the government of transition, the constitutional congress, and a call for eleven basic needs—work, land, housing, food, health care, education, independence, freedom, democracy, justice, and peace.[55]

✦✦✦

While Habermas's institutions are procedurally and formally revolutionary, Marcuse reminds us of a crucial lesson from Marx. One must root democratic procedures and law in the political economy of institutions. To give an example of what is at stake in this dialectically concrete thinking, note how Habermas defends the procedural adequacy of the agreement in the U.N. on the legitimacy of the 1992 joint allied attack on Iraq.

> We've discussed the fact that the United States and its allies appealed to the legitimation of the UN. . . . The institutions of the UN, and the basic principles of international law expressed in the UN charter, embody what Hegel would have called a piece of "existential reason"—a small portion of the idea that Kant had already clearly formulated two hundred years ago.

Having in mind Habermas, Haller cautions against all forms of "false universalism."[56]

Likewise, Derrida's tenth plague of the NWO places "two limits" on Habermas's optimism. One, our international institutions are rooted in particular historical cultures, specifically, *the idea of Europe*. Two, "[t]his supposedly universal international law remains, in its application, largely dominated by particular nation-States."[57] Must not a specter of Marx haunt Habermas's "hybrid," i.e., the "politically convincing . . . piece of reality" about the Gulf War? Could a materially more concrete critique of the hegemonic imperial politics and of the neoliberal economy still hope for the enlightenment "ideal," celebrate the "claim to legitimation," derive the "normative implications" in the same way as does Habermas? What might it mean, then, "to try to make the best of the Gulf War—the best not only for the Middle East but for the order of international relations as such"? What is *best* here?[58]

Why Not Imagine a Concretely 'Radical' Democracy but for a Failure of Nerve?

Must our age grow up from lyrical revolutionary fanaticism, well ironized by Kundera's *Life Is Elsewhere*, into a liberal politics with nothing but the neoliberal economic and the conservative monocultural imaginary? The communications theory envisions multicultural and social democracy yet does not venture from political to economic democracy. Even after 1989 one may ask both the deliberative critical theorists and the postmodern social theorists of radical democracy, is political democracy possible without reciprocal economic justice? Ingram and Marsh, among others, insist that it is not. They are inspired by Habermas yet vouch for an unapologetic, more concretely democratic version of his deliberative democratic model. Both follow arguments for unoppressive community and free individuals, yet come to endorse a more complex view than either side in the liberal-communitarian debate. Both learn from the failed Soviet etatism and the advances made by liberal politics and law, yet critique the neoliberal and the conservative world orders. While Habermas's communicative reason sustains liberal politics in the institutions of democratic will-formation, they ask whether or not one can tolerate the neoliberal or the conservatively communitarian facticity of the NWO and remain democratic.[59]

✦✦✦

The meanings of 'radical' have come to designate very strange bedfellows. Radicals are skinheads attacking the Roma and Turkish populations, the neo-Nazis commemorating Hitler's birthday, and all those longing for the Old/New World Order. Mayans in Chiapas, Greenpeace activists ingressing into the French nuclear testing site at the Pacific Mururoa, and African Americans in the L.A. urban uprising of 1992—all are described as radicals. Radical feminists are branded as feminazis by a radical culture-critic Limbaugh. There are radical world views, from the Oklahoma bombing squad to the Freemen (White anti-U.S. separatists) to Buchanan's salvation crusade for the American soul to Robertson's religious war on the NWO to varieties of radically democratic, post-modern, or Marxist rejections of the same. Lonesome radicals come with missions from god: unibomber, suicide-bomber, leaders of mass marches or conservative revolutions. In a night of all mad cows, 'radical' says as little and as much as 'democracy'.

If this were all! One may get tired of radicals and discard their radical slogans. Stalinists and Nazis make peculiar examples of the red-black coalitions of radicals—both are the radically founding and the radically destructive kinds. When neoliberals get tired of radicals, they ridicule those party or in-group sectarians and their catechism lessons. Tiredness with intolerance yields to surface diversity, a sort of radically ironic in/difference. We find some former '60s radicals after 1989 allied with some tired critical theorists and tired postmodern theorists. Allied, neither group draws lines between the neoliberal/monocultural and radical/multicultural democracies. The neoliberal imaginary of surfaces capitalizes on fragmentation. The conservative imaginary admits only one kind of radical, the second-generation ideological offspring inherited and transmuted from the red-black coalitions. Both imaginaries produce radicals who block a radical critique and radical democracy. Radicalism without democracy is blind; democracy which shies from its radical promise is empty. Critical theory without apologies aims at radical overcoming of domination, at liberation praxis of radical democracy. Even radical democracy may fall short of being radical existentially-materially. The latter radicality casts sociopolitical or economic decidabilities upon normative questions, such as in unmasking any surplus scarcity (i.e., hunger). 'Radical democrats' Laclau and Mouffe appeal to Lyotard's postmodern condition, but they seem precociously allergic to Habermas's normativity precisely where Habermas remains rather helpful. Yet they do not go for Derrida's radical multicultural and economic democracy—but what else may a new Inter-national mean?—as a critically post/modern hegemonic project of liberation today.

✦✦✦

Habermas aims at politically reforming our human interaction in the public sphere, and he relegates human labor into the acommunicative realm of systems rationality. He overstates the immunity of these systems (neoliberal markets and administrative power) to democratic critique and transformation. Liberal procedural politics may only check and balance the functionalism of markets and power, but it should not try to change the equation in some radical fashion, he implies. Yet if we do not sever democratic theory from an imaginative, existential, and material overcoming of all human exploitation, is it then wise to rest content with a job half done? Severing material life (body) from politics (mind) seems counterintuitive.

For example, since an autocratic rule over towns violates the public sovereignty of citizens in these towns, it is counterintuitive that any sort of tyranny should be all right in the workplace. Learning from George Pullman's failed nineteenth-century experiment in running a company township, and from the worker-resident revolt against this twofold tyranny, various authors argue for extending democracy from political interaction to the economy of the workplace. Ironically, the Illinois Supreme Court ordered Pullman to give up the township, yet it let him keep his enterprise unchanged. Would not democratizing the law without doing the same in the workplace resemble the lopsided political democracy of this court? With the manuscript on law by the nineteen-year-old Marx lost to us, one may in vain seek clues to an answer in Habermas's radically democratic transformations of Hegel's *Philosophy of Right*.[60]

And yet, the demand for a multicultural and politicoeconomic democracy follows from Habermas's own antiauthoritarian pragmatics of communicative rationality, just as it can be distilled from Hegel's institutionalization of Kant's idea of ethical life and perpetual peace. For this reason, at least, Marx stuck with Hegel's project, and we would not fare worse in lending a careful ear to Habermas. One needs to situate his pragmatics in a concrete human activity, albeit for Habermas, no less than for Adorno, this can no longer be a concretistic blueprint for the substantively utopian form of life. Still, one should avoid reifying the lifeworld- and systems-rationality in the way Habermas's analytical split between communication and labor suggests. Real workers, just like judges and juries, live and interact in both realms in a single temporal embodiment.

If one remains an observer of concrete labor, one fails to theorize a key dimension of human interaction. What if we are compelled to elaborate the sociopolitical and economic conditions of possible discourse ethics? This materially expanded ideality is not a concretistic blueprint—for that nuance, Habermas should lend us an ear. And now: the full ideality demands *validly* that we democratize equally state-run (state socialist or capitalist) and private (market liberal) workplaces, not just debating clubs, seminar rooms, or law courts.[61]

Let us say we side with Habermas; Marx romantically hopes that Communism delivers us to a life free from profit- and power-politics. Habermas finds modern lifeworlds too complex to be able to function without efficient markets and administrations. And market liberals minimally restore to Eastern Europeans this functioning efficiency which the Soviet *apparatchiki* either robbed (getting ready for the capitalist phase) or simply screwed up (nothing is left to steal now by anyone). Habermas argues as follows: When cultures undergo a one-sided rationalization, their lifeworlds become tyrannized by one cultural sphere, e.g., education and political deliberations by the instrumental ends of the technocrats. The problem increases if lifeworlds get colonized by the unchecked demands of efficient markets and state bureaucrats. The task of critical theorists is to limit these encroachments by functionalist rationality; but it is not their task to eliminate the beneficial efficiency of these autonomous systems. Now, let us say that after reading Kundera and Habermas, we do grow up from an unfruitful romanticism and sober up from the scary lyrical revolutionary fanaticism. Should *we* throw overboard the not so romantic but realistic and contemporary core of Marx's analysis of alienation and immiseration—now that it applies to the former so-called Marxist regimes? Marx reiterates Kant's Enlightenment question, what constitutes genuine growing up or sober maturity?[62]

Besides the systemic colonization of lifeworlds *from without* (Habermas), there figure active tyranny, marginalization, and the domination of one group by another *from within* the lifeworld (e.g., Bartky, Gordon, Marsh, or Young). Marsh shows that the latter forms are evident in "a lived, phenomenological dimension": in the undemocratic workplace, in civil society and the family structures distorted by patriarchy and racism, in ongoing economic and political tyranny, in outright marginalization and other forms of public manipulation. "Where Habermas needs to be more Marxist than he seems willing to be is in recognizing both colonization and domination." "Contrary to what Habermas says, therefore, the face-to-face confrontation of the laborer with the capitalist is an ethical one in the life-world, grounding or founding the systemic aspects of capitalism and the colonization of life-world by system."[63]

As a dialectical phenomenologist, Marsh has an advantage over

Habermas in that he need not split the perceptual from the linguistic life-worlds, nor descriptive from explanatory accounts. In lived dimensions of markets and power, motivated tyranny and domination occur *within* the lifeworld. Habermas limits his explanation to systems-autonomy, whereby a colonization can take place from *without* the lifeworld. In this he is right but incomplete. A concretely grounded discourse theory of democracy can integrate microanalyses, e.g., postmodern descriptions of the disciplined body, with the explanatory macroanalyses of systemic exploitation.[64]

While accepting Habermas's critique of Marx's romanticism, we can introduce a complex critique of the faces of oppression created by capital-logic. At least one face occurs via anonymous systemic colonization and another via motivated lifeworld distortions. The former carries extrinsic intrusions into the lifeworld by neoliberal markets and administrations. The latter infects communicative interaction and liberal procedural politics within the lifeworld. Marsh drives this home succinctly: "If making some money is good, then making more money is better, and making the most money is best; and this 'good', 'better', and 'best' is both intentional and systemic." The logic of profit or power expands *functionally*, increasing in greater complexities of systems, and *inwardly*, entering "into the very psyche of the worker" and citizen.[65] We must either concur with Habermas's total "skepticism about 'simple recipes of workers' self-man-agement'"[66] or imagine that *concretely radical* democracy affects the entire human existence—its existentially material (economic, political, cultural) dimensions. Is the latter path merely a romantic, or a disenchanted mod-ernist, or a frightening longing—simply a utopian-cum-nightmarish dream displaced by the revolutionary, postmodern gains of 1989?[67]

If a human communicative interaction were all that is required for self-determination (morality, democracy, and law) and self-realization (identity-formation), then political rights would be their sufficient conditions and the liberal creed (even in its postmodern version as radically democratic) their true banner. Our markets and technocracy, as we know them, would be just the necessary, unavoidable surds of living in the big city or the rural outskirts. The surds would be chastised periodically by a postideological communicative reason or displaced by counterhege-monic gestures of a postmodern radical democrat. Perhaps this is a bad caricature of these options, even though I am not sure that it is entirely unfair to how the mainstream U.S. reception of them presents itself. A phenomenologically grounded discourse ethics evinces a strong *prima facie* evidence that communicative freedom, even in hegemonic struggles, provides the necessary formal but insufficient existential and material conditions of free action. Liberty and the possibility of hegemonic strug-gles begins with equal rights for all participants in discourse. Yet consistent liberalism and political democracy extend to all lived conditions of communicative freedom. These comprise democratically structured life-worlds, not just abstract talking heads. Workers do not just sit in a seminar room debating possibilities, but they organize workplaces and distribute burdens, benefits, and material resources democratically.[68]

Habermas harnesses the pragmatist response to Hegel—"this American version of the philosophy of praxis"—in order to focus on law and democratic politics, something Marx's and Kierkegaard's productive responses to Hegel did not do.[69] Why should one—can one—cut off the praxis of radical democracy and law from the praxis of creating and existing? If Marx was naïve about what it took legally and politically to form and sustain permanently genuine democracy for all, the Hegelian-Kantian or, for that matter, the mainstream North American naïveté about what it takes materially and existentially need not be repeated. Communicative, moral, and legal liberty without the material conditions for free action is empty, just as efficiency without political democracy is blind. Liberty is one dimension of human freedom.

✤✤✤

It is no infallible dogma in the Frankfurt School that Soviet Marxism or romanticism about direct workplace democracy are or were our only options. I contest claims that the Soviets represented democratic economy and only suffered from the political form of class domination. It is debatable that this state economy was democratic even in a socialist sense. We have here a peculiar form of the welfare-state capitalism: workers do not own the means of production. They are taxed by the totalitarian state, the sole owner and employer and jailor. This state bows down to the inefficient needs of the military-industrial complex and of a new aristocracy—the Communist Party mafia and bosses. The shifts of 1989 represent a displacement within this capitalism: from a totalitarian Pullman-like company state to private markets. The astonishing readiness with which the past nomenklatura *transformed the state Party capital to private enterprise—with which western companies were quick to enter into joint business—testifies that they were historically a* sui generis *class of robber-barons. Our tiredness with state socialism seems to mask our yet undiscovered exhaustion with one sinister form of capitalism.*[70]

✤✤✤

I agree with Habermas: avoid prescribing the 'simple recipes' of command and invisible-hand economies. Therefore, I would argue that democratic workplaces could be demanded and instituted in regionally autonomous as well as in publicly, even globally determined markets.

Democratically structured firms and markets are likely to become more efficient in our complex world where environmental problems and structural or real scarcity of resources need more attention than unlimited growth and competitive profit. Democratically managed firms seem less prone to institutional and class conflict, they admit a greater inclusion of various groups before the law. By a democratic overcoming of economic domination—not by a welfare state or neoliberal tinkering with it—the discourse model of justice might come to prevail with greater consistency. Demanding a performative consistency of deconstruction, may critical theorists apologetically leave themselves off the hook? I can envision that critical post/modern social theorists—if joined without needless polemics and apologies—would, first, reject dogmatic scientistic Marxism and, second, acknowledge the material limits of the real existing liberal imaginaries (whether classical or neoliberal or left-leaning or radically democratic).[71]

In search of anticolonial coalitions and postcolonial solidarity. There is a related issue of concrete justice which comes to us from a different angle than the foregoing correctives to Habermas. This angle returns us both to the need for recognition, discussed in chapter 1, and to the specters of a joint venture among critical post/modern social theorists, discussed above. Marsh holds, "Racism and sexism . . . to an extent are indirectly displaced forms of class domination and colonization, . . . they are not equal in importance to class domination."[72] This is my question: What distinguishes patriarchy or racism within capitalist or state socialist economies? Can one hold that the economy as well as race and gender categories should all be kept distinct and yet at the same time insist that an economic class take priority over race and gender classes in the analysis of the core form of domination? An insistence on an analytical priority of economic class would mark only its *accidental distinction* from race and gender categories. *Real distinctions* would imply, however, that freedom from economic oppression need not yet overcome patriarchy or anti-Black racism—the reverse being *prima facie* true. The two analyses indicate different diagnoses; this affects proposed prescriptions and prognoses.

Once one assumes that complex relations exist among these three categories—and the faces of oppression they theorize—the Hegelian-Marxist holistic category of one social totality needs rethinking. This is a salutary consequence of Habermas's twofold model of the lifeworld- and system-integration, even if we need not split them off in ways suggested by a dual-systems critical theory of recognition and redistribution. Granted all this, can one view an economic class as the more basic social category? Do sexism, homophobia, or racism represent a 'moral evil', hence, only that which is foundationally derivative of the market pathologies of modernity? Is economic domination materially more fundamental than would be a materiality of a sexualized or racialized body in bad faith? While racism and patriarchy serve as supplements to economic domination, is not the reverse also true?[73] Could not race-, ethnie-, or sex-based classes survive as core problems plaguing even advanced social democracies, such as were the early Yugoslav experiments in the socialist and self-management markets?

Thinkers like Firestone, Hartmann, and Young make strong cases for revising the dialectical method used for social analysis. Firestone argues for a transformation of historical materialism into the dialectics of sex and economy:

> For unless revolution uproots the basic social organization [of reproduction], the biological family—the vinculum through which the psychology of power can always be smuggled—the tapeworm of exploitation will never be annihilated. We shall need a sexual revolution much larger than—inclusive of—a socialist one to truly eradicate all class systems.

And her position carves out a dialectic of sex in the gap between the scientistic, economistic reductionism of diamat and the psychosexual ahistoricism of orthodox Freudianism: "we can attempt to develop a materialist view of history based on sex itself."[74]

Many argue that race-based struggles are likewise not reducible to economic categories. Racism haunts state socialist economies just as it flourishes in liberal politics. Hence, racism may not be overcome by the dialectical critique of an undemocratic politics in state socialism and an undemocratic workplace in liberal democracies. While bell hooks holds out for integrating gender and race analyses, West and Outlaw focus on the intersections of class and race. These moves theoretically close the gaps between gender and race and class in classical Marxist and Critical Theory. They do not offer mere descriptive and factual concessions to the forefront role of certain social struggles today. Rather, they articulate a nuanced hermeneutics of racism and patriarchy as distinct modern pathologies. The move prevents absorbing race classes and gender classes into economic classes, thereby facilitating broader coalitions and even solidarity.[75]

✢✢✢

I venture with confidence one genealogy of how the social constructs of gender and race experience a reduction into an economic class analysis: it might seem more obvious to a White male how to relate to economic class oppression. I might have suffered this in some derived forms as a refugee, immigrant, and a graduate student in a profit-driven economy. It changes little that state socialism of my native Czechoslovakia declared sexism and racism overcome along with the purported equality of all citizens. I come to diagnose the dialectics of sexual reproduction and racialization through a dialectic of economic privileges and their overcoming. Yet do women or Roma or Blacks or gay people focus only on the means of economic production when they attack patriarchy and racism and homophobia? Systemic racism and homophobia and sexual classes were not absent from the workers' paradise. Indeed, hatred toward Vietnamese or Cubans or Chinese did well in East European socialism. And anti-Semitism flourished only to be promoted by and hidden behind an anticapitalist rhetoric. Even though we may discern economic reasons for some forms of hatred, many hatreds are first to appear in post-1989 East Europe even where they offer no economic gains. Feminism becomes here a dirty word associated with the past regime because of its ambiguous economic-and-gender equality which suppressed one's individual style as well as minority cultures. This would be so even if we could argue that White women in East Europe did gain their greater sense of workplace and repro- ductive self-determination, something which, e.g., the German unification threatens to take away from East Germans. Don't we need a distinct critique of anti-Black racism and of the male ownership of the means of reproduction? (I venture that a straight White Man has a need for this as much as does a White gay male benefiting from 'passing' within the economic and racial privileges of White patriarchy.) If yes, can we concede to antiracist and gender-based strug- gles their practical but omit their critical-theoretical roles? I fear not, lest in con- sidering the dialectic of sex we fail to heed the judgment on our future omissions: "we can learn a lot from Marx and Engels . . . [but] about the conditions of women as an oppressed class they know next to nothing, recognizing it only where it overlaps with economics."[76]

✤ ✤ ✤

Would not an antiracist and antipatriarchal attitude make struggles for economic justice more consistent, phenomenologically adequate, hermeneutically comprehensive, and politically fruitful? Would not this criterion test the scope and concreteness of one's fallibilism? If yes, we must admit that social democracy *could* emerge with patriarchy and racism intact, still to be overcome. In pursuing radical critique and democracy, it seems unnecessary to hold onto those asymmetrical dis- tinctions which grant theoretical primacy to economic class over the social location of race and gender. Moreover, *this* asymmetry robs critical social theory of a more positive alliance with pluralist and even post- modern politics. And finally, it severs critical theories from complex struggles even where they may concede to gender and race their practical equality with or even priority over the economic-class-based social movements.[77]

The hermeneutics of postmodernism as a new French or Euro-American ideology, justifying real existing late capitalism, hits its target well in the self-containing western academy and in the media or advertising used by multinationals. However, must not this hermeneutics miss other of its targets, i.e., "critical theory in a postmodern mode"? Discourses from the Euro-American margins, often by people of color, raise the specter of new post/modern alliances against the political economy of the post/modern NWO. From their vantage point, the undifferentiated hermeneutics of *the post/modern* rehashes boring inhouse debates of the West—it becomes a form of Eurocentrism.[78]

An excursus: existential correctives to certain holisms and foundationalisms. A consistent fallibilism contravenes both the holistic and foundationalist claims for the exceptionality of western development. Short of resurrecting an absolute, there is no standpoint from which one may redeem such exceptional claims *fallibilistically.* If *this* insight covers what one may claim validly, then claims to exceptionality are either vacuous or they must be democratized.

It is in this sense that Kierkegaard claimed exceptionality for the category of the individual through which the present age and all its social concepts must pass. Each individual narrative is a totally existential claim. Simply put: each individual apart from a conventional socialization may become a unique species-being. In facticity, even if learning to will absolutely, no single one can turn exceptional uniqueness into an absolute. Kierkegaard was aware that the individual may recover at most an ironic exception. Sartre harnesses this lesson into his skeptical study of sustainable human self-development. The skepticism stems from the unlikelihood that groups-in-fusion could once for all learn from past failures of other group formations, that fraternities could once for all nurture ethical solidarities without the terror of the pledge, and that institutionalized politics could fully sustain an existentially attenuated deliberative democracy. Heidegger is right that certain historical possibilities of development are granted to *us* first by changes of *our* historical horizon, not by intentional willing as if humans could jump out of the horizon of historically contingent possibilities (this is a sound Hegelian insight). Kierkegaard and Sartre, however, find the difficulty of becoming the individual to be the same for everyone in all ages. Sartre is intuitively more right than Heidegger that even if a god existed, humans could not be saved (god would either make no difference or come too early) without learning to coexist as humans. No wonder that Sartre's skepticism about fraternity's survival sounds more realistic than his or Marcuse's 'hope now' and Rorty's prognosis of its future reign. Cycles of decline do not show respite, no gods or extraterrestrials hover around the corner to rescue *us* from this difficulty! Yesterday's radical progress in historical consciousness—irrelevant whether religious or secular—could in the next generation serve radically regressive venues. Still the human difficulty of beginnings is no smaller but no greater now than it was in yesteryears.[79]

✤ ✤ ✤

Among the youth growing up after the civil-rights, gay, and women's liberation movements, a spiritually inclined, pull-yourself-by-the-bootstraps high-school kid may today have pierced body-parts, wear ethnically eclectic fashion, and display at least in clubs an openly polyvalent sexual identity. One was unlikely to be individualized and socialized in this manner with ease as a baby-boomer. Yet one may judge progress or decline in all this just as little by externals or labels as Kierkegaard thought one was able to discern inwardness by monastic garb. To wit, one also encounters in the new generation antifeminist women leaders, free-market Black nationalists, and transgressive gay sex with patriarchal or racist identity structures. Children of reformed Communists and religionists, both, may become ruthless capitalists.[80]

✤ ✤ ✤

Kierkegaard could not claim an exception for messianicity as a tradition, though he tried to become a Christian, wrote from a Eurocentric town, and was limited by a nineteenth-century White-male perspective. An egalitarian distribution of the difficulty of becoming the individual qualifies the exception one may claim for oneself or for any messianic faith in liberation-to-come. This exceptionality solicits a pluralist view of traditions, groups, and individuals within them. No individual could become exceptional through another or via an ascending group and era. We may democratize 'exceptionality' as a claim to one's own unique difficulty of beginnings. This may allow for a revolutionary shortening of the historically reactive cycles of decline through more intensified cycles of learning the difficulty within a single generation. The vanishing point of liberating self-development would be neither a foundationalist cogito nor a holistic spirit of the age but a memory of learning. Individuals-in-groups in each generation learn from historical failures (e.g., that both real existing socialism and capitalism were driven by competition for profit and power) and untried historical possibilities (viz., multicultural and existential democracy motivated by a nonreactive, shared need for sustainable self-development).[81]

Democracy is not immune to patriarchy or racism, unless by the *singular universal* (Sartre's Marxian-Kierkegaardian answer to Hegel) one means a totalization without a totalizer. If the 'individual' performs as the vanishing critical point for one's standpoint (existential fallibilism) and an entirety of a life (existential holism), then theoretical claims to a qualified exceptionality or uniqueness of western development remain indeed ironic. This existential irony is entirely at odds with ethnocentrism, albeit the latter is inscribed into a liberal-postmodern ironism.[82]

With the latter meretriciously aestheticizing irony, just as with apodictic foundationalism and absolutist holism, one can maintain neither a genuinely radical critique nor a multicultural, multigender, and antiracist democracy. In alliance with postmodern social theory, critical theorists can now appreciate postmetaphysical and even existentially performative thinking. This dissuades them even further from holding out for an ultimate transcendental grounding of claims or an uncritical affirmation of a received form of life. Perhaps *we* can learn to avoid both problematic foundationalism and holism in theory, and their practical consequent as well as antecedent in 'human' cleansing. Sober in the salutary skepticism about all messianic totalizations of what is *our* human history, yet imbued with existentially material passion and hope, *we* need not be late in awaking the lifegiving specters of liberation. Will *our* radical democratic theory and praxis—*our* political economy of recognition—dare to imagine a more just world?[83]

Conclusions: An Existential Either/Or with a Constant Reference to Dissent and Democracy

A critical modernist need not be implicated by the deconstruction of traditional theory. Liberation theory, emerging from concrete critical traditions and their communicative praxis, antedates and now can join with the postmodern case against instrumental reason and society. Consistent critical theorists offer differentiated accounts of fallible normativity and egalitarian yet concrete praxis. They aim, even after 1989, for a democracy capable of an unapologetic dissent on behalf of liberation. A consistent deconstructionist need not be implicated by this critical social theory. It is legitimate to care for the singular kinds of marginalization and thereby share the starting point of a normative theory grounded in critically appropriated traditions. This deconstructive critic may warn how procedural, liberal politics *could* become unjust. Men and women of color debate this danger both with Marxist economistic reductionists and with formal proceduralists. If gender and race apartheids become subsumed under concerns with capital-logic or under striving for liberal politics alone, then real injustice, marginalization, even colonization, *could* still occur.

A fourfold complementary shift becomes apparent in this reflection: the symmetrical politics of democratic identity and recognition comes to join the asymmetrical politics of multicultural, multigender, and multiracial difference; the struggles for recognition come to join the struggles for socioeconomic democracy; an individualist diversity becomes transformed into dissenting individuals in complex communities; and the deconstructions of existing laws and institutions come to empower communities in forming the new institutions of radical critique and democracy. While there is a phenomenological symmetry with regard to shared bodily needs, material scarcity, and the overall ethical project of creating humanity, there is likewise an ethical and moral asymmetry of individuals-in-communities, with the resultant justice conceived of as a politics of difference. The singular universal and radical multicultural and existential democracy are notions integrating the spirited as well as appropriated dimensions of a/symmetry in a manner that endeavors to avoid the liberal pitfalls of the generalized other and the nominalistic pitfalls of dispersed anecdotal revolts without institutions.

Consistent postmodern theorists arrive at those concerns where consistent critical social theorists wish to begin. And consistent critical social theorists learn from this postmodern theory how to defend the newly emerging radical democratic pluralism. The interesting topic is no longer locating the border between the modern, the postmodern, or even critically traditional.[84] Fractures of life importance appear between the failed state socialist-cum-state capitalist undemocratic economies and the dissenting projects of radical socioeconomic democracy. There is no just totality that could sublate this disjunction. This either/or choice seems more philosophically compelling and politically urgent than the boring disputes between postmodernism and modernism. In many cases the sought-out options emerge for the sake of those without hope—and hope is their democratic and dissenting specter of liberation.

A sympathetic reader of Derrida and Habermas might say at the end of the day: reason, albeit politically liberal or institutionally incarnate, without passing through its material and existential revolutions, ends up supporting established neoliberal and monocultural realities. A liberation theory which gets its draft from the margins is possible. These margins exhibit individual and institutional dimensions. Suffering people implore for a social theory with human faces and liberating agencies. The blowing wind urges critical post/modern social theorists into coalitions, to work in solidarity with emancipatory struggles. Theirs is hope and refusal, the existentially material specters of liberation which ironize and unmask all ghoulish apologies.[85]

5

HOPE AND REFUSAL

Where there is power, there is resistance. . . . [P]oints of resistance are present everywhere in the power network. Hence there is no single locus of great Refusal, no soul of revolt, source of all rebellions, or pure law of the revolutionary. Instead there is a plurality of resistances, each of them a special case.

—Michel Foucault, *History of Sexuality*, vol. 1

✣✣✣

The critical theory of society possess no concepts which could bridge the gap between the present and its future; holding no promise and showing no success, it remains negative. Thus it wants to remain loyal to those who, without hope, have given and give their life to the Great Refusal. At the beginning of the fascist era, Walter Benjamin wrote: ". . . It is only for the sake of those without hope that hope is given to us."

—Herbert Marcuse, *One-Dimensional Man*

✣✣✣

Marcuse's meditations on hope and refusal sounded as untimely in the 1960s as they would have in the 1940s, indeed as they do today. Foucault is more skeptical than Marcuse about the 'Great Refusal' or any other unique source of revolutionary hope. Foucault pluralizes sites and sources of refusals and situates them within the interstices of power relations. Does this double movement (limiting and proliferating resistance-and-power complexes) stifle or intensify the specters of liberation? Does it sidestep the question in social critique, or does it empower a more radical critical social theory without apologies? I consider the unfashionable: possibilities of an untimely hope in liberation—Marcuse's obstinate critical social theory—persist.

Any such consideration runs into a heap of questions: Can hope be won through self-mastery? Does hope lie in an agent's sovereign self-possession? Can hope arrive via a determinate world-historical revolutionary subject of social change? Or, if a 'no' be given to all above questions, is hope granted to *us* through some gaps in Being, in language, in destiny, in resistance-and-power configurations? Must any and all such gaps be transgressions but never an agency? But can transgressive gaps alone (i.e., without becoming a form of critical agency) always already resist attempts at closing the untrue social whole of the present age?

In these questions one meets the end of hope: the rhetoric of possessive self-mastery flips into its mirror image in a single revolutionary subjectivity; or both are replaced by anonymous transgressions. Enter a combined end of liberation. The NWO celebrates this as the good tidings of having arrived at last at this hope's end. A stupid hope has always been nothing but despair. The NWO's grinning feast of the end of history only mimics laughter. Being merely different—one has not laughed at the established order, one has not refused hope or hopelessness.

Even if possessive agencies or anonymous transgressions fail all hope for *us*, must hope against hope be a bad social theory and, confessing to the 'death of god', an obsolete path? That the emperors of the NWO wear no clothing is comically hopeful. Don't clowns and *refuseniki* in this *ordo* show how to laugh, how to imagine other than a hopelessly stupid world?[1]

I wish to harness into a critical social theory great refusals of stupid hopes and hopelessnesses alike. Nietzsche's 'death of god' might not be of disservice in this transvaluation of hope/lessness. I intend to read anew the Marcusean Refusal, now as pluralized by the transgressions of disciplined bodies and oppressive institutions. Clowning within the matrices of disciplinary power, refusing to close out liberation specters— I join Marcuse's new sensibility with Foucault's aesthetics of reciprocal ethical existence. The living sources of hope arise within multiple struggles. They emerge across the dimensions of economic, gender, sex, and race classes. Hope in liberation can imbue the singular transgressive body-performativity as well as the performative uses of fallibilist pragmatic presuppositions of human communication action. This risky hope—it is another name for the coalitions and the communities among *refuseniki*—appears under the figures of a radically existential and multicultural democracy.[2]

In his contentions with both classical liberal and Marxist social theory, Foucault gives a misleading impression that by rejecting the "single locus of great Refusal," *we* are somehow beyond Marcuse's "real spectre of liberation." Foucault puts on the brakes against a critical social theory and decisive praxis of liberation, and so somewhat does Derrida. Both gain a compelling sobriety vis-à-vis the former Soviet totality and the liberal-market realities, yet their skepticism about the possibilities of critical social theory and praxis can be traced to not-so-politically sober (un-Marcusean) dimensions of Heidegger. Derrida's spectral Marx, however, admits that the microanalyses of human sufferings provide a macroscopic evidence against the one remaining grand narrative: global techno-power and markets. Thus, Derrida's specter disperses Marcuse's "spectre of liberation" into a myriad of refusals, but does not thereby end it.[3]

One can learn from Foucault's skepticism about Marcuse's refusal. Yet there are no grounds in Foucault, Derrida, Adorno, or in the innovative developments of their approaches (e.g., in Butler and Cornell) to prevent *us* from rethinking the matters of hope and refusal. I propose here precisely this rethinking via Foucault's unfinished project of ethical reciprocity. Thus, I will highlight the possibilities and limits of his genealogical approach, and then link body-performativity (Butler) with postconventional ethics (Benhabib, Cornell, Fraser, Honneth, and Young). The latter two notions fruitfully complement Habermas's formal-pragmatic performativity and communicative ethics. The next chapter will discuss the possibilities of ethical community. I take up the Marcusean refusals again in chapter 7.

1. Foucault's Genealogical Liberation Theory and Praxis

Poster distinguishes three phases in Foucault's work. These follow Foucault's very early interest in existential phenomenology. In the first phase from the 1960s, Foucault elaborates an archeology of the rationalist, Cartesian self. In the second phase from the 1970s, he develops the genealogy of a decentered self. And in the third phase from the 1980s, he renews his earliest interests in existential self-creation. It is in this last stage that he transforms his early existential concerns in the most interesting fashion. Poster sums up Foucault's path from early existential thought, through three phases, to late studies of the *aesthetics of existence*:

In this last phase of Foucault's theory of the subject one senses a return of sorts to the problematic of Sartre and the existentialists. In place of the hermeneutics of suspicion in Positions 1 and 2 there is an affirmative effort to comprehend a process of self-constitution, a genuine search for an ethics.[4]

Since my study of transgressing dissent and democratic agency benefits from this last period most, I need not be tracing the well-documented development of Foucault's theory of power. My questions build from his positions on power (the middle period) and on the historical aesthetics of existential self-constitution (the unfinished last period) without needing to posit discontinuities or unities in his work. I limit myself to this working query: Is it possible to fashion pluralized Marcusean *refusals*—an *ethos*, aesthetics, and ethic of a new existence—within the complexes of resistance-and-power struggles projected by Foucault?[5] What options does a historically concrete ethic of self-creation hold for deliberative democracy? Can a Foucauldian performative microapproach challenge the more global aspirations of the NWO? My inquiry highlights seven interrelated dimensions where the transgressions of limits and the limitations of agency occur. I make my way at last to Foucault's existential ethics and new enlightenment.[6]

Power: margins without centers. During his second phase, Foucault abandons the repressive-oppressive schemata of dominating and juridical power and adopts a more diffuse or capillary notion of power. With this move, he must give up an intentional subject of power. Thus, he develops a methodology which describes the microscopic configurations of power relations in the service of various productions of knowledges, institutions, and human subjects. Power does not form a homogeneous or sovereign totality aspiring to domination. Because power operates in the flexible fields of accumulation, power relations are always already shot through with openings for local resistances. Capillary power inhabits margins without centers. Resistance within margins of power-configurations must employ the performative, lived body-politics. Resistance is, thus, not a result of intentional agency but a productive effect of this very same power. "One needs to be nominalistic, no doubt: power is not an institution, and not a structure; neither is it a certain strength we are endowed with; it is the name that one attributes to a complex strategical situation in a particular society."[7]

The repressive-oppressive doublet presupposes intentional, royal, sovereign subjects. These embody the legitimate right, the possessive loci of power, and the distribution of its mostly negative effects. The "polymorphous" approach to power replaces the royal sovereignty model. Foucault describes power as a field of relations: power transgresses fixed borders and, yet, produces subject positions and agencies. The latter emerge as effects of power relations. The field does not form a totality. It operates through a capillary- or body-cyberspace, "a net-like organization." Transgressions of fixed limits define, nonpositively, the existing configurations of power; critical agencies are limited by the gaps in these very power relations. Foucault's genealogy transforms what was once an existential insight into a performative notion of subject-formations: "individuals are the vehicles of power, not its points of application."[8]

The early existential Foucault (echoing the well-known challenges to Hegel's identity logic) locates one's authenticity in radical self-creation. If we could genealogically intensify the Sartrean thesis that existence precedes essence, we would arrive at Foucault's middle phase when he proceeds by decentering existential phenomenology. He becomes at that point the genealogist who no longer raises questions of authenticity. When at last this genealogy of self gives way to the performative attitude of an enlightenment critic, or to the proposed new ethics and politics of self-constitution, Foucault still retains this distinct hermeneutical, even historicist horizon.[9]

These shifts in Foucault's concerns with 'existence' do represent a welcome advance which I wish to exploit further. Foucault gets rid of the Cartesian—monological and decisionistic—elements of subject-centered existentialism. Yet focusing on the aesthetics of existence, he wins a performative, postmetaphysical sense of postconventional ethics. In this move, which for him is never a mere formal affair, he preserves an existential ethic. Foucault, thus, opens doors also for postconventional-existential ethics: this would enflesh the formalism of those linguistic methods—post/structuralist or formally pragmatic—which have done away with the lived body (viz., of existential phenomenology) to begin with.[10]

One issue remains, however, unresolved even in this advance. Given that Foucault retains the emphatically descriptive and microscopic methodology, can his hermeneutics, ethics, and politics of self-constitution challenge the rhetoric of the NWO? This *ordo* tends to hegemonize the local narratives of ethicopolitical self-constitution in a grand macroscopic, global narrative. Don't we need that embodied and institutional performativity, whereby hope and refusal, both, pragmatically project an aesthetics, ethics, and politics of liberation?

Microanalyses: performing descriptions. Another key innovation occurs in Foucault's second period. Foucault records a genealogical shift from the intentional to the strategic questioning of power. He requires theorists of power to begin with local (rather than global) descriptions, with ascending (rather than descending) deductive frameworks, and with microanalyses (rather than macroanalyses). This approach marks a preoccupation with a diffuse or "molecular" marginality without centers. Forms of "global domination" are produced or exercised locally—in the lived margins of medicalized, criminalized, regimented human bodies. A focus on microanalyses favors assumptions of performative body politics. Global refusals of domination function in this context as other effects of this very same performativity.[11]

Foucault retains the microfocus all the way into his latest discussions of ethicopolitical self-constitution. Even as the hegemonic power clusters are being displaced, a new self or a new *ethos* may be constituted only within its multiple historical margins. A counterhegemonic power-configuration is equally the productive effect of such margins. Yet Foucault solicits our commitment to justice in marginal and body matters. And his studies of disciplinary power and of the ethic of self-constitution open up the political possibilities of reversing injustice. These reversals never deliver for Foucault some normative conditions of possibility. And so one wonders whether or not there is a difference in how one transgresses power centers (from actual margins? from the textual margins at the centers of academic postmodernity?). Must not Foucault's politics of difference project an aesthetics of liberated existence, that is, a revolutionary agency of change? Would one necessarily err by asking whether or not the localism which does not empower an existentially responsible and institutional agency of social change can resist effectively the global colonization of our lifeworlds by the NWO?

Disciplines: performing transgressions. Foucault limits his local task to an interventionist and strategic attitude toward the debilitating effects of disciplinary power. He identifies this task in the essay from his first period as a nonpositively affirmative transgression of limits. His ultimate concerns with self-constitution retain this local, interventionist, and nonpositively affirmative approach to ethicopolitical self-creation. Once again, we may note some key advantages of Foucault's historically specific transformation of existential*ism*. Performativity articulates those material and historical refusals which any concrete justice demands. There remain, however, deficits in any merely nominalist interventionism. Some of these deficits echo the problems others had with decisionism—charges, to be sure, leveled in the 1960s and still today against all existential thought.[12]

In his 1963 essay Foucault writes, "The limit and transgression depend on each other for whatever density of being they possess: a limit could not exist if it were absolutely uncrossable and, reciprocally, transgression would be pointless if it merely crossed a limit composed of illusions and shadows." He characterizes the relation of transgression and limit in a nondualistic manner as a certain "flash of lightning in the night." As if echoing Albert Camus's *Myth of Sisyphus*, with self-creations in one's desert and polar nights, Foucault insists that the "singularity" of transgression lies neither inside nor outside, is neither Black nor White, can be neither prohibited nor lawful, but rather, it "lights up the night from the inside" of the dark itself. Foucauldian transgressions reject not only the linear Hegelian-Marxist teleology of progress but also the existential dialectic of dissenting transgression and democratic agency:

Transgression is neither violence in a divided world (in an ethical world) nor a victory over limits (in a dialectical or revolutionary world); and exactly for this reason, its role is to measure the excessive distance that it opens at the heart of the limit and to trace the flashing line that causes the limit to arise. *Transgression contains nothing negative, but affirms limited being—affirms the limitlessness into which it leaps as it opens this zone to existence for the first time.*[13]

Can such interventionist leaps be equated with an existential attitude? Can they assume the role of a postconventional ethic articulated in Foucault's last phase? (Is radical self-choice just some violence in the divided world of values?) Would not nominalist leaps fall short of any concretely political justice? (Is the radical agency of sociopolitical change simply a victory over limits?)

Foucault's characterization of a "nonpositive affirmation" as the form of "contestation" need not exhaust other possibilities for transgressive agency. Words such as 'contestation' and 'intervention' are postmodern markers for a textual radicality. What Foucault says of this radicality here strikes me, however (from the ethical and political angle of concrete activism), as emphatically contentless: contestation "does not imply a generalized negation, but an affirmation that affirms nothing, a radical break of transitivity." Can a Nietzschean-Heideggerian radicalism, if left on its own, help those who must contest the NWO? "[T]o contest is to proceed until one reaches the empty core where being achieves its limit and where limit defines being. There, at the transgressed limit, the 'yes' of contestation reverberates."[14] Certain radicalism does quite well in the dominant power-centers. Can one remain existentially and democratically radical (*this* radicality would refuse the NWO and all its globally regional works) while assigning to various uncritically ontological or invisible hands what is to be done by the historically concrete human beings carrying on their material struggles?

Marcuse's objection (it transforms transgressions into a liberation praxis) that any uncritically ontological radicalism is blind and abstract stands firm today as it did during his Freiburg studies with Heidegger. The most promising aspect of Foucault's last phase goes beyond the limits placed on a responsibly self-constituting and social agency. His last ethics is no longer a productive effect of functionalist power. Here Foucault rejoins a sort of Marcusean and Sartrean trajectory: the structural or ontological view of power and historicity gives way to a performative, historically and materially concrete, and activist human existence. Foucault's ethics of self-constitution learns from the failures of early existentialism, anonymous post/structuralisms, and linguistic formalisms alike.[15]

Power and resistance. The method of Foucault's middle period demands that the microanalyses of power be limited to multiple, asymmetrical, and local forces. Power is produced, effected, institutionalized, hegemonized, contested, but not intentionally deployed by an agency. "Major dominations are the hegemonic effects that are sustained by all these confrontations." This power's transgressive limit-condition of possibility lies in resistance. "Where there is power, there is resistance." If one must doubt that power should emanate from single choices, decisions, power-centers, then there can be no outside for hope and refusal either. "[O]ne is always 'inside' power, there is no 'escaping' it, there is no absolute outside."[16]

This thorough loss of an 'outside' standpoint for *any* historical and revolutionary subject does not define the ends of resistance. Foucault does not glorify domination. He describes through these power-nets the relational character of concrete existence. Relations are impossible without the points of resistance. Both power and resistance define, rather broadly, a complex social ontology, not clear possibilities of an all-out political resistance to dominating power. How helpful for any concrete refusals would be this formal structure of power-and-resistance? What can Foucault provide beyond offering a descriptive social ontology? Even if power is not equal to domination, but ontologically always already admits resistance, is there not a concrete sense of dominating power to be resisted for ethical and sociopolitical reasons? Even if there is "no single locus of great Refusal,"[17] are there not radically activist forms of resistance which launch multiple 'great refusals' in the NWO? The descriptive angle (it limits itself to an abstract ontology of power-and-resistance) is theoretically blind and politically ineffective.

Fraser is on this issue quite right. Foucault offers great empirical insights into disciplinary power configurations; but his theoretical and political nominalism is not necessarily an option for the marginalized. This is true of Foucault's theory (even if not true of his lived politics) insofar as his emphatic nominalism shies away from expanding the phenomenology of enslaved bodies into a fallibilist critical theory of slavery. The celebrated nominalist descriptions—do not they abandon all real struggles to a normatively confused inside/outside of the NWO? Are not NAFTA and GATT describable—quite accurately—as configurations of power-and-resistance? So what? Good grief! Or put otherwise than in terms of the NWO: what is to be done?[18]

Specific refusals. Should *we* settle on agreeing with Foucault that there is no single locus of Refusal (and on this, there is agreement among the earlier Frankfurt School thinkers), then critical post/modern theorists could no longer work as abstractly global intellectuals. In spite of Foucault's target (Marcuse), both Marcuse and Adorno offer excellent early examples of drawing on the multiple theoretical and practical sources of refusals. The Foucauldian genealogists in addition develop the micro-analyses of the present age. As microcritical theorists, they become specific intellectuals: geologists, topographers, geographers, body-anatomists of power-and-resistance. One cannot speak for one truth or universal institution. There is no one agent of revolutionary change. The totalizing angle is undone at the proletarian base and in the intellectual superstructure: this very Marxist binary of base-superstructure is finally debased. World and body-maps reveal how cultures and civilizations constitute hegemonic identities, and they disclose which loci can erupt against oppressive geographies.[19]

Such specific intellectuals may learn from ongoing struggles by the oppressed how to confront the same opponent. This centrifugal movement results from breaking down the totalizing perspective of one universal expert consciousness. The shift occurs at a time when the globalizing effect of multinationals becomes much more entrenched. Instead of a singular intellectual agency, Foucault envisions a "polymorphous ensemble of intellectuals." Their work might be related to the academy, yet none of them is an expert in the total field. Experts are both situated and in need of collaborating with others. The specific intellectual is able to pose a critical threat to the hegemonic system precisely because of the specificity from within which any resistance is projected.[20]

Since Foucauldian refusals function as genealogical transformations of the Sartrean concrete universal, one is able to avoid irrelevant critiques or ineffective struggles. This genealogist is sociopolitically positioned and, thus, achieves descriptive generality through specificity. One is not suspended in transparent truth apart from or against all power. One inhabits a position of the counterhegemonic "politics of truth." One need not stand outside of power or even ideology. One's specificity is to some degree always already an effect of power. At best, then, the genealogist problematizes the very regimes and economies of truth.[21]

I discern in Foucault's historical specification of critique distinct affinities not only with Sartre's 'singular universal', to be developed further in the next chapter, but likewise with Marcuse's demand for concrete philosophy, which I will follow in chapter 7. Common to all three thinkers is their search for a postconventional-existential ethics and politics. If my specific existence precedes any essence one could ascribe to me, then my and our ethical and political projects present the performative task of self-creation, and all critique of their established shapes becomes reconstructive or genealogical. Marcuse argues that a philosopher becomes concrete by rooting all critical categories in ongoing human struggles. He depicts Socrates, Kierkegaard, and Marx, but no longer Heidegger, as examples of a philosopher becoming concrete. Liberating refusals begin at the street corner and on the public square, not within some abstract categories of historicity or nationalist fate. Sartre's singular universal learns from Kierkegaard's concrete category of the single individual—it is through this singular, not via transcendental categories, that history takes its shape. The universal enters history through the specific and the singular, argues Sartre no less than Marcuse.[22]

I emphasize that getting rid of abstract universalism and essentialism does not necessarily annul all provisional essences and universals. The need for recognition might have a better use of the latter than of theoretical nominalism, which in some sense likewise abstracts from living. Pragmatically speaking, however specific one's critique becomes, individual standpoints inevitably project alternatives beyond their immediate specificity. Nominalism is descriptively and *de facto* true of these specific positionalities (of individuals or groups) where our struggles originate. But a theoretical nominalism or a nominalism in social struggles cannot cut it; indeed, both are counterintuitive. Granted that any inquiry into the regimes of truth (prison, hospital, academy, government) must be specific in order to be critical; still, "detaching the power of truth from the forms of hegemony, social, economic and cultural, within which it operates at the present time"[23] requires generalizations about these regimes and their forms of oppression.

Genealogies: performing theory and praxis. The foregoing reflections mark the advantages and disadvantages of a generalized genealogical method. The genealogist with feet planted in local liberation struggles can offer distinct advantages over the global revolutionary avant-gardes. But there are the disadvantages of any merely speculative genealogy. And these echo abstract universalist and transcendental approaches to history. I believe that theoretical and practical nominalism results from such abstractions, and is not warranted by experiencing and theorizing diverse struggles. Insofar as genealogists do not relapse into abstract theorizing, their method is quite welcome for keeping theorists concrete. And it is necessary for dialectically pluralizing the scope of a single great refusal.

The local character of genealogical method arises as a historical corrective to the totalizing "communistological" figure of party politics. Foucault declares the death of 'Marx' as *the* author of liberation, of Marxism as his revolutionary catechism: "As far as I'm concerned, Marx doesn't exist." (What about specters of Marx?) Insofar as Marxian and Freudian discourses were liberated from their totalizing "theoretical unity," they have become transmuted into the "non-centralized" local forms of critique. Therein one can seek today's relevance of the Marcusean refusals (i.e., in what Foucault describes as *"an insurrection of subjugated knowledges"*). Foucault's just as Marcuse's resources for great refusals refer to the marginalized and subaltern voices, "the immediate emergence of historical contents."[24]

Marcuse taps into historical forms of dissent against one-dimensional mentality. Likewise Foucault finds there the possibility that one can "rediscover the ruptural effects of conflict and struggle that the order imposed by functionalist or systematizing thought is designed to mask." The subaltern, disqualified, abject, subjugated knowledges manifest resources for refusals—disrupting the hegemony of dominant hierarchies. Marginalized or disqualified—repressed contents haunt us with "a *historical knowledge of struggles.*" From "margins of knowledge" comes dangerous memory—human history's 'truth commission' and specter of liberation.[25]

Foucault's genealogy emerges from a dangerous memory, not a fireside cogitation. His genealogical method is shaped in reflecting on experience, "as a painstaking rediscovery of struggles together with the rude memory of their conflicts." It is true that Foucault gives up on "the tyranny of globalizing discourses" of "a theoretical *avant-garde,*" and resists all "positivist returns to . . . exact form of science." It is also true that his genealogy invigorates the Marcusean refusals whose obstinacy is concrete yet antiscientist. Refusals can be disorderly, transgressive, and still imbued with a hopeful memory (an agency) of liberation. "The role for theory today seems to me to be just this: not to formulate the global systematic theory which holds everything in place, but to analyze specificity of mechanisms of power." Foucault's descriptive theory depicts specific power-and-struggle constellations. With the genealogy as a critical social theory begins then our historical reflection on domination and social struggle.[26]

I submit that a meaningful opposition is not between theory and antitheory. This seems to be a false binary. Beyond positivist scientism and ahistorical transcendentalism lies what Marcuse calls a critical theory which "preserves obstinacy as a genuine quality of philosophic thought." This theory would be (re)constructive. It runs against certain facts and their systematization, such as the fact of racism. Yet a critique of facts is empowered by social struggles. Transcendence is, thus, within the world—if not of the world as *we* have established it. Likewise a critical genealogist who is concrete need not be antitheoretical and, as a theorist with practical intent, indeed, cannot be uncritically nominalist.[27]

A new enlightenment: searching for ethical reciprocity. There is a Kantian dimension to Foucault's Nietzschean genealogy. Foucault recovers the memory of liberation struggles. Instead of seeking some originary source of authenticity, he articulates the 'existential' as "the practice of creativity."[28] In spite of this latter disclaimer of authenticity, Foucault's

Nietzschean rereading of Kant and Sartre innovates rather than jettisons the possibilities of an existentially rooted social theory. A deep sense of selfhood gives way to a regulative (Kant), self-created (Nietzsche, Sartre), and performative (Foucault's body politics), that is, self-authenticating, attitude. One may not get authenticity *qua* essentially fixed being. The 'existential' viewed in a performative attitude leads to Foucault's critical ethic of self-constitution. I wish to discuss existential performativity—the aesthetics of existence—as Foucault's new enlightenment.[29]

Let me now inscribe Foucault's critical attitude into that enlightenment performativity which is deployed in formal pragmatics. We meet the latter in Habermas's communications theory. Poster sets Habermas's ideal speech situation in opposition to performativity. But if one reads performativity, in Foucault and Habermas alike, in more existential terms, this opposition becomes problematic. Foucault's search for "an aesthetics of existence"—the novel forms of ethical reciprocity—places him squarely in alliance with Habermas's efforts to formulate communicative ethics. In both thinkers, I claim, we meet postmetaphysical limits constraining any a priori principle for what Foucault calls "a new ethics."[30]

I propose below to rethink Foucault's genealogical attitude (transgressive performativity in body practices) along with Habermas's communicative attitude (agent-centered performativity in speech acts). The dissenting transgression and the democratic agency, both conceived as social performatives, require one to adopt an existential attitude of self-creation.

First, Foucault describes transgressions as the "body politic." This politics denudes the "political anatomy" of disciplinary power-techniques over bodies. The human "soul" and humanism, both, are viewed as effects of this power. The 'soul' is not an ideological superstructure; it is produced by the technologies of power over the body. The political economy of disciplined bodies must account for the re/production of souls: "The soul is the effect and instrument of a political anatomy; the soul is the prison of the body."[31]

If power defines the points of resistance and vice versa, it is crucial to find where the cleavages in power are. For this, we need to recall the memory of struggles against the hegemonic forms of knowledge productions (identity, morality, and law). Thus, one must study "the history of the body" (demography, geography, hospitals, asylums, prisons, army, sexual practices, academic institutions, etc.). "[T]he body is also directly involved in a political field." The body is productive and produced. It is invested "with complex reciprocal relations" of the political economy of power and resistance.[32]

New helpful directions in the sought-for critical social theory and politics take on inevitably the shape of body-transgressions. Descriptive theory can microanalyze the political technologies of the body. And the latter can be further analyzed through the genealogies of power relations, e.g., under the historically specific forms of governance and self-constitution. Therefore, if "the body itself is invested by power relations," then the needed critical theory and practice must involve likewise a body politic. Foucault does abandon the globally theoretical standpoint and no longer puts all his eggs into one basket with the single agency of social change. Yet his transgressive theory and body politics spring from and foster multiple refusals.[33] If power produces knowledges—shaping, imprisoning, disciplining the bodies—then any critique of power hegemonies proceeds likewise via power-knowledge complexes. Again, critique must comprise a body politic. The production of power over bodies operates through a "micro-physics." The ruptures of the hegemonic disciplinary relations occur on this microlevel, "whose field of validity is situated in a sense between these great functionings [institutions] and the bodies themselves [microlevel] with their materiality and their forces."[34]

I conclude, first, that there can be no *discursive validity* which might be able to claim itself apart from the *body-field of validity*. The transgressive dimensions of social struggle must be retained in critical social theory and practice in order to account for this post-Cartesian inclusion of the body. The materiality of the body, and of the subjugated body or the body in bad faith in particular, is what continues to prompt shifts from traditional to critical theory.[35]

Secondly, to the key question whether there are disciplines which need not fall under the relations of domination, Foucault says: "there are consensual disciplines." This is an astonishing admission, if one considers his emphatic methodological nominalism. If we can link 'consensual disciplines' with the genealogical attitude, then concrete transgressivity is not necessarily opposed to consensuality, hence against critical agency, as such. Consensus and agency can function nicely as useful fictions, each being "a critical principle." Why not concede that Foucault holds out for a minimalist use of critical principles? "The farthest I would go is to say that perhaps one must not be for consensuality, but one must be against nonconsensuality."[36]

Foucault allows for a degree of nonconsensuality in all power-truth relations. In this he comes quite near Adorno's ethic anchored in critical modernism. That Auschwitz inflicted unique damage on human bodies, on that there is a high degree of consensuality. So what agency of social change is possible (given *our* dangerous memory) that one may affirm at least negatively? Adorno articulates only negatively the damaged forms of life. Foucault, like the early Frankfurt School and Nietzsche, admits Judaic prohibitions of idols—positive material utopias of a happy life. He intimates "a non-disciplinary form of power" which can be found neither in the classical nor the modern natural law. Foucault envisions "a new form of right" which would be "anti-disciplinarian" and free from the strictures of power as sovereignty.[37]

The search for a new form of rights gives us more than an antinormative reading of Foucault. Abundant evidence points to Foucault's new enlightenment. His query solicits a modernist, genealogical yet, I argue, existential ethics of self-constitution. The new right describes "an ethical attitude." With this in mind, one should not hold out for some *ethos* as a traditionally given ethics. Foucault's genealogical and existential performatives need not contravene each other. I constitute myself as a performative principle on the move. That is a logical extension of my ethical situation—a genealogical/existential self performs an ethical principle. If thought through in a pragmatic way and within a social context, this performative self stabilizes itself in new forms of ethical reciprocity. The reciprocal self remains a regulative principle, not a fixity. As a performatively regulative ideal, one may derive from it a concrete procedural morality and radical democracy. This ethical ideality assumes pragmatically ongoing resistance to disciplinary hegemony and to total nonconsensuality. Foucault's postconventional-existential selves, shaping complementary ideals of ethical reciprocity and procedural democracy, are not givens. Both perform/exist in relations that one assumes to oneself in relation to others.[38]

Foucault decries the violations of reciprocity in pleasure among men and women; he criticizes the nonexistence of reciprocity in the homosexual love between a boy and an adult man. In Greece and Christendom, both kinds of sexual relations, unlike friendships among free and adult White males, were not open to ethical reciprocity. This marks the deficits of patriarchal and racist relations to date. Foucault describes an ethical reciprocity of pleasures as that existentially regulative ideal which many might want to seek nowadays. He defines ethics in nonmasculinist terms of the reciprocal self-constituting existence. And yet he does so without any dependence on classical natural law, modern law of sovereign rights, or even contemporary marital conventions—whether for heterosexual or gay relations.[39]

Foucault's aesthetics of existence. I come full circle to Foucault's ideal of ethical reciprocity. He learns from the Greeks, medieval Christians, and moderns by performing a genealogy of their ethics. The new ethics is a question for humans today. And this is a modern, Kantian way of posing the question. The question cannot be answered by given religious and social institutions or mores. What Sartre once called a pessimistic toughness, Foucault now names "a hyper- and pessimistic activism." An existentially rooted postconventional ethical attitude defines well a new enlightenment principle of self-constitution. Foucault hopes that this ethics not only structures existence but also nourishes creative forms of radical reciprocity. Ethics as an aesthetics of existence has no truck with juridical power, authoritarianism, or totally nonconsensual disciplinary structures.[40]

I do not, however, share Foucault's implied separation of this new ethics from sociopolitical and economic needs. Such a one-sidedly apolitical move needlessly falls behind Sartre's gains in integrating existential with sociopolitical perspectives. I argued elsewhere for going in the opposite direction: bringing together an existential, nonpolitical politics with procedural justice. If "ethics is a practice" and "ethos is a manner of being," then ethics and politics do come quite close. Unless I misread what Foucault implies, in other texts he prohibits all severance of ethics from politics. He distinguishes the political impact of an ethical attitude, e.g., dissent and protest, from deliberative or strategic politics. This is also my position. One side represents, e.g., Havel's dissent and the other his presidency. The former appears strictly ethical and nonpolitical only from the side of the latter's contaminated professionalism. The latter is severed from the former at the price of sheltering problematic attitudes. The worst case scenario of split separation infects procedural politics with attitudinal distortions—by disciplinary power-relations of patriarchy and racism. Foucault calls us back to this microlevel.[41]

I think that it could be more promising to root the ethics of self-constitution within a postconventional ethical reciprocity and radical democracy. If the ethics of self-constitution aims at a singular universal, then the opposition between the singularly ethical and the sociopolitical, and between the universally ethical and the sociopolitical, becomes a false binary. Marcuse's search for a new *ethos* of liberation requires overcoming this binary—refusals have both strictly agent-centered and transgressive political dimensions. If ethics need not define a fount of authenticity or a natural law, then the modern existential ethics cannot be a communitarian given; then an *ethos* of liberation depends upon an ongoing critical attitude.[42]

An interesting thing about Foucault's retrieval of Kant's enlightenment and about the ethics of self-constitution are their postliberal yet noncommunitarian aim. I say post- rather than antiliberal because Foucault does not rehash the liberal-communitarian debate. He poses the issue of self-constitution in dissent from each. He examines existential self-constitution and the histories of politics genealogically. This blocks any return to the disencumbered individualism (whether the liberal or the voluntarist-existential*ist* kinds) and to the uncritical communitarian grounds of legitimating politics (classical or contemporary). Foucault reclaims the critical attitude towards the present. And still more concretely than Kant, he affirms ethical self-constitution and a critical *ethos* as lived regulative ideals and projects of liberation.[43]

2. Performativity and Ethical Reciprocity

Butler takes the notion of performativity out of its formal-pragmatic framework into the fields of lived bodies. This embodiment of speech acts suggests one way of expanding Foucault's unfinished aesthetics of existence. A concrete idea of the postconventional ethics of reciprocity and difference (variously envisioned by Benhabib, Cornell, Fraser, Honneth, or Young) nicely complements Habermas's formally pragmatic idea of communicative ethics.

Performatives that Matter

Butler's category of performativity is inspired by Derrida's reading of the speech-acts theory of J. L. Austin. Besides Derrida's linguistic turn, Butler adopts Foucault's body politics. She articulates a critical queer theory and develops a phenomenology of the body performance. In an example I discuss below she analyzes the Los Angeles urban uprising. These are the body performatives that matter—ought to matter—to formal pragmatics. Since Habermas draws on the linguistic turn, albeit in a formal pragmatic analysis and not body-deconstructions, the two views of performativity allow me to elaborate a meaningful link between transgression and agency.[44]

Butler defends her use of performativity against the emphatically idealist or constructivist readings which worry the critics of her earlier work. She does not put forward any essentialist notion of self. Yet she does want to hold out for a substantive notion of gender formation. That she rejects with Nietzsche and poststructuralists "a doer behind the deed"—this cannot mean that one may take gender identities on and off as pieces of clothing or surface behavioral gestures. Selfhood cannot be achieved as if outside of performativity, i.e., apart from one's socially expressed existence. Yet neither Butler nor Foucault wish to speak of ethical self-constitution in purely behavioral or even disembodied terms. "A performative act is one which brings into being or enacts that which it names, and so marks the constitutive or productive power of discourse." Human agency surfaces as a field which must become at first "legible."[45]

Texts become legible *for us* because one begins by repeating or (re)citing prior texts. Performatives are not free-floating signifiers or protocol propositions; and even textualities cannot perform somersaults in an existential and ahistorical vacuum. Kierkegaard insisted on a paradox that one become *what* one is and, thereby, in existential repetition undergo a radical self-transformation. Derrida and Wittgenstein agree that no citations or repetitions (no *how* of textualities) construct languages, traditions, histories, bodies *ex nihilo*. In Butler's assessment,

when words engage actions or constitute themselves a kind of action, they do this not because they reflect the power of an individual's will or intention, but because they draw upon and reengage conventions which have gained their power precisely through *a sedimented iterability*.[46]

Butler emphasizes transgression. The doer (intentions, agency, subject) is constituted through and in performing. Those performatives matter which have an embodied life. It is for this reason that Butler now rejects the behaviorally constructivist notions of performativity. And she abandons all naturalized or essentialized notions of self and gender. Any concretely self-constituting existence requires a temporal dimension. The temporality of an agent or a transgressor is neither natural nor behaviorally constructed nor legible through formal pragmatics alone. The temporal "'I' and 'We' will be neither fully determined by language nor radically free to instrumentalize language as an external medium."[47]

A philosophy of existence could be invigorated quite well with reference to Butler's recent work. True, just as other post-Beauvoirean feminists, she might not spontaneously and explicitly take to this methodological alliance. *But what if a novel existential approach provides the needed terrain wherein to articulate that performativity which is concrete but not naturalized, social yet not behaviorally constructivist, communicative and pragmatic and yet not emphatically formalist?* Then a second look at this alliance would not be the worst one could do. Indeed, it is most interesting to note how Butler contributes to an existential study of performativity.[48]

Butler describes transgressive body performances in order to elaborate a critical queer and race theory. In her analysis of the film *Paris Is Burning*, she searches for an agency conceived of as "resignification." The term defines agency by its temporal field in which the new discursive and subject possibilities become first manifest. Butler asks, how can one exist within a culture which marks anything slightly queer by its continuing abjection and subjugation? The film shows some spaces in which queer possibilities emerge and even at times succeed. One can repeat the genocidal cultural conventions in a disloyal, resignified manner. One can affirm them in a transgressive manner. One can create a community of kinship in defiance. Butler's analysis of this film shows that subversions are not free from unsubversive appropriations; that critical appropriations can function subversively. The subjects of liberation live at a border. Their liberating specters are neither fully constructing nor constructed.

Border-subjects exist in temporal spaces, within the performances of liberating possibilities. The specter of queer is not a liberated doer behind the deed of liberation, "drag is a site of a certain ambivalence." Its appropriation, just as the repudiation of hegemonic cultural norms, expresses the performative-existential possibilities of transgressive agency.[49]

Butler critiques oppressive cultures likewise from an opposite angle, i.e., via describing the body-performatives that disable possibilities of liberation. In analyzing the beating of Rodney King by the Los Angeles police, she asks how the video recording of this event could serve as a visual evidence that King's body *intended* to hurt the *peace* officers who subjugated him. How can the disciplined body (seen on the film clip over and over) be "read" by numerous audiences as the continuing origin of real violence, threat, and danger? Butler's phenomenology of the racialized perception within the field of distorted visibility facilitates a critical theory of how this body becomes a threat. The Simi Valley verdict sided with the L.A. police officers and against King. In trying to decipher this occurrence, Butler uncovers the construction of the beaten Black body as "the *agent* of violence." The doer does not exist behind the deed but is produced along with the inscribed intention. This production itself is not explicitly intentional. Notice that the jurors *really* "saw" King's body as the agent of violence. Thus, it is the "transvaluation of agency" and the "racist modes of seeing" which resignify (in the disabling sense of the term) the very field of what can be visible and what remains invisible.[50]

What can possibly count as the validity claims to truth, normative rightness, and sincerity in the visual field which is hegemonized by racist perception? The formal discourse ethics—in its liberal procedural assumptions—is inadequate to detect this hegemony by its own resources. If one claims to have seen King's body posing the vital danger to a peaceful society, what discursive or legal claim can get at this piece of *visible* evidence? Sartre reminds us that a good democrat can act consistently as an anti-Semite. And Butler's existential phenomenology of an evidence provided in bad faith echoes Sartre's insight into the limits of proceduralism:

> [T]o the extent that there is a racist organization and disposition of the visible, it will work to circumscribe what qualifies as visual evidence, such that it is in some cases impossible to establish the "truth" of racist brutality through recourse to visual evidence.[51]

Given the prevalent hegemony of the anti-Black racist episteme in the Euro-American modernity, White speakers and hearers are systematically deprived of true, right, and sincere appreciation for visible evidence. The fact and problem of Blackness (Fanon's and Du Bois's existential markers for a racist episteme) distort in their incipience the celebrated formal force of the better argument. Butler indicates how this facticity is always already imbued with a certain validity: the fact is "always already performing within that [W]hite racist imaginary, has always already performed prior to the emergence of any video."[52]

For the sake of those who have been rendered invisible, for the sake of those whose visibility is daily shaped in media clips of 'Black' intentionally violent bodies, for the sake of those without hope . . . , what communicative ethics and critical theory can one fashion? How can one refuse the racist facticity and its public space of validity? The jurors, viewers, and hearers constructed by racialized evidence are not amenable to seeing differently—no matter how many argumentative appeals to evidence are made and how many rounds of democratic voting are taken. The appeals to the true, truthful, and sincere agency of racist agents—even in well established democracies—remain practically counterproductive. And insisting on a singular recourse to formal pragmatics in this scenario is theoretically counterintuitive. Hence, the undoing of a distorted field of facticity and validity must be launched via active resignification. Butler depicts this 'great' refusal as an "aggressive counterreading" of the racist episteme.[53]

This transgressive agency acts for the sake of genuine democracy. Refusals proceed behind the intentional agency of the jurors or viewers or hearers infected by the racist epistemic fields. The task of this body politics cannot be reduced to an empirical issue to be relegated to the applied practices of formal pragmatics or to a political action in aid of formal pragmatics. Since one has to do with a racist episteme (that is, an infection of the entire validity field of claims), one must confront an issue that is intrinsic for a critical social theory as theory. Therein lies one existentially concrete role for transgressive critical theory and politics: body performatives must appropriate and unmask those structures of democratic speech which have become distorted by the racist episteme and have been deployed by the racist readings of validity claims. In sum: the material conditions of the possibility of undistorted communication require an active restoration of the body (and its evidence) to the fields of facticity and validity.

Butler's rethinking of performativity in its embodied dimensions, thus, inaugurates a promising corrective enhancement of formal pragmatics. First, her body-performative category integrates the formally pragmatic with the deconstructive renditions of speech acts. Secondly, elaborating performativity as a form of transgressive agency (bypassing the voluntarist idealist ego and even the Cartesian cogito inscribed into some body-intentionality) expresses "the reiterative and citational practice by which discourse produces the effects that it names." Butler helps us to get beyond the aporia of naturalizing essentialism and linguistic idealism or one-sided social constructivism. Neither everything is body-nature nor everything is discourse-society. And we may not assume an individual or social agency behind such totalities. Apart from performativity, in which natures and social constructs become at first available, there can be no 'I' or 'we'. Claims about facts (constative speech) are to some extent always performative.[54]

Even if performativity is not an all-out constructivist, voluntarist act behind the deed, nonetheless something originates in performance. Butler's recent writings allow me to return to her earlier positive rereading of the Beauvoirean claim that one is not born but becomes a woman. I have been claiming that performativity should be read as a category of formal pragmatics and existential politics alike. Performativity produces what Butler calls "an ontological puzzle" that gender results from existential choices. With Beauvoir, Butler raises anew the question found in the Kierkegaardian repetition: "If we are always already gendered, immersed in gender, *what sense does it make to say that we choose what we already are?*" (emphasis added). It makes little sense to choose/repeat the Cartesian disembodied ghost who is ontologically severed from language and culture. On this Kierkegaard agrees with contemporary critiques of existentialism— all of which misconstrue the "doctrine of choice" without reference to one's context. A lived repetition shows that one's self-choice in received traditions and within communicative interaction implies critique and refusal.[55]

I conclude that Butler's Derridean-Foucauldian expansion of performativity does not detract anything from formal pragmatics. Derrida enhances the formal scheme of performatives: discursive power to produce what one names—to do things in the world with one's words— hangs on citing other such practices. None of us is an author who creates *ex nihilo*. Butler adds a Foucauldian suspicion: "The paradox of subjectivation . . . is precisely that the subject who would resist such [regulatory] norms is itself enabled, if not produced, by such norms."[56]

Yet I find that Butler needlessly conflates the possessive liberal individualist with that existential individual who becomes a self only through the risky acts of repetition, that is, critical citationality. Like her, I reject the prelinguistic, self-mastering will to be oneself (this is an existentially disproved doctrine of a despairing self-choice). I consider, however, no need to jettison thereby the relational view of self-choice which can never precede its performative contexts. Adopting Butler's poststructuralist category of performativity, we are certainly not precluded from newly retrieving a richer existential approach. On the contrary, retrievals of *existential performativity* within this combined methodological innovation (i.e., an existential model of communication) promise to enhance and complement rather than disqualify radical existential democracy.[57]

An Unfinished Task: Ethical Self-Constitution and Reciprocity

Even as one grows inspired by the Foucauldian body-politics, one cannot easily put aside Marcuse's Benjaminian concern: are today's transgressive performers able to refuse hopelessness for the sake of those without hope? That one should be able to refuse so seems implied by Foucault's and Butler's critical analyses of disciplinary cultures! Yet Butler (with Foucault, against Marcuse) locates the "radical invention" of sex and gender in the fields of power-and-resistance. She situates all refusals within such cultural power-matrices:

> In that Foucault seeks to subvert the binary configuration of power, the juridical model of oppressor and oppressed[,] he offers some strategies for the subversion of gender hierarchy. For Foucault, the binary organization of power, including that based on strict gender polarities, is effected through a multiplication of productive and strategic forms of power. Hence, Foucault is interested no longer in the Marcusean dream of a sexuality without power, but is concerned with subverting and dissipating the existing terms of juridical power. . . . In effect, Foucault writes in the disillusioned aftermath of Marcuse's *Eros and Civilization*, rejecting a progressive model of history based on the gradual release of an intrinsically liberating *eros*.[58]

The Foucauldian pluralized and denaturalized refusals must face the objections brought against the voluntarist readings of Sartre's existentialism or Marcuse's "liberating *eros*," Butler admits. First, there is the naïve romanticism of positing some badly utopian agency behind radical inventions. And there pivots the conservative tragedy in any project which only refigured what one badly is. Secondly, her distancing from Marcuse notwithstanding, she defends Foucault with the Marcusean and at the same time Sartrean and Beauvoirean appeals: the received reality principle (e.g., the real existing capitalist and state socialist realities) is only a historically specific and thus *contingent reality*.[59]

Remember that Butler hopes for the *radical inventions* of sex and gender, even if these operate in the Foucauldian fields of power-and-resistance. The charges that her performatives lack some novel reality principle could be legitimate only if one assumed that the given historical performance principle (e.g., patriarchy or the racist episteme) were somehow inscribed into our human natures. This is not Butler's position. Now Marcuse, too, imagines radically inventing wholly other reality principles. This he would argue against the conservative uses of instinctual drives in Freudian and post-Freudian psychoanalysis alike. Yet in opposition to the romantic and cognitivist oversights of the depth dimensions of human existence in some Marxism and existentialism, he does not espouse a radical social constructivism or voluntarism. He joins Freud with Marx, and both to a socially situated existential praxis. Butler's performatives call for these Marcusean refusals of what necessarily is; they raise the hope of inventing new realities.

I argued that Foucault (just as Derrida and Habermas) strives for a *new enlightenment*. The heart of this project is an ethical and socially transformative regard for the other. The Foucauldian and Derridean enlightenment rejects both the possessive individualism and the abstract universalism of instrumental modernity. Existence, concretely inhabited, is at odds with the hegemony of calculative rationality. Philosophies of existence inevitably promote a sort of antihumanism: consider Kierkegaard's critique of the Christians of Christendom, Fanon's of the Whites of an anti-Black world, Sartre's of anti-Semitic democrats, Merleau-Ponty's of the Communists of the Stalinist era. This existential antihumanism strives for a transformed human existence. Must not other celebrations of antihumanism (and I do not mean our care for nonhumans) be out to lunch? The possibility of a *new humanism* is implied by the deconstructively genealogical and existential critiques of the present age. Insofar as *we* speak of existence with a human face, for the sake of those without hope, ethical and sociopolitical regards for the other set forth a human task.[60]

The Foucauldian performativity as a philosophy of existence. It is, thus, not without interest if we return to the early Foucault. We find here his philosophy of existence contained as if in a nutshell within a long introduction to the major work on dreams by Binswanger. Foucault discovers in dreams an entry into an imaginative world; and therein they open new possibilities by evoking and transfiguring hidden memories. Human imagination is stirred up by the dangerous memories of unoppressive life. And the same imagination awakens with an impetus for change. Hope, then, emerges from imagining a radically different existence than one's present unjust world. The transgression of the given and the agency striving for the new—both are the subject and object of dreams. Dreams, not dreamers, form the subject-object unity. As Merleau-Ponty shows later in his analysis of the primordial body-intentionality, one begins existentially within this unity. Subsequently humans may develop symptoms of a Cartesian cogito-complex. Human situations, wherein one starts and where one returns, are always already post-Cartesian.[61]

In the same breath as Foucault portrays the post-Cartesian subject-object unity, he insists on the human core of dreams:

If the dream is the bearer of the deepest human meanings, this is not insofar as it betrays their hidden mechanisms or shows their inhuman cogs and wheels, but on the contrary, insofar as it brings to light the freedom of man in its most original form.[62]

Human existence is freedom. The flight from freedom—from the task to embody it in existence—engenders bad faith. The latter, and only the latter, inaugurates bad humanism. Antihumanism at times mimics the very same flight. Foucault's philosophy of existence is anti/antihumanist.

Dreams explore the human possibilities of freedom. While possibility contains necessity, death is a worldly horizon of lived existence, not life's simple destruction: "in announcing death, the dream exhibits the fullness of being which existence has now attained." Freedom and death—the possibilities of existence—form a "dream subjectivity." This subject is not one of masks; the subject-object is constituted and constitutive of an existential whole. One becomes this whole in the present via temporally repeating the past as open to its future-in-process:

[T]he first person of the dream, is the dream itself, the whole dream. In the dream, everything says, "I," even the things and the animals, . . . the empty space, . . . objects distant and strange which populate the phantasmagoria. The dream is an existence carving itself out in barren space.[63]

Foucault locates in dreams "the first condition of . . . [imagination's] possibility." Dreams (and imagination) reveal the irreality of the real, of what is otherwise than being. The possibilities of ethical self-constitution and reciprocity (i.e., of another than the historically received reality principle in racism, patriarchy, economic oppression) are grafted into the transformative power of imagination. Just as dreams express in time the total subject-object of transgression and agency, so also the performative "I" responds always already to an experience of one's own dreaming and imagining the transformative possibilities.[64]

In his last writings on ethics, Foucault adopts, Sawicki suggests, a genealogical method for harnessing "resistant subjectivity." She views genealogy "as a form of resistance." And she confirms what I take to be Foucault's view: since there is no privileged standpoint, no "fundamental coalitions in history," refusals emerge within the configurations of power-and-resistance. She counsels against the despair of a "disappointed traditional revolutionary." The realization that *we* cannot control history (a nod to Foucault) does not justify anyone against hope and refusal (a nod to Marcuse). Her caution about the positive utopias of global transformation and yet insistence on remembering ongoing injustices are as much true of Foucault as Adorno and Marcuse. The voices of the marginalized and the victimized in history "are the sources of resistance, the creative subjects of history." The body-politics harkens to these voices, thereby becoming a multiple fount for inventing specters of liberation. Must one, then, insist that "Foucault's method requires a suspension of humanistic assumption"? It is not wise to concede to the Cartesian or to the liberal that *they* stand for a full sense of embodied human existence. A new aesthetics of ethical existence and its performative body-politics integrate much better the advances made by pragmatic, existential, and genealogical methodologies.[65]

Recall how Butler expands Foucault's ethical genealogies and Habermas's formal pragmatics into what I named an existential attitude, specifically, the performative body-acts of resignification. This vantage point allows her to elaborate an antipatriarchal and antiracist body-politics. It is noteworthy for my line of thought that Fraser discerns in Butler's denaturalized notion of critical agency a distinct "Sartrean parlance." Fraser's characterization of Butler's critical genealogy confirms my reading of performativity in existential terms. Says Fraser: "By thematizing the performative dimension of signification, she [Butler] spotlights the *act* in the speech act . . . the praxis in practico-inert." The acts of critical resignification are neither voluntaristic nor structuralistically anonymous. "Paradoxically, these acts are performed from, and indeed enabled by, subject positions that are themselves constructed by the very discursive regimes they contest." Fraser offers a succinct insight into Butler's transgressive agency: "Butler posits a linguistic subject that is nontranscendental yet capable of innovation."[66]

Postconventional ethics as a philosophy of existence. D. Cornell, like Butler, depicts ethics more concretely than Habermas. In the context of her feminist politics of difference, quite promising is a multilayered view of ethical reciprocity as "the aspiration to a nonviolent relationship to the Other and to otherness in the widest possible sense. This assumes responsibility to struggle against the appropriation of the Other into any system of meaning that would deny her difference and singularity." A nonviolent integration between oneself and another is discernible in Adorno's negative dialectics as much as in Kierkegaard's individualism. Adorno and Kierkegaard stress that one is ethically responsible to a radical, nonreducible singularity. (This is so in spite of Adorno's polemic against *The Jargon of Authenticity*.) And even though Cornell never speaks in explicit existential terms, she poses the ethical as a task: "such a definition of the ethical demands that we pay attention to what kind of person we must become in order to aspire to a nonviolent relationality." To make these hidden markers of an existential attitude even more apparent, note how Cornell sets off her definition of concrete ethics equally in contrast to conventions (*Sittlichkeit*) and the rule-governed procedures (*Moralität*). "The ethical as I define it is not a system of behavioral rules, nor a system of positive standards by which to justify disapproval of others. It is, rather, an attitude towards what is other to oneself." This is not all! Even more exciting is her innovative move, whereby she links what I wish to call an existential attitude with Peirce's critical attitudes of fallibilism and musement. "Fallibilism implies a challenge to one's basic organization of the world, while musement indicates the stance of amazement before the mysteries and marvels of life." Transforming an attitude to oneself in relation to others through a radical revaluation of one's singular historical existence—these are the core topics of philosophies of existence from Kierkegaard to Sartre to Beauvoir to Fanon.[67]

Discovering this link between the existential and the fallibilist attitudes parallels an already established insight into the internal links between body performatives, adopted by Butler from Foucault, and linguistic performatives, adopted by her from Austin and Derrida. And it should not escape the perceptive reader that the performative attitudes of communication and fallibilism (inspired originally by Peirce's regulative ideal of a communication community) form the cornerstones of Habermas's ethical and democratic theory. While an existential attitude houses concrete ethics and body-politics, the attitudes of fallibilism, musement, and linguistic performatives enable critical speech acts. The phenomenologies of existence, such as Butler's of Rodney King, show that one must integrate the bodily and linguistic levels of performatives in order to imagine the nonviolent forms of ethical reciprocity and democratic politics. In this regard, making explicit the existential paths shared by the body- and speech-performatives seems more helpful for a coalition-building than making explicit contentions among their proponents.

There is another sense in which Cornell's adoption of the Peircean fallibilism and musement confirms the discovered existential markers. These markers are intrinsic to her definition of the ethical. If her ethics were a classical virtue ethics, then her move would have to be discernible as a retreat from critical moral-liberal procedures to emphatically communitarian normativity. This is not so, and Cornell is quite clear about this. "The ethical as I understand it *should not* be grasped as a determinable, theoretical reflection on morality." In order to defend "the virtue of public reason," she defines the ethical by a lived critical attitude. The ethical is defined within that existential positionality which allows for both moral rights and the good life in the first place. Appeals to goods and rights presuppose "an ethical appeal . . . to expand our moral sensibility." One can describe a postconventional existential ethics "as a call for us to re-imagine our form of life so that we can 'see' differently." This ethics helps to explain and challenge, e.g., the racist epistemic fields described so well by Butler.[68]

Recognition and community: the dialectics of symmetry and asymmetry. Other attempts at concretizing Habermas's formalism in communicative ethics can be found already in Benhabib and Honneth. Like Cornell, the latter two seek a new postconventional ethics of the concrete other; unlike her, they do not show in what consists the corrective to Habermas's generalized other. If the corrective lies in integrating a communitarian into a proceduralist position, which is what Benhabib's and Honneth's notions of postconventional *Sittlichkeit* ultimately suggest, then we are simply replaying the old argument between Kant and Hegel. This would be so even if we crafted a post-Hegelian compromise, e.g., Taylor's ethics of recognition. If I am right, then an unfinished task of recognition can still learn from existentially material critiques of Hegel.[69]

Fraser and Young show that focusing on cultural recognition at the expense of bypassing the economic issues of redistribution represents a retreat to uncritical theory.[70] Moreover, the questions of race and gender fall in between those of recognition and redistribution. They cause ongoing legitimation crises to liberal theories, notwithstanding whether these are classical or left-leaning. The validity fields of the human body are affected by racist and patriarchal attitudes. This distortion cannot be reversed by appealing to the good any more than to the validity claims of speech. If this is a correct assessment, it justifies encountering ethical and sociopolitical needs for recognition after having exhausted all variants of the liberal-communitarian debate.

Adopting an imaginative view of ethical self-constitution, one may critically search for nondisciplinary reciprocities. Cornell's ethics and Butler's performativity break with the self-possessive liberal/libertarian and the emphatic communitarian models. Cornell makes a helpful rejoinder to Young's skepticism of community ideals as such. I cannot go into the differences between Young and Cornell on this issue. As Young shows by offering narrative case studies, it seems *prima facie* intuitively right to eye with suspicion any community ideal which would be shaped through a projected symmetrical reversibility of singular perspectives. This suspicion derives from *recognizing the need to recognize difference*, i.e., ethical and moral asymmetries of concrete existers. Here come to mind Young's "asymmetrical reciprocity" and Cornell's "ethical asymmetry." Like Benhabib and Honneth, above thinkers elaborate Arendt's Kantian enlarged thinking; unlike them, they envision likewise enlarged asymmetry as a social ontology with the vanishing point in an irreversible singularity of however otherwise imaginatively and interactively expanded perspectives. With this corrective I consent to a double emphasis on asymmetry in order to preclude the substantive communitarian (ethical) as well as the formal consensual (moral) homogenizations of singular perspectives.[71]

Such emphases are necessary if one is to avoid the dangers that worry Young in her rejoinder to Benhabib: that *we* level differences among distinct perspectives; that *we* strive for an impossibility of directly communicating to others the perspective of a singular individual; and that *we* derive a politically "suspect" if not dangerous ideal of a homogeneous community. The ethics of an enlarged mentality—when read by Young and Cornell via Adorno, Derrida, Irigaray, Kristeva, or Lévinas— prohibits reconciling singular perspectives by projecting their direct reversibility. Nonviolent recognition of perspectives, let us say in ethical community, must retain in itself a post-Hegelian singularity (difference) or it is not worth much.[72]

Why, then, does Cornell's argument for ethical asymmetry build from a "phenomenological 'symmetry'"? How can she explain the insistence on both an ethical-moral asymmetry and a phenomenological symmetry? One's respect for another human as another must recognize this other as nonetheless "phenomenologically symmetrical to me," as one's alter ego. Cornell, not unlike in Willett's notion of tactile sociality and correspondences, locates a universally primordial symmetry in human existing that one shares with others. "Without this moment of universality [that the other is the same as me] the otherness of the Other can be only too easily reduced to mythical projection."[73]

There is no need to read into *this* symmetrical recognition a Cartesian or Hegelian or WhiteMan's/WhiteWoman's identity logic! The focus on a certain symmetry Cornell shares, I venture an interpretation, with Derrida, Foucault, Lévinas, Sartre, Beauvoir, and Fanon. Here is why I think this is so: Any critique of misrecognition (Fanon's of anti-Blackness, Sartre's of anti-Semitism, Beauvoir's of the patriarchal gaze, or Butler's of homophobia) presupposes that an appeal to misrecognizing another is minimally possible. A radical untranslatability (incommensurability) of frameworks would deny—at a descriptive level—the performative possibility of speech acts and tactile body-politics alike. Merleau-Ponty locates sympathy in a body-intentionality of an emergent self. Yet he retains an existential singularity (what Willett identifies as an infant's preintentional capacity for spirited resistance of the other) at the ethical and sociopolitical levels. Sartre's social ontology assumes a shared material level of the need to fight scarcity along with affirming an irreducibility of individual temporality in social groups, institutions, and their praxis. Lévinas and Derrida appeal to the singular face in the shared face-to-face encounter with alter. Foucault's postdisciplinary reciprocities admit as much.[74]

The feminist and other contentions with Habermas's (and Benhabib's or Honneth's) communications model are of different sort. The charge is that the model collapses the levels where symmetry is necessary and sufficient with the levels where it is merely necessary. Within the generalized other of ethical, moral, and political domains, the projected symmetry of liberal, egalitarian, and universal discourse invokes a strictly formal ideal. The phenomenological symmetry is, however, concrete and existentially necessary, thus of preethical and premoral significance. Projecting such a symmetry formally as an ethical and moral ideality is insufficient, even pernicious, from the viewpoint of concrete justice. Young's stress on asymmetrical reciprocity or Cornell's on ethical asymmetry seems to be about this contention that the dialogic models developed from Habermas's purview by Benhabib or Honneth still lack concrete justice. Young is not concerned with prenormative phenomenological symmetry; she notes the insufficiency of a formally moral kind of symmetry. With the move to postconventional ethics, which Benhabib or Honneth undertake, and to the politics of difference in Young and Cornell, appeals to asymmetrical reciprocity become intelligible. The ethical and moral levels of asymmetry need not be contested by a descriptive symmetry, nor vice versa. A postconventional ethics of responsibility and the morality and politics that recognize difference require reciprocal asymmetry: it is their normative corrective to the idealizations made by the formal symmetry of communication. Therein lies the new enlightenment core of that singular universality which is nowadays shared by some critical modernists and postmodernists alike. Benhabib invokes the concrete other; Honneth admits, with Derrida and Lévinas, the other of justice; and Critchley speaks of a "marriage" between Derrida and Habermas. Their joint venture in imagining new and theorizing existing communication communities-in-process is needed. Why not pursue this track, especially if both the regulative community ideals and actualities, just as the individuals-in-process, did not kill but rather enhanced difference?[75]

Conclusions

There is a margin of hope for the sake of those without it. By discovering the greatest degree of universality in the tactile sociality that humans share at a phenomenological level of spirited body-intentionality, in correspondences with concrete others, one may affirm (with a healthy dose of historical skepticism) the possibility of fraternal, or better, communal selves. Even the most singular aesthetics of existence implies a shared social form of life. This is another way of harnessing theoretically a lifeworld insight into the existentially material horizon of needs experienced and cared for cooperatively by all humans. Fight unto death and fraternal terror derive from historical traumas. They account for skepticism, they do not explain hope and refusal.

A qualitatively new mode of human existence inevitably solicits a critical theory of individualization through socialization. For this reason, I think, *we* cannot escape considering whether and how the facticity of basic material needs can empower a normative idea of community. I have been trying to circumvent the shortcomings of the liberal-communitarian terms of the debate. I learned by joining the efforts at rethinking the ethical. As I show next, Hegel's ideal of ethical community remains a precarious task, not a given. *We* are conflicted strangers to ourselves and others (pace Kristeva). That strangeness within, too, marks our shared life. The discovery of a stranger in one's own abode should ideally make one refuse all xenophobia. The denial, on the contrary, renders the desire for community even more suspicious (pace Žižek and Sartre). A suspicion of fuzzy symmetries seems at times all that communities may be able to share. The living communities require an ongoing attitudinal transformation of their shared ideas in order to admit more than a suspicion of the established bonds. They require justice as the politics of difference. The failures of concrete justice warrant coming together in the senses theorized by performative and reciprocal asymmetry. And yet, in resistance, concrete communities raise credible specters of liberation in the present age.

6

Communities in Resistance

The Communities of Population in Resistance are an example and a seed of the new society in Guatemala, the hope of the poor of Guatemala.

—*Declaration of the Unnumbered*, January 1991

✤✤✤

[Human] solidarity is founded upon rebellion, and this rebellion, in its turn, can only find its justification in this solidarity. . . . Each tells the other that [s/]he is not God.

—Albert Camus, *The Rebel*

✤✤✤

The foreigner comes in when the consciousness of my difference arises, and . . . disappears when we all acknowledge ourselves as foreigners, unamenable to bonds and communities. . . . [S]hall we be . . . able to live with the others, to live *as others*, without ostracism but also without leveling?

—Julia Kristeva, *Strangers to Ourselves*

✤✤✤

[T]he coalition of trade unions and churches that toppled the military dictatorship in 2044, has retained control of Congress by successfully convincing the voters that its opponents constitute "the parties of selfishness." The traditional use of "brother" and "sister" in union locals and religious congregations is the principal reason why "fraternity" (. . . "siblinghood") is now the name of our most cherished ideal.

—Richard Rorty, "Fraternity Reigns"

✤✤✤

We still have a choice today: nonviolent coexistence or violent coannihila-
tion. This may well be mankind's last chance to choose between chaos and
community.

—Martin Luther King, Jr.,
Where Do We Go from Here: Chaos or Community?

✤ ✤ ✤

Would *we* have to be afraid of *community*, if its instantiations appropriated the tactile sociality of infants into the maturing needs for recognition? Why not draw on the discovery that one-day-old infants exhibit
a/symmetrical correspondences with adults without fusing with them,
and that they demonstrate prediscursive communicative competencies
for spirited resistance yet without fragmenting social bonds? If to be an
underdeveloped infant does mean neither to be unrelated, nor fused into
sameness with the adult, nor unaware of primordial, integral frontiers,
then why should atomism or fusion define the possibilities of adult
sociality? I have redefined the 'existential' as embodying from infancy
and carrying into adult competencies the a/symmetrical dimensions of
tactile social resistance-in-relation to others. A communicative ethic of
self-realizing and self-determining adults must account for its possibility
by the concrete existential situation of the one-day-old. Existential individuals as adults can be shown to exhibit a tactile sociality of self-in-
another within their identity formation. Humans need coalitional bonds
and even ethical solidary communities because of the risks to and the vul-
nerabilities of the feeling selves they always already are.[1]

That Kierkegaard was suspicious of the Hegelian community ideal
of the nation-state as the aim and end of history should not surprise
anyone familiar with his spirited individual dissent. Many contemporary critics of identity and organic community ideals benefit from
Kierkegaard's hermeneutics of suspicion. It is less obvious that his existential individualism, adapted to these times, ironizes now the neoliberal and conservative celebrations of the NWO. Yet this is the case! If an
adult's existential dissent, harnessing early competencies for spirited
resistance, cannot be conceived apart from a social form of life against
which it projects another mode of existing, then even a singular dissent
can imagine communities of free and equal persons. These communities
emerge often in resistance. Nowadays communities resist communitarian fusions and neoliberal fragmentations. If 'communitarian' might not
define 'communal' and if 'liberal' or 'libertarian' should not define
'existential', then the fear of *community* in its *resisting* instantiation is
theoretically premature. A critical social theorist may stay a bit longer
and learn.

Compare Kierkegaard's attack on Christendom in the nineteenth century with Derrida's twentieth-century return to Marx. They disconfirm Fukuyama's revival of the Christian-Hegelian peak of the struggle for recognition. And they ridicule emphatic communitarian readings of Hegel on the end of history. Kierkegaard refuses the Christian nation-state—whether its market individualism (where authoring the self is gained for a good price) or its conservative taste (where popular culture dispenses family values for bourgeois philistine middle classes). He prefigures Foucault's unmaskings of one-dimensional state panopticism. "[T]o be improved by living in the state is just as doubtful as being improved in a prison. Perhaps an individual becomes much shrewder about his egotism, his enlightened egotism, that is, his egotism in relation to other egotisms, but less egotistic he does not become."[2]

When Marcuse exposed the German political existentialists of the Nazi period, he echoed this worry about atomistic market individualism and fascist etatism. They represent convex mirrors. A radically democratic philosophy of existence may have no pact with the market manipulation of disencumbered individuals or the political manipulation of oppressed communities. Kierkegaard dramatizes an ethical individual as a corrective to the nation-state—in both its possessive liberal and communitarian confessions. He does this so well and carries it so far that he eclipses imagining any viable democratic sociality or even more intimate ethical solidarity. And he fails to theorize coalitional politics suited to *our* post-Hegelian world.[3]

Communitarians stress the necessity of anchoring individual moral rights in communally shared substantive goods. Their focus follows at least two paths. The nostalgically gazing communitarians search for such shared goods in some golden age of virtue or a life closer to land; the utopian gazing ones project such goods as revolutionary possibilities. Against both, political liberals begin with a modern impossibility of agreeing on any shared substantive vision of the good. Economic neoliberals celebrate this impossibility with the rhetorical toast to the end of ideology and history, and with the rhetorical kickoff for the beginnings of the NWO and new free-market individualism. Left-liberal proceduralists aim for deliberative democracy which offers a formal corrective to the impersonal imperatives of the state power and money. Liberals tend to be urbancentrist individualists, communitarians tend to prefer rural communities.[4]

Other positions confirm neither of the above one-sidedly communitarian or liberal readings of Hegel on the end of history. From the side of Critical Theory, Benhabib and Honneth correct a certain procedural liberalism and emphatic communitarianism. They hold out hope for an ethical life under the conditions of plurality. Yet they find it necessary to formulate procedural alternatives to substantive communitarian commitments. This leads them to argue for a nonpatriarchal and materially just postconventional ethical life. I will describe these options as *a procedurally formal idea of ethical community and coalitional politics*.

While Young remains suspicious of community ideals as suited for a politics of difference, there are postmodern social theories which affirm possibilities of community. Martin, Nancy, and even Laclau and Mouffe admit, respectively, a postmodern possibility of unnameable community, or inoperative community, or radically democratic politics. All share with Young, Benhabib, and Honneth objections to the emphatic communitarian politics of identity. All likewise oppose abstract liberal humanism and universalist identity politics; and all question the NWO. Yet, in contrast to Young's affirmative politics of group difference and Derrida's loose affinity of a new International, Nancy and Martin positively conceptualize what I will call *a substantively an-archic idea of ethical community and coalitional politics*. What differentiates postmodern community ideals from uncritical communitarians (nostalgic or utopian) is either the negative affirmation of a shared form of life or the an-archic articulation of its substance. What differentiates them from liberal variations as well as from someone like Young is a qualified 'yes' to a sustainable community life.

Are ideals of an economically and ecologically sustainable community life viable under the plural conditions of post/modernity? Can sustainable solidarities be compatible with a global coalitional politics of difference, and not just in rural settings but also in urban life? And even if amenable to post/modern pluralism and coalitional politics, do *our* theoretical affirmations or *our* fears of community admit the spirited and active subversions of the NWO already found in the border imaginary of hybrid identities-in-difference and in the communities in resistance?[5]

I begin with a tension in Hegel—between a postconventional ideal of ethical community integrated into the nation-state and the classical liberal view of inter*national* relations. I show, then, how Habermas reforms Hegel's communitarian inter*nationalism*, which admits warfare among nation-states, through Kant's cosmopolitan globalism, which hopes for *Perpetual Peace*. Even while dissenting from Hegel's identity politics, I will ask next, what may *we* learn from an ideal of ethical community and coalitional politics? I conclude that a consistent critical theorist and activist must learn today from the deposed vision of a holistic state socialism and the now dominant world vision of the globally regional, transnational, and flexibly multicultural capital: the task becomes to join wholesome yet open communities formed in solidary resistance yet capable of globally regional, flexible, and multifaceted coalitional struggles for liberation.

1. Hegel's Nation-State and Its Discontents

Does Hegel's nation-state throw oil into nationalist fires or does it provide antidotes for this fever of inter*national* relations? Is Hegel that nationalist who might allow the ethnic nationalisms of conquest among old and new nation-states? Or is he that nationalist who would support the nationalisms of liberation from imperial domination? Or is he neither a consistent nationalist of either kind nor an inter*nationalist*?

Avineri defends Hegel against those who depict him as a German romantic nationalist of liberation. Before and after Napoleon's defeat, Hegel held pro-French, West-oriented hopes for Germany. Unlike Helmut Kohl after 1989, he did not desire a reconquest of a unified German Nation. Hegel rejected the German nationalism of his day, just as he would likely do after the fall of the Berlin Wall. Eschewing ethnic intolerance and the supremacy myth of the Aryan *"Ur-Volk,"* Hegel championed political equality for the Jews. So, "how did it happen that a thinker who expressed himself in such unequivocal terms against the German national movement over a long period of years came to be regarded, as he still is today, as the intellectual and spiritual father of German nationalism?" Avineri asks.[6]

One of the explanations given by Avineri lies in Hegel's relation to Prussia: while after 1870 Bismarck's Prussia became a vehicle of German nationalist unification, the Prussia of the early 1800s and at the time of the Congress of Vienna was opposed to this nationalism. Hegel's pro-Prussianism exemplifies his critique of classical liberalism. But this view cannot support a defense of the movements which identified the nation-state with the romantic notion of origins. When Hegel uses Herder's concept of *Volksgeist* (the spirit of the people), Avineri shows, he means something else than an identity of the state with some original national Thing or *Ur*-ethnicity. A modernist imbued with concrete historical consciousness, Hegel may not hold out for some ahistorical national origins to constitute a nonsectarian state. A century before postmodern thought surfaced in the First World academies, Hegel understood that nations are just as much emergent constructs of historical developments as are their states. The modern nation-state may not seek its legitimation by reviving a nationalist romantic myth, whether ethnic or racial. People's national character is not produced by an unconscious force or a Thing, an enjoyment of which must be won at any price and once for all. This character is shaped in the historical traditions of the people. Their traditions must be institutionalized in the ethical life of national communities and universalized laws. "The Hegelian *Volksgeist* is *identical* with the features it is describing, and does not *create* them." People's characters, like the institutions which embody them in a universal form, develop historically.[7]

Avineri concludes that for Hegel international arrangements are "antinational." The "Germanic world"—comprising most of Christian Europe, western civilization, and today's Russian Federation—cannot be based on "need for the subjectivist nationalist consciousness or for the ethnic-linguistic links." Hegel does not expect a world civilization; yet he posits a world order guided by providential historical reason and freedom. In Hegel's philosophical theodicy, the world reaches *at the end of history* (the realized need to recognize a mutually reciprocal necessity) a more humane inter*national* community of nations—not a global government.[8]

Avineri notes an instance, key to my analysis, in which the claims to self-determination find support in Hegel's view. Does Hegel admit "the grafting of the national *idea* into the political *structure* of the territorial machinery produced by monarchical absolutism"? He does not celebrate romantic nationalism—whether that of liberation or conquest. Yet theoretical etatism provides safe grounds for the modern political movements of national self-determination:

The political sphere, by becoming dominant, makes modern state strong in comparison with other historical arrangements, and, though it was not Hegel's intention, this powerful state became an instrument of nationalism—for without a clear-cut idea of a modern, strong and rationally-organized state, nationalism could not have laid its claim to primacy.[9]

I may be satisfied with Avineri's defense (that Hegel's contribution to modern nationalisms was at worst marginal and from "an unexpected angle") if and only if I am permitted to sever the genealogy of the modern nationalist Thing from the genealogy of nation-states. Yet if Hobsbawm is correct that "nationalism comes before nations," then our age cannot afford this severance. It is not nationalism that aspires to enjoy its nation-state. The reverse is true. Nation-states either invent the nation-Thing for their own legitimation or provoke its multiple births because of oppressing some other groups within their borders—which supposedly frustrate the enjoyment of the Thing. In either case, the exploitative institutions of modern states invent ethnic and cultural nationalisms to mobilize and discipline fragmented or exiled individuals dispersed within shifting political borders. Nationalisms hire etatism and capital production: together they create its *imagined nation-state community*. Today's NWO exchanges the nation-state imaginary for a multinational village, a global capital regionalism. Says B. Anderson: "Nationalism's purities (and thus also cleansing) are set to emerge from exactly this hybridity." 'Nationalism', 'nation', and 'ethnie' are emergent, hybrid political concepts, just as political and economic *maps* of the World are. Nation-states, nationalisms, multinationals have never existed apart—whether in Old or NWOs.[10]

To answer my opening questions, Hegel is not a nationalist of conquest. He rejects the romantic nostalgia for originary national identity. He fails, however, to theorize the ethical life of the rational state globally. In that key sense he does not provide a communal ethic of resistance to offset the warring nation-states and their futile desire for the supreme enjoyment of the national-Thing. Worst of all, his *laissez-faire* view of *international* relations fuels what Derrida calls the "manic" optimism—awakened in Fukuyama's neoliberal reading of the end of history. Whether or not Fukuyama's or Kojève's end of history is exactly what Hegel had in mind seems beside the point here. Hegel's failure to forge a global ethic of mutual recognition leaves him checkmated by the unholy alliance of multinational corporations and imperial nationalisms spearheaded by an imagined global village/pillage of the NWO.[11]

Laissez-faire relations among nation-states allow for nationalist wars. If states are left to their national enjoyment-in-cleansing, we are not free from wars. When legitimate liberation struggles regress to conquests, we are not free from nationalist propaganda or genocide. Multinational capital cannibalizes multicultural borders and the national-Thing for profit— no less than the Soviets did to safeguard the empire. Yet today, multinationals close borders to immigration at will, not to lose profit from cheap labor. The NWO is not free from xenophobia, chauvinism, immiseration, and imperial warfare in the name of the global village.

✦✦✦

There was a virtual simultaneity to the passing of the multinational NAFTA (January 1, 1994) and GATT (December 1, 1994) free-trade agreements and the passing of the nationalist, racist California Proposition 187 (November 8, 1994). The former ruptured the borders between North American and Mexican cultures for trade. The latter erected a new Iron Curtain, a new Berlin Wall, between them. The former legitimated a free ride for North American companies, exploiting cheap labor and the lack of regulation. The latter legitimated exploitation by keeping cheap labor cheap—South of the wall. Some U.S. unions, even Perot and Buchanan, opposed NAFTA and GATT on nationalist and pro-North American grounds; others passed the anti-immigrant proposition with the same nationalist and protectionist rhetoric echoed once more in passing the California antiaffirmative action Proposition 209 (November 5, 1996). Nationalism mobilizes U.S. citizens to enhance production and consumerism along imagined nationalist lines. In times of economic hardship nationalism mobilizes popular resentment (or as Žižek would psychoanalyti-

cally enhance Marx: it mobilizes the diminishing rate of enjoyment of the national Thing) to divert attention from the multinational exports of flexible labor, the lack of national health care, and the missing education reforms. Nationalism shifts attention from economic theft to a resentment of the joy those concocted others have presumably stolen from us: and thus ruffled and rallied and generally pissed-off exploited people at times vote to deny political rights, labor protection, health care, and education to the undocumented migrant workers or Blacks or Roma—having at hand no vulnerable Jewish or gay people to blame. Judged from the perspective of the winner (and nationalism just as multinationalism ends with its global capital as but one winner), it makes no difference that the U.S. automobile has become a world or multicultural car (produced in many lands) or even a new people's car. Remember, it was Hitler's populist expansionism that rejoiced in Volkswagen—the people's world-order-car.[12] The nation-state fashions nationalism to mobilize workers within national homes for production and profit. The imperial state transforms nationalism to mobilize workers for the same reason. But now, by its use of multicultural and ecological marketing for a globally regional pillage, it distracts all of us from the multinationally flexible money-and-power fiefdoms.

✠ ✠ ✠

Nationalism by eschewing global solidarity is never an ethical whole. This severe verdict is true on Hegel's holistic criteria. The world of nationalist wars remains imperfect, at worst it is a world of Thrasymachus. Domination calls the game of vital national interests. The cards are stacked for the strongest states. The Newspeak of the national-Thing is: Upholding Democracy.

Westphal succinctly calls this contradiction in Hegel "the failure of nerve."[13] Hegel has all the tools to envision global solidary relations: both his *Phenomenology* (para. 670–71) and his argument for relations within the state in *Philosophy of Right* (para. 257–320) culminate in the affirmation of a nonsectarian community based on reciprocal recognition. In the latter work he regresses into an atomistic liberal view on national sovereignty and inter*national* law. Minimalist contracts define relations among the nation-states. Hegel affirms ethical life within the nation-states. He, however, launches their wholes, as if they were some insular Hobbesian monads, into a largely hostile world of unethical inter*nationalist* relations.[14]

Does not Hegel's holistic argument—his affirmation of the historical need for reciprocal recognition and ethical community—demand that global relations become free of war, propaganda, and humanly caused immiseration? Can nation-states sustain ethical life within while retaining neoliberal contracts to other states—as if these were possessive individualists? Hegel's historical realization of ethical life bespeaks a regulative ideal of more rational global institutions. Westphal concludes such reading of Hegel against Hegel very nicely:

> To follow the implications of his own dialectical holism for an understanding of both knowledge and intersubjectivity which underlies it, Hegel would have to say that no human society yet corresponds to its concept, that the present world order is in specifiable respects irrational, and that a specifiable different state of affairs ought to exist. . . . [T]he requirement for a new international order free from war and propaganda . . . did not arise out of a "conceptophobic" emotionalism, but rather out of the severe conceptual discipline of Hegel's own dialectical holism.[15]

2. Perpetual Peace or an Entrenchment of the New World Order?

In an ingenious move, Habermas projects Kant's essay *Perpetual Peace* into a Hegelian ethical life as this might or should evolve within global political relations. Habermas develops a reading of Hegel through Kant in the context of the East Central European revolutions of 1989. Habermas's initiative raises questions that Hegel should have asked. Can the politics of reciprocal recognition hold out for the nation-state? Ought the failed Kantian and European practices of *perpetual peace* get another chance? If the rhetoric of the NWO (a half-Kantian and half-Hegelian caricature of the end of history) is not to seal *our* global future, what society ought to correspond to the concept of just global relations and institutions?[16]

Nation-States: Nothing but Possessive Individualists and Sovereign Egos?

Defending "sovereignty at home," Hegel argues that "the state has individuality," i.e., an "awareness of one's existence as a unit in sharp distinction from others."[17] He divines that war on behalf of the sovereign state operates behind our backs as a providential ethical "agency." "Sacrifice on behalf of the individuality of the state is the substantial tie between the state and all its members and so is a universal duty." So, against Kant's vision of perpetual peace, Hegel argues that the nation-state needs "a standing army."[18]

It seems that someone could appeal to Hegel's text, arguing that the war machine and the military-industrial complex nurture in humans the self-sacrificial spirit for the fatherland. When the federation of ex-Yugoslavia breaks up into nation-states, then national warriors, in spite of Hegel's possible protests, discover the *need* for ethnic cleansing. There

is no originary stopgap for desiring one's recognition via some pure ethnie. The pruning of organic communities, the *Volk*, functions as a measure
of one's sacrificial duty to the state. Enter this dubious idea: "corruption
in nations would be the product of prolonged, let alone 'perpetual'
peace."[19]

One must not crudely accuse Hegel of a warmonger mentality. He
relies on the world-historical providence: reason recognizes a more sane
conduct than found in the sniper alleys of Sarajevo's or Jerusalem's urban
guerilla. Yet he never comes to question the irrationality of his view of
inter*national* community. He abandons nations without any ethical or
institutional basis for reciprocal recognition. Because "[t]he nation
state . . . is the absolute power on earth," "states are to that extent in a
state of nature in relation to each other." Hegel's "fundamental proposition of international law" rejects a Kantian moral compact against all war.
States enter into expedient treaties, breakable contracts. "It follows that if
states disagree and their particular wills cannot be harmonized, the matter can only be settled by war." So there we are![20]

Habermas confirms Avineri's assessment that Hegel does not support romantic nationalisms of the nineteenth century. Habermas would
agree that in inter*national* relations Hegel operates with the possessive
sovereignty of liberal individualists incapable of satisfying the need for
recognition. Habermas aims to overcome such arbitrariness in global
affairs. He locates an opening for more just arrangements in the historically evolving social institutions of the West. He pursues Hegel's argument where Hegel refused to venture. To protect the ethical life of states
from an exposure to Hegel's "external contingency" globally, Habermas
reformulates Kant's and Rousseau's views of sovereignty.[21]

Let me conceive with Habermas that the modern state is not to be
a subjectivity but a higher-level intersubjectivity. Thus can be overcome a
surd between the ethical life within each state and the Hobbesian state of
nature among them. Habermas's *Aufhebung* of Hegel and Kant appears
possible when states articulate a normative validity for global laws and
institutions. Enter the Habermasian radical democratic republic: expanding ethical relations into procedural globalism, Habermas projects Kant's
perpetual peace into Hegel's dialectic of reciprocal recognition. As a
global configuration, this political community can no longer bear the concretistic, substantive terms of Hegel's emphatic communitarianism.
Habermas limits the expectations of political democracy both within and
among states to the radically plural conditions of the present age. The
normative criteria that can appeal to all concerned today (i.e., not only
after the Thirty Year War of religions but also after Gulag, Auschwitz,
Hiroshima, or Sarajevo) are the formal presuppositions of rational discourse and the procedural terms of popular sovereignty.[22]

Habermas disagrees with the following Hegelian verdict while agreeing with some of its reasons:

There is no Praetor to judge between states; at best there may be an arbitrator or a mediator, and even he exercises his functions contingently only, i.e. in dependence on the particular wills of the disputants. Kant had an idea for securing "perpetual peace" by a League of Nations to adjust every dispute. It was to be a power recognized by each individual state, and was to arbitrate in all cases of dissension in order to make it impossible for disputants to resort to war in order to settle them. This idea presupposes an accord between states; this would rest on moral or religious or other grounds and considerations, but in any case would always depend ultimately on a particular sovereign will and for that reason would remain infected with contingency.[23]

If sovereignty resides neither in the monarchical head—however symbolic in Hegel—nor in the individuality of nation-states, but rather in a radically democratic formation of popular meaning and will, then indeed, *we need no Praetor*. The monarchical idea of the *head* is inherently antidemocratic, and modern pluralistic institutions seem at odds with it. Substantive grounds, such as fixed religious and moral goods, on which communitarians wish to legitimate politically a democratic and constitutional republic, are likewise superfluous. Radical contingency invades relations among particular wills of all citizens. The popular sovereignty of a radically democratic republic must rely now on the normative grounds of rational discourse itself. These remain—as a regulative ideal—pluralistic, open, and egalitarian.[24]

Habermas characterizes these grounds as formal pragmatic presuppositions. They operate in the performances of reciprocal, dialogic recognition. Speakers raise and accept or reject claims to truth, normative validity, and sincerity. Speakers assume subject positions in discourse wherein they are viewed as agents who are capable of offering moral and political reasons for their claims; and they are viewed as capable of acting in accord with them. For Habermas, only this formally performative sense of agency can be normative. Morally speaking, participants in rational discourse cannot but be viewed as individually responsible loci of agency. Politically speaking, participants in public deliberations cannot but be viewed as socially responsible loci of agency. The locus of popular sovereignty lies in one's egalitarian access to procedures in which concrete material needs and reasons are evaluated. A radically democratic republic enshrines such access in the laws and institutions of popular sovereignty. The sovereignty of each state and constitution is popular, procedurally formal, and in that minimalist or thin sense universal. 'Nation' and 'state' are not religious doctrines to be preserved as invariant dogmas or endangered museum icons or zoo species. Rather, they, just as our vulnerable, tactile, feeling selves, are emergent concepts and existential tasks: "A constitution can be thought of as an historical project that each generation of citizens continues to pursue."[25]

Habermas argues that an ethical community project after Hegel immigrates into global political and legal relations. This becomes possible, he surmises, with "the cosmopolitan condition [which] is no longer merely a mirage. State citizenship and world citizenship form a continuum whose contours, at least, are already becoming visible." Habermas does not celebrate an end of history or the last man: rereading Hegel via Kant, he hopes for "a piece of 'existential reason'" in institutions such as the U.N. and their international charters.[26]

Global Public Sphere or Global Pillage?
A Second Chance for "Perpetual Peace"?

Habermas hopes that political rationality may bring sanity into human affairs. If "prepolitical" communities learn to overcome conflicts politically, they may foster perpetual peace in "the practice of citizens who actively exercise their rights to participation and communication." Inveighing with Rousseau and Kant against Hegel's constitutional monarchy, Habermas honors Foucault's request and chops off the king's head in the practical grammar of social theory. Perpetual peace fosters a perpetual revolution. This requires transferring authoritarian residues of royal sovereignty to the popular self-determination of free citizens in democracy.[27]

Habermas's admixture of perpetual peace with revolution immigrates into a formal politics of legal and democratic institutions. This partially explains how the peculiar Hegelian optimism, trust, and hope return in their Habermasian disguise. The envisioned rationality, read by Habermas into the existing republican constitutions (e.g., the U.N.), is en/trusted to deliver our age to a more just world. "This idea of a self-determining political community has assumed a variety of concrete legal forms in the different constitutions and political systems of Western Europe and the United States." As is obvious from my discussion of the need for recognition, Habermas argues against Taylor that the link between the war-torn facticity of nationalist worlds and the normative ideality of these republican constitutions is "only a historically contingent and not a conceptual connection."[28] Habermas invokes secular hope—like Derrida no longer affirming Hegel's realized, Eurocentric eschatology, and yet unlike Derrida or Fanon no longer worrying about Kierkegaard's fear and trembling—that 'Europe' gets "a second chance":

And today it's not without sympathy that I observe that world history has offered a unified Europe a second chance. . . . Today, however, that force that Max Weber attributed to Western rationality could once again be gathering—and this time, I hope, free of all imperialistic ambitions and with so little narcissistic self-absorption that a Europe that has learned from its own history can help other countries emerge from *their* nineteenth centuries.[29]

Habermas projects Kant's cosmopolitan vision into "a future Federal Republic of European States." Europe's perpetual peace might be possible if particular national cultures were to relativize themselves vis-à-vis others to form "a common political culture." Deliberative democracy envisions no longer some supra-agency, class, or "the macrosubject of a communal whole." It requires an open and multilevel "political public sphere." This sphere comprises agents, networks, and themes with an interplay between an informal communicative pluralism and institutionalized procedures for forming collective meaning and will.[30]

Habermas's guarded optimism draws on the perceived historical trends toward the single market, the multicultural societies composed of immigrants, and a growing political culture that seems more capable of resolving nationalist conflicts. He welcomes new social movements since they satisfy the need for mutual recognition by engendering global cooperation on ecological, peace, racial, and gender issues. He locates in these trends (not by returning to a papal vision of "the European Middle Ages") the possibilities for overcoming Eurocentrism and enhancing "a nonimperialist process of reaching understanding with, and learning from, other cultures."[31]

While invoking Europe's *second chance*, Habermas nonetheless jettisons the idea of 'Europe' as a self-enclosed fortress. Perpetual peace cannot be upheld by keeping out from Europe the expected twenty to thirty million immigrants. What he says about the European asylum debates is no less true about the U.S. anti-immigration policies of California Propositions 187 and 209, sponsored by Governor Peter Wilson, or about the problematic, both racially and economically motivated, policies of keeping out Cuban and Haitian refugees. "Economic immigrants, more than asylum seekers, confront members of the European States with the problem of whether one can justify the priority of special membership-based duties over universal obligations that transcend state boundaries."[32] If there are "legitimate restrictions of immigration rights," these cannot discriminate against non-White or poor groups, or be based on a "particularistic" understanding of political community. Political citizenship should expand the Kantian criterion of a "world society." "The identity of the political community, which also must not be violated by immigration, depends primarily on the legal principles anchored in the *political culture* and not on an *ethnical-cultural* form of life as a whole."[33]

One of the more radically democratic proposals (postliberal and postlibertarian alike) is raised by Habermas's problematization of the divide between the political and economic senses of immigration. Answering his own question about the right to immigrate from immiserating conditions, he defends the legitimacy of "a moral claim" that the poor of today's "global society" may lay upon wealthy nations. He notes the "overall political responsibility for safeguarding life on the planet"— a role increasingly assumed by the U.N. Both the validity of the moral claim raised by immigration and the corresponding political responsibility of global institutions must be read against "the history of colonization and the uprooting of regional cultures by the incursion of capitalist modernization." I dare to characterize the immigration policies implied by Habermas's query as a form of affirmative action, or better an affirmation of a common democratic economic and political culture, which would redress inequalities of "intercontinental migratory movements" occurring in last two hundred years. Eighty percent of all world migrants were Europeans (citing P. C. Emmer, Habermas estimates sixty-one million since 1800). European migrants and Europe gained from the New World Order. Today's "European chauvinism of affluence" (note the rhetoric of anti-immigration propositions) suffers a Eurocentric amnesia of conquest, slavery, genocide, and colonialism.[34]

Habermas limits the *moral-economic claim* to a demand for "a liberal immigration policy." The moral claim of the poor on the rich becomes for him neither a *political* nor an *economic right* which would draw radical democratic consequences minimally from libertarian/liberal notions of self-ownership. One may detect here still too much of that old-world European paternalism. The irony of history—from the time when St. Augustine wrote *The City of God* to Columbus's gold-rush crusade to save America's soul (Buchanan hopes to finish the job) to the Vietnamese-Haitian-Cuban boat people—is the fact that the waves of migration prevail in such outcomes which libertarians might have difficulty protesting. Europe's *second chance* is inscribed into this irony. Habermas's voucher for "a liberal immigration policy" points beyond its restricted moral scope. The wretched of the earth have little to lose by disrespecting the liberal policies of "affluent and peaceful [?] societies." These specters raise prospects of that global liberation which Habermas also wants: "an existence worthy of human beings."[35]

That there are claims to global economic justice is obvious if one considers post-war Germany or the North American South after its Civil War. Can one speak of Europe's chances without repaying debts for its long colonial period? Would not moral claims raised vis-à-vis any NWO

require a step from affluent countries minimally as fair as were war repa-
rations by Nazi Germany or those administered by the U.S. Freedmen's
Bureau and Bank (not the World Bank or I.M.F.) to freed slaves? If *we*
want to avert a civilizational clash, must not *we* pursue worldwide civil
and economic justice, analogical to that claimed within civilizations by
other marginalized minorities? Can there ever be perpetual peace on
'European' (liberal/libertarian?) terms alone?[36]

Habermas does not pursue the global, anti-imperialistic political
economy of immigration as an existentially material key against "a chauvinism of affluence." Might not such a key alone safeguard hope for perpetual peace within the League of Nations? Habermas does not expand his
radical democratic communications ideal into a consistent critical theory of
global procedures, laws, and institutions. Might not *this* failure of nerve be
reminiscent of the one we encountered at the end of Hegel's *Philosophy of
Right*? Habermas limits himself to a Kantian-Hegelian political vision of
the U.N. and to a liberal argument on behalf of a "common political culture." "Only democratic citizenship that does not close itself off in a particularistic fashion can pave the way for a *world citizenship*, which is already
taking shape today in worldwide political communications." Thus, he
curbs his democratic revolution by downplaying its sound existential intu-
itions gained from an ingenious Kantian conversation with Hegel.[37]

Habermas supports his optimism by a list of examples—"the Vietnam War, the revolutionary changes in eastern and central Europe, as
well as the Gulf War." This laundry list seems odd since it leaves an
unproductive ambiguity about the comparative status of each item. How
can these "first *world-political* events in the strict sense" aid the marginalized who must resist the chauvinism of prosperity? The "superpowers"
could recognize "the reality of worldwide protests." Yet does the League
of Nations, by policing their perpetual peace, necessarily overcome the
uneven world development? Habermas does not tell us how to distinguish a democratic perpetual peace from an imperialist fiction.[38]

By emphasizing the politics of the world public sphere in "the elec-
tronic mass media," did Habermas overlook the political economy colonizing cyberspace, the Worldwide Web, the tele-media from within? Or
does his self-limitation abandon us to live like the Television Man, in the
text of the song by Talking Heads, who cannot tell the inside from the
outside of the world-political events? In the wake of the TV-War versions
of justice in the Persian Gulf War, this perverse possibility is *also* "no
longer merely a mirage." Can the global institutions of procedural justice,
e.g., the U.N., deliver justice as the historical "piece of reality" (safeguard
the Hegelian historical reason and the Kantian perpetual peace in human
affairs) apart from paying attention to the political economy of these very
institutions, their structures, and uses?[39]

3. Border Identities and Global Relations

It is time to reap some fruit from the historical failures of universalisms and particularisms, whether in their individualistic or group forms. Much criticism is leveled at both homogenizing traditions and fragmented modern life. And an equal force of objections targets possessive individualistic or collectivist agencies and singular or group transgressions. Both agencies and transgressions are at times incapable of coalitional politics or larger solidarity. So how can *we* imagine life on the other side of oppressive, racist, and patriarchal societies?

Even if transgressing Hegel's identity politics, why not retrieve ethical communities on less organicist, more politically solidary and coalitional terms? This revised ideality already exists within communities in resistance. They foster an interlocking of oppressions, a solidary and coalitional politics of difference, and critical agency—all well suited to complex societies.[40]

Breaking down my general suggestion analytically, one cluster of questions points to what I called at the outset *a procedurally formal idea of ethical community and coalitional politics*. The second cluster of possible directions comprises *a substantively an-archic idea of ethical community and coalitional politics*. These two clusters learn from Hegel. The former dissents from substantive identity-logic; the latter harnesses the politics of difference. The third cluster takes to heart worries about identity-logic igniting some desires for community: I argue for *a dialectical idea of ethical community and coalitional politics*.

A Formal Idea of Community and Coalitional Politics

Honneth, in his Hegelian-Marxian rejoinder to Habermas's Kantian Hegelianism, argues that formal proceduralism begs the question of the material conditions of its possibility. Such conditions pertain to reciprocal recognition. This question raises more than an empirical issue of ethicopolitical integration (socializing individuals, transmitting cultural identities). A material reproduction of the lifeworld cannot be severed from the normative issue of its sociopolitical integration (citizenship in deliberative democracy, constitutional culture).[41]

As I discussed in chapter 1, Habermas, like C. Taylor, couches the issue of material justice in the culturalist terms of diversity, i.e., as an "ethical-political self-understanding on the part of the nation" or "the differences among the ethical-cultural communities within the nation." Under the heading of "The Permeation of the Constitutional State by Ethics," he defines concrete global institutions by the terms of the communitarian-liberal debate. This debate keeps alive the arguments about the priority of either the good or rights in constituting ethical communi-

ties and political institutions. Neither Taylor's communitarian multiculturalism nor Habermas's proceduralist multiculturalism delivers us yet
to material justice. Honneth (as in Fraser or I. Young) evokes material limits in the sociopolitical theories of recognition which are critical of political institutions but not of their political economy.[42]

Honneth's approach is intensified in the gender and race studies
which go beyond a libertarian, formally liberal, or popular postmodern
jargon of diversity. What are the intersubjective and material conditions
of self-determination and self-realization? A path to radical multicultural
democracy envisions justice in terms of the politics of identity *and* difference. Benhabib searches for a "participationist" view of postconventional
(critically self-related) ethical community (*"a postconventional Sittlichkeit"*)
and postnational identity. She insists that deliberative proceduralism
must not ignore the concrete other. Gender and race, just as class for
Marx, mark concretely material loci for any democratic politics of identity and difference. Love, in her rejoinder to Benhabib, shows that there is
a tension between the generalized symmetry of equal rights and a concrete justice met in reciprocal asymmetry.[43]

An existentially material postconventional identity-in-difference
admits neither a purely formal nor an uncritically substantive agency. So,
what about Hegel's insight that communities in our complex world will
breathe freely solely by achieving reciprocal recognition? Benhabib shows
that this cannot be done without practicing an "enlarged thinking"; thus,
a concrete universal must be "interactive." If procedural justice demands
interaction and deliberative reciprocity among concrete humans, it is
impossible to prefabricate its existentially material conditions formally.
Benhabib's theory carries implications for the praxis of critical theorizing.
How should *we* travel to meet concrete others? Short of cultural and economic imperialism, *we* must not predesign relations with others on our
terms. Such terms could mask a thinly veiled, self-serving neocolonialism.
One should be suspicious that even a concrete *Sittlichkeit* could become a
home for anti-Semitic, anti-Black, dehumanizing democrats. Imperialism
invades at times not only emphatic communitarianisms but likewise liberal procedures. Both, I argued in preceding chapters, are insufficiently
attentive to the material conditions of the concrete other.[44]

Ricoeur links his 'yes' to concrete morality with a 'no' to Hegel's
etatism. Like Honneth and Benhabib, he agrees with Hegel's idea of postconventional ethical life, and he warns against the *Sittlichkeit* that would
function behind backs of individuals and groups as a third superagency
of the nation-state. He has, furthermore, a keen sense of not wanting to
heed his own warning with mere formal reciprocity. Thus, he recognizes
the special role of Havel's powerless. Ricoeur's existential retrieval of
concrete morality becomes here quite impassioned:

When the spirit of a people is perverted to the point of feeding a deadly *Sittlichkeit*, it is finally in the moral consciousness of a small number of individuals, inaccessible to fear and to corruption, that the spirit takes refuge, once it has fled the now-criminal institutions.[45]

Hegel's institutionalism, transformed by individual and group dissent, engenders a critical theory of local and global ethical life. The limits of refiguring Hegel formally (e.g., via Kant alone) are existentially material. This insight into the limits of any procedurally formal critical theory is not lost on post-Hegelian critics of institutions, Marx and Kierkegaard, nor on the liberation theorists who have confronted Nazi, Stalinist, one-dimensional, and today's NWOs.

A Substantive Idea of Community and Coalitional Politics

An affirmation of concrete but decentered ethics saves Hegel's insight into community for democratic dissent. This insight is shared by all positions in the second cluster of community ideals. I find this common ground even should one adopt I. Young's politics of group differences or accept her objections to antiurban, rural-centrist community ideals. This common thread connects furthermore with Cornell's notion of gender as that radical difference which must mark *our* imaginative universals on the other side of patriarchy. This commonality runs through unnameable and inoperative community ideals projected, respectively, by Martin and Nancy. And singular sufferers join together within Derrida's global affinity as much as in Laclau and Mouffe's Gramscian civil society and postmodern radical democracy.[46]

Young criticizes the ideals of community for their hopeless logic of identity, unity, and closure. Contrary to a market atomism and fragmentation, her politics of difference supports group bonds among city dwellers. They can join in political coalitions against the homogenizing centers of domination and material oppression. Lawson reiterates this in a discussion with Young and Gordon: to give up in theory and practice on urban life is to relegate to a new invisibility Black and poor America. In dialogue with them Young invokes alternatives to an assimilationist logic permeating not only certain humanist universalism but also the received models of racial and gender integration. She views individual or group differences as irreducible. Each individual inhabits multiple and heterogeneous loci. Politically, city strangers empower Kristevian nations without nationalism. Must this fair criticism of "usually antiurban" community ideals exhaust all such ideals? And can outright rejection of community ideals sustain actual communities in resistance while forming global coalitions? Can an anticommunity spirit of cosmopolitanism heal modern fragmentation and anomie?[47]

We need to imagine and experiment in forming plural, regional solidarities capable of coalitionally global politics. This would require developing urban-rural models of economically and ecologically sustainable, locally rooted, yet flexible borders and political governance. Multinational corporations, cyberspace technologies, as well as global ecological and human crises have advanced ahead of individual and group identities. Individuals in dissent and multicultural communities in resistance meet new needs for recognition in multilayered border solidarities (below current nation-states); their flexible and postnational political coalitions offer some vantage points from which to launch regionally global refusals of that unwanted corporate advance (above current nation-states). A vision of ethical life *after sovereign and possessive nation-states* solicits what all must learn—sharing and sustaining resources locally in urban-rural solidarities, and regulating local needs and global burdens in political coalitions against global scarcity and crises. Young recently pleaded for a renewed Marcusean Critical Theory: imagining and articulating from within the existential experience, desire, and "felt lacks" of our existing societies the viable ideals of liberation to develop normative principles and motivate action. This study is an installment in that direction.[48]

Green launches a communitarian retrieval of Young's urbancentrist politics of difference in order to allow for unoppressive and nonhomogenizing communities. Green does not disvalue Young's critique of identity, instead she aims to sustain *the city ideal as a form of sustainable community*. With this urban-community move, one could minimally offset some of the purist, invidiously separatist, survivalist, generally conservative nostalgia found among emphatic ecological and ruralcentrist communitarians. Now Martin, who does not get much excited about the big city-life, conversely advances a communitarian corrective to emphatic anticommunity positions. He draws on Derrida's an-archic logic of difference. (One may find a parallel in the Foucauldian stress on the unfixity of social relations and their articulation in Laclau and Mouffe's Gramscian politics of radical democracy.) Martin's deconstructively communitarian rejoinder to Young's deconstructive politics of difference questions her urbancentrism. Martin seems to perceive her urbanity as yielding to a liberal tendency to overlook city-imperialism over resources; he searches for a more self-sustainable development in agricultural models. In doing so he, however, overlooks whether or not a politics of difference, even Derrida's, itself can be sustained within the strictly rural type of community, for which he discloses as much affective as argued sociopolitical and economic preferences. Can the real existing rural communities become comfortable with the critical demands of unnameable (nonidentitarian) community ideals? This substantive yet unnameable solidarity is appealing politically insofar as no historical community could own the realized eschatology of togetherness as such. Remember, Willett's analysis of the one-day-old infants requires us to assume a spirited-relation-in-resistance as the point of departure in thinking about any (solidary or political) human sociality. It is unclear that rural life, where Martin wishes to find exemplifications of his community ideal, historically corresponds to the unnameable concept, or to the preferred point of departure, any better than would the cities. Young's urbancentrism may become a welcome partner to Martin's ruralcentrism, and I ask why not! The two might have to collaborate before the solidary bonds as well as coalitions among gays, lesbians, Blacks, Jews, migrants, refugees, disabled, the mainstream, and the poor across the entire spectrum can coexist in the city and the country at all. This calls for new self-sustainable urban-rural centers by imagining and inhabiting them out of necessity (in response to regional-global crises).⁴⁹

Lugones and Anzaldúa conceive of solidary bonds and the coalitional politics of identity as a thoroughly 'hybrid' affair. Border solidarities and coalitions are to be based partly on friendship, however otherwise loosely defined. Substantive bonds may spring up across group boundaries. It is this permeable and unfixed hybridity, rather than one—rural or urban—locus, that one may read back into the matrices and lines of Martin's unnameable ideality or Laclau and Mouffe's articulation of Gramscian hegemonic political struggles. The multilayered communal ties should be able to interlock multiple faces of oppressions—not only among Latina or *mestiza* lesbians but also among Black, gay, Jewish, and caucasian peoples.⁵⁰

Lugones and Anzaldúa think that to be capable of resisting oppression in complex societies, one must articulate to ongoing hegemonic struggles a multiple borderland and in-between subject who, however, by crossing cultural or gender borders, need not become fragmented. The high price of fragmentation worries these critics of urban cosmopolitanism (as found, for example, in Young's model of subject-positions and sociality). So they join some communitarian correctives to the notions of multiple self, and they might then argue as follows: without affirming the thickness of self, or of one's group otherness within society, any politics of difference remains too thin to be able to empower coalitions against fragmenting society's thick members. The urban politics of difference seems to undo the identity logic of homogenization or social fixity at the very high price of separation or fragmentation or ghettoization of difference. Yet, as I note above, not all these critics accept the communitarian postmodernism which would privilege a rural or some such *ethos* of community. This *ethos* pays another high price to pacify its urban worries and advance its postliberal yet antiurban sustainable development. However much it rallies against urban or even multinational imperialism, might not such *ethos* still have difficulties crossing the race/gender/sex, etc. borders? Is rural life ready to embrace the struggles of the urban poor, Blacks, women, gays? Is any particular community defined by uncritical communitarian *ethos* ready? Would not a one-sidedly antiurban position fail to unseat the pernicious 'maturity' of "Disney, Benetton, and Beyond?"[51]

Theorists and activists unwilling to pay either of the above prices reclaim a dialectic of the border self and a concrete border thinker (in place of the thin or even fragmented subject-in-process). This allows for a critically communal agency (in place of liberal atomic selves in estrangement). If the organic communitarian ideals do not articulate best the real coalitions and solidarities of the communities in resistance (rural and urban), yet if we cannot but embrace and join the reality of communities in resistance, why not then interlock struggles against oppression not only regionally but also in globally local refusals of the NWO? The notion of a one-day-old emergent baby-self already sketches a model of hybrid tactile sociality without a fusion with the other, and a spirited dissenting relation developed into communicative competencies for refusal.

Drawing on conversations in the preceding chapters and above, I agree with Young that the debate between "liberal individualism and communitarianism [does not] exhaust the possibilities for conceiving social relations." Her critique of any "collapse [of] the temporal difference inherent in language and experience into a totality that can be comprehended in one view" seems all but necessary. I agree likewise with Lugones who worries about the separation and incoherence in certain models of subject-positions. Additive identities-in-difference would fare poorly in practices of social integration and coalitional politics. They are theoretically inadequate accounts of what goes on in child development and adult relations. Disagreements aside, nothing Young says blocks the concrete existential dialectics found in tactile sociality (see chapter 1) and in performative ethics and body politics (see chapter 5): I affirm the "basic asymmetry" or "difference" among subjects without postulating additive identity-in-difference.[52]

✠✠✠

Lugones should be right not only when speaking about mestiza *as that "dual, hyphenated, personality," which is mostly an "Anglo creation." I should be able to verify this description as likewise apropos to my Czech-Slovak-American-Jewish-Christian-post/secular . . . migrant life between borders. Identities, however much set in contexts and bodies, are historical, emergent forms of invention. The issue is not to invent or not to invent, but how to imagine unoppressive subject-positions and how to narrate self and community ideals critically. When I try to cleanse one part of the hyphen by the other part, the hyphen becomes a contested political space: during World War II with the hyphen cleansed, Japanese-Americans become 'Japs'; today the southern border of California becomes a hyphen severing undocumented aliens from public services. In the separation of Czecho-Slovakia a struggle was waged about the hyphen (literally), creating a political fiction supplemented by national and even racial myths. It does not serve anyone now to privilege either Czech phenomenologists who are distrustful of Critical Theory (who in the post-Communist East can trust thinkers from a Marxist lineage?) or the North American Critical Theorists coming to lecture in Prague who don't find much originality among Czech phenomenologists (what wisdom can come from those who trained their skills for forty years mainly on Heidegger and Patočka and the Greeks?). Communities, even if battered by struggles or when procedurally fair, don't easily cherish in their midst allegiances to hybridity by concrete others.*[53]

✣ ✣ ✣

Nowadays, refusals enter an ecologically cleaned up "global localism" of the flexible accumulation of capital. Dirlik shows how the NWO benefits from a postcolonial aura of hybrid identities invented by the first-world academy and multicultural marketing specialists. Thus, resistance cannot succeed without explicit anticolonial coalitions. Yet, Lugones suggests, this move should not mean postcultural purity. Refusals today cannot do, likewise, without a postcolonial solidarity. Yet, Dirlik contends, a new solidarity may have to intervene against the first-world postmodern imaginary of postcolonial hybridity and the vapid liberal culture of diversity. Multinational capital is projected even into the most hidden rural gender-and-race-free cyberspaces. In the Web, it will not help to privilege the coalitions and the solidary communities of the countryside. Given that the language of postcoloniality is neocolonized by the multinational lingo of postmodernity, one may not innocently appeal to received community practices either. Transgressive performances of hybridity, border crossing, in-betweenness—all require *our* collaboration with critical agency, not a flight to the immediacy of anti-theory. If border crossing is possible (in this age it seems a matter of justice), what stops *us* from expanding rural solidarity across its close-knit intimacy to the struggles within city centers where so many live in immiseration? Why not take dissenting individuals and groups in the cities of discontent and in the jungle communities in resistance, and engage both dialectically?[54]

A Dialectical Idea of Community and Coalitional Politics

What would a solidary and coalitional politics of recognition on the other side of patriarchal and racist sociality be like? The question raises a degree of concretion met neither in Kant's perpetual peace nor Hegel's ethical community, neither Taylor's nor Habermas's rejoinders.[55]

In her suspicion of community ideals and identity politics, Young articulates reasons not unlike those held by Kierkegaard against Hegel's organic community ideal of the nation-state, or those which powerless dissidents mobilize against totalitarian politics. Her suspicion shares much in common with an existentially material protest because she defends unoppressive city coalitions. Their dissent (as seen with the Czech and Slovak *Charta 77* or Polish *Solidarity*) fosters pluralistic group-ings, not homogeneous fusions. (This is so in spite of a certain nostalgia for fusions among some culturally conservative East European dissi-dents.) With an existential politics of difference, one may embark more safely upon Martin's project of unnameable community. Communal life may occur among unnameable subjects-in-process and even among city and rural strangers. Martin finds responsible autonomy growing out of solidarity, just as Willett theorizes that an emergent self is growing always already out of a bonded and yet resisting locus of human tactile sociality. Communal solidarity and coalitional politics, to nurture justice globally, locally, and on terms other than the communitarian monocul-tural and monogenealogical headings, must grow out of identity and dif-ference dialectically conceived.[56]

I want to intensify Sartre's insight that human existence precedes essential definitions of individuals and groups. Notions of tactile social-ity and the emergent existential self allow me to refigure Sartre's social ontology of individual freedom, fused groups, or fraternity-terror con-textually, as in case of radical freedom, and historically, as in struggles for recognition. One's self is always already related to another (phenomeno-logical symmetry). Yet relational correspondences exceed a total group fusion or fraternal terror: the self discloses from the start a spirited resis-tance to others (phenomenological asymmetry). Infant and adult live in a Lévinasian or Kafkaesque exile from a possessive self-mastery and, while decentered at home, resist mastery by others. Building from this phe-nomenological a/symmetry, I argued in the first five chapters that possi-bilities of recognition, dissent, radical multicultural democracy, and ethi-cal performatives defy liberal, communitarian, and certain postmodern categories. Likewise, self-ownership, fusion, and the fight unto death (of the self) are but masculinist fictions of sociality. The *struggle* unlike the *need* for recognition is a historically derivative, not a socially ontological fact. An ethics of a/symmetrical reciprocity is more performatively suited to communities in resistance.

The 'singular universal'. The general horizon for a critical theory of global relations is, thus, suggested by refiguring key existential-social categories. The vanishing point for the politics of identity and difference (i.e., a point beyond or behind which it is impossible to pass further in either type of politics) directs us to the Sartrean category of the 'singular universal'. Given the legitimate critiques of possessive and existential*ist* individualism, one must exercise great caution in unfolding this category. A workable existential-social category may not fit a disembodied, disencumbered, transparent individualist. Ethical solidarity and coalitional politics are born from unmasking racist, chauvinistic, and patriarchal universalisms. The desired category becomes unhelpful, further, if fixed by a separate or insular essential social identity. One needs to unmask the particularisms which shut off identity in unsolidary and anticoalitional difference—regardless whether closures beget essences nominalistically in individuals or groups.

Sartre's "Kierkegaard" can be helpful in taking a nonstandard, potentially fresh approach to some current debates on community. This is because he identifies with the core of existential-social dialectics. Learning from Kierkegaard and anticipating postmodern rediscoveries of singularity, Sartre argues that the universal can enter history only through the singular. This relationship marks the reciprocities between a historical temporality and a "transhistorical contemporaneity." Their link prescribes the parameters for a possible liberating cohabitation of identity with difference: identity must be free from homogeneity and transparency. Yet by allowing for bonding, difference must resist its own fragmentation. Sartre defines such a/symmetry as a "relationship of reciprocal interiority and immanence." Between *us* and Kierkegaard's plural subject-names, and among other contemporaries, there exist *"multiple subject"* positions. The dialectical relations, in Sartre's improvement on Derrida's International, mark "an inner bond linking our singularities." Existential reciprocity, indeed, improves on the linear or nominalist relations between identity and difference—conceived of as either an identical symmetry or a differential asymmetry alone. Temporality signifies "a transhistorical dimension of History." Existential reciprocity and social recognition transpire "not in the relativity of circumstances, but rather at the very level where each of us is an incomparable absolute."[57]

I hope that it need not upset post-Beauvoirean thinkers if I take the liberty to characterize Friedman as making an insight in feminist theory parallel to Sartre. Taking issue with "new communitarians," she argues that while people find themselves in "communities of origins" or "place," they live out *all* origins by always already becoming within "communities of choice." The singularity of individuals and groups cannot operate behind our backs as a genetic, naturalistic, racial, gendered, market myth of the given. Whether one speaks of singularity or universality, selves or communities, each term is, thus, a hybrid, emergent, dialectical notion.[58]

There are valid objections to a certain existential*ist* feminism. Yet a performatively refigured ethical life of the singular universal, as suggested in the previous chapter, disqualifies voluntarism, assimilationism, essentialism, or fragmentation—the core issues in such objections. The category of singular universal invents a concrete ideality receptive to community strivings cognizant of class, gender, and race differences. This category may complement the dialogic symmetry of Benhabib's "enlarged mentality," Young's "asymmetrical reciprocity," or Cornell's "ethical asymmetry" read into imaginative universalism; and it may help to articulate the dialectically a/symmetrical models of community in Caraway's "crossover politics," Friedman's "community of choice," or Outlaw's shift from "universality via conceptual strategies to universality in the form of democratically based shared unity as an existential project."[59] Note Sartre's view:[60]

For a Jew, conscious and proud of being Jewish, asserting his claim to be a member of the Jewish community without ignoring on that account the bonds which unite him to the national community, there may not be much difference between the anti-Semite and the democrat. The former wishes to destroy him as a man and leaves nothing to him but the Jew, the pariah, the untouchable; the latter wishes to destroy him as a Jew and leave nothing in him but the man, the abstract and universal subject of the rights of man and the rights of the citizen.

Sartre only intimates that a viable alternative to the intolerant and the liberal standpoints of bad faith replaces homogenizing democratic procedures with a radical multicultural democracy:

What we propose here is a concrete liberalism. By that we mean that all persons who through their work collaborate toward the greatness of a country have the full rights of citizens of that country. What gives them this right is not the possession of a problematical and abstract "human nature," but their active participation in the life of the society. This means, then, that the Jews—and likewise the Arabs and the Negroes [pace Sartre's preface to Fanon's WoE]— from the moment that they are participants in the national enterprise, have a right in that enterprise; they are citizens. But they have these rights *as* Jews, Negroes, or Arabs [he says below, men and women]—that is, as concrete persons.

The singular universal, which I would dare to defend today, can be neither formal in the abstract liberal-voluntarist sense, nor material and particular in the uncritical communitarian sense. The same must be true of individuals-in-community. The sought for existential-social category must satisfy the critics of the assimilationist dangers; and its concretely material key must enhance critical community ideals, whether in procedural or an-archic models of ethical life. Individuals-in-community, whom I envision satisfying the a/symmetrical ideal notion of the singular universal, embody a concrete dialectics. They inhabit a middle positionality between pure proceduralism and insular communitarianism. With this aid, a critical theory of global relations can support both an oppositional identity politics and the agencies capable of the solidary and coalitional politics of difference.

Dialectics of solidarity and coalition. I detect three thematic areas which chart the dialectics of the singular universal. In the first area, Sartre's category anticipates 'community' held via radical alterity, found now in Nancy's *Inoperative Community*. Supported by what is radically other than its mastered self-conception, this community can disable the reality and the ideality of closure. Community exists thanks to a temporal gap. Community is constitutive of/constituted by temporal relations among singularities:

> Being *in* common has nothing to do with communion, with fusion into a body, into a unique and ultimate identity that would no longer be exposed. Being *in* common means . . . *no longer having, in any form, in any empirical or ideal place, such a substantial identity, and sharing this* . . . *"lack of identity."*[61]

The singular universal is inoperative since, in principle, community cannot be communitarian. Community could mean existential (a/symmetrical) reciprocity, a union of an ideal distance.

> By inverting the "principle" stated a moment ago, we get totalitarianism. By ignoring it, we condemn the political to management and to power. . . . By taking it as a rule of analysis and thought, we raise the question: how can the community without essence (the community that is neither "people" nor "nation," neither "destiny" nor "generic humanity," etc.) be presented as such? That is, what might a politics be that does not stem from the will to realize an essence?[62]

Possessive individualists and nation-Things (macho self-owners writ in small and large letters) miserably fail community—practically and in theory; ethically, morally, and politically. Democracy suited to complex multinational cyber-societies ought to be articulated existentially in anti-

colonial coalitions and postcolonial solidarities. Being-in-common transforms dissenting individuals-in-communities into performative sites of
resistance.

✦✦✦

*The Guatemalan Communities of Population in Resistance (CPRs) devel-
oped new forms of community organization across several religious and multiple
linguistic borders. The political struggle of communities for bare life can help us
to refigure and then concretize Nancy's thought of "the impossibility of community." CPRs already know how this impossibility ("death as community")
applies to the homogeneously "communitarian being" of community. Struggle
requires imagining communities on the other side of the aporia of identity and
difference. Resistance communities share a being-towards-death ("the death of
others") as their political and historical reality, not as their ontological destiny.
Death signifies positively a closed fate only in the desire of the oppressors who
eagerly visit death on others. "Community is, in a sense, resistance itself:
namely, resistance to immanence." Yet what is being resisted in common is not
my being towards death but rather the oppressive death of ethical relations. The
shared sense of the death of others may never justify a prior ontology of a heroic
war or apolitical quietism or vapid transgressions—something that a certain
Hegel, Heidegger, and Bataille glorify at times. Resisting oppressive death
inspires being-towards-revolution, that is, a stance of being wholly-other-than-
the-world, when the world is devoid of ethical bonds and alterity.*[63]

✦✦✦

Accordingly, the second area depicts the singular universal as a corrective to the emphatic desire of wanton transgressions. If there is no historical or universal truth that must identify the postcolonial with the
postmodern, especially if the latter is derived by the new affluent centers
that make profit from imagined margins and imagined decenterings,
then transgressions should be checked against actual anticolonial struggles. It would not help much in coalitional politics to foster an-archic
communal bonds in opposition to forming new social institutions.

Thus, Young's urban politics and Mouffe's and Laclau's radical
democracy strive for more just social institutions. Each opposes homogeneous community ideals without embracing an emphatic singularity of
transgressions for their own sake. The issue for transgressions conceived
in hegemonic struggles is how to overcome this or that form of oppression. When dialectically conceived, transgression theoretically enhances
and practically supports agency.[64]

The notion of the singular universal solicits a dialectic of transgression and agency, and it comprises singular and social transgressions as well as singular and social agency. A full existentially material dialectic brings us to the most radical vanishing point of singularity beyond or behind which we are unable to conceive of it. At the same time, the dialectic articulates this vanishing point through reciprocal bonds, "linking our singularities."[65]

In his essay on Kierkegaard, Sartre provides, *avant la lettre*, insights for a viable joint venture of postmodern and critical social theory; and this warrants shifting from the skepticism of *Critique* to *Hope Now*. The transhistorical singularity of a historical event gathers the transgressive difference of sporadic refusals. Historical, material, and existential situations define a responsibility for and a choice of this event—emerging into great refusals. An existential dialectic of community is circumscribed by both parameters: it "remains within History as a transhistorical relation between contemporaries grasped in their singular historiality." Sartre insists that, lest we become abstract, this "Kierkegaardian immanence" of "the human singularity of the concrete universal" must be integrated within a Marxian "historical dialectic." He hopes for Kierkegaard's and Marx's "full reality and reciprocal interiority." Both inform *our* "theory and practice." The task challenges any new solidarity or coalition: how could *Kierkegaardian-Marxian CPRs*, i.e., after Hegel, raise a specter of liberation for *us today*: "how can we discover the singularity of the universal and the universalization of the singular, in each conjuncture, as indissolubly linked to each other?"[66]

The third area marks how the idea of the singular universal contributes to many a move in critical feminist and race theories. Not only must the age pass through the category of the singular individual, to paraphrase Kierkegaard, but theoretical categories must become existentially material in thematizing the dialectic of singularity and universality in race and gender matters.[67]

I find very exciting the innovations which variously confront the accommodation with the dominant patriarchal and racist symbolic, thereby fostering new existential and institutional performatives. Concrete performatives generate reciprocal or interactive universals, but not before dismantling oppressive communities. Material praxis must inform formal theory constructions. One cannot accomplish the former via an imaginative universalism of the latter alone. I would not want to confuse this latter with doing critical social theory. Only a die-hard formalist could declare with a straight face that race or gender is not a philosophical category suited for critical social theory. Only a proceduralist with feet floating in clouds could come to another culture, carry on an in-house debate, and expect reciprocal dialogue with the locals on imported terms. Such oversights damage the best in Habermas's communications theory.

Unless a critical theorist is informed by the oppression and needs of concrete others, how can she or he not be ironized by those who are affected but ignored?[68] Habermas's sharp separation between the questions of the good and right overlooks that proceduralism and antiracist and antipatriarchal struggles need to collaborate. Race, sex, and gender may not be conceived of as separable ethical goods. Racism and patriarchy, since both at times infect deliberative procedures, are likewise not formally separable as inverse goods or as evil items. These categories do not have the same status as ethical life-projects among the plurality of items available to us. Life-projects emerge from the ethical question of who I am or who we want to be. These projects change and grow. Being a Black or a gay or a woman is both a concrete material situation and a self-choice of oneself in that situation. That I might be a racist or a homophobe is inseparable from how I adopt and employ deliberative procedures. This inseparability does not invoke a problematic essentialism of gender or race. Existential-social performatives—describing and inhabiting these situations—provide a basis for the substantive and at the same time nonessentializing, concretely perspectival critical theory. The question is now about how I embody my existence, how I embody procedural justice, in my racialized and gendered lifeworld. This question is materially concrete just as my body and economy are. A liberal-communitarian cut or fusion between good and right does not even touch this question; bypassing it relives a post-Husserlian "Crisis of the European Man."[69]

The critics of substantive community ideals and identity politics do not tire of pointing out that the affirmative retrieval of racial, gender, and cultural symbolics must be sober. The politics of difference, in offsetting not-so-sober cultural homogenizations, must not ignore side-effects— marginalization of cultures. The love of one's local group identity or difference, even of one's regional 'hybridity', cannot duck from expanding *our* narrow borders to global responsibility.

Border a/symmetries and other real or imagined groupings. Friedman hesitates about feminist retrievals of "the social self." I highlight in her discussion the pros and cons of the Hegelian critique of abstract individualism. She agrees with the retrieval and critique, and she shows that "communitarian philosophy as a whole is a perilous ally for feminist theory." To reiterate my claim, suspicions of communitarianism hardly amount to an all-out jettisoning of community. The strength of Young's critique of organic community ideals may produce as a side-effect an undesired weakness. Can such a critique empower or theorize communities in resistance? Friedman's insight into a critical community formation can offset the unwanted weakness: "Communitarians invoke a model of community which is focused particularly on families, neighborhoods, and nations. . . . By building on uncritical references to those sorts of communities, communitarian philosophy can lead in directions which feminists should not wish to follow." Friedman argues that alternatives to the organic "family-neighborhood-nation complex" are found in models of community based on "friendships" *and* "urban relationships." Imaginative expansions of tactile sociality (with its correspondence and resistance) invite a new alliance between feminist critical theories of community and the politics of difference.[70]

Friedman does not object to one's having inherited traditions and bonds. She worries that they become "the points of reference for self-definition by the communitarian subject." She offers now a more common example: migrants do not find their communities but choose their neighborhoods, cities, nations. Living communities become what they are by choice or resistance, rather than by remaining the communities of place. To be a good German or American, it is insufficient to discover just one's having been born German or American.[71]

Friedman translates the 'hybrid' life between borders into a critically communal agency, that is, "radically different communities from those so often invoked by communitarians":

The whole tenor of communitarian thinking would change once we opened up the conception of the social self to encompass chosen communities, especially those which lie beyond the typical original community of family-neighborhood-school-church. No longer would communitarian thought present a seemingly conservative complacency about the private and local communities of place which have so effectively circumscribed, in particular, the lives of most women.[72]

She prefers urban relationships not because they are anticommunal, but because they shift from the communitarian-conventional to the democratic-communicative associations. While CPRs embody this possibility quite well in the Guatemalan jungle, we could accept Friedman's claim that modern life and existential living *per se* do not lead to the loss of community and emotive bonds "but [to] an increase in importance of community of a different sort." CPRs emerge as deliberately chosen, critically traditional, even 'modern' defenses of endangered bonds. Chosen communities constitute their members by reconstituting them, communities of place are reconstituted through choosing. Choice need not mean possessive decisionism; but pragmatically and dialectically speaking, it is an existentially communal act of critique.[73]

With this perspective, I come to appreciate how Caraway harnesses the critical ideal of community to empower multicultural and crossracial solidarity. Her "crossover politics" interlocks "long-silenced hybrid populations." How may one achieve "a crossover model of community"— bridging globally political, racial, and gendered borders? She questions equally 'Whitewomen' and 'women-of-color'. Breaking from insularity, "organic collectivities" and "segregated communities" learn to imagine and live in expanded (say: a/symmetrical) borders. Critical communities become "alert to the imperialist moment of identity creation *per se*."[74]

Caraway inquires into "margins without identities and centers." She worries about *our* romanticizing the oppressed; and she rejects the vanguardism or standpoint theory and practice which would emerge from this romantic view. I agree that folklorizing the indigenous can be *de facto* racist; yet I think that abstract care for margins can keep dominant (at times postmodern and at times liberal) centers well in business. Margins without centers, in a performative-existential sense that matters, must signify (from the standpoint where *we* stand) the undoing of *our* own centers first. Who are the marginalized in the flesh? Caraway worries about who determines the authority of marginal consciousness. This strikes me as precocious *for us*. Richard suspects the worry: "[t]he fractured syntax of postmodernity allowed the center to be the first to meditate about its crisis of centrality and about recovering the transversal proliferation of its margins."[75]

I am enthusiastic about Caraway's Marcusean urgency to fashion "new conceptions of community." She rejects communitarian homes (e.g., Whitewoman 'sisterhood') but affirms coalitions and solidarities across race, sex, class. Concrete dialectics of formal and substantive community ideals brings me to her "constructed arena for unassimilated others to politically engage themselves and the larger society." Shielded by an antitotalitarian sobriety, capable of ironic self-distantiation, *this* enlarged mentality may foster "mediated [critical] community."[76]

This sobriety germinates in an emergent tactile self-in-community as a relational and yet resistant locus. Adults, politically sobered up, undergo a Kristevian detox from xenophobia:

Strangely, the foreigner lives within us: he is the hidden face of our identity, the space that wrecks our abode, the time in which understanding and affinity founder. By recognizing him within ourselves, we are spared detesting him in himself. A symptom that precisely turns "we" into a problem, perhaps make it impossible.[77]

The Kristevian communities of 'AA' (Alcoholics Anonymous) fit this politics of difference; their sober postliberal/postcommunitarian identities admit political coalition and ethical solidarity:

[O]n the basis of that contemporary individualism's subversion, beginning with the moment when the citizen-individual ceases to consider himself as unitary and glorious but discovers his incoherences and abysses, in short his "strangeness"—. . . the question arises again: no longer that of welcoming the foreigner within a system that obliterates him but of promoting the togetherness of those foreigners that we all recognize ourselves to be.[78]

4. Perpetual Peace and Global
Singular Universals from the Margins

Our century is bleeding in discontented nation-states. Habermas projects a Hegelian hope for reciprocal recognition into a Kantian hope for perpetual peace. He holds out for global rights as well as democratic reciprocity. Thus far, this is excellent. He skirts the need for recognition in radical economic and existential democracy. He limits his economic demands to left-liberal welfare state policies (such as refugee asylum), accepting that there *can be* in principle a noncolonizing systemic profit. To wit, the NWO of affluence is happily reaping the advantage of this story that capitalism, pacified a tad by liberal democracy, is *our* best hope.[79]

Lest one commences with coalitional, solidary, border communities in resistance, can a reading of Hegel via Kant alone overcome the discontents? I argue throughout the book that this research program (the dialectics of formal and substantive needs for existentially material recognition) must be verified in liberation struggles of dissenting individuals and resisting communities.

⚜ ⚜ ⚜

Not only cultural identity but also critical theory and practice need to cross borders and inhabit 'hybrid' loci. The masked face of Subcomandante Marcos from the Lacandón jungle in Chiapas, Mexico, represents one globally cultural, political, and economic crossing. 'Marcos' stands for margins without center. The masked face—a Marcusean 'new sensibility' of nonconformist existence—signifies a vanishing point of individual and communal resistance, wherein one can meet the wretched of the earth. In this in-betweenness, I am still learning of the need to go as far and wide within and without as I can beyond my local borders to meet myself and others as ever new. I must learn of 'hybrid' life in solidarity with struggles I do not directly know or wage, lest my procedures are blind to sufferings bordering on my own; lest I ignore, compare, fragment pain.

At times local communities, such as the Zapatistas, invoke the Habermasian criteria of procedural justice and even employ modernist technologies, e-mail, and satellite communications, to bring their voice into the global public sphere. At other times they need to invoke concrete material justice. A formal procedural justice, such as the U.N. resolutions on the Persian Gulf War, can be willfully ignorant of the racial and imperial motives driving even the rationally achieved international consensus. Marcos's use of cyberspace to reach the global village from his Mayan jungle village is an excellent application of proceduralism worldwide and from within local communities. His January 1994 refusal of the NWO reached global consciousness, yet focused the affluent worlds on what had been missing from formal democratic procedures. Habermas's trust in the rational core of the U.N. legitimation of the Persian Gulf War was not safe from manipulations by the TV coverage of this War. Some public intellectuals did not escape this same blunder of naïve trust any more than those whom Norris gathers under the Rortyan 'hybrid' identity as "North Atlantic postmodern bourgeois-liberal neopragmatist[s]." It is not always just or safe to expect global justice in formal procedures (ratifying NAFTA was achieved in the same spirit of democratic meaning- and will-formation prescribed by Habermas as the above U.N. consensus, and yet Marcos deems it lethal for the indigenous) or in substantive decenterings, if carried by intact dominant centers.[80]

✦✦✦

Kant arrives *avant* Marx at some key insights for a critical theory of global relations. These insights conjure up specters of a radical Habermas of the asylum debate. They conjure up specters of Derrida's and Foucault's new enlightenment. Kant offers resources for refusals of the NWO—the specters of hope echoed in the language of the CPRs in Latin America and civil society elsewhere. How would resisting communities read *this* Kant on global justice?

Though Kant was no Marxist radical, his *Perpetual Peace* unsettles the NWO.

1. Article 3, section 1,[81] states that all "standing armies" must "in time be totally abolished." This is a more revolutionary proposal than the debates about whether the dominant centers of power have some obligation to intervene in or remain in isolationism from the *international* conflicts at the periphery. Kant's condition, reread today, questions the global order based on the prevalent axes of center and periphery. These axes remain unquestioned in the U.N. and other debates about inter*national* rescue. The U.N., as we know it, increasingly relies on an army of inter*national* recruits. Even as a peacekeeping blue-helmet army, it acts at the service of the Security Council, which today is basically a world arm of member states and their global economic policies. The distinction between actions by allied

armies (NATO) and the U.N. force has been blurred in numerous instances. The allied forms of intervention, such as the ones in Iraq or Haiti, and the U.S. role of the Globocop, contradict the condition for perpetual peace. The U.N. *as we know it* resembles the rationality of Hegel's inter*national* relations and institutions, not Kant's League of Nations. *Pax Americana*, that faith underwriting an insurance policy of the NWO, replaces the ill-fated Hegelian Providence.

2. Article 4, section 1,[82] states that "national debts shall not be contracted with a view to the external friction of states." This stipulation radicalizes the reflection on economic immigration (as in Habermas) or on the innumerable human suffering due to an economic exploitation (as in Derrida). Kant argues that the world credit system (e.g., our International Monetary Fund and World Bank) "constitutes a dangerous money power" through which creditor states plunder poor countries and stimulate domestic industry and trade. He proposes that this credit system be forbidden, lest "it must eventually entangle many innocent states in the inevitable bankruptcy and openly harm them." He goes so far as considering that these states are "justified in allying themselves against such a [creditor] state and its measures." World debt by poor countries creates the major cause of immiseration and of the global imbalance in resources and consumption. Kant's objection to foreign debt and his intimation of a global democratic alliance against it stand firm today. The elimination of world debt of the poor—a Derridean 'gift' in concrete material terms—would meet this Kantian condition. Only then, not before, may we begin to regard the U.N. in a regionally global, procedurally democratic way.

3. The "league of peace" is not a treaty which ends a preceding war, but is a condition of global governance without borders and sovereign territories that would end all wars. Kant performs here an *Aufhebung* on the Hegelian rump-international. One picks up from Kant a hint that this enlarged mentality requires us to take a step beyond neoliberal politics and economy. The hint marks Kant's "law of world citizenship," i.e., the "universal hospitality" to strangers. This law is echoed in Derrida's critique of Eurocentrism, in Habermas's view on immigration, by the theorists of border-crossing or hybridity, and in the ideals of regional-global environmental communities. Kant affirms what Habermas sets aside in the asylum debate: universal hospitality "is not a question of philanthropy but of right. Hospitality means the right of a stranger not to be treated as an enemy when he arrives in the land of another."[83]

Kant's moral and political universe anticipates the political significance of postnational governance and hybrid borders. His hospitality clause becomes a radical idea with the growth of the global public space. Reading *this* Kant becomes subversive against the Nazi and Cold War periods, in East and South Europe, in Germany or France after 1989, or on Miami and California shores after November 8, 1994 and November 5, 1996.

✦✦✦

The several different types of passports I have been issued in my lifetime document some political realities of local and global borders. The Czechoslovak passport, which I no longer own, was taken from me in an Austrian refugee camp when I requested political asylum in August 1977. There began a span of time when I was stateless and passportless at the same time. When Austria granted me asylum, I was issued a light-blue travel document. This was not a passport but a Geneva Convention (28 July 1951) identification of my stateless status. From a utopian political perspective, this U.N. document is still the most desirable I.D., and perhaps the only global I.D. I have ever owned. On the first page it stipulates that this is a travel document in lieu of a national passport: "It is without prejudice to and in no way affects the holder's nationality." Practically, these were the least desirable papers. The I.D. authorized me to return to Austria within one year unless I took up residence in one of the democracies named on page 4, where I was allowed to travel from Austria. None of these countries has been eager to see me cross their borders with this document in hand. I needed a visa for each country, a round-trip ticket to Austria, or a sufficiently high bank account or a letter of invitation with a financial and medical guarantee—things that refugees do not readily possess or obtain.

I was sponsored by an agency to immigrate to the USA in 1978, traveling on the U.N. document. After two years I received a white U.S. equivalent of my Austrian stateless-resident travel document. The new papers were, however, no longer an unprejudiced asylum I.D. but a U.S. document. I was allowed to return from abroad to the United States for the purposes of establishing my continued residence there. When I became a U.S. citizen, my new dark-blue passport stated that I was born in Czechoslovakia and my 'nationality' was USA. The U.S. passport prejudicially stipulates the holder's nationality, and this is so in spite of the fact that USA is not a nation-state in a European sense but a multicultural immigrant state comprised of many national, racial, and ethnic groups. In 1994, I replaced my expired U.S. passport. The new green document still claimed that my 'nationality' was USA, yet it retroactively affected my place of birth. I am no longer born in Czechoslovakia but in Slovakia. The letter from the U.S. State Department explained that Czechoslovakia no longer existed in their computer listings. It made no difference that I was born of a Czech father and a Slovak mother of Jewish descent. The split of Czechoslovakia prejudiced and affected one's nationality—in terms of one's birth-nationality and political rights while living in that territory. One could opt to be a Czech national though be a citizen in a Slovak nation-state, or vice versa; either move would decrease one's social benefits.

Europeans are less confused than North Americans about what is a state and what a nation since they have a longer practice in ethnic cleansing or genocide. Political manipulations of nationalism from below or above are no less constructed on one than on the other continent. The rise of U.S. imperial nationalism is as devastating in cultural and economic terms as local tribal wars in the post-Soviet lifeworlds. Kant's world citizens will recognize one another by a nationless-stateless travel document. To its geographical map-concept corresponds another than our world order. The imagined radical multicultural and economic democracy is a locally global freedom-agreement to live without borders and territories, i.e., only with those regional-global political regulations which resist war, hunger, environmental collapse, and propaganda. In this imagined world, our agreement would be like my one-time refugee-asylum travel document which is "without prejudice to and in no way affects the holder's nationality."

❖ ❖ ❖

4.   The position that a migration from immiseration or environmental catastrophe is a legitimate political-economic demand by all affected (that is, they have a right to rebel against imposed or structurally sustained poverty) renders Kant's conditions for perpetual peace through the marginal specters of Marx and Kierkegaard. Kant gives us more to go on than any neoliberal world-procedure would:

> A special beneficent agreement would be needed in order to give an outsider a right to become a fellow inhabitant for a certain length of time. It is only a right of temporary sojourn, a right to associate, which all men have. They have it by virtue of their common possession of the surface of the earth, where, as a globe, they cannot infinitely disperse and hence must finally tolerate the presence of each other. *Originally, no one had more right than another to a particular part of the earth.*[84]

Ethical solidarities and coalitional politics issue from enlarged perspectives. This insight is descriptively and normatively true. Beyond epistemic concerns, an expanded perspective must challenge any motivated deception and bad faith. This challenge pertains minimally to hidden classist, patriarchal, homophobic, and racist standpoints. Concrete justice crosses these lines in theory and practice; coalitional politics can unify around anticolonial agenda; while solidarity admits closer postcolonial ethical bonds. Critical theory and practice, both, are today more than ever hybrid and not single-issue affairs. After Hegel, communities in resistance re/fashion traditions and hybridity critically. This expanded perspective need not repeat problems of standpoint theories. Options for the poor and outsiders and the earth out of balance remain. The communities formed in one or more of those options have variably, depending on their needs and context, appealed to the local or global, substantive or formal, criteria of justice. It would be wise for this reason, if no other, to let *our* critical theory constructions be open to their spirited sociality in resistance.

Conclusions

Imagine that the oppressed in one of the unnamed hellholes of the world found one day the above four fragments of Kant's conditions for perpetual peace. Black or South American or East Indian or Timorese indigenous communities of civil society might interpret *this* Kant with a less naïve or less tired neoliberal veneer. Who has the right to define what civil society can or cannot accomplish after Marx? Mayans know through their living traditions, even before Kant and Marx and after John Locke and the World Bank, that land is a common life-thread which nobody can sell or buy or own. Self-ownership of what we share in common—this earth that carries our bodies—is an odd fiction even when read with moral help from Kant. If it originally was as Kant says above, then the fact that some claim more ownership to parts of the earth cannot be just—locally or globally. CPRs show themselves to be more hospitable and solidary than even a Habermasian formal tolerance to migrants admits. They might demand a post-Hegelian ethical life for themselves and other communities. And they might ask for this by political birthright, not while waiting for a European philanthropy or even WhiteMan's *second chance*. Thinking globally and regionally, i.e., ecologically, might justify inhabiting unjustly accumulated *latifundios*. The indigenous slave on them but live landless and in poverty, similar to North American urban poor Blacks who after the U.S. Civil War never received the promised acres and mules. If Kant is correct above, then a communally determined takeover of sustainable rural or urban territory could not be viewed as a riot or looting; it would be a 'million man and woman march' that matters. Communities would claim a share to what the robber-barons stole in the first place—the common stewardship of the earth, the very existentially material, ecologically sustainable ground of tactile sociality. What passes as the imaginary of the NWO continues a Eurocentric war and propaganda for the baron-robbery by other means; it immiserates those who have nothing. If it is as Kant says (I repeat: Kant was no Marxist radical), would not putting an end to this robbery demand an emergence of a more socially, economically, and ecologically just global public sphere?

Does not this valid claim cry out for a cosmopolis in which popular democracy means regional and economic self-determination and self-realization? Is this not a missing, existentially material key to ethical recognition, communicative reason, and deliberative democracy, to new global solidarities and their political governance by perpetual peace?

Today's globally regional refusals of the flexible market immiseration can be enhanced in theory by a new multicultural enlightenment critique in the present age. Marcuse anticipated the 'great refusal' in this fashion; and this is how actual *refusals* are emerging against the multinational reign of robber-barons. Hopeful *refuseniki* employ neither a unified field nor a standpoint theory (something that Foucault, Derrida, and Habermas variously place in doubt), nor get much excited about disjointed atomistic gesturing (something of dubious service to critical social theory and not very helpful to the oppressed). Derrida expands the otherwise useful nominalist microphenomenology of power and resistance into critical standpoints of justice gathered into a new International. Derrida's and Foucault's new enlightenment shows the limits of neoliberal and formally poststructural *laissez-faire* approaches. Still, their transgressions of canonical texts and disciplined bodies justify no metatheory which could block marginalized agencies from joining in the Marcusean hopeful *refusals* today.

I will next link this Derridean deconstructive global politics with the Foucauldian performativity—but now in order to reread Marcuse's existentially material critical social theory. The last two chapters will consider how a critical social theory can imagine new social forms of existence, indeed how it may become invigorated by concrete social struggles that have already introduced such imagined novelty into existence.

7

CLOWNING AND REFUSAL

I do not know whether it must be said today that the critical task still entails faith in Enlightenment; I continue to think that this task requires work on our limits, that is a patient labor giving form to our impatience for liberty.

—Michel Foucault, "What Is Enlightenment?"

✤ ✤ ✤

[T]he rebellion often takes on the weird and clownish forms which get on the nerves of the Establishment. In the face of the gruesomely serious totality of institutionalized politics, satire, irony, and laughing provocation become a necessary dimension of the new politics.

—Herbert Marcuse, *An Essay on Liberation*

✤ ✤ ✤

Marcusean dissenting refusals embody hope for a radically democratic agency of personal and social change. That specters of liberating change are given for the sake of the wretched of the earth prompts one to imagine a wholly other than our real existing unjust worlds. These wretched do not share today one standpoint of deliverance. Hope emerges in regionally global intersections of liberating struggles. Hope, while being neither transparent nor metaphysical, neither owned by any one party nor an invisible hand, marks off an existential emancipatory dissent rather than ineffectively dispersed, or even naïvely dangerous, transgressions.

Marcuse's promissory refusals are not fashionable these days. He no more shares fundamentalist reasons for opposing the NWO than liberal reasons for supporting it. And Marcuse has one advantage over those transgressive strategies which downplay individual and institutional agencies of social change. He analyzes domination, human development, language, and culture by theorizing actual liberation struggles. The post-1989 rhetoric of the NWO—however much it exports the idea of democracy—tends to lobotomize open discourse by flexibly homogenizing global and regional lifeworlds. This *ordo* might rely on bad social theory, and its projected rhetoric might turn out politically and economically to nothing. Yet its pseudo-multicultural, pretend-ecophilic, transnationally greedy, and locally flexible imaginary (e.g., replacing the 1936 Nazi aesthetics of the Aryan Olympics with the 1996 Coca-Cola aesthetics of the NWO Olympics) must be met with genuine multicultural, ecological, postnational, yet existentially material alternatives. I reject the comfortable view, shared among many a Habermasian or radical democratic theorist, that the danger of one-dimensionality is passé. Some would like to presume that the NWO as such *really* does not exist (did the Gulf War take place?). Precocious comforts offer convex mirrors of the Fukuyamaesque gospel proclaiming the end of history. What distinguishes the commercial babble from a critical theory and praxis?[1]

Our age accommodates with a sigh of relief not only the latest trends celebrating (smugly grinning) an end of critical theory, but also descriptive accounts of what C. West calls an inner-city nihilism. This binary celebratory-reactive nihilism signifies an end of humor and living narrative. The portraits of fragmentary life are elevated into an extratheoretical norm of what humans in our self-proclaimed posthumanist age can or cannot think and do. Even while wielding the formal pragmatic presuppositions for ethical reciprocity, one is not sufficiently immune to sustain competently any such reciprocity or democracy: there are infections attacking one's liberatory imagination from within. What if *our* tired, old 'European' hope for ethical and democratic recognition needs to be empowered from the margins of today's clowning and refusal?[2]

Critical social theory benefits from a dose of existentially material concretion. Marcuse's embodied performative politics from the margins (pluralized, humorous, and earnest refusals by oppressed outsiders) proffers such benefits. Even if *we*, as critics of this age, rightly give up a teleological philosophy of history or liberation, in Marcuse we meet with a timely query. Can *we* in good faith abstract from those who are suffering under the historical and material conditions of oppression, to whom a radical hope of inventing and introducing liberation into existence is addressed in the first place? What is the political economy of the festivities that are celebrating the end of critical theory and liberating agency? Whose life would such joy support? There are hidden treasures in Marcuse that bridge certain impasses between critical and postmodern social theorists today. He can help us to refigure performative transgressions critically without enforcing his use of Freud's theory of instincts. Thinkers and activists could fare much worse than to learn from Marcuse how to invent analogical moves for existentially material critical theory and praxis. What would it mean to link categories of transgression—existentialist or poststructuralist—with dissenting democratic agencies? Occasioned by Derrida's *Specters*, I first situate Foucauldian performativity vis-à-vis concretized Habermasian critical theory. Next I will examine a transgressive body politics and ethics of difference, taken up in previous chapters, by updating the Marcusean hopeful dialectic of clowning and refusal.[3]

1. Which Specters? Whose H(a)unting?

H(a)unted by the Faces of Clowns and *Refuseniki*

In chapter 4, we witnessed Derrida's recent turn to Marx taking place against the backdrop of the evangelical rhetoric that the NWO has come to embody "the ideal of a liberal democracy which has finally realized itself as the ideal of human history." It became apparent that Marx has gone out of fashion among many a post-1989 critical social as well as radical democratic theorist. Derrida's Marx-book invokes specters of a global solidarity among all suffering in an untimely timely fashion (irrespective of how Derrida might be read otherwise). The book disrupts celebrations of the end of history and emancipatory discourses—celebrated in East Central Europe, the postmodern temples of the American academy, and the U.S. State Department. Neither Fukuyama nor the U.S. or European public policies can rely easily on this text. If we return via Marcuse with *this* Derrida to chapter 5 where I highlighted seven dimensions in Foucault's genealogical liberation theory, we get a set of complementary shifts.[4]

From the marginalized lost within the margins to counterhegemonic struggles. Locally global movements for social change invent certain Kierkegaardian-Marxian leaps. Singular sufferers dissent from an untrue and unjust universality of the NWO. They teleologically suspend the homogenizing pseudoethical trends by *this* purported universal. Yet, pace Marx, Sartre, or Fanon, they introduce their inventions into existence, inhabiting a singular universal.

I read nominalistic transgressions dialectically as inventing liberation agencies. Singular individuals join in social unions. (In Kierkegaard liberating sociality can be only an existential universal of *Works of Love* set against untrue universals of crowds or abstract thinkers; in Marx it becomes the liberating agency of immiserated workers of *The Manifesto* raised against the hegemony of universal capital.) Yet singular individuals refuse the social *ethos* of nation-states. Liberating agencies gather leaping singularities to rupture the hegemonic aspirations of the NWO—e.g. a Coca-Cola regional globalism or fake eco-multiculturalism. In such acts, counterhegemonies by clowns and *refuseniki* are a must. The sufferers leap to justice as singulars, singularly. As dissenting individuals in communal resistance, they meet in a realm where, for Derrida too, "suffering" and "hope" are joined dialectically by a "link of affinity."[5]

From microdescriptions to micro- and macroanalyses. Let us say that postmodern social theorists and activists are clowning with disgust within the NWO, unmasking its side-effects—unemployment, hunger, poverty, ecological collapse, wars of religions or nation-states. This carnival is an earnestly joyous *Kehre* from *performing* nominalist analyses or deconstructions within intertextual micropractices alone to existentially material lifeworlds of humans. The latter require macroscopic, institutional, body-performances on behalf of social justice. Marcuse prompts us not to hesitate about links, such as joining singular transgressive clowns into coalitions, even solidarities. These linkages empower responsible agencies and deliberate social refusals. I find nothing to block a dialectical thought—expanding single transgressions into global agencies, grasping activist and critically theoretical contours of ongoing struggles. I would find it unfounded if one's politics theoretically or practically blocked this concrete dialectics.

From nominal transgressions to dissenting and radically democratic agencies. I am not interested in nitpicking whether or not the 'Derrida' who prefers extranormative singularities coheres with the globally responsible 'Derrida'. Let me suggest instead that the former (like a one-sided nominalist Foucault) becomes h(a)unted by the specter of the latter and by Foucault's last search for an integral ethic of reciprocity. Why not celebrate this h(a)unting as a promising slippage in deconstructive and performative practices? A good undecidability between two 'Derridas' or two 'Foucaults'—at least on singularly odd calendar days or during *leap* years, such as was 1989—heightens the urgency of bringing emphatically postmodern and critical theory to collaborate on new projects of liberation. Dissent—in irony, humor, earnest refusals—which does not equivocate with oppressors, should it not *empower* critical and radically democratic agency?

From immanence of resistance and power to a postdisciplinary critique of domination. Today's urgency harkens to the emancipatory perspectives of the 1960s on both sides of the old Cold War frontier. One encounters the urgency of Marcuse's *Essay on Liberation* two decades later in the wake of the revolutionary events of 1989.

✣✣✣

The 1960s were marked by the 'great refusal' of one-dimensional individuality and society, whether in the Strawberry proclamation; Paris, Copenhagen, and Berkeley revolts; or during Alexander Dubček's Prague Spring. The 1990s show that the most radical demands of the Velvet Revolutions are incompatible with the NWO that took their place. From Los Angeles of April 1992, to the Europe of Sarajevo, to the Zapatista democracy movement of Chiapas, to the massive strikes against the 'welfare reform' in France, 1995–96, to South Korea, 1996–97, the NWO shows preference for homogenizing cultures and the sociopolitical and economic status quo of the always already privileged. Must not the refuseniki of dissenting years before 1989 transmigrate among the refuseniki who resist the disciplinary side-effects of neoliberalism today?

✢✢✢

The rhetorical imaginary of the NWO colonizes the local and global levels of culture, civil society, and the economy. Singular transgressions, apart from engaging the existentially responsible and social agencies of emancipation, remain what Kierkegaard ironized as the short-lived spasms of enthusiasm. These knee-jerks are a poor imitation of clowns; they mark dubious radicalism. They get stimulated by an idealist pseudoheroics of Kierkegaard's knight of resignation. The specters of liberation imagine life beyond resigned, lonely, herd heroics—a postdisciplinary overcoming of domination. This 'beyond' marks a 'way' between Soviet imperial etatism and market imperial neoliberalism, between Cold War dualisms and new disciplinary democracies. This overcoming of domination—Habermas's narrow passage through an eye of the needle of our post-1989 age—requires hope on this side of the world.[6]

Towards coalitions and solidarity among clowns and **refuseniki.** Who but those within the worlds of relative security and affluence have the luxury to engage in restricted sporadic and nominalistically theorized gestures? If one earnestly demands genuine social change, is it enough to describe specific singular sufferings by the wretched of the earth without theorizing their liberation struggles? Would not any new coalition and even solidarity among the immiserated that now rests satisfied with "an alliance without institution" be less than earnest about itself?[7] Are not such transgressions—which neglect to envision more postnationally integrated multicultural communities, more politically just international laws, and more genuinely democratic economic relations than those of the present world order—but shortlived spasms of clowns manqué whose jokes no longer embarrass the kings and robber-barons? Are not ineffective refusals mere luxury items in occasional middle-class European thoughts of 'revolt'?

If one projected specific refusals of locally active theorists and activists into global issues, there would be nothing to disvalue (theoretically) a coalitional politics of difference. It seems that liberation practice runs ahead of hesitating theorists. Critical theory for our age may help practices by imagining those institutions that allow for effective yet polyvalent alliances.

Towards new humanist specters of liberation. Can one raise an existentially material hope and specters of liberation? Let us be h(a)unted by body politics and liberation specters. Let us position antihumanist genealogies and "Ends of Man" near *Marcuse's specters of liberation* in the Paris of May 1968. Let us then take up a site within today's imaginary of the NWO, viewing Derrida's transgressive post-1989 *Specters* and Foucault's postdisciplinary ethical reciprocity from the shores of their 'other heading'—Marcusean refusals.[8]

Marcuse imagines a new, radical and critical, humanism. This hope he shares with many thinkers whose intellectual and political trajectory runs from the 1960s to the present.[9] Unlike Heidegger in the 1930s and in his shortlived mentorship of Marcuse, Derrida proposes that after 1989 we are (finally) free to *read* Marx. Derrida sighs with relief that many of his leftist colleagues, who are still alive, no longer seem interested in Marx. This attitude is consistent with Derrida's style of reading against the stream, especially against the new East Central European and the U.S. neo/liberal mainstream. Is it not fair to demand that Foucault's ethics, just as Derrida's return to Marx, improve on Heidegger's rejection of Marcuse's original Freiburg project of radical philosophy (joining Kierkegaard and Marx)? There lurks a type of Heideggerianism which is just as unhelpful to liberation as would be a certain Marxism. Marcuse offers a most timely point of departure since he revises both schools of thought (steering clear of market-liberal letting be), anticipating postmodern returns to critical social theory.[10]

Is there no historical possibility left to throw off the shackles of existing oppressive social situations? After all, such specters and hope for the twenty-first century would have to promise a multicultural, multiracial, multigendered, existentially material radical democracy, namely, a concrete humanism with a human face yet without a humanist totalizer[11] on the other side of the Eurocentric East/West/South divides. Would not anything short of inventing and inhabiting these possibilities legitimate an anonymous and functionalist, *bona fide* antihumanist, NWO?

Towards a new enlightenment: ethical reciprocity and radical democracy. Foucault and Derrida, echoing a certain Heidegger, distrust Marcuse's 'great refusal'. Both condemn it as an heir of bankrupt anthropology (abstract humanism) or eschatology (Hegelian Marxism). Don't we get in this severe judgment but a repackaged nominalist retreat from a liberation hope of 1968 if not a quietist echo of the Nazi events of the

1930s? Foucault's last ethics of self-constitution remains unfinished; Derrida, in spite of invoking Marx, jettisons Marcuse's existentially critical social approach. Marcuse, Sartre, or Fanon stand here much closer together than either one of them might with Derrida. We could bring Foucault's early and last existential insights to inveigh against his own emphatic, to be sure Heideggerian, antihumanism and nominalism since the latter square so poorly with ethical and liberation projects. Marcuse's own critique of phenomenology and existentialism can be accounted for in a twofold productive way: by his rejection of an impersonal and apolitical ghostly Heideggerianism (herein lies a Marcusean bridge to critical post/modern social theory); and by his wanting to socially integrate (into liberation struggles) the rebellious individuals. This twofold approach is equally true, e.g., of Sartre's and Fanon's liberation projects.[12] In all fairness to Derrida and Foucault, one could let nominal clowning (Heideggerian transgressions) be h(a)unted by specters of liberation; the latter must earnestly be demanded in actual living (Marxian-Kierkegaardian refusals).

I question the other of a binary gap between faceless transgressions and abstractly global agencies. Even the late Foucault and the spectral Derrida speak mainly of nominal affinities, not active coalitions or solidarities. How can leaping singularities translate into the a/symmetrical ethical and moral reciprocities and liberation struggles discussed in preceding chapters? The h(a)unting specters of liberation manifest from the other heading of an undecidable knighthood of resignation. I mean a concrete, singular universal, human other of anonymous antihumanism. Do not Foucault's and Derrida's new enlightenments, hoping for postdisciplinary ethics and postliberal affinities, need an aesthetics of liberated existence with a human face?[13]

"The question of Derrida versus Marcuse," raised in the American public twenty-five years before Derrida's book on Marx, and the question of Heidegger versus Marcuse, broached in the 1930s, offer poignant crossroads for *our* present. I do not think, however, that one must choose between Foucault and Derrida on one side and Marcuse on the other. (In preceding chapters, I did not find it necessary to side with Butler and Cornell against Benhabib and Fraser, or with Fraser against Young, or vice versa.) If Foucault's and Derrida's implied hope for liberation philosophy, ethics, and politics are taken earnestly, then Marcuse is the most obvious fellow traveler, not an antagonist. The 1960s disputes between Derrida and Marcuse, Marcuse and Sartre, have a sociological or antiquarian-historical, not a critically theoretical, value.[14]

One need not ignore that receptions of Marcuse, e.g., his reading of Freud, will have been enhanced or corrected significantly through recent developments. Yet Marcuse's key critical ideal remains utterly contemporary in its timely untimeliness—this is the specter of a world that would be free and the refusal of any theory or practice that would influence us otherwise.[15]

Revisiting the Dialectics of Antitheory and Critical Theory

Dialectic of Enlightenment in a post/modern world. Horkheimer and Adorno introduce a thesis that myth is always already enlightenment, and enlightenment reverts back into myth. They elaborate the dialectic of myth and enlightenment within a two-track notion of domination. Depending on how one approaches this conceptual ambivalence, their thesis can become a setback or an opening. Should we view formal pragmatics in light of performative body-politics and its liberation specters, should we thus take up Horkheimer and Adorno's *Dialectic*, the result is a set of complementary revisions or shifts in critical post/modern social theory.

Enlightenment, broadly understood, is to affect all major human cognitive activities: understanding, identity formation, language, and communication. The dialectic under discussion refers to the unthought, the unsaid, the mythical. Myth is to permeate the very communication process of coming to an understanding with another about something in the world. Myth underpins human development and grammar. This is the dialectic: as one reflects on myth, one already lives disenchanted about myth; when one abstracts from the process and context of this reflection, one obfuscates the origins of thought in what is unthought. Humans fall *badly* back into myth: humans use reason, yet they mystify themselves and others with this very process.[16]

The authors view the mutual links between myth and enlightenment as a slippery slope of increasing domination. Because human thought objectifies, we pay a heavy price for becoming intelligent, civilized, and linguistic beings. The price is identity formation that engenders repression of human existence. Struggling for self-preservation, humans sacrifice spontaneity in exchange for oppressing their body and its habitats. Speech acts become contaminated by the logic of the same. The communicative medium—grammar—in reifying the lifeworld into fixed essences tends to abstract from and even homogenize the living particular.[17]

What *reasons* do the authors find for this regressive character of progress? (Evidence for regression is visible in the aftermath of the crisis of European modernity, whether in the period of the 1940s when the *Dialectic* is written or the one after 1989 when liberal democracy reverts to barbarism.) At one level, they view domination as the by-product of human thinking, development, and conceptuality as such. Domination is a civilizational side-effect of western rationality. The source of this view goes back as much to a critical 'postmodernism' of Freud and Nietzsche as to Weber's critical 'post-Marxian' skepticism. All of the above identify western civilization with progressive domination (most poststructuralists follow the suit).[18]

Still Adorno and Horkheimer (unlike Freud, Nietzsche, Weber, and some poststructuralists) trace domination to its sociopolitical and historical roots in commodity production. At this level, domination results not so much from rationalized lifeworlds (Weber), or repressive socialization and individualization (Freud), or our very linguistic being (Nietzsche, Heidegger, and most poststructuralists), but rather from historically specific forms of economic and sociopolitical relations (Marx, Lukács, Marcuse).[19]

Since there are these two levels of diagnosis, *Dialectic* exhibits ambiguity, or what Habermas later calls the paradox of rationalization. One diagnosis gives us a global genealogical notion of domination, traversing the prehistoric origins of western civilization. Authors read modernist discontents into the rationalization of human understanding, development, and conceptuality. Thought, identity, and language are defined as logocentric. Reason cohabitates with violence, and agency lives on transgression. Enlightenment *is* domination. Myth *is* already enlightenment. The birth of civilizations and conceptualities entrenches human socialization and individualization in domination. There is no exit, at least not a normative one.

The second diagnosis invents a critical genealogy. One is led through a material analysis to historically concrete forms of life, specifically, the modern culture industry and commodity and labor relations. This approach finds the exploitative political economy, not the birth of concepts, to be at the root of domination. Alienation results from reified forms of understanding and not from objectification in thought as such. Repression emerges from the oppressive forms of life and not from human development per se. And domination reflects specific institutionalized ideologies. They and not thought justify and entrench domination. Hence not all language and communication can be exposed as having always already dirty hands.

Holding such a two-track view of domination is ambivalent. One cannot but envision or presuppose in the standpoint of critique some emancipated form of life. But without the dialectical link between the two—genealogical and existentially material—poles of the *Dialectic*, global attacks on rationality leave one no other option than to proclaim the end of theory already in the 1940s if not always already in human prehistory. *We* did not need to wait on disputes between Paris and Frankfurt to tell us this news at the twilight of the twentieth century.

Habermas develops his democratic theory in response to the perceived deficits in the early Frankfurt School and against the postmodern turn. In the ambivalence of the *Dialectic*, one may discern a path untapped by this response and turn alike. Some of the most innovative moves within critical and poststructuralist social theory, as discussed before, now acknowledge a greater *rapprochement* precisely between the two levels of diagnosis found in the *Dialectic*. The question turns on this: what makes theory materially concrete and sober about its radical limits? This query leads beyond answers proffered by formal pragmatics alone. A new concern becomes establishing existentially material conditions of sober communication and sociality.

Genealogical materialism. Influenced by Cornel West, my provisional name for a path tracing this question is "genealogical materialism." Why not strengthen *Dialectic*'s key gesture of an unrelenting, unapologetic critical social theory as a form of resistance? This gesture upholds an intensified resumption of enlightenment. The move would *integrate* the Foucauldian, Derridean, and Adornian transgressions of reified thought with singular dissent, performing now as agency against actual domination: "true revolutionary practice depends on the intransigence of theory in the face of the insensibility with which society allows thought to ossify."[20]

A genealogical materialist can learn from both diagnostic moves—transgressive clowning and concerted refusal—in the *Dialectic*. Transgressive strategies aim to disrupt all unhelpfully idealist conceptualities known mainly in the Occident (this is a critical genealogy of the West). Individual dissent and communities in resistance may join with normative agencies of individual and social change (this existentially material approach envisions and theorizes alternatives within the historically concrete forms of life). An advantage of a joint venture is the rise of a multidimensional oppositional theory with the practical intent to undo concrete local and global domination. Habermas's formal pragmatics provides structural aspects for a discursively based critical social theory. As my discussion indicated in chapter 5, nothing blocks integrating a genealogical materialism (modes of body performativity and validity) with procedural justice (domains of speech-acts performativity and formal validity). Indeed, a joint venture is a must.

Abstract idealism and uncritical materialism. There remains a problem with theorizing about theory or even about its ends. The genealogist must avoid fancying pure transgressions, e.g., becoming an abstract thinker. The materialist must resist gravitating to the given, when existence becomes historically determinist, positivist, uncritical. While Horkheimer and Adorno argue, I believe correctly, that there is no interiority apart from sociality, they do not explain how one can clown or refuse in the shadows of even a partial domination. Ahistorical, psycho-analytical, and poststructuralist categories can be a "straightjacket," an iron (c)age leveling individual and group sources of liberation. A critique of concepts alone may be nothing but an idealist flight to myth. Engaging in or taking leave of theory, in the dual sense of abstract idealism and uncritical materialism, commits one to a bad dialectic of theory vs. antitheory.[21]

If all sociality were reified, and if there were no sites of spirited resistance apart from a fused or reified or commodified sociality, one would have no standpoint from which to take a measure of existing. Socialization would *de facto* entrench progress in domination. Individual-ization would titillate ego with semblances of freedom. Meanings and choices would be prepackaged as are other commodities. If all meanings (grammar, communication, democracy) and choices (identity, delibera-tion, freedom) were fused or contaminated, it would be inconsequential to speak either of clowns, who still might know how to laugh, or of *refuseniki*, who might know what or why to refuse. One might be able to admit then a practical exercise in transgressive strategies. One could admit descriptive facts or textual metaphors that show that no totalizing is ever total. (*Discipline and Punish; One-Dimensional Man;* or *Dialectic* could not have been written otherwise.) But it would be hard to show how transgressions may be weighted against one another once they emerge. Why aren't they equal? Could they offer anything better but a warmed over, uncritical liberalism—postmodern, even radically democ-ratic?

Marcuse insists that to launch transgressive strategies against the rhetoric of an untrue whole (logocentric reason, patriarchy, racist epis-temic evidence or validity, homogenizing identity logic, contaminated grammar), oppositional humor and sober refusals must be (made) possi-ble. This possibility must be continually imagined, discovered, and theo-rized. Formal pragmatics simply assumes ready-at-hand uncontami-nated fields of validity. I am not unfair to Habermas since he would not deny that his communication theory relies on the transparent and sym-metrical structures of validity claims. This sort of (ideal and existentially material) naïveté is bothersome in a critical theory so complex and nuanced on so many other issues. Habermas leaves his model ill equipped to deal with classism, racism, and patriarchy insofar as each distorts a performance of speech acts within lifeworlds. I introduce here local and globally aimed body performativity to correct and complement the formal performativity in discourse ethics.[22]

Not just any performative clowning/transgression inhabits con-crete justice. Liberating specters define those sites wherein transgressions are possible and just. These sites of clowning and refusal that are possible and just are those that respect ethical reciprocity, empower liberating agencies, and join in radical existential democracy. How else can *we* take stock of novelties that emerge in transgressions *practiced by us* or because of *new constellations* bringing forth transgressive options *for us*? It might become historically true that a contamination of all cognitive resources for irony, resistance, and liberation could—*per hypothesis*—one day become total. Here both the possibilities and justice of any change (whether by transgressive dissent or agency) would become a moot point. From this vanishing instant in reflection to admit to such a fused totality as my/our actuality would be a ruse, a smokescreen, since it is inaccurate even for the one-day-olds. I agree that one need not give up transgressive (genealogical, intertextual, deconstructive) forms of critique and praxis, from whatever sources these might become justly possible. Still, descriptive claims about the end of liberating agencies could turn out to be a too-welcome settlement of ludic postmodernity with the political nihilism of the NWO. Welcome fests for ends of theory, history, and humanism may *also* signify the rhetorical beginnings of a global functionalist one-dimensionality. Should not one want to keep the primordial aim of festival true to its liberating promise? True sobriety prescribes clowning in and refusals of any too timely accommodation with one-dimensional logic and politics of the age—with its anti-(critical)theory.

✦✦✦

Without theorizing a critical agency of local and global social justice, transgressions might become but a sideshow for the trends of late industrial society.[23] *Postmodern art claims to be an heir to what is truly radical, but it decorates nicely the sleek business buildings; the transgressive antitheory sells well on the commodity market. In the post-Communist East, these new artifacts replace the monumental revolutionary sculptures which once adorned the corridors and gathering squares of the Soviet empire. Language is the house of being, and humans are effects of language. Today's language speaks of globally local, flexible profit and power. One untimely thought in the post-Communist East would read the genealogies of concepts along with the political economy of theory formation. Another untimely thought would adopt dissent and agency from the margins of the wretched of the earth. Academic theories about the margins of theory easily fall short of unmasking the political, gender, and racial economy that supports their theorizing in the present institutions. They can fail to account for those who do not have the luxury to romanticize their lived marginality in our societies.*

✦✦✦

What if the end of theory, just as genuine ends of humanism (Man), might not be extratheoretical (extrahuman/e) but rather solicit a radically critical social theory (existential humans)? There is a need for social agency empowered by the transgressive possibilities and justice found among dissenting individuals and communities in resistance, and in their complex yearnings for recognition. Clowns joined into sites of critical agency transgress not only problematized semiotic or cultural symbols but also their historical and material careers. In such refusals springs up a hope for specters of radical multicultural and existential democracy.

2. Marcuse's Dangerous Specters— Hope of Clowns and *Refuseniki*

Towards a Critical Theory of Domination

One could fool around with the notion of domination by parading the limits of rational claims or the impossibilities of texts. One could apply this notion to reverse domination. The first strategy is that of an abstract genealogist. It might rupture, e.g., Freud's biological determinism. This move, however, does not refigure either one's instinctual or civilizational needs. For the latter *we* must employ the combined approaches of a materialist genealogist and a critical social theorist. Enter Marcuse's dialectics that intimates such refiguring.

An uncritical theory obtrusively and ideologically blocks alternatives to nonoppressive forms of life. Who benefits from a position that takes the descriptions of actual exploitation and oppression as explanations for why things cannot be otherwise? This Marcusean query interrogates the political economies of domination. The theoretical position that depicts domination as inevitable "has always provided the most effective rationalization for repression." Questioning this view concerns the economics and politics of theory construction and the forms of life that the claim—"a non-repressive civilization is impossible"—legitimates.[24]

An existentially material genealogy and critical theory. Note how Marcuse's Freud becomes a genealogical materialist. Marcuse invokes Nietzsche's transvaluing of all values and yet forges a genealogy of domination. Since any theory lives out a material (institutional and historical) career, genealogies "suggest its reversal." Marcuse argues that reason and repression are situated in sociohistorical formations. They are not offsprings of pure theory or unsocialized biology. Ideologies are driven by the political economy of concepts, neither by presocial instincts nor unsituated thinking. Genealogies of domination engender theory as critique and resistance. This is not, therefore, an end to the praxis of theorizing.[25]

The materially concrete genealogy and critical theory of domination must move from descriptions of general, ontological, or supramoral power to explanations of exploitation and oppression as historical events. Marcuse interrogates metatheoretical claims about the transhistorical nature of repression, scarcity, or the civilizational strife for recognition. If one can demonstrate that specific discourses of power are effects of socialized forms of domination, then attending to historical instantiations of oppressive social organization makes very good sense. Marcuse explains established orders of real existing domination by their performance principle and surplus-repression. The former term refers to the exploitative organization of labor; the latter refers to the historically established reality principle as governed by profit, production, and the excess regimentation of needs. This historical performance reality occurs via its specific distribution of scarcity. The level of unnecessary repression required for the maintenance of scarcity is existentially and materially contingent. Contrary to ontologically ahistorical views of social relations, Marcuse holds a concrete material hope that a high level of technological development allows for eliminating surplus scarcity. Historically specific repression is not only unnecessary (surplus) but likewise reversible.[26]

A comprehensive theory of domination would integrate two methodological standpoints—dialectic and genealogy—in a materially concrete way. There are benefits in strengthening the socially emancipatory potentials of both Freud and Nietzsche. All benefits are weakened by a sweep of ahistorical genealogies. Marcuse challenges Freud with a possibility of unrepressed civilization, confronts Nietzsche with a possibility of nonalienated labor, expands on Heidegger (and Habermas) with a possibility of humane technology in the service of free development, and proposes a possibility of critical theory and unregimented praxis that should interest not only any reader of Sartre's social theory but also of Foucault's ethics *qua* aesthetics of existence. I am not concerned with whether these possibilities are all Marcuse's proposals or how far they exist within the positions of his interlocutors. More interesting is to discover how his dialectic of civilization allows us to reconceive all such possibilities in a critical social theory.[27]

Specters of laughter, critique, and resistance. Marcuse raises a problem for any earnest clown and *refusenik* in the present age: if domination becomes internalized via socialization, and if individualization occurs in the same process as socialization, then what are the available sources of irony and liberation? If human development as we know it already bespeaks a progress in domination, such resources should all be defunct. Through socialization one would come to inhabit domination in one's very perception, identity formation, and language. That humans are effects of history would have to mean something even more sinister than a hermeneutical claim about the context for all development. Given genealogies of *our* history, *we* should become knowers, subjects, and participants in discourse via power configurations that speak us, that house our being. Because knowledges, subject-positions, and grammars are effects of power, they cannot aid liberation. They erect an iron (c)age, become masters of disciplined life. The reader arrives at familiar claims about the end of Man, history, and theory.

Marcuse antedates Derrida's hauntology and invokes multiple specters disturbing our waking reality. Notice that only the first specter below is decidedly that of Marx. In contexts of a totally disciplined society/body, "the real spectre of liberation,"[28] of Marx's *Manifesto* of 1848,[29] gives way to "the spectre that . . . the impossibility of speaking a non-reified language, of communicating the negative . . . has ceased to be a spectre. It has materialized."[30] The NWO, as if to dash all chances for change, makes out of this impossibility rhetorically a *fait accompli*. Human efforts at liberation stumble across the undecidability of language itself.

Has a Heideggerian apocalypse materialized on this side of the world? Not so, says Derrida. For this reason alone, he can celebrate an impossibility and an undecidability as ethical virtues. He might agree with Marcuse that some untrue whole *could* absorb "the transcendent elements in ordinary language," indeed our unique "transcendence within the one world" available to linguistic-communication and poststructuralist turns alike. Derrida's impossibility serves as a condition of ethical possibility. At the threshold of all grammar, an unlocalized locus in language is to occasion a spectral reversal of the whole, of all linguistic closures.[31]

Does Derrida any longer need Marx's specters—Marx's transgressive revolution or democratic agency? Liberation is granted via postapocalyptic undecidabilities of closure. This is an undecidability of specters and ghosts. But which ghost or whose specter is it then? Must one still care?

For Marcuse, unlike Heidegger and Freud, this postmodern *Ereignis* (shift from possibility to impossibility) happens for historical and institutional reasons. Marcuse thematizes gaps, fractures, or subversive subaltern motives within the rhetorics of one-dimensional life. He offers different explanations than found in the line of thought following Nietzsche, Heidegger, or Freud. Marcuse offers us more than an invisible (neoliberal?) hand of undecidable genealogical, instinctual, linguistic, textual, discursive gaps. There exist historical grounds for irony and dissent. Such grounds, not pure transgressivity, reveal marginal gaps; materially concrete gaps inform emancipatory agencies of social change for suffering individuals and groups. Looking through Marcuse's glasses, ghostly specters take on a bit more solidity.

If there is no interiority apart from sociality, then a contingent historical possibility of ascending total domination might materialize. One way to theorize and actualize an alternative to a totally internalized reality of social domination, Marcuse insists, is to distinguish between its descriptions and critical explanations. It would seem that if one lacks a new "critical theory of socialization,"[32] it would be impossible to draw any such distinction. The intertextual radicalism, harnessing the impossibilities of closure in discursive games, gives us ethical possibilities but not in itself sociopolitical alternatives to the institutionalized practices of domination. Deconstruction or microanalysis facilitates ethics; it is not a critical social theory.

It is widely accepted in the hermeneutical, post/structuralist, and linguistic-communication turns of philosophical methodology that humans are individualized insofar as they are socialized. Given this basic insight, one must still explain how humans *do* adopt some critical distance from that culture in which they become knowers as well as responsible and linguistic subjects. To be a good American, is it sufficient to be just that—an American individualized through American socialization? Best common sense tells us that it is not. The obvious point calls for some explanation. Existential philosophy provides an answer to this issue by thematizing that there is a mode of inwardness which is incommensurable with conventional sociality. This answer, for the most part, has not taken seriously the linguistic-communications turn. Some existential thinkers might even consider the turn to have been a bad idea. Yet most of those who do take the turn give up on an existential approach of any sort. This rash trashing of the existential attitude, most critical theorists and poststructuralists share with analytic philosophers. I find such one-sidedness to be an error for sociopolitical liberation theory.

Marcuse retains key insights of concrete existential thought and critical social theory in his category of refusal. He finds resources of liberation in the cleavages within pure or binary notions of nature and culture. We are socialized into both notions; resources of irony, critique, and refusal are situated within the human capacity to adopt some distance from both. This harnessed competence empowers a dialectic of critical individualization through socialization.

Critical Individualization through Socialization

Someone may object, how do you distinguish true and false needs and yet hold that there is no interiority apart from sociality? This doubt drives home an outcome of the divorce (unhappy marriage?) between existential philosophers and critical as well as postmodern social theorists.

Marcuse's critique of one-dimensional individuality and sociality affirms the possibility, even the necessity, of this distinction by jettisoning abstract individualism. He decries an eclipse of individuals "who are free to give their own answer," and the rise of those who are "incapable of being autonomous." The latter type cements—always and already—the end of a spirited resistance in the one-day-old, a demise of liberating sociality. Marcuse mourns that in an unfree society nobody has real possibilities of social choice. The "contrast (or conflict) between the given and the possible" is being flattened or, in Kierkegaard's parlance, leveled down.[33]

Inner and outer. Hegel's principle that the inner is the outer and vice versa emerges with pernicious consequences in the rhetorical and historical possibilities of one-dimensionality. Marcuse, then and now, describes actual institutions. He does not offer a universal indictment of western conceptuality. The thesis of one-dimensionality discloses depths of domination now. After Nietzsche and Heidegger, Marcuse anticipates Foucault and Derrida. The NWO-individual is produced and disciplined by bodily and textual controls and by technologies of power.[34]

Marcuse's analysis of domination goes beyond a Heideggerian-Foucauldian, descriptively genealogical notion. His analysis carries an ideology-critical ring to it. This critical edge need not subscribe to a grand philosophy of history. Just as Derrida finds it silly (in his Marx-book) to jettison macro-narratives, so likewise Marcuse invokes fallibly formed critical universals. For an effective and consistent critique of the age, these must emerge from the concrete dialectics of empirical evidence (e.g., singular immiseration) and its possible overcoming.[35]

Marcuse acknowledges that Marx, Nietzsche, and Kierkegaard were suspicious of uncritical immediacy. It is moreover true that Hegel's negative phenomenology anticipates Adorno's negative dialectic and a post-Husserlian dialectical phenomenology: all three resist reconciling conflicts in a factual or ideal positivity. Marcuse's negation is, however, more concrete than Hegel's; it joins to any project of liberation an empirical evidence of struggle.[36]

Marcuse's hermeneutics of recovery sobers up in a hermeneutics of suspicion. "[T]he transplantation of social into individual needs is so effective that the difference between them seems to be purely theoretical." Under the conditions of the NWO's leveling, Hegel's principle—that the inner is the outer, etc.—could indeed become bad totality. Marcuse, like Sartre, suspects liberal democracy. "The rational character of . . . irrationality" implies that *we* can achieve reciprocal recognition in formal democracy, and yet mutually recognize one another via commodities or racial and gender phobias: "The very mechanism which ties the individual to his society has changed, and social control is anchored in the new needs which it has produced."[37]

That the inner is the outer, etc., could mean under the rhetorical NWO that the capacity for dissent has been hijacked. The "inner dimension" of oppositional identity *and* difference, thinking or language, vanishes. "Today this private space has been invaded and whittled down by technological reality. Mass production and mass distribution claim the *entire* individual."[38]

When critical dimensions are leveled to the facticity of the established order, opposition is easily cooptable. Resistance itself could be an effect of the productive technologies of power. Marcuse intimates the Foucauldian warnings about disciplinary power. Yet Marcuse views its hegemonic ascendancy as a historical, not a transcendental or ontological, possibility. Thus his warnings of the historically realized anti-eschatology (namely, one-dimensionality) suggest a refreshing take on the above Hegelian principle. Note that this move sustains hope around the corner. In his critical rereading, Marcuse allows—in the pragmatic sense of soliciting it—for the standpoint from which one can attack the status quo in the first place. Here comes the missing question in the puzzle, whether and how one may give birth to dissenting individualism and resisting groups under the conditions of the disciplinary administration of the inner and the outer.

First, there could occur in history piecemeal materializations of the principle that the inner is the outer, etc. Secondly, the oppositional subject-positions to this bad facticity can never be at home among the classical market-liberal, formally left-liberal, or existentialist-voluntarist kinds of individualists. All three kinds are compositional individualists. A compositional identity is undialectical since in it the inner precedes or determines or composes the outer. Thirdly, what replaces this undialectical view is an affirmation of the linguistic-communications turn. Yet, fourthly, an undialectical communitarianism, whereby the outer would precede or determine or wholly produce the inner, is just as unhelpful in theorizing and resisting one-dimensionality as would be compositional individualism. Fifthly, theorizing refusals today must aim at a critical individualization through critical socialization.[39]

If we can accept Marcuse's agreement with Hegel's principle as no longer a descriptive sociology linking particularity and universality, but rather a description of particulars and universals, each becoming one-dimensional, then Marcuse offers a critical sociology and politics. The Hegelian principle would describe a leveling reciprocity, what Marcuse calls a "flattening" of the tension between the given and the possible (as captured in the word one-dimensional).[40]

That the inner is the outer and the outer is the inner signifies historically that a one-dimensional Man mirrors the Weberian-Foucauldian iron-disciplinary cage of one-dimensional sociality. The outer produces subjects of one-dimensionality; the inner celebrates one-dimensionality as democratic freedom. These are the historically specific, ideology-critical social forms of the East/West Cold-War mentality. Marcuse coined his one-dimensionality thesis in response to these or any such ghostly times.[41]

Concrete universals and critical particulars. One-dimensional universals incarnate "a false concreteness" and "misplaced abstractness." "The concreteness of the particular case which the translation achieves is the result of a series of abstractions from its *real* concreteness, which is in the universal character of the case." *Bad* materialism and empiricism affirm sinister facticity. *Bad* idealism and rationalism translate one-dimensional universality into a speculation or functionalism. Both pure transgressions and formal agency—adopted in one-dimensional situations—turn out to be tragic comedies of themselves (a travesty of clowns and *refuseniki*).[42]

Against "ideological empiricism," Marcuse sketches a factical untruth of the age.[43] Against the established global order, he raises the negative specters that "[d]emocracy would appear to be the most efficient system of domination."[44] This situation can be extremely comic or tragically hopeless. Indeed, we arrive already with Marcuse at Derrida's ironically harsh indictment of "the ideal of a liberal democracy" as a realized "ideal of human history."[45]

Our age is skeptical of universals. Singular transgressions are a fashionable high—even on a road to nowhere. If Marcuse is right, then just as the aporias of the inner and the outer, inside and outside, present false problems, so must those of marginality and institutions. These are false binaries. Genuine promises of liberation confront certain one-dimensional particulars and certain one-dimensional universals. They confront each kind in theory and in practical politics. Thus, in place of disencumbered transgressions, I prefer speaking of one's critical dissent; instead of formal agencies, there are concrete agencies of radical democracy.[46]

Let us flush out the false binaries, their abstract either-or: either the inner or the outer, either transgression or agency, either marginal singularities or institutionalized universals. I hope for a concretely material and historical critical theory. This is consistent with a praxis of an existential either/or: either drift within the one-dimensional inner-outer, or adopt a radically honest relation within the inner-outer; either celebrate the fragmentary transgressions and homogenizing agencies, or affirm excluded difference and open identity; either be a dupe of disconnected marginality and abstract universality, or empower the disenfranchised, who suffer in the margins, and establish emancipatory institutional coalitions as well as solidary communities; either promote diversity as a form of nominal gender, race, and class tokenism, or strive for the concrete universal of a radical multicultural, multiracial, and multigendered democracy. *This* either/or envisions a concrete singular universal by refusing its one-dimensional impostor.

Considered by Marcuse from an angle of political economy, i.e., the material dimensions of theory construction, "no mode of thought can dispense with universals." The need for the normative agency of social change is obvious. "In social theory, recognition of facts is critique of facts" and "of the ideology that sustains the facts."[47] Reason *can* become logocentric and violent. To pass such a judgment on reason, one must admit to a one-dimensional either-or and still hold for a critical either/or.[48] How else could one acknowledge that "[r]eason is the subversive power"?[49] How else could reason mock and refuse the established order?[50] And how else could one affirm that critical reason "projects another mode of existence"?![51]

Without anchoring *our* theoretical as well as activist clowning and refusal in historical struggles, transgressions can be "quickly digested by the status quo as part of its healthy diet." Transgressions of normative agency thus join the cultural logic of late capitalism.[52] Clowns can, however, turn into digestive catalysts. Like a Socratic-Kierkegaardian *correctio*, they would occasion severely and yet radically democratic, antiracist, and transgender indigestions within the established order. Without this upset diet, there is no way to stop even very sophisticated deconstructive gestures from becoming one-dimensional in the hands of their practitioners or institutional promoters. Should not one be h(a)unted by the prospect that seemingly radical ruptures may only serve to enhance the select diets of late post-Communist and neoliberal worlds?[53]

The worry that this *tasty* diet could become ours returns me to my opening questions: whose deconstruction? which refusal? what transgression? Not to inquire into such worries implicates one at best in an adolescent evasion and at worst in playing around while spreading the one-dimensional virus. I branded this attitude at the outset of this section as fooling around with the notion of domination. Transgressions bereft of social change are blind. Formal agencies alone might be too immune-deficient to resist one-dimensionality within existing democracies. The prophylactic task is to disrupt the one-dimensional rhetorics at both ends. Another set of false either-ors becomes moribund: either theory or activism, either theory or the end of theory. Critical theorists and activists learn to clowningly dissent in democratic refusals.

An Essay on Liberation in a Post/Modern World

This is how refusals may become timely in the context of the NWO. First, Marcuse (as Sartre) comes to implore that western middle-class existential revolts join with the wretched of the earth. Critical theory and praxis must expand from a narrow Eurocentric angle. Way before Derrida's *Other Heading* and *Specters*, Marcuse (as Sartre) imagines a post-Eurocentric critical theory. Secondly, refusals without democratic institutions remain a shortlived blind rage; without a counterinstitutional opposition, democratic agency tends to either slumber in a *modus vivendi* or tolerate fascism. Thirdly, refusals are dialectical in an existentially material sense. They close an unfruitful gap (plaguing the nominalist character of Derridean and Foucauldian explanatory methods) between pure transgressions and formal agency.[54]

Inventing refusals within a new rhetoric of one world order. The jargon of the NWO inaugurates a homogenizing reality. The NWO valorizes the end of the Cold War as a victory for the canons of western culture, it interprets prodemocracy movements as the vindication of western political interests, and its universal doctrine of free trade is locally partial to the global reign of the first-world multinationals. Celebrating multiculturalism, democratic pluralism, and open trade on terms of a globally regional pillage by the West is by all commonsense standards deceptive. Can a critical theory resist this outcome without theorizing in its praxis the standpoints of the immiserated? Marcuse searches for an anticolonial critical theory. He does not envision this as one of many issues brought into *our* democratic discourse *after we* have established a procedural framework for *this* democracy. His quest marks the core of a radically democratic starting point for a true liberation theory and practice.[55]

Marcuse makes *us* aware that theorizing from the standpoint of western, middle-class, existential*ist* (and deconstructionist) rebellions alone does not give *us* any right to speak for the wretched of the earth. A European decentering of the 'European idea' by a European post/modernity suffices rather poorly in delivering the perspective of colonial lifeworlds into those of the colonized. Striving for some reciprocal reversibility of such perspectives would be a tragic joke. These are the limits of a textual view from nowhere. Can the descriptive evidence for a 'new International' improve on the solipsism of European preoccupations with its own texts? Can I become decentered without knowing the immiseration of others who might not even make it into the margins of my text— not even as Derrida's Shakespearean-Marxian ghosts? Are the textual deaths of the author and the agent the good news to be brought to the colonized who were denied as an authoring agency by *our* colonial worlds in the first place?

Abstractly reversible positions fashioned from nowhere are liberally radical but in a conservative sense. Marcuse defines as radical someone who struggles for a historically material liberation of the immiserated. Radicals are not those who sketch textual otherness, who exhaust radicality with textual hermeneutics, who never venture to meet concrete others. To cite Gordon, erasing all concrete perspective out of existence "manifests two forms of bad faith":

> the evasion of the body as seen and the evasion of the body as consciousness/freedom in the flesh. . . . [E]ven the positive project of deconstruction—*de*-constructing, re-building an interpretation from a de-centered world-view, from the "margins," after revealing its faulty, centric foundations—would be rather limited without consideration that no one is marginalized without a perspective, in the flesh, of marginality. . . . [A]bsence without a point of view is a form of bad faith that turns out to be the form of consciousness that it condemns.[56]

A concrete embodiment of refusals demands that western middle-class revolts be rooted in the struggles waged by "the wretched of the earth."[57] Critical theory and praxis may not retire on the Euro-American soil; it cannot continue forever sentimentally crying over the death of the White European God(s) and Man as the only worthy themes. If the NWO emerges on the heap of the bankrupt *idea of Europe*, must not one resist it with globally local, cultural, sociopolitical, and economic hope? Is it wise to wait for this *idea of Europe*'s "second chance" that would deliver itself and the globe into the good life? Should a battered woman give a second chance to a rotten lover who pleads that she really cannot live without him, who begs her to take him home only to beat and rape her once again? Should a slave wait on the master? Who has the luxury to wait on *this* 'Europe' to sober up?[58]

Consider the offense of another thought. If there is to be a chance of liberation even for this *our* Europe, it might not originate with 'Europe'. Not only critical theory but also deconstruction cannot escape the specters from the margins of the tired 'European' idea. If nobody waits on its second chance, why should the colonized spend the next century on deconstructing its texts? The reformulations of 'Europe' in critical theory or in nominalist deconstructions of this idea are still by and from European perspectives in which the colonial West is not compelled to meet the colonized worlds. Fanon brings forth what Marcuse understood: if emancipatory claims are not in coalition (striving for solidarity) with the "struggle . . . waged outside," then liberation will not come to be for the White European Man.[59]

Great refusals must provide bridges for coalitions and solidarity of the middle-class revolts with the struggles by the immiserated (both in affluent cities and at the world margins). To be sure, Fanon speaks about western intellectual alienation with a definitive and understandable disdain. Some students of existential despair, particularly if coming from an economically secure background, might resort to quietist inaction or even self-distancing nihilism as responses to their anomic and fragmented worlds. Herein lies a key to Marcuse's Fanonian notion of refusals. The missing key opens existential rebellions within the colonial empires to the material struggles of the colonized. The latter, pace Fanon and Sartre, would not be antinomical to existentially positioned critical social theory and practice. This opening has come to be obvious in works of existential theorists of the African American and Caribbean experience. For example, Gordon shows that European existentialist texts about anguish and bad faith alone may not wake one to gender and race apartheid. For this one must confront sexism and racism in its embodied forms of self-evasion. C. West provides many descriptions of inner-city nihilism. With this background, one can better grasp Marcuse's claim that it is often the outsiders who genuinely raise the specters of great refusals.[60]

The term *Great Refusal* is inspired by André Breton's surrealist dissent against alienated reality. Marcuse identifies the term throughout his corpus with the positionality of nonintegrated outsiders.[61] Being an outsider does not mean that one's rebellion is to remain detached in a private bourgeois *intérieur*. This famous Adornian caricature of Kierkegaard's existential inwardness is expunged by Marcuse's active irony and refusal. Paradoxically, not only Marcuse but also Adorno is influenced in his own critiques of untrue totality or one-dimensionality by Kierkegaard's category of the individual. Adorno limits critical theory to ambivalent hopes of the dialectic of enlightenment. In the wake of Auschwitz, all that non-identity logic could hope for is a negative image of absent hope and justice. Marcuse develops the logic of nonidentity into an activist negation (refusal) of an unjust social order. His refusals generate existentially political acts. He stands closer to Fanon's and Sartre's views of existential dissent than to Adorno's negative or Habermas's formal rendition of it. Marcuse (pace Fanon) introduces negating leaps of outsiders into fashioning a truly democratic existence.[62]

Marcuse depicts the 'outsiders' living on the urban outskirts of the West as genuine resources of liberation. They often stage their clowning and refusal within an increasingly nihilistic world (as in Los Angeles, April 1992). These kinds of rebellion, by mirroring the nihilism of an established order, project hope in another than this hopeless world. The refusals are thus decentered by multiple non-Eurocentric foci of struggle. Kellner points out that we would be misreading the 'great refusal' if we equated Marcuse's appeal to the outsiders with anarchistic movements. Kellner argues somewhat analogically to Derrida's vision of a new International. But Marcuse goes beyond Derrida's singular stress on singularity. An existential contempt for an uncritical crowd expands into Marcuse's material critique of mass culture or consumerism. The latter have come to colonize our very needs.[63] Refusals also cannot be identified with the philistine bourgeois individualism. The clowns and *refuseniki* preserve and imagine revolutionary possibilities as much within the hegemony of one-dimensional mentality as in confrontation politics or in an age of nihilism. During the Cold War era, there was a crisis of liberating possibilities. The NWO brings about a similar crisis. One meets a certain irony in wanting to theorize great refusals in the age after 1989. In order to avoid retrieving merely middle-class revolts of academic textual interventions, one must link *our* transgressions to the postcolonial sources of humor and refusal. Textual margins of deconstructive decenterings cannot stand for the margins of western discourse. The nonintegrated textualities do not yet speak for excluded or oppressed minorities.[64]

Inventing refusals within real existing democracies. What is the link between refusals and established democracies? Given the rhetorical project of the NWO, can we do without dissent? It is hard to sustain the gains of liberation struggles; these must be institutionalized in democratic procedures. Whether in transitional civil societies or in established democracies, transgressions without democratic agency are but shortlived and blind rage, indeed, possibly also right or left fascism.[65] Yet democracy without permanent, even counterinstitutional, opposition tends to preserve a *modus vivendi*. Neo/liberal democracy that first waters down its radical promise, later learns to tolerate misery and, at the end of the day, succumbs to fascism.[66]

Already in his early phenomenological period—against the stoic and quietist inwardness prevalent among the German political existentialists of the 1930s—Marcuse depicts a unity of existential and democratic change. His youthful sympathy with Heidegger's phenomenology notwithstanding, one is not justified in branding radical democracy and its radical action as forms of left fascism. This would be just as premature, ahistorical, and tendentiously ideological as if we branded in this way Havel's dissent and Czech presidency. Neither Marcuse nor Havel share Heidegger's antidemocratic and antihumanist political aims.[67] Marcuse does abandon his early attempt to integrate Marx through Heidegger's existential phenomenology. He, however, never gives up a key insight that democratic solidarity requires existential self-reflection, and vice versa, and that sociopolitical transformation cannot sustain itself without existential self-transformation, and vice versa. He quite early unmasks the bad theory and fruits yielded by Soviet Marxism—the one vintage candidate for the label of left fascism.[68]

✠ ✠ ✠

Let us say our preferred radicals were the self-limiting revolutionaries of the Czecho-Slovak "Velvet Revolution." The velvet hope of clowns and refuseniki of 1989 gave way to the gravity of the daily politics of compromise. There is nothing amiss with democratic compromises. Havel, the dissident, has become the president, thus a professional. Democratic compromise is prima facie preferable to antidemocratic radicalism. A 'new' conservative revolution of Gingrich or the radical projects of Robertson, Buchanan, and Limbaugh are the cases in point. Note, however, that there is but a short step from the market neoliberal tolerance of oppression, e.g., in Pinochet's Chile or Fujimori's Peru, to outright government fascism. What true compromise can democracy offer to the immiserated except a true, rightful, and sincere change of their plight? The fear of revolutionary change, of violent forms those who are exploited might adopt as their last resort—is this fear not water on the fascist mills?

✤ ✤ ✤

Fascism shows not only left or right Janus-faced sides, it also produces liberal and radical progeny. Neo/liberal democrats might be no more friends to Jews or Blacks, women and gays, poor and marginalized, than White supremacists or White FreeMen. A fruitful nonreductive relation between critical dissent and democratic agency should be theorized to meet this challenge. I want to sum up some consequences of such collaborative efforts. First, an ethic of authenticity—individual or group— cannot be legislated. Legislating it could produce political leaders who would moralize from on high. Even benevolent moral leadership could prepare grounds for antidemocratic radicalism. (This should worry charismatic humanists like Havel.) Second, autonomous morality and formal democracy, if severed from an ethic of authenticity, may lack concretion in two regards: by failing to meet political and economic rights of oppressed groups and by failing to detect racial and gender supremacy due to systematically deployed bad faith. Yes, there are dangers of left fascism. Yet formal morality and neo/liberal democracy are often too tolerant to a class-biased self-determination, racist contractual relations, or a patriarchal consensus. Yes, there is prima facie historical evidence that formal democracy, in principle, can normalize anti-Black racism, patriarchy, and outright immiseration.[69]

Inventing refusals as existential and sociopolitical specters of liberation. The received gap between historical materialism and existentialism vanishes with revisions of the nominalist, one-sidedly antihumanist methods. Marcuse's refusal offers to be a "real spectre of liberation" that subverts the rhetorical and really existing specters of one-dimensional orders. Effective refusals cannot but ironize and subvert such orders existentially and sociopolitically. The one-dimensionality of the inner and the outer is undone by an obstinate thought, a counterhegemonic gesture; by communicative, sociopolitical, and economic action. Without opposing one-dimensionality as at once inner-outer, we get abstract either-or: either opt for margins or for institutions. Each option is projected undialectically. Abstractly celebrated margins, formal delimitations of institutional democracy—both can lead to dead ends.[70]

Those on the margins are anything but unnameable tokens for radicality. They do not seek a decentering via anonymous others. They do not long for an intertextuality without a human face. In the margins of the West lie the voices of those to be heard in oppositional speech, the faces and hands to be made visible in ironical grimace and clenched fist, the persons to impact us as agents of personal and institutional change. Are the marginalized served by remaining the perpetual margins—that is, postponed texts, undecidable gestures, sporadic transgressions? An economically secure romantic or academic might think so. The aporias of marginality and institutions are not set in stone. They disappear when the struggle for justice becomes informed by the concrete material analyses about and the plight of the marginalized. One had better stop babbling about margins as something that makes *us*, theoreticians in the Eurocenters of the West, decentered and posttheoretically radical. If projects of liberation aim at radically multicultural democracies with human faces, then these must admit an existential dimension. This existentiality issues in a reconstructed historical materialism, not in the wasteland haunted by spiritual ghosts. Democracy concerns the entirety of human existence or it is abstract. Revolution concerns the entirety of human existence or it is abstract. Dissent and democracy concern the entirety of human existence or they are abstract.

Thus, Sartre can argue for concrete liberalism against a communitarian anti-Semite and against a formal liberal democrat. Marcuse can argue against the capitalist performance principle and the Soviet performance principle and for the pacification of human existence beyond surplus-scarcity and for harnessing the new structure of nonrepressive needs. And dissident democrats, from Havel to Fanon to hooks and West, can argue for radical existential democracy, i.e., the politics with a human face. The character of their humor and refusal offers at once existential, historically concrete, and radically democratic hope.

Erecting the bridge between dissent and democracy proffers a threefold success. First, in spite of grumbling from some critical theorists, communitarians, and postmoderns, nothing any longer prevents *us* from sensibly rehabilitating the category of the individual. My argument affirms a dissenting clown, a *refusenik*, that is to say, a critical individual, not a possessive individualist. Dissenters think and act for the sake of those without hope/in hope of a better social form of life. They shed grand historical narratives. They jettison the humanist transparency of Man. Yet such dissenters retain human faces, nor do they vanish in anonymous intertextuality.

Second, in spite of discontented hope for ideal community, nothing stops *us* from sensibly rehabilitating hope in its border ideality. As I argued in the previous chapter, *our* ideal community can be critical, not sedimented in unproblematized traditions. Critical traditionality and ethical community both emerge in spirited relationality and resistance, not out of total fusion or self-ownership. The need of community arises for the sake of those without hope/in hope of a just form of life. Freed from a grand idea of the totalized community, in the midst of unjust global relations and amidst anticosmopolitan ethnic cleansing, hope now for globally local relations retains a human face.

Third, there is a tension between the politics of identity and difference. Radical existential and multicultural democracy could integrate insights from each politics. The need for recognition calls for individual and groups rights as well as for autonomy, authenticity, and communal self-realization. *We* can learn from Taylor and Outlaw (arguing for communities of meaning), and Butler and Young (stressing body politics, performance, and justice—all domains of difference). *We* can benefit from Gordon and West (highlighting critical ontology and material genealogy) and Habermas (marking the institutional possibilities of democratic and performative proceduralism).

A dialectical thinking about liberation—in dissent and democracy—is preferable to existential or social one-sidedness. Our age wants *us* to learn from the failures to integrate existential and historically material perspectives. One should judge concretely what is needed, and do so by mocking, refusing anti-Black racism as well as patriarchal and class domination. This can help to integrate existential with critically social analyses, proceduralism with substantive community ideals, and the oppositional politics of identity with the performative politics of difference.

Hope and Liberation—Ghosts of the 'Third Way?'

What about the Marcusean hauntology? Great refusals in the NWO articulate dimensions of a critical social theory which are missing from the specters haunting Derrida's recent returns to Kierkegaard and Marx and from Foucault's nominalism. And Marcuse's specters no longer haunt liberal Habermasians. But is Marcuse a ghost, a worldwide discredited 'third way'?

By offering us dialectically oppositional refusals, Marcuse pays attention to the "innumerable singular sufferings" (Derrida). He, then, links singular dissent with democratic agency. A liberating agency would resist all pretense to democracy driven by techno-capital; it refuses social identities systematically distorted by bad faith. Such refusals intertwine socioeconomic, political, and existential dimensions into a more complex critical theory.

It is this nuance that is most fruitful in moving beyond the modern/postmodern polemics about the sufficiency of either the nominalist or the universalist strategies of critique. If transgressions are not dialectical (that is, in the existentially material sense of dissenting refusals), one gets their one-sided presentation. Fears of a pseudo-utopian-nostalgic fascism in some transgressions are here on target! Yet one must resist both horns of reified formal democracy and of the "complacent positivism" of the Party, Nation, Church, or Corporation.[71]

Marcuse counsels against ignoring the aporias of the inside and the outside, marginality and institutions, the particular and the universal. He warns against a complicity with the *de facto* undecidability of the given inner-outer. An antitheoretical attitude will not advance anywhere, given that this actual undecidability *can* settle into a one-dimensional world. Clowning and refusal, formed within a concrete universal, have an interactive character of qualitative human relations; they offer existential and materially historical possibilities.[72]

I dare to draw the following conclusions: if great refusals are to become earnest specters of liberation in the NWO, and if they are to foster a concretely interactive universality, then they must be conceived of dialectically. And this concrete dialectics marks the positionality of a certain existentially material *thirdness*.[73]

Great caution must be exercised as to avoid the pitfalls of a fascist political existentialism and the variety of 'third ways' criticized by Lukács and Marcuse alike. These are the ways of pseudoradicals espousing linguistic and conservative forms of revolutionary idealism; these are the ways of publishing houses or politicians profiting from postcolonial texts within neocolonial academy and society; and these are the ways of elitist exceptionalists shooting beyond idealism and materialism, or formal and material democracy. I beg to separate off from such ghostly specters of abstractly radical 'third ways' what I mean by specters of liberation and an existentially material critical social theory.[74]

The Marcusean *thirdness* can be neither that of Germany in the 1930s nor that of the present age of undecidability. By *thirdness* would be designated a position beyond *bad* materialism and idealism, beyond possessive neo/liberalism and etatist socialism. This *thirdness* ironizes and refuses the seeds of fascism in an empty liberal tolerance of market immiseration and the heavy-handed orthodoxy of a state Party. One raises instead hope in liberation not only via textual clowning but also in conjunction with a concretely historical and culturally material dissent.

Imagination and phantasy become utopian with reference to existing material conditions.

This *thirdness* aims to overcome the East/West, North/South binaries of the NWO. A theory, if it wants to grow critically, must articulate transgressions cognitively, not vitalistically, as invisible hands operating behind a theorist's back. Critical theory introduces possibilities as historical agents of change through an ongoing transformation of the entirety of human existence. I find no need of replaying the mind-and-body problem. I do not hope to discover a pineal gland—that Cartesian 'third way'—where the two (ethics and politics) meet. It is beneficial to view an existentially material dissent and procedural democracy in dialectical terms of liberation.

✦ ✦ ✦

Fascism—left or right—was not the 'third way' projected in the Prague Spring of 1968 or November 1989. Comparisons of either Prague event with the German young conservatives fail miserably. The Czechoslovakia of the magical realist numerology of '68/89' is not the Germany of the 1930s. Czech existential phenomenology—particularly in Patočka's text of "Charta 77" and Havel's existential politics—is a far cry from German political existentialism. The Spring of '68' hoped for democracy with a human face just as much as did the Velvet Fall of '89'. Both revolutions aimed at self-limiting yet radically democratic transformations of the equal rights, liberty, and political coalition, even solidarity, of 1789. Yes, these revolutions aimed to do a bit more than move from a real existing dogmatic socialism into a dogmatic market neo/liberalism. This democratic revolutionary invention is hardly introducing a fascist aesthetics or sensibility. The 'third' invents and introduces here the refusals of the neo/liberal fear of radical democracy, and coterminously the refusals of the neo/liberal tolerance for the material seeds of fascism, and the refusals of the revolutionary terror and totalitarianism in its mixed secular-religious forms.

The often misunderstood notion of nonpolitical politics is a case in point.[75] From the vantage point of professional politics, one should strive for effective power. Dissidents in East Central Europe had high moral ideals and personal courage yet were, unlike Lenin before them, unprepared for harnessing power. Their nonpolitical dissent has been morally admirable. Reality demanded an admirable professional response: organizing a political party, winning elections, amending the constitution, resisting nationalism, making democratically economic reforms, etc. Václav Klaus answered Vladimir Iljic Lenin's question—what is to be done?—in two Parliamentary elections and in the 1997 crisis of his government by seeking, gaining, and keeping power. Havel's moral leadership was unable to stop the split of the country or a constitutional weakening of his presidential power. Is it the idea of nonpolitical politics that is to be blamed? Per-

haps Havel was not at the outset professionally smart. Perhaps revolutions by dissident intellectuals are a comic if not disastrous idea. Perhaps moral refusals should not meddle in professional politics or markets. Perhaps there should be separation between ethics or morality and politics or economy just as between Church and State. Perhaps . . . Havel's ethicopolitical role in 1996 and 1997 proved to be a stronger mediating partner than Klaus's neoliberal and Miloš Zeman's social democratic parties.

✤ ✤ ✤

My argument is not about mixing up domains of ethics and politics. I argue for a fruitful, nonreductive collaboration between critical dissent and radical democracy. If a dissident is unprepared to be professionally savvy, this does not mean that a professional politician can dispense with culture and ethics. Technocratic politicians seem often a bit obtuse about the latter questions. They often lack distance on their own polished professional efficiency.

✤ ✤ ✤

Klaus's arrogance in subsuming ethics, education, and culture under markets creates an ongoing need for critical dissent in what would otherwise become just a lopsided democracy. Not even George Soros, who made billions on currency speculations, thinks that education and culture can be run by market profit imperatives. The Czechoslovak totalitarian ministries of culture and education after 1968 fired hundreds of intellectuals—they, among others, have built the Prague metro. Current proposals to abolish the cultural ministry and place educational institutions under market pressures threaten to finish off independent culture and education, something that the previous regime was unable to do. Havel pointed out that coopting culture, actors, and pop-stars for the June 1996 Czech Parliamentary election campaign by the right-coalition parties is disingenuous given their disregard for the critical role of culture. "It reminds me a bit of those comic expressions of brotherhood between the Communist Party and the artists which were at times organized by the previous regime."[76]

The conservative revolution of the U.S. Congress, led by Newt Gingrich, lies 180 degrees apart from Havel's existential revolution (articulated in Havel's "The Power of the Powerless"). Because formal democrats travel hand-in-hand well with nationalistic and imperial radicals (they are but a short distance from embracing an antidemocratic social and political form of life), U.S. politics exhibits the need for cultural irony and critical dissent. The former radicalism is espoused by conservative revolutionaries; the latter need conserves the task of existential clowns and refuseniki.

✤ ✤ ✤

I rest uneasy with the claims of those who tell *us* that 1989 is the end of ideologies, the end of history, a victory for neo/liberal democracy or even multicultural NWO. I do not place my confidence in those who now would like to curb the roles of critical intellectual and active dissident. If dissent is deemed antidemocratic, unpatriotic, fascistic—what are humor and critique? Rebellion without affecting institutions democratically can be shortlived; liberal institutions and traditions, emptied of ironic and critical voices—what are they but well-managed and lobotomized corporations, just "another brick in the wall"?[77] Existential democracy celebrates clowning and refusal; they are democracy's own unique life and way of validating, legitimating, and sustaining itself as always open to genuine democratic change.

Conclusions

I adopted Derrida's specters of Marx in order to harness Foucault's body politics against nominalist readings of such specters and politics. Thus, I updated Marcuse's dialectic of hope, in clowning and refusal, against its disregard in certain critical and postmodern social theories.

The notions of pure transgression and transparent normative agency might present unfair caricatures of more complex positions, caricatures that, admittedly, no thinker criticized above would subscribe to. Regardless of the possibly dubious rhetorical role of such stylized extremes, I find it legitimate to agree with Marcuse and Fanon in their adaptations of Kierkegaard's responsible individual and Marx's revolutionary, that inventing emancipated life, leaping out of the rhetoric of one-dimensionality (out of the hegemonizing NWO), demands transformations *"within* the established society."[78] If there were no transcendence, there would be no liberation from "ideological empiricism"; one could not claim from within any existing space and time that "that which is cannot be true."[79] *Bad* materialism affirms a real existing socioeconomic and political reality. But if transcendence meant a flight from "bad facticity" into "arbitrary inwardness," then liberation would leave "everything in the external world as it was."[80]

Bad idealism can easily uphold, e.g., abstract religion or "beat ways of life" or textual politics as the conservatively radical "modes of protest and transcendence" that "are no longer contradictory to the status quo and no longer negative."[81] The fake carnival of the established order even hurries to permit all that is merely "academically controversial."[82] This feast for "society and nature, mind and body" emboldens conservative revolutionaries who leave everything intact. Accepting the good old ways, a conservative revolution levels the private-public dimensions of humor and refusal. Leveling "integrates all authentic opposition, absorbs all alternatives" into its "permanent mobilization for the defense of this [totalitarian] universe."[83]

A more complete theoretical and practical dimension of great refusals finds all sources of liberation always already anchored within the political economy and historical conditions of fighting domination. I limited myself to depicting some conceptual contours of hope in clowning and refusals within the NWO. These contours show that genuine refusals do inhabit a concretely operative middle term or *thirdness*. They do so both in theorizing and in praxis. In both realms, clowns and *refuseniki* learn to safeguard critical traditionality and culture, existing margins and mainstream institutions, antitheory and theory, etc. against the horns of *bad* materialism and idealism. These horns invade traditions; and they distort escapes from bankrupt traditions. One must envision subversions of the existential and sociopolitical entirety of their false either-or choices. This comic and earnest subversion affects "the very structure of human existence," inventing and introducing "a qualitatively new mode of existence."[84]

An existentially material critical theory and praxis embrace neither a flighty normative leap nor an uncritical infatuation with facticity. Even the most individual mode of human existence implies a shared social form of life. Thus, a qualitatively new mode of human existence requires a critical theory of individualization through socialization. This leads me to consider next whether and how the hope of radical multicultural and existential democracy proffers credible resources for liberation. For this one must both seek actual or historical instantiations and theorize the axes of ongoing great refusals across a wide dimension of needs for recognition.

8

SKI MASKS AND VELVET FACES

While the Moscow-imposed government in Prague would degrade and humiliate reformers, the Washington-made government in Guatemala would kill them. It still does, in a virtual genocide that has taken more than 150,000 victims. . . . [T]he main explanation for the fearless character of the students' recent uprising in Prague [is]: the Czechoslovak army doesn't shoot to kill. . . . In Guatemala, not to mention El Salvador, random terror is used to keep unions and peasant associations from seeking their own way. . . . [This terror] can easily compete against Nicolae Ceasescu's Securitate for the World Cruelty Prize.

—Julio Godoy, Guatemalan journalist

✤✤✤

Must I argue the wrongfulness of slavery? . . . Is it to be settled by the rules of logic and argumentation, as a matter beset with great difficulty, involving a doubtful application of the principle of justice, hard to be understood? . . . What! am I to argue that it is wrong to make men brutes, to rob them of their liberty, to work them without wages, to keep them ignorant of their relations to their fellow-men . . . At a time like this, scorching irony, not convincing argument, is needed.

—Frederick Douglass, "What to the Slave Is the Fourth of July?"

✤✤✤

So there are two approaches, and both are human but seem not to be compatible; yet we must try to live them both at the same time. There is the effort, all other conditions aside, to create Humanity, to engender Humanity; this is the ethical relationship. And there is the struggle against scarcity.

—Jean-Paul Sartre, *Hope Now*

✤✤✤

What could Subcommander 'Marcos' and Václav Havel have in common? Even if I found that they shared something, why should I seek here family resem-

blances? And if I discerned more than loose affinities, would they be meaningful and relevant rather than utterly bizarre? I am trying to get at credible instantiations of great refusals. I meet these in multidimensional expressions of the need for recognition. An active hope for radical multicultural and existential democracy already raises specters of liberation.

The more obvious is how different Marcos and Havel appear. Marcos is a ski-masked face of the Chiapas insurrection, Havel is a public face of the Czecho-Slovak Velvet Revolution. Marcos leads an armed social revolution, Havel heads the revolutionary tradition of a nonviolent protest against a sociopolitical totality. Marcos has defended the immiserated Mayans against the effects of private markets run by and for power elites. Havel has engaged a mainstream struggle against the state-command economy of the Communist rule. Marcos decries the real existing neoliberal rule and open trade borders because he suspects them of serving North American and European business agents. Havel decries the real existing socialism and state economy because these were the agents of the nomenklatura, its business and power interests.

Still, both Havel and Marcos are two philosophically inclined poets and dissidents. Both embrace a performative style and rhetoric in their activism. Each engages a dramatic staging in communicating his ideas. This dramatization empowers others to open spaces for social change. Havel took part in theater actor strikes in order to energize civil society in November 1989. Marcos announced the 1994 Chiapas rebellion to Mexico and the world from his ecologically and agriculturally self-sustaining natural amphitheater of the Lacandón jungle. Unlike Heidegger's quietist, false-peasantphilic, urbanophobic, generally antimodern questioning concerning planetary technology, modern media, and global culture, and unlike Sartre's ambivalence on the possibilities of ever pacifying nature and overcoming material scarcity, Marcuse creatively adopts modern technology to humanize the realm of necessity with play and to combat unnecessary, i.e., surplus scarcity. In this instance, Marcos—among peasants and in a deep forest—vindicates Marcuse not Heidegger. Employing a technologically savvy struggle against dehumanization and material want, while hooked on-line to the information highway with a battery-operated laptop and a satellite dish, Marcos does not suffer from an antitechnology apocalyptic or antiurban rural sentimentality. He stages in his jungle setting a broad, serious and yet humorous, rural but also urban, local and yet globally appealing and videotaped National Democratic Convention (1994) and An Intercontinental Encounter for Humanity and against Neoliberalism (1996). The core of Havel's and Marcos's staging lies in existential drama. Trust responsible individuals and radically sovereign publics to make the best judgments, to facilitate spaces for genuine changes! Both Havel and Marcos utilize self-irony and humor in politics. Both use indirect communication to empower citizen action. The masked and the velvet leadership, both energize and mobilize civil society—away from creating a Party of the State. Neither the Chiapas rebellion nor the Velvet Revolution required a formation of the vanguard professional party for social change. On the contrary, Havel's Civic Forum and Marcos's Zapatistas intentionally reversed Lenin's drive (his answer to what is to be done) for vanguard power. The Czech Civic Forum, the Slovak Public Against Violence, or the Mexican Civil Society promoted self-limiting revolutions with radically democratic means.

I do not overlook that Marcos, Ramona (the famous female subcomman-der), and other Zapatista rebels cover their faces with ski masks, while Havel beams with a jovial face. A struggle against hunger does not find itself in the same locus as another's velvet struggle for ethical and civic life. Objections to neoliberalism by the wretched of the earth seem to contradict Havel's desire for restoring posttotalitarian, so-called 'normal free markets'. Hard questions are pressed by the great refusals in both the self-limiting violent and the self-limit-ing nonviolent revolutions in the NWO. Reflecting on a Prague of 1989 and a Chiapas of 1994 can shed some light on the liberating specters of democracy-to-come.

1. The Velvet Faces of Great Refusals, Or Why Dissent Today?

I used to say about myself that I feel to be a socialist. I did not iden-tify by that with some concrete economic theory . . . or an idea, that all should be state-run and planned; I wanted to say by that only that my heart is so to speak on the left. . . . [Y]esterday's feared Com-munist is today's quite unscrupulous capitalist.[1]

✠✠✠

Fragments from a Damaged Lifeworld

In the post-Communist paradise, the nomenklatura becomes an East European representative to western companies. Which victory, whose justice is served by a state robbery, laundered into a private market robbery (often by the same bosses), and legitimated by the same 'free' markets?

✠✠✠

Behold the visual landscapes—massive billboards and enterprise logos loom in place of pro-Soviet slogans, which have been transfigured into slogans for Volkswagen or IBM or the new lingerie! A popular buffet near Prague's Charles University is replaced by the unhealthy and overpriced fast food Ken-tucky Fried Chicken. The Prague Radio, Kiss 98.7, sponsors the opening night full of lights, speeches, and status sharing. Elsewhere, the golden Communist Creed printed on red and surrounded by red stars melts into the Big Mac ad printed under MacDonald's golden arches against a red background. Where once

*hovered Stalinist monumental sculptures, there triumph today sleek postmodern
ads promising power and a piece of beef—the ads obscenely stick out in the city's
organic, urban-rural horizon.*

*A larger than life goddess of revolution yields place to a panty-hose cen-
terfold billboard, inviting all to indulge in a free enterprise. Captions: "It is me."
A video for Levis 501 suggests one should exchange an old Škoda car for a pair
of jeans; what a "škoda" ("pity"). A TV ad promises the car "Infinity"—on
Prague streets. The text: "What do you want . . . ?" The North American "Bud-
weiser" invests in the original "Budějovické pivo" brewery in České Budějovice
in Southern Bohemia in order to gain west European markets for the U.S.
"Bud." The Czech Škoda car transfers 70% of ownership over to the German
Volkswagen; flexibly accumulating capital assures that the Czech strikes can be
offset by VW moves to Mexico, and vice versa . . .*

✦ ✦ ✦

*Czech prime minister, Václav Klaus, was until 1989 an active member of
the Communist Party flagship Prognostic Research Institute. He has been on the
list as a candidate for his full membership in the Party whose research directives
he dutifully fulfilled. Early in 1989, we can still find him on Czechoslovak TV
espousing the benefits of rigidly directed state-socialist economics. As a non-
Party member who has, however, learned the spirit of five-year planning, he was
chosen (after Valter Komárek also from the Prognostic Institute) to be a prime
compromise candidate for the transitional government. Many former Party or
non-Party members of the Prognostic Institute now have government posts.
Some, like Miloš Zeman (de facto victor of the 1996 Parliamentary elections),
work in the social democratic opposition. Under Klaus culture, education, health,
and social welfare are starved in salaries and investment; state and enforcement
apparatus—government, judges, courts, police, military—grow in salaries.*

*There are many Czech newspapers. Despite obvious pluralism, most,
except paradoxically the Communist Rudé právo (Red Law), are foreign-
owned.[2] Dissent controlled some of the renewed papers at the post-1989 incep-
tion, today's editorial controls serve German, Swiss, or other owners. Too few
offer critical discussions about the government or the past profile of its members.
In Slovakia, the state censorship of media is exercised directly by Vladimir
Mečiar's government just as before by the Communists; in Bohemia, pressures
are those of the 'free market'.*

*The absence of political discussion and public culture is matched by the cir-
culation of strange views. That Klaus preaches Thatcher-Reaganism but practices tight etatism is not questioned by the voting majority; and this is so even
when Klaus's attempt to gain a free state apartment in Prague was leaked to the
public. His defense that many politicians get state apartments without incurring
harm was as naïve as it was cynical. Housing construction is at its all-time low,*

the need has increased. Yet if the government placed state rents on the market, it would itself most likely experience a fourth Czech defenestration.
Klaus was able to curb legitimation and motivation crises of his policies (e.g., those experienced by Hungary or Poland) because he practices strict controls in housing, in state and power apparatus, and to some extent in health care and education. He, however, applies a minimalist market neoliberalism in politics, culture, research, and education. He is in no hurry to decentralize Prague power. In its style and approach, a five-year socialist prognosticating becomes now a dutiful and meticulous, even dogmatic and intolerant, laissez-faire gospel. The rhetoric of the Communist paradise gives in to the rhetoric of free markets. In neither case does theory meet practice. The Communist technocracy was not a paradise but a badly run state based on an illiberal capitalism of one state Party. The market technocracy does not meet its own politically economic and liberal democratic criteria when it flirts with an etatist absolutism. Given that education has been until 1989 a vehicle for the one-Party directives, and is after 1989 taking a back seat to etatist economism, culture and education have become doubly orphans.

A New 'Noble Lie', Or Which Story about 1989 Shall We Tell?

Brodsky and Havel: "The Post-Communist Nightmare." Havel, after having written "The Post-Communist Nightmare," engaged in "An Exchange" with Brodsky. Havel claims that a "misunderstanding has occurred between two people who essentially understand each other." He disagrees with Brodsky that all dissidents in all former Soviet block countries were dismissed by friends and acquaintances as an "inconvenience." He agrees that some dissidents might have been used by conformist masses "as a source of . . . moral comfort."[3]
Maybe both views are right; maybe they speak at cross-purposes. Dissidents in Central Europe were an inconvenience, dissidents in the Soviet Russia allowed conformists to justify bad faith. Perhaps one should not universalize one local context onto another, Havel objects to Brodsky. What if the dissident "has had it" in both cases? Either dissidents are nothing but naïve romantics whose "living reproach" (says Havel) falls prey after 1989 to "the vulgarity of the human heart" (Brodsky's suspicion); or they are the gadflies who turn out to be more irrelevant than inconvenient to existing democracies (Klaus's wish).[4]
These distressing parallel possibilities would make an engaging topic for the conversation to which Havel in his reply invited Brodsky before the latter's death. Still their purported misunderstanding is not the most important issue. Given Havel's invitation, it might be wiser for me to discuss also that to which Havel did not respond; further that which Brodsky's criticisms reveal; and finally that which Brodsky did not note in Havel's own position.
Havel could have addressed some basic differences in his and Brodsky's assumptions about the world. Brodsky's world reveals tragic dimensions. These seem to be absent from Havel's less dark world. Brodsky condemns "the better

part of this century as a reminder of Original Sin." Havel hopes for existential revolution and the awakening of human spirit.[5] Brodsky worries about "human negative potential." Havel focuses on 'the post-Communist nightmare' recorded in the paradoxical anxiety of freedom that accompanies every exodus from total-ity/prison.[6] Brodsky warns that humans are dangerous, prone to betray and com-mit murder. Real civility lies in giving up the illusion about human goodness. Havel envisions a deeper "metaphysical order" of the universe. This allows for the "moral order" and, in crisis or in the experience of the absurd, sustains the possibilities for improved human relations.[7]

    This exchange does not sound like a case of people misunderstanding each other. They offer two views of the world. Havel's concrete existential humanism adapts to the postmodern and post-1989 NWO realities. Brodsky's portrait of total human depravity is tuned to these same realities: he partakes neither in a postmodern carnival (its rejections of human reason), nor in a conservative dogma about the brave new market-world. I suspect that in the exchange on post/Communism, Brodsky and Havel are beating around the bush.

How stories become one-dimensional. Brodsky did not beat around George Bush's lead story about 1989 as the victory of pure capitalism over dirty Communism. Brodsky brands this sort of narrative as playing on cowboys and Indians. His antihumanist skepticism about vulgar human hearts reveals that although Klaus eagerly and Havel reluctantly beat to the Reagan-Thatcher-Bush (and Clinton) drums, their joint story is but one among myths one may tell about 1989. Is theirs a good story or a lyrical kitsch? Is life after 1989 still "else-where"?[8]

    Is a dramatic line about cowboys and Indians really about the Velvet Rev-olution? Or is this line more about something else into which the hope of 1989, just as that of 1968, has been historically molded, melted, smothered? Brodsky thinks that Communism, the post/Communist age, transitional civil societies— all too conveniently externalize human evil. Cowboys in the West and their cronies in the East, he reminds us, both overlook the fact that totalitarianism was about mass democracies of "the world's future." Each regime shows a timely mir-ror to the other. Each avoids its deceptively disclosed or demoniacally masked face.[9]

    Extending Brodsky's Beckett-like 'happy days', one arrives at the global position with one-dimensionality as a zero-sum-game. Here all possible resis-tance is exhausted. Derrida hopes to find cleavages in language, Foucault seeks resistance within power constellations. But Brodsky gives credence to a Heideg-gerian technological apocalypse mixed with a tinge of Marcusean doubts about retaining any nonreified language of critique. Both sides of the post-1989 East/West conflict have become more like each other: more cynically imbued with power, more ruthlessly money hungry, more intolerantly nationalist or smugly fundamentalist, more hateful across racial and gender worlds, more eager to *engage in regional-ethnic and global-imperial cleansing. For all that liberal anxiety about left fascism, there is no energy in 1989 to seek a 'third way' between Soviet command and western market economies. Brodsky's reply to Havel's daytime nightmare marks a way of muddling through. The neoliberal market way cannot appease the misplaced liberal political anxiety. These sketches of 1989, no matter where they come from, or how much liberals or proceduralists protest that the thesis of one-dimensionality is passé, become part of a postmodernly cynical, conservatively glib whole. Welcome to a NWO!*

There is one advantage in Brodsky's tragic, at times nihilistic, conservativism. It presents a corrective to an insipid conservative fairy tale about western civilization as a cultural salvation and capitalism as the conquest of evil. Brodsky and Derrida could agree about the silliness of the Fukuyamaesque dogma of the new posthistoric age with free markets bulging in commodities and ideas. Perhaps there are no specters of Marx (Brodsky might protest to Derrida), only the specters of original human depravity. This latter ghost ruined the Soviet dream; it raises havoc within the American dream too. Too bad for Samuel Huntington!

Brodsky refuses to be sentimental about humanity. Thus, he secures a margin of dissent from a seemingly seamless whole. The margin pivots in the gaps between smug aperitifs for NWO victories and the cover-up of self-justifying narratives. For Brodsky, 'velvet' revolutions and 'free' markets are roughed up each by vulgar human hearts. Sentimental stories and carnival parades cannot cure a masked vulgarity or a pretentious innocent face. This critique of left-liberal optimism does not vindicate market-liberals or the politically minimalist dogmatists either. Like Freud or Nietzsche, like Brodsky—all sober conservatives—S. Huntington and Pat Buchanan are not. Brodsky's plague on all houses of post/Communism and Americanism may not offer an exit from Havel's nightmare. Its wake justifies neither a willed naïveté about one's lifeworld nor a willed colonization of lifeworlds by the imperatives of profit and power.

Brodsky proposes to Havel that he resist equally the paths of self- and other-deception. (The possibility of deception applies when the lifeworld imperatives of the Velvet Revolution become colonized by the functionalist imperatives of Klausonomics and when this colonization of lifeworld by systems of gain and technocracy is justified by court philosophers.) Philosophers from Plato to Heidegger to Khmer Rouge to Mihaijlo Markovič—insofar as they tried to beat to/for someone's fascist power drums, rather than serve as a dissenting nuisance to the people and the established order—have been bad ethical news for politics. Which world shall our age embrace, which story about 1989 will it tell itself or its posterity: beating naïvely around the bush, beating to power drums, accepting the new beat ways of neoliberal carnivals or even of a new apocalypse? Can we do better than offer another Platonic not-so-noble lie about people's natures and their newly constituted republics?

Brodsky calls the reader to self-examination. If this call does not transform present civil societies, what does one get but an escape to some false either-or? False either-or models abound equally in some forms of existential philosophy and in functionalist sociopolitical and economic theories. On the one hand there pivots privatist, objectless inwardness. (This bad idealism is practiced in most totalitarian regimes when bereft of dissent; in consumer democracies it is practiced through an apolitical withdrawal from democratic participation.) On the other hand there pivots a quietist acceptance of our world in which human vulgarity and fraternity-terror reign as eternally given realities. (This bad materialism issues today mainly from market conservatives; before it was espoused by Stalinist economistic reductionists.)

Brodsky's conservative margin of sobriety, just as that of other intelligent conservatives, deconstructs the market and cultural legitimations which underwrite the naïve or cynical cowboy-mentality. Does he offer any earnest choice of alternatives or just a false, because amoral, either-or? Does one have to accept either his ascetical thesis of the total human depravity (a secularized Calvinism adapted for a postmodern world order) or the unreflective conservativism of the new market-gospel? Are these the best stories left in the marketplace? Are there any other stories—unrestrained by the Hobbesian-Nietzschean-Freudian insights into humanity, and not driven by profit and power imperatives?

Fragments from a Damaged Lifeworld II: Ends of Critical Theory

Consider these tragic-ironical developments after 1989. The one-time Communists and stasis (secret police) praise the coupon privatization (the sale of the state), just as they applauded the economic determinism of prior state enterprises. New mutual funds offer instant wealth. They replace five-year plans: ads promise double-triple digit returns to those who invest the privatization coupons. Mutual funds continue the East Central European traditions of building a Potemkin-like economic air-castle. Potemkin Village names a nonexistent entity—built, dismantled, moved around for home propaganda and foreign visitors. People used to believe in the dogma of central state planning. Many now, especially senior citizens, trust the dogma of fair markets. Promises of an instant paradise once again cover billboards. Instead of 'With the Soviet Union for Ever and Ever' or 'With the Communist Party towards Bright New Future', one reads 'With Western Market Economy and Privatization to Interminable Growth, Prosperity, and Happiness'.

***

Havel's call for the "second [economic] revolution" against the new Communist-turned-capitalist mafia has never materialized. Instead he got himself embroiled in the political witch hunt and the debate over the Czech "lustrace law," which was supposed to prevent former collaborators from taking high polit-

ical offices for five years (another of the five-year plans just renewed—temporarily—for five more years?). While the media and the Parliament argued with Havel whether this was a good or a bad law from the standpoint of global human rights, highly placed collaborators (such as Klaus's Slovak counterpart, Mečiar) managed to stash away the compromising files. Havel received a lot of bad rap at home for his opposition to the early version of the lustration law, and bad press in the West for not launching a stronger opposition. The law does not avoid implying the notion of collective guilt to which Havel objects on existential-humanist grounds. Ironically, the law does not even touch the nuevo riche *who gained wealth because of their past collaboration. Business is business! Unlike in the post-Nazi Germany, the law neither names the former* nomenklatura *as a criminal group (and this provision would differ from collective guilt), nor offers means that would criminalize the use of wealth amassed over the years by various sectors of the past regime. Today as in the past, the real power resides among those who have the resources and market connections. Those in politics who are lustrated 'clean' need those who stashed away the funds, albeit dirty, to wield over the old market monopolies. Market's invisible hands absolve the dirty hands. If money proves God's favor, there can be no dirty money. If money is the postideological pimp of the nations, then sale of innocence becomes the general law. The market launders dirty history.*[10]

✦✦✦

One hears from some people in the East that George Soros's Open Society Foundations promote his leftist (read: Jewish) ideological agenda. An appeal to Sir Karl Popper's notion of open society should allow one to characterize Soros as a somewhat progressively thinking and politically liberal philanthropist. This is how he stylizes himself in his book 'on Soros' (see Tucker's review essay). He hardly contradicts the U.S. tradition of anti-Communism. This U.S. legacy—from McCarthy to Nixon to Reagan, Bush, and Gingrich—is really conservative. It is, thus, ironical that the academics and politicians who are against Soros think of someone who made billions by speculating on world currencies as a raging leftist. Soros promotes free markets just as passionately as, if not better than, Klaus. It, however, irritates the market dogmatists that Soros does not entrust to markets the foster care for culture and education. So the suspicion—that Soros's open societies offer too much freedom in the eastern market of ideas and too intense a competition with the unreformed academy—is indeed a comedy if not a farce with unhappy end.

In September 1993 the Czech Parliament voided past university contracts in order to open competitions for all existing and new university positions. A number of old cadres found a loophole in the new law. Many resigned but immediately renewed contracts before the ordinance took effect. Thus, they fell outside of the law's reforming intent. (It is a local hiring practice to find suitable candi-

dates first and only then announce a competitive search describing the chosen candidate. While this communitarian custom can work well with benevolent rulers who single-handedly reform a Ministry, department, or school by placing in them trusted dissident friends, it provides no democratic checks on tyrants or incompetent apparatchiki *who rule by decrees or who block genuinely democratic reforms.) The new law aimed at improving the quality of higher education via competitive searches; and some of those old cadres who criticize Soros's purported leftism used this law to remain in place. Another irony: tenure was abolished by this Parliament law; and most positions are* de facto *lifetime, albeit badly paid, posts.*

Klaus wants to charge tuition to university students; but he is not eager to allow the growth of other competitive universities. This strange bird of a market-nationalist-etatism offers Czechs the worst mix: uncompetitive state-run institutions with an obligatory tuition cost. There exist solid anti-imperial reasons for protecting a Czech institutional and professorial autonomy from being coopted by western interests. But note that market-nationalism is one of the reasons why Soros's university never took legitimate roots in Prague. By canceling Havel's agreement to pay state rent for the Prague location of The Central European University, *Klaus did his utmost to get rid of Soros. A related reason is that it is not enough to have locals dance around a big bag of money: without sharing accreditation and salaries with Czech institutions and academics, Soros cannot become a Czech entity even with his generous bankroll operation.*

How *Apparatchiki* and Commissars Became Capitalists and Nationalists

The post/Communist nightmare II. One need not unfairly link Havel to the goldrush in a wild eastern frontier, to the nationalist fever, to closed-mindedness. His story—that after 1989 there opens a path to capital markets with a human face—nonetheless echoes Klaus's story about the special calling of central Europeans in transforming Communism into model capitalism. Are these stories the ghosts of a 'third way'? Such ghosts would threaten an offensive analogical nightmare: Havel defends a heresy of moral, democratic capitalism (1989 velvet-idealism), Klaus defends capitalist normalization (post-1989 market-realism). Havel is to Dubček (Prague Spring 1968 socialism with a human face) as Klaus is to Husák (post-1968 normalization).

Are 1968/89 the same story, or is this the end of all narratives? If the former were true, then there would occur a tragic reversal. For some the November velvet turned into gold, for others into a nightmare. (Which post/Communist nightmare should one worry about?) If the latter were true, then the U.S. State Department philosophers and some Czech court philosophers celebrate what Havel had feared most during his dissident years—Fukuyama's end of history and man means the end of all human story. Some faces hide cynical grins, some masks disclose struggles for bare survival. The Black skin of Roma becomes invis-

ible, i.e., bereft of economic rights, citizenship papers. Can velvet faces—not resisting a grin—have truck with such antihumanism? There pivot two ends of theory and practice here! There is the manifest non-ideological, market-liberal, politically pragmatic, even nonsentimental view. And there is a hidden view (the overnight transformation of Communist thieves to respected capitalists or populist-nationalists) which the story about the end of theory legitimates. If a critical theory of this transfiguration of Stalinist logic into capital-logic (were the former always-already participating in the latter?) is blocked, then how is it possible to expose this most successful theft of power and money? (Some in the East characterize this line of questioning as dogmatically left, others among western leftists call it emphatically anti-Communist.)

The story about ends of critical theory and practice does not tell much directly. It sets a laissez-faire *stage for cynical acts in which the theorists of postvelvet normalization serve cynical reason. The lead story covers up how* apparatchiki *and commissars turn into robber barons or nationalists. Michnik unmasks in the velvet of anti-Communists the faces of the walking dead, the souls of Stalinists. One learns to refuse an impostor velvet face masking but a commissar!*[11]

Remembering existential democracy. *Havel's position on markets, politics, and human hearts does not harbor within as much naïve innocence about itself as Brodsky would have us believe. Havel argues already in his 1984 essay, "Politics and Conscience," that the totalitarian logic of the Communist East represents a "convex-mirror" of consumer mass democracies. And in 1978 (PP) he hopes for that posttotalitarian democracy which would resemble neither the established western regimes nor his present nightmare. He envisions a lifeworld on the other side of the nightmare, learning to resist functionalist rationality and the politics of the apparatus. Havel's hope implies Marcuse's and Sartre's suspicions of western commodified lifeworlds. Life beyond* apparatchiki *and technocrats must empower some form of concrete democracy.*

Contrary to Brodsky, Havel does not build his prognosis for the better world on a "self-flattering basis" of the humanism that relies on "illusions" about "global responsibilities." Havel's civility is nourished by thinkers of the absurd, and not by cowboys. He appeals to Kafka's prison anxieties in order to laugh at the power and other privileges he enjoys as a professional politician.[12] *Havel invokes Camus's* Myth of Sisyphus *to exorcise his own political conceit as a victorious intellectual. And he suspects any nationalist justification since its power emerges in the vacuum of a functioning democratic culture.*[13] *In the more recent monograph* Letní přemítání, *he criticizes the dogmatism of the markets. He records differences with Klaus most urgently by objecting that yesterday's bosses laugh at that same worker whose paradise has been postponed on Communist billboards—'for ever and ever, Amen'. Today's delayed or repressively sublimated gratification grants happiness via the new consumer culture industry.*

If this marks legitimate suspicions, how can one draw a straight line from November 17, 1989 to the lead story about restoring a 'normal market economy'? Husák's 'normalization' of Dubček's 1968 reminds us of one sinister story. Should it not be in doubt what 'normal' means under the normalized robbery of the past monopolies? Destalinization requires democratic refusals of such 'noble' normalizations. (Denazification of Germany extends today into an inquiry concerning Nazi loot, stolen Jewish gold, deposited in secret Swiss bank accounts).

A former Prague dissident told me over a cup of coffee that Klaus's market story—perhaps because of the considerable initial success of the coupon privatization, perhaps thanks to Klaus's politics of permanent campaign—has already domesticated the existential democratic narrative of the Velvet Revolution. The two of us, however, agreed that Havel's postsecular humanism allows one to envision a possibility of "existential democracy."[14] *Instead of a nostalgia for the 1989 velvet, or the 1968 Spring, we need to forge coalitions and solidary bonds—with a human face.*

Havel's nightmare about post/Communism becomes intelligible when we distinguish that there are at least two ends of theory and practice, or two stories about 1989. The question is not whether or not x is left or right, or anti/Communist. I could agree with Havel that in a post-Stalinist and post-Cold War climate, it helps to get off these high ideological horses. Why not leave out all words that have become sacred cows (for discredited cowboys)—bereft of anything remotely sacred about them? Perhaps the 'S' and 'C' words have had it! If one is honest, the question our post-1989 lifeworlds share is, how to resist earnestly and critically what the old 'Communist' cadres represent (this comprises what they represent in the U.S. anti-Communist demonology of the Cold War)? When thinking of these deposed regimes, I would consider all items that the most anti-Dubček or anti-Havel, indeed anti-Soros, even anti-Castro, and pro-neoliberal and conservative, forces of the right wing claim that they stand against. And, then, would not one let the very same old cadres right back in, if one were unable to unmask in theory and resist in practice the 'capitalist' robber barons and the political economic theorists who legitimate the story of their new normalization? I plead for a fair immanent critique, measuring with the same rod the robbers of the 'Communist' and of the 'capitalist' normalizations! A liberation from the normalization rhetoric of the NWO may not rest with less. In a democracy-to-come, dissenting velvet faces refuse easy settlements with one-dimensional stories about 1989.

Unmasked democratic faces need not necessarily feel like velvet. Ski-masked faces must not necessarily hide terrorists or commissars. A White face could deceive itself and others about its received colors of innocence. A democratic face could be of other colors than White; it could be covered by a ski mask to boot. Dissenting democratic faces of all colors and trans/genders, masked or not, refuse deception in any form. They haunt us with specters of liberation.

2. Masked Faces in Great Refusal,
Or Why Radical Democracy Today?

Humanity lives in the breast of every one of us, and, as a heart, it prefers the left side. It is necessary to find it there, it is necessary to find ourselves.[15]

✤✤✤

We do not want that others, more or less of the right, more or less of the center, or more or less of the left, decide on our behalf. . . . We do not fight for getting power; we struggle for democracy, liberty, and justice. Our political proposal is the most radical that exists in Mexico (and perhaps in the world, but it is early to say that). It is that radical that the traditional political spectrum (right, center, left, and others of each extreme) criticize us.[16]

✤✤✤

Michnik worries that anti-Communist faces often mask faces of Bolsheviks. Sartre worries that faces of liberals can mask dirty hands of anti-Semites. St. Augustine worries that a key difference between Alexander the Great and a pirate is that the former has a fleet, and is worshiped as an emperor, but the latter operates from a bark, and is snubbed as a robber.[17]

Such worries describe well the post/Communist and real democratic nightmares. The worry does not, however, make all hope for concrete democracy undecidable. Neither wearing a ski mask nor operating with a small fleet proves that one is a robber. Formal democracy proves that it too can legitimate robber barons, basking in their smug faces at the noonday. A ski mask does not make one naturally a fascist (left or right); democracy in peace time proved that it can breed fascists quite well and on its own. For example, the attraction of Buchanan for many U.S. citizens in 1996 has a scary parallel to Germany of the 1930s. When the democratic face becomes a zombie, then must not the dissenting masks hide the faces of radical democrats? A dissident face may go masked—underground— for the sake of greater democracy.

Beyond Augustine's despairing, soberly conservative spiritualism, note the markers of the following difference. First, faces and masks can disclose or hide either laughter or grins. Second, laughter and grins (through both faces and masks) represent two modes of interest here: either dissenting refusals or defiant, pure, exceptional transgressions. And third, the two modes, laughter and grin, dissent and defiance, further differentiate radical democracy from surface, sham democracy.

Laughter and Grins

What distinguishes an emancipatory irony from the political correctness of conservative revolutionaries? Are survivalists funny? Do fascists remember the tragic justice of humor?

Remembering the comic. *When at midnight of January first, 1994, the Zapatista rebels quietly and with local indigenous approval took over several cities in Chiapas, Mexico, Marcos dialed from San Cristobal the headquarters of the Mexican government military chiefs:* "Feliz Año Nuevo, Cabrones!" "Happy New Year, Jerks!"[18]

✦✦✦

At the largest Prague demonstration of the Velvet Revolution about one million people pulled up keys from their pockets and rattled them for the end of the totalitarian regime. Hated rulers escaped their defenestration from the Prague Castle but were locked out from power.

✦✦✦

The Greenpeace movement countered Jacques Chirac's French 1995–96 nuclear tests in the colonized Pacific. In major cities the streets bearing the word 'French' were repostered/renamed as 'The Street of Atomic Blasts'.

✦✦✦

After 1989, Czech students gave a fresh pink coat to the Soviet tank-monument commemorating the 1945 liberation of Prague. The Soviet Embassy was furious. Next day the tank was forced into its military green. By the following morning, the tank was cross-dressed in pink again. In the end this tank-monument to 'liberation' had to be moved elsewhere.

✦✦✦

Jan Palach, the first of the two students who immolated themselves in 1969 protesting the 1968 invasion by the Soviet-bloc armies, was buried at Prague's Olšany. People used to come there to lay flowers, light candles, and place poems or letters. The normalization authorities removed Palach's body to an unknown location. They buried in his grave the body of Marie Jedličková. It is not known whether 'Marie' was a real dead person or a pseudonym for the Communist-regime fear of the dead dissident ghosts. From the 1970s people ignored the dead 'Marie'. They honored this location as Palach's 'empty tomb'. And that it is still today.

✦✦✦

For a long time, this town has existed where the men are Zapatistas, the women are Zapatistas, the kids are Zapatistas, the chickens are Zapatistas, the stones are Zapatistas, everything is Zapatista. And in order to wipe out the Zapatista Army of National Liberation, they will have to wipe this piece of territory from the face of the earth— not just destroy it but erase it completely because there is always the danger from the dead below.[19]

✤ ✤ ✤

Kierkegaard contends that our age fails to distinguish a comic laughter from a grimace. He was cartooned because of the uneven length of his pants; Copenhagen children ridiculed him as Mr. Either/Or. Having become an object of the tabloid, Corsair, *which conflated irony with an agitating mass envy, Kierkegaard sought to demonstrate that fake fun has its own indirect defense in genuine irony. Abusive powers err in overassessing their effectiveness. In confusing relative human ends with absolute, abusive power attracts on itself the wrath of the comic. The tragic comedy first targets, then denudes hated power. (When the powerful and despised ones forget that they too must preside over a toilet, over a pile of shit, their power is stripped down to its bare arse.) The comic invades the incongruity between highminded projects and a human incapacity to sustain them in godlike manner. Laughter in irony and humor mocks a key sociopolitical fact—the stupidity of unjust power. Such power is pitiful; in itself it is never humorous. Humor for Kierkegaard indirectly though communicably marks off other's existential inwardness from its fake impostor. Remembering laughter earnestly can empower liberation.*[20]

✤ ✤ ✤

There is no humor among those fed by envy and ressentiment—moral majorities, religious fundamentalists, dogmatic revolutionaries, survivalists. Forman's film biography of Larry Flynt, the founder of Hustler, *dramatizes the TV-evangelist Jerry Falwell's as well as the U.S. political establishment's utter lack of self-irony and humor. A television comedian, Al Franken, writes a bestselling title:* Rush Limbaugh Is a Big Fat Idiot. *This book, like Forman's flick, is comic not because there is anything morally wrong with being fat or simple or religious. It is the publicly displayed and arrogantly, hatefully served pretense to live God's honest truth that is here exposed as a fat lie, an idiocy, a vapid seriousness. What marks off Forman and Franken or Kafka, Kundera, Havel, and Hašek from excitable hate-speech is the ridicule of another's stupid power through a heightened performance of self-irony. If stupid power were capable of the latter, it would no longer be stupid or ridiculous to others. But envy is neither a source of laughter, nor remembers the tragic justice of irony and humor; envy, like hatred, is a specter from hell, not one of liberation. A conservative revolutionary, parading itself with a certainty of gods, one day becomes comic to others. Those who help us laugh in refusal of tyrants do us a fine service. (There is hope when the TV-nurtured public elevates such 'divine comedies' into Top Ten titles. I disagree with Kundera's* Testaments, *9, that "religion and humor are incompatible"; on the contrary, if there are gods for us, humor is our shared divine nectar.)*

✤✤✤

Remembering the comic II: ends of laughter. When Prague's demon-strators in 1969 greeted the riot police with a chant, "long live the police force!" this unit was dislodged as an aggressive force. The chant cast a disarming, per-haps castrating charm over the phallus. Stupid forces in power do not easily yield to public denuding acts. Chinese and Prague students, bearing flowers to a Communist army or police, were suppressed by riot units; and this may still await students in Burma and Beograd. Empires collapse—as they will—when they become tragically comic, ridiculous, empty.

✤✤✤

A Czech colleague from a prestigious Czech think tank raised the specter of U.S. Political Correctness coming to haunt East Central Europe. Entering a con-versation at a dinner for one distinguished U.S. philosopher, this well-educated Czech suggested: "There is a neo-Stalinist PC brigade taking over democracy in the U.S. and in the academy in particular!" (Kundera, in his Testaments, *31, sub-scribes to this view of 'America' from Europe's self-idolized novelistic shores.) One proof seemed sufficient for this view of multicultural and antiracist debates, i.e., that several U.S. women academics, guests at this dinner, did not find this person's racist and sexist jokes a bit funny. "You see, you are not even free to laugh!"*

✤✤✤

There is a curious law prohibiting in several U.S. states masked individu-als from speaking in public spaces. Using this statute, some progressive groups have brought charges against the KKK whose hooded representative delivered a hate-filled sermon on public TV. One's uncovered face is to guarantee that gen-eral disapproval may deter irresponsible behavior and promote democracy, so the argument goes. Yet cannot one be deceived equally by a pious and clean-shaven face, such as that of a candidate in the New Hampshire 1996 Republican Pri-mary? The deceptive candidate's winning of the primary indicates a yes answer. How different is his appearance on TV from our KKK-hooded comrade? The law does not help us to unmask the face of a respected, Church-going, tax-paying, family-bread-winning, value-loving, homophobically and epidermically chal-

lenged primitive with a pitchfork bent on conquering the barbarians in Washington. Should not such an impostor velvet face be masked by the hood of the Great Wizard of the KKK? The chilling effect of the hood is conjured up by the candidate's grimace and righteous-sounding hate speech-acts.

✦✦✦

Is there a difference, in principle, between the shopkeeper who refuses one day to put the slogan, "Proletarians of all countries unite" into his shop window and a Mayan peasant who one day declares to the Party of the State, "Today we say, Basta Ya!" "Enough!"? Does not each refuse (note that this is not done via excitable hate speech-acts) faces of oppressive power?[21]

These refusals diverge from the populism of left and right fascism. Marx distrusted bursts of enthusiasm in the lumpen proletariat just as Kierkegaard did in the enthusiasm of the crowd. The very same sentiments fuel any populist hate speech. They are syphoned for pseudoproletarian, conservative, national socialist revolutions. These considerations, rather than superficial differences between faces and masks, are intersubjectively verifiable. The oppressed denude self-certain, idiotic gods who grin but who lack irony and humor. The strength of humor empowers the powerless in a godless world. Nietzsche's word, "God is dead,"[22] can be a happy tragic comedy. This comic can become terrifying to the powers that be. A mask, just as a cleanly washed and manicured face, can laugh either for liberation or with a resentful grin.

Refusals and Tantrums

Can one think of dissent and revolution without a cocksure warranty (I intend the antipatriarchal and antiracist allusions), yet meaning it all for real? Can one differentiate fanaticism from fear and trembling? Are one's—our—freedom projects ever certain, exceptional?

Remembering the comic as refusal. *Posters, shouts on October 12, 1992, in Mexico City:* "Colón al Paradón!" "Columbus to the firing squad!" "Discovery is Extermination!"[23]

✦✦✦

[W]hat would be the repercussions for the "EZ" if the true Marcos was unmasked? "We are all Marcos." . . . "Why do you wear that ski mask," a feminine voice called out. "Actually, only the most handsome of us are required to wear them, for our own protection," bantered the Zapatista spokesperson.[24]

✦✦✦

In ancient Mixteca cultures, men put on masks and became beasts, the shape-shifting "nahual" who channel nature's magic. . . . "Hombres sin rostros"—"men without faces"—Marcos calls his compañeros. "What do we look like?" . . . "just look in the mirror. . . ." Will Marcos ever remove his mask and reveal his true identity? "I'm prepared to take off my mask when Mexico takes off its mask. . . ." "Does this mean that Mexico is getting ready for a mass revolution—or a masquerade?"[25]

✛✛✛

In 1968, two forms of resistance to the Soviet invasion occurred: an active, nonviolent, noncooperation campaign (altered street and road signs directed Soviet army units to the W. German border); and performance art fostering resistance bonds and undermining the occupying power.

✛✛✛

Havel and others noted a carnival-like staging of the 1989 Velvet Revolution—though there were no masks involved. Instead of masked actors, striking theaters evolved into living political clubs. Artists and students changed into political actors. A boiler-room attendant became a foreign minister. A poet and a philosophizing playwright was elected the president.

✛✛✛

Kierkegaard's pseudonym, Johannes Climacus (PF), meditates on Socrates's teaching style. Socrates is, for this pseudonym, a radical egalitarian. Socrates lacks the positive vis-à-vis others; teacher and students are equal, and teacher relinquishes all authority. Kierkegaard follows this critical pedagogy. His pseudonyma become masks—not out of fear but to hide the teacher's own person from being set up as an example or a proximate cause of transformation, followership, etc.

The Socratic lesson defines civil society and empowers today's pedagogy of the oppressed, prohibits the icon-worship of revolution, and curbs the cult of parties or leaders. Why continue the masquerade? In real struggle the masks protect from the oppressors. They may serve as ironical-erotic gestures (e.g., Zapatistas are handsome and pretty, vulnerable without masks). The masks mark undiscovered spots of transgendered, transracial beauty. Until liberation—this beauty and truth are deferred by hope. Revolution and leaders never incarnate the sublime.

An erotic dimension visits Kierkegaard's performativity. Note his desire for a liberated singular reader. Eros imbues the poetic beauty and gay carnival atmosphere of today's complex revolutions. Havel and Marcos partake in poetry and eros—without that Jacobinian lyricism unmasked by Kundera. A key to all this is offered by the Socratic Climacus. Masks empower egalitarian relationships among all liberation struggles. Masks help to resist central power figures or a dominant gender or race of revolution. Masks need not hide faces of terror.

Note that while Havel does not veil the velvet face with a ski mask, he veils his political speeches and acts by indirect communication. Alluding to Kafka's Trial, he suggested, early in his first presidency, that he had been uncertain of his own position as a leader in the seat of power. Could he one day wake up in his old prison cell? He warns, one must not be cocksure (hypermasculinely challenged, lacking self-irony)! This is true for revolutionaries and lovers.

Remembering the comic as refusal II: from tantrum to fundamentalism. "EZLN leaders wore ski masks as 'a vaccination against Caudillismo (domination by one leader)'."[26]

✣ ✣ ✣

When in 1995 the Greenpeace ships trespassed into the French nuclear test site at Atol Mururoa, they did not put themselves up as guarantees of world peace. The claim was a modest appeal to check the posture of imperial nations. The French president, Chirac, was unprepared to relinquish a drive to national self-certainty. When this ego-mania becomes even more important than the manifest desire for nuclear security—while damaging international relations and sales of French wines—one witnesses a political tantrum. The Mexican government today finds itself in that emotive state, while accusing Zapatistas, ironically, of being in a "delirium."[27]

✣ ✣ ✣

Abraham was not an armed rebel with a justified cause. He lived in fear and trembling concerning the divine command to sacrifice his son Isaac. There exist today acts of a violent refusal of peace, e.g., between some Israelis and Palestinians. Israeli prime minister, Yitzak Rabin, is shot dead. Lacking Abraham's fear and trembling, forgetting the tradition of Jewish self-irony and humor, there are morally self-righteous settlers on Israel-occupied territories, the religiously smug assassin of Rabin, and the unyielding new Israeli prime minister; their partners are the ruthless Hammas and suicide-bomb missions. Did Abraham excuse himself from all human communities? Could he be called not a father of faith but of every religiously political fanatic? He knew that he might have been quite wrong about the command to sacrifice Isaac. He owned no red telephone to a Party of God or to family values. He never even owned the positive certainty that his own exception was granted—whether by the God of Israel or by that of a fascist-nationalist state.

✣ ✣ ✣

During the normalization years in Czechoslovakia (1970–89) school boys were ordered to cut their long hair. Elementary and high school students were forbidden to wear blue jeans. And neither long hair nor blue jeans were looked upon favorably at the universities. Such prohibitions were to protect civiliza- tional-Communist values against all that western decadence.

Civilizational and family values clashed on the earlobe of Jimmy Hines. In 1992 Jimmy was suspended from an Indiana high school for wearing a gold stud earring. The school board ruled with this monocultural decree: "earrings are female attire. Allowing boys to wear them . . . would open their world to gangs, cults, drugs, homosexuals and rebellion."[28]

During my first return to a prevelvet Czechoslovakia (1988), I visited, with my companion, Prague's National Gallery. We were chastized for behaving immorally (i.e., subverting state values) when my friend played with my earlobe while we viewed some socialist-realist art.

A moral: Fundamentalist, racist, patriarchal, homophobic values are undermined by their comic underside; what appears as their Enemy, or a queer contrast, becomes their undoing. For example, East Europe has preserved since the 1960s and after 1989 more long-haired young men than there are, perhaps were, anywhere else in the West. U.S. high school and college classrooms have today short-haired, cleanly shaven types. The marine or jock hairdo would have satisfied the desired pre-1989 East European aesthetics. We meet skinheads—if to be cleansed, then why not all the way?—as the netherside of an old appa- ratchik *and Aryan aesthetics for the New WhiteMan! They have a scary resem- blance to the poster images for the 1936 Berlin Olympics or the 1950s propa- ganda for building the socialist motherland. We meet in the U.S. rugged long-haired individualists as well as conservative revolutionaries who never tried to be hippies. The length of a person's hair seems as unlikely to be a credi- ble marker of liberation politics as the length of a skirt. Would nowadays one's piercing of ears, noses, eyebrows, tongues, lips, nipples, belly buttons, genitals, etc. transfigure these into feminine or even unnatural body parts? Do body appendages and openings come with one set of instructions for use? Are they like forks, knives, spoons, or rules at the dinner table? Imagine that an extraterres- trial being (or, for example, anyone who learned to use knife and fork according to Old World etiquette) has just landed in the U.S. and is brought to dinner: since many a North-American-born eats with one hand with the other hand sus- pended in his or her crotch, our visitor might seriously consider that erotic play with oneself belongs among mainstream U.S. family and even religious values, that such pleasure is practiced as one's pastime at meals.*

✦ ✦ ✦

Why should one wish to own the positive? Climacus raises this Socratic lesson over and against the misunderstood laughter of his age. A nonphobic erotic dimension becomes available when one realizes that neither truth nor beauty nor love can be had in a private ownership, by assault, or on command. Disciplining the sexed, racialized, queer bodies would thus demand, unfairly, the positive. Absence of positive grounds defines the performance of loving, its masked-disclosed risk. Revolts that take exception from this critical pedagogy tend towards the spirit of a serious, fundamentalist (divine command), phobic certainty. Transgressions must have no truck with a hierarchical exceptionalism, no matter how much our common sense or scholars may conflate the (disappointed) fascist tantrums for the (lost) positive with existential refusals.

Radical and Sham Democracy

Are clowns too weak and refuseniki *too idealist to challenge the NWO? If fascists nowadays attack this very same* ordo, *would not great refusals resemble Sartre's and Michnik's anti-Communist, or Havel's post/Communist nightmares?*

Gathering the fragments of democracy.

To those of you who are wondering if Marcos is homosexual: Marcos is a gay person in San Francisco, a Black person in South Africa, an Asian person in Europe, a Chicano in San Isidro . . . a Palestinian in Israel, an indigenous person in the streets of San Cristobal . . . a Jew in Germany . . . a housewife . . . a peasant without land . . . an unemployed worker . . . and a Zapatista in southeastern Mexico. In other words, Marcos is a human being in this world. Marcos is every untolerated, oppressed, exploited minority that is resisting and saying "enough already!" . . . This is Marcos.[29]

✦✦✦

Of an estimated 100 million indigenous peoples who populated the Western hemisphere from the Arctic to Tierra del Fuego before the Conquest, 40 million resisted the genocide and survive today.[30]

✦✦✦

The National Democratic Convention, held in August 1994 on the Zapatista territory, and The Intercontinental Encounter for Humanity and Against Neoliberalism, held first in April on all five continents and subsequently in Aguascalientes, Chiapas, from 27 July to 3 August 1996, were to empower, organize, and defend the civil expression of a popular sovereignty. These aims do not contravene the Habermasian democratic meaning- and will-formation. They, however, introduce correctives against any rigged consensus. Formal pragmatics alone, while structurally necessary, is insufficient to resist the imperial and one-

sided nature of elections in Mexico or a tilted negotiating table with Mexican business and political powers. Democracy in dissent assures that the popular will is that of the indigenous, not that of the established ruling consensus. The indigenous popular will comprises, e.g., the Revolutionary Women's Law (January 1, 1994).[31] *This popular law makes women equal to men in all civil and military respects. They are responsible for their uncoerced decision about intimacy, marriages, and the number of children they can and will care for. Children and women have rights to nutrition, health care, and education. The bottom line: concrete democracy may have no contract with the faces of oppression. Democracy must not mask terror with painted velvet faces.*

✛✛✛

During the last years the power of money has presented a new mask covering its criminal face. Across the borders, without importing races or colors, the power of money degrades dignities, insults honesties, and assassinates hopes. Renamed as 'Neoliberalism', the historical crime of the concentration of privileges, riches, and impunities, democratizes the misery and hopelessness.[32]

✛✛✛

Gathering the fragments of democracy II: when fascists march against the NWO! "Like Mussolini, Buchanan synthesizes Left- and Right-wing political themes; moreover, like Il Duce, he lards his speeches with military metaphors."[33]

✛✛✛

If Buchanan did not exist, the U.S. politics would likely fashion one. When fascists attack the NWO, they suck on the revolutionary energies of people disaffected with real existing democracy. Comparisons to Vladimir Zhirinovsky or Marković, two East European left-and-right nationalist extremists, is not inappropriate. 'Marcos' attacks the NWO; so do Buchanan and the above-named East European demagogues. 'Marcos' points out the damages of NAFTA, GATT, and corporate globalization, and so do the other three. 'Marcos' and Havel demand more humor in politics, and so do Buchanan and Zhirinovsky—with a smirk and grin. All of them root for the small guy or the nation in the margins. Babies are picked up and kissed as part of a softer TV-image. This is enough to scare me into dreading that Buchanan, Zhirinovsky, Marković, perhaps Perot and Farrakhan, and 'Marcos' are on the same track, and so am I!

✛✛✛

Sham democracy opts for elitist politics at one end and a populist lumpen leftism at the other end. Here feast the worms of right and left fascism in their radical cohabitation. It matters little that the elitist rhetoric resembles a progressive left or even radical thinking. One needs only to study Leni Riefenstahl, "Triumph of the Will," a 1934 propaganda film on Hitler's Nuremberg rallies, or the story of Evita Perrón. A fascist activist can appeal to hungry workers clutching shovels, then with a dose of some monogenealogically cleaned up, symbol-waving spirituality (pagan or Judeo-Christian or Moslem, etc.) turn them into the blood-and-soil soldiers marching for the National-Thing. This face of a democrat hides a bigot; this face of a champion of a proletarian or other minority masks the antisolidary, parochial fundamentalist; this face of a patriot displays the sentiments of the xenophobe and homophobe. At the end of the day, the fascist radical dresses in halloween costumes of a death-dealing revolutionary, stealing winds from the windbags of tired liberals or from those who no longer rely on the general seriality of a voting booth or on the ruling elites to secure even the semblance of formal democracy.

Our born-again spooky radical may reincarnate as either a pro-NAFTA elitist and multinational globalist or an antitrade Ausländer-basher, protectionist, conservative revolutionary. The spooky radical grasps the importance of new social and multicultural movements and the rise of civil society. The deceptive face wears proletarian denims, bears the gun-toting tinge of an antigovernment grudge and ludic anarchism (ready to blow up those hated State Buildings); and it covets family values and church populism (it is for everyone *but Asians, Blacks, gays, Jews, lesbians,* mestizas, Roma, Slavs, *women, etc.).*

A superficial democratic face cannot deceive anyone who manages to strip away its facelift. A spooky radical marches against the new ordo *from racist, xenophobic, fundamentalist, imperial platforms. Genuine dissent opens fora of multicultural democracy. The spooky radical is a seriously White macho—grins at everyone but the pink face. I enlist irony in self-defense against emerging facts of White patriarchy—their anti-Black narcissistic halloween "white masks"!*[34]

Democratic dissent globalizes from below, against the "globalization" which "assassinates and forgets" by conceiving "a new world war" for "a new division of the world."[35] *Elitism and immiseration must be fought by empowering a universally coalitional politics with local solidarity, each in popular sovereignty. I think that civil society can generate radical democracy even in the global Information Age. If cyberspace is becoming a new "workerless" workplace and "virtual" corporation, then political and economic democracy must be fought likewise on the field of these service and leisure sectors of the Information Age revolution.*[36]

✦✦✦

From East Central Europe to Chiapas, movements of civil society gather a dangerous memory of liberation. From their jungle, the forgotten voices of civil society speak on-line:

I write you in order that together we remember that we have
a memory, in order to remember that we should remember. . . .
For the powerful our silence would be its wish. By being silent
we would die, without words we would not exist. We struggle to
speak against forgetting, against death, for the memory and for life.
We struggle out of the fear to die the death of forgetting. . . .
It is not the armaments that give us radicality; it is the new
politics which we propose and in which we are engaged with thou-
sands of men and women in Mexico and in the world: a construction of a new political practice which does not seek a takeover of
power but rather an organization of society.[37]

✤ ✤ ✤

*Cyberpunks and hackers of the world's workerless corporations unite! Let
us inveigh not 'ludically' against but with help from the labor-saving technologies and world communication!*

*Cyberspace can be a mask of sorts. One can appear as a Santo or a Zorro;
one can wear jewelry on any body part, embody trans/gender roles, become a
shapeshifting nahual animal. One enters a queer space known from the texts and
art of magical realism. It may be objected that cyberspace replaces an existential
concretion of human faces with a keyboard-and-screen anonymity, with promis-
cuity bereft of intimate eros. As I have noted in the excursus in chapter 4, neither
faces nor masks carry direct markers of earnest humor or genuine interiority.
There are shiny velvets and fake democracies—both at times masking what is not
there—i.e., democracy with a human face. The objection should be a Marcusean
critique of this deficiency in real existing social forms of life and not a pseudo-Hei-
deggerian invective against new technologies. Masks remain just as much a mys-
tery as faces since one must meet self and others critically. Cyberspace, just like a
book, public city, village square, only promises a face-to-face (globally local)
encounter. Gathering democratic possibilities, even from fragments, is a task.*

*The specter of this promise with its deliberate task demands the public own-
ership of information. (For example, the Internet got Chiapas and Beograd on-line
even though the ruling Party tried to close down the information highway. Such
a close-down would have hurt its economy tied to the world markets.) The specter
raises the imperative of a reduced work-week and an increase of pure play time.
(Marcuse envisions a pacified nature replacing the artificial scarcity induced by
protectionism, downsizing, xenophobia. Without a reduced work-week for more
people, the global economy can burst with the unemployed who cannot buy what
technologies make possible.) The specter is the need for an equitable distribution
of cost-savings earned due to new technologies. (Ludic responses to modernity—
whether popular, conservative, or postmodern—are regressive. Health, culture,
education seem to be obvious candidates for public uses of surplus.)*

An Excursus on the Violence of Faces and Masks

Violence is not intended by democratic dissent. Sham democracy as a social form of life masks both the overt and structural forms of violence. What can one intend by overcoming this mask—even when it requires, besides ringing one's key chain, wearing a rebel mask?

I think that Ash rightly agrees with 'Václav I' (Havel) rather than 'Václav II' (Klaus) that the critical role of public and independent intellectuals in the NWO does not and must not vanish with the fall of the Berlin Wall. All kinds of folks were dismantling the Wall; other bricks and walls have gone up since. Klaus's story about the end of dissent is just as precocious as is Fukuyama's about the end of history or S. Huntington's about the entrenched spheres of power. While I take Klaus to be more sophisticated than either Limbaugh or the neoliberal (read: conservative) rhetoric of Gingrich's U.S. Congress; still, his anti-intellectualism drags the Czech Republic to this sad common denominator. Klaus flagrantly disregards the role of civil society and culture in sustaining genuine democracy. How does this arrogance repair the damage to culture and critical education by the past Communist regime?[38]

I, too, am suspicious (pace Ash's Kantian retort to Plato's ideally just polity run by philosopher-kings) that Havel's second presidency might become a "velvet cage," wherein "his image and voice as an intellectual have become blurred." While Havel insists against Klaus on keeping the distinction between politicians and intellectuals, he wants their fruitful collaboration. He desires this to the point of integrating intellectual criticism within the confines of political institutions. In Havel's view intellectuals should at times serve as public servants. Ash worries that Havel confuses the roles of intellectual critique and partisan politics, even though Havel's confusion lies at the very opposite pole from Klaus.[39]

Yet, Ash, like many others in Havel's homeland and abroad, does not credit a third possibility for which Havel gropes. Havel holds that politics need not be a dirty business—neither that it is nor that it is not.[40] I understand him to be raising a critical, ethicopolitical, not naïve, hope. He does not offer a positivist fact about politics but counsels radical honesty for intellectuals and politicians. Since some in each group are often dirty, the task is not forging an additive or hyphenated intellectual-professional role but rather achieving a collaborative transformation within both. Democratic dissent must be launched independently of oppressive powers that be. 'Václav I' needs this form of critical distance from faces of oppression as much as 'Václav II'. Transgressive dissent must invigorate not only the outskirts of urban and jungle rebellions but also the very hearts of democratic institutions and professional politics.

This type of collaboration between dissent and professional politics has a long tradition in the U.S.—from the Civil War to civil, women's, and gay rights struggles, to the most recent mobilization of Jesse Jackson's Rainbow Coalition, to five hundred years of anti-Columbian resistance. There is a time when dissent operates marginally, there is a time when dissent affects our institutions from within. I believe this to be Havel's point. Being a longstanding student of the U.S. counterculture, Havel's contribution lies in searching for ways of integrating both dimensions of dissent in a coalition between cultural critique and professional politics.

In my unlikely comparisons, 'Marcos', the leader of the Chiapas post-1989 movement against oppressive Mexican policies, is like Havel both a poet and a dissident. He stands both outside and inside professional politics, acts both as an independent critical intellectual and a facilitator for a new democratic constitution and transitional government. Marcos opted for a ski mask over a velvet face. As the August 1994 National Democratic Convention and the 1996 Encounter for Humanity and Against Neoliberalism demonstrated, armed resistance is not an aim, not even the preferred means to justice, liberty, and democracy. Ultimately, the radically democratic logic of nonviolence prevails: the goal is to have the rebel army disappear in the process of genuine democratic transition. The task is to activate the self-determination of local communities and of national and global civil societies.

The following examples are overlooked by the conservative-neoliberal and the left-liberal alike: a dissident-intellectual, who exercises an independent critical role in empowering civil society to organize itself against an oppressive regime; and a politician-intellectual, who plays a professional role as a leader of the rebel army and speaks for emerging political institutions. Regardless of one's preferences for the textuality/texture of velvet faces or ski masks—each represents an antifascist, indeed, radically democratic aesthetics of resistance.[41]

My hope is that individuals and communities learn how to keep such complex positions honest against any dirty business. One must relinquish the cycles of declining into vanguard or elitist leadership or into ideologically deployed mythical narratives of community. This insight marks one salutary outcome of postmodern correctives within social theory, and of self-limiting revolutions in 1989 and after. Relinquish the cult of the group or personality as well as uncritical myths of origins—the food of Jacobins, Stalinists, and ethnic cleansers; integrate the needs for recognition and economic justice as these emerge within dissenting and democratic civil society! Havel, in Central European contexts of political and market liberalism, must resist moral elitism (dissidents are not a vanguard, and they do not always know best) or irrelevance (whether as a professional politician or a critical intellectual). One can sustain self-development of emancipated individuals and groups only in alliance with other democratic projects.

Self-corrective processes of learning may benefit from meditating jointly on the existential and political aesthetics of refusals by velvet faces and ski masks. Havel and Marcos push the outer bounds of imagining as well as instantiating existential and democratic dissent in the need for multicultural enlightenment and recognition; for broad coalitions and more intimate communal solidarity; for civil and uncivil rebellions or velvet and belligerent revolutions; and for hope, clowning, and refusal in the NWO. Havel and Marcos, just as King or Gandhi and Fanon, from the velvet and belligerent perspectives of dissent and rebellion, represent distinct though humanly fallible correctives to previous forms of struggle. Benefits of learning outweigh the risks of appealing to historically finite examples of individual human beings and their contingent social contexts. Neither of these instantiations—in failure or success—frees any one of us from the difficulty of beginnings.[42]

The first dramatic acts of the Zapatistas in January 1994 were to free prisoners, open a free city market of goods for the poor, and use the Banamex money for the common needs, such as health and education. There were no executions, no cleansing, no retribution. Some have named the New Year 1994 in Chiapas a "poem." The rebellion was armed, yet with remarkable self-restraint. No vanguard leadership was set up. The command lines were democratically sensitive to gender and race inclusion. Later that year, EZLN declared the National Democratic Convention to be its decision-making body. The convention called for basic human needs. "Those were the demands of the long night of 500 years."[43] This belligerence did not call for war. Mexican military responded and still does to their requests with aerial bombing and brutal retaliation.

We find students offering flowers to the riot police both in 1968 and 1989, yet in each epochal moment, students are brutally beaten, and they continue to be beaten from Tiananmen Square to Beograd to Burma.[44] The 1989 Velvet Revolution is praised for its self-restraining character. Students hoped for a more humane world. Communist rulers were not hanged on street lamps as in Hungary of 1956, they were largely let go with generous pensions. This fact made many suspicious later of dirty business. The lustration law restricts the old cadres from holding high political posts; they have been free to make money as they wish. Havel, just as Marcos, released numerous prisoners in the first revolutionary act. Past injustices were to be redressed in courts. Yet old nomenklatura and secret agents retaliate with shady business practices and corruption at all levels. Nationalist leaders sow envy and hatred.

My point is simple: a nonviolent change can occur in the contexts where preceding structural or other violence does not make active, nonviolent, civil disobedience impossible. Civil society acts mostly civil, but at other times resorts to uncivil rebellions. Tragic comedy in each case dramatizes the violent demise of gods with clay feet. It is not, then, Fanon or Malcolm X or Marcos who first introduce violence. Even the logic of nonviolence produces the 'violence' of radical social change. Thus, it is really not Havel or Martin Luther King, Jr. or even Mahatma Gandhi who offer here such an entirely different approach. The nature of undoing domination produces structural violence in each regard as a tragic and indeed comic effect. Decolonization solicits at times both tragedy and comedy. If the hated regime would not have left the Prague Castle in 1989, Havel *would not have apologized, I am convinced, had people lost patience and thrown the bastards out of the Prague Castle windows. In Prague, defenestration, too, is a cherished tradition, and not every thrown-out government has the luck to land on a pile of cow shit, or slide down with the forgiving tears of the velvet face.*

Being for nonviolent change, do we *have a right to counsel the sufferers of total violence to wait, to restrain themselves? King argued to the contrary against some U.S. White Southern clergymen as well as for the end to Vietnam War. Heaven and justice cannot wait! I repeat, the logic of nonviolence is not a logic of inaction. And even a well-addressed loving can produce violent effects in those who love not. Malcolm X's biting irony and his "by any means necessary" mark the refusals restrained from their self-seriousness but not held back from immiseration. I read both violent and nonviolent options (in contexts of the tragic comedy of undoing domination) as two forms of the same demand for radical democracy and hope now.*

Conclusions: The Dangerous Memory of Radical Democracy with a Human Face

I am not saying that everything is the same—before or after 1989, on both sides of the Atlantic. Yet certain affinities remain frightening. One can witness red-black coalitions in the post-Soviet life as much as, e.g., in Slovakia, ex-Yugoslavia, and U.S. politics. Nationalists or disappointed democrats espousing family or moral values, these are the name brands on the rise in the Euro-American world order. The academy is not immune to these political shifts. The sins that brought me on the red carpet before the Communist and secret-service establishments in 1977 are the sins which can block professional approval for anyone in the U.S. today. These are the sins of thinking and speaking critically against unholy alliances between power and ignorance. Note that this ignorance need not be simply stupid; it is willed and educated ignorance for the sake of keeping domination. If one ironizes its reactionary epistemic and political correctness, refusing to submit to enticements of secure existence in a secure institution, this merits total punishment. Ironizing or refusing to take part in abusive power is a capital offense. Offended, in despair willing itself to be, power goes for the jugular and the head. It attacks critical thought, an integrity of dissent, the sanity of wanting to stand apart.

A solidary memory of those in struggle against any willfully ignorant and despairing power, joined across historical times and spaces, can perhaps save our age from moving within vicious circles. I have learned that one cannot emigrate from the state socialist capitalism of the Soviets to a corporate jungle of private capital as a solution to this problem; and one faces extinction in trying to demo-cratically transform an existing totalitarian society. Russian escapist artists might have been right that we need to imagine another than this unjust world. One cannot get to that other world by ordinary means such as immigration or exchanging one set of robber barons with another set.

I return to the dangerous memory of struggling against totality. It may help in recognizing a willful ignorant power in its many shapes. I would want to join my memory, laughter, and active forgetting with those of others. I travel in these essays along but a few specters of refusals today—great refusals of misrecognition by dissenting individuals, democratic multiculturalists, critical post/modern social theorists, those who hope against hope, the communities in resistance, and others. Some refusals take on Marcos's poetic, ironically sad ski mask; others exchange ignorant power for a velvet face. Ski masks and velvet faces carry dangerous memories of liberation; I cannot repress my memory of either of them.

Perhaps more people will come to remember across borders and experiences, reversing the long cycles of decline, and within a single generational self-correcting process of learning. This intensified, existentially material, and historical time and space of struggle, too, raises specters of liberation, of its globalization from below. The memory of those who join together such concrete experiences of struggle against domination seems dangerous insofar as it refuses to accept the historical judgment of declining cycles, but rather practices critical thought, liberating action, and hope against hope. To refuse in this sense—in season or out, across historical places and times—means to take the risk of incurring capital offense in its unexpected, unlikely, or obviously painful forms. To refuse in this great yet always vulnerably coalitional sense (may we hope for solidary links?) means to ultimately bar any straying from the task of refusals and all merely reactive, in the end declining changes in regimes and forms of life. Do we have today escape passages other than the ones discovered by the escapist artist-revolutionaries—in order to imagine another than this unjust world and introduce this invention into concrete existence?

9

RADICAL MULTICULTURAL
AND EXISTENTIAL DEMOCRACY

The issue . . . is whether there is sufficient commonality in our sufferings . . . hopes . . . joys and accomplishments, to allow our . . . forging a concrete universal. . . . [W]e must move from . . . universality via conceptual strategies to universality in the form of democratically based shared unity as an existential project.

—Lucius T. Outlaw, *On Race and Philosophy*

✤ ✤ ✤

[W]hat Eastern Europe needs most now is . . . the establishment of an 'alienated' state that . . . would be embodying no particular ethnic community's dream. . . . Otherwise, the vision depicted by Margaret Atwood in her *The Handmaid's Tale*, . . . where a moral-majority fundamentalism reigns, will come closer to being realized in Eastern Europe than in the United States itself.

—Slavoj Žižek, "Eastern Europe's Republics of Gilead"

✤ ✤ ✤

[I]f nationalism is not made explicit, if it is not enriched and deepened by a very rapid transformation into a consciousness of social and political needs, in other words into humanism, it leads up a blind alley.

—Frantz Fanon, *Wretched of the Earth*

✤ ✤ ✤

Against the international of terror, which represents neoliberalism, we should raise an international of hope. Unity across the borders, languages, colors, cultures, sexes, strategies, and thoughts—of all who prefer a living humanity. . . . Hope is this rebellion which refuses conformism and defeat.

—Marcos, "Contra el Neoliberalismo y por la Humanidad" (1996)

✤ ✤ ✤

I began by suggesting that it was to Habermas's credit that he reintroduced existential topics into the architectonic of critical social theory. I argued, in turn, that a formal communications theory of multicultural recognition, while procedurally necessary, was not sufficient to safeguard its regulative ideality of concrete justice. At the end of the day, I remain suspicious of the hope for *Europe's second chance* which is not sought for the sake of those without hope, i.e., those who struggle and theorize from non-Eurocentric shores. The other of the idea of 'Europe' might not need to designate exclusively other geographies or non-Euro-American peoples. Indeed, barbarians are once more at Rome's gate: Euro-Americans come from many shores. If so, then hope of remaking the NWO emerges with a new multicultural enlightenment rather than by theorizing how to buttress *our* fortress 'Europe' against the perceived clash of civilizations. Proper names of monogenealogical dominant cultures no longer define best what can be a Euro-American, *our*, any future. It is the dispossessed and marginalized at the street corners and fields of all major civilizations for whose sake hoping for second chances still makes any sense. Marcuse is forever right, social "revolution would be liberating only if it were carried by the nonrepressive forces stirring in the existing society. The proposition is no more—and no less—than a hope." The existentially material concerns from the margins, raised increasingly in each preceding chapter, occasion a 'crisis' even within Habermas's more concrete communications theory. Perhaps the personal copy of *One-Dimensional Man*, which Marcuse dedicated to Habermas with the words, "to the hope of those without hope," was a prophetic gesture of the unfinished, urgent task today.[1]

I theorized that democratic projects of liberation learn to resist ethnic cleansing in regional and global forms. The communitarian and liberal variants of modern nation-states are inadequate insofar as they fuel local or imperial nationalisms of conquest. A refigured multicultural category of the singular universal marks the vanishing point of democratic dissent against the faces of oppression. Unlike emphatic communitarianism and possessive individualism, or unified and dual-systems theories, this category subverts homogenization and anomic fragmentation haunting nation-states as well as a certain politics of identity and difference.

In my concluding reflections, I wish to take advantage of Cornel West's insight and demand that liberation projects usher in *existential democracy*. West adopts existential terms in order to portray engaged intellectuals. What makes this orientation inviting for my argument is his interpretation of existential categories under the sociopolitical and activist perspective. He calls for "*the existential imperative* to institutionalize critiques of illegitimate authority and arbitrary uses of power; a bestowal of dignity . . . on the ordinary lives . . . ; and an experimental form of life." He unites personal and political dimensions of struggle—two joint dimensions constituted in and constitutive of "existential democracy." West's project draws at once on existential and social phenomenology, the early Frankfurt School of critical social theory, and pragmatist race theory. This proposal, whose suggestive image promises much, remains programmatic in West's preface and undeveloped throughout his work. There is nothing to prevent me from taking his program to its conclusions.[2]

Existential democracy proffers alternatives to fragmenting particularism and closed communitarianism. West's use of existential terms to speak of political culture neither confirms voluntarism nor privileges fate. The existential attitude emerges intersubjectively in already problematized traditions. Critical ontology if harnessed into social theory aims at "a democratic mode of being in the world inseparable from democratic ways of life and ways of struggle." This aim recalls Marcos and Havel, Marcuse and Fanon, and in the latter two, Sartre's preface to Fanon's *Wretched of the Earth*, even if each faces different situations. Existential democracy solicits concrete multicultural sociality with a human face: that is, relation to self and others beyond possessive liberal humanism or its convex mirror in anonymous antihumanism.[3]

Existential democracy becomes for West one's prophetic praxis, "a self-critical and self-corrective enterprise." Such praxis operates at the crossroad of particularism and universalism. For example, in the Americas, radical praxis must draw on Euro-American and New World African modernities, not just the idea or the heading of 'Europe'. What is the ethicopolitical possibility of this crossroad between the particular and the universal? How can one develop a critical theory and praxis of existential democracy? Accepting this challenge, I expand West's *existential imperative*. I am prompted along by hooks's "movement beyond accepted boundaries," or by Lugones's (following Anzaldúa) "transgression of rigid conceptual boundaries" to "the borderdwelling self." This imperative invokes the existentially concrete, multidimensional theory and praxis of resistance.[4]

How can one join difference (multicultural, multiracial, multigender) and identity (national or racial or gender) of any kind? Can one sustain difference in solidarity? Is identity formation possible while open to difference? What individual and group identities fit with democracy which is becoming multicultural and existential? Are not transgression and agency—each both singular and social—two moves at odds with one another? Can one maintain both?

West inscribes the double movement into existential imperative. The imperative demands that *we* transgress borders or limits of conventional identities and received traditions. It requires that *we* transform the sites of transgressions into singularly and socially responsible and institutional agencies. Dissent harnesses transgression dialectically, it inhabits responsible and institutional agencies of democratic change. The heart of this liberation project is the specter of multicultural and existential democracy *qua* anticolonial coalition and postcolonial solidarity.

I want to lay my cards open once more at the outset: I do not derive the categories of anti- and postcoloniality from the first-world intellectuals. True, one finds an academic postcolonial discourse—such as Bhabha's literary metaphors of hybridity—serving ongoing coalitional struggles. Here comes to mind also Lugones's adoption of *mestizaje* border identity in terms of plural (rather than Anglo dual or hyphenated) cultural personality. Yet articulating postcoloniality from within hybrid texts and regions does not necessarily deliver *us* to the anticolonial coalition of Young's politics of difference or the postcolonial solidarity of West's existential democracy. Unless extended in the way that, e.g., Zapatistas formed their coalitions and declared solidarity with other struggles, border identities might not shed all anti-Black racism or other xenophobias. The anti-Black color-line in the U.S. provides the color-horizon of racial oppression long before Californians passed the anti-immigrant Proposition 187 or the anti-welfare rights Proposition 209. A *mestiza* or a ladino can pass as 'White' not only within native American populations but also in anti-Black contexts. Anti- and postcoloniality *qua* resistance must be more thorough. One must not be blind to the globally local, flexibly porous borders of the multinational economy. This is the hybrid politics of identity and difference practiced by neocolonialism as it emerges within the rhetoric of the NWO. Any jargon of hybridity which is blind to these realities becomes a mere convex mirror for the flexible accumulation of profit and power. Global corporations have good uses for the production of textual undecidables. They market the "ideology of postcolonialism"—to cannibalize multicultural worlds, conserve power, reap profit.[5]

Anti- and postcoloniality *qua* dissent and resistance may learn again from Marcuse's great refusals. With this (now pluralized) category of liberation, I invoke once more a need for an existentially concrete, critical post/modern social theory conceived in multidimensional practices of dissent and resistance. I attend first to a particularity of historical refusals where the liberation and the conquest of difference and identity originate. Next, I set off the homogenizing agencies of modern nation-states from the open agencies of multilevel global coalitions and solidarities. Viable democracies, I argue in turn, admit global and regional dissent. I conclude that the viable politics of identity and difference may jointly empower liberation struggles of the immiserated.

When their stories become partners in radical multicultural and existential democracy, globally and locally, they no longer need exclusionary myths to sustain cultures and civilizations from decline or clashes deployed as invisible universal hands under their noses or behind their backs.

1. Liberation and Conquest

In transgressing the borders of identity formation today, we confront the particularly modern issue of nationalism. Nationalism appeals with a promise of immediate deliverance to the marginalized lives of colonized individuals and groups. This promise empowers regional cultures and modern national consciousness. Yet the nationalist principle of integration inscribes political self-determination into a highly contentious interplay between the politics of difference and identity. I agree with Balibar that, politically, we should distinguish nationalisms of liberation from those of conquest, but acknowledge formal symmetries between them because of the aporia shared by both.[6] Social movements safeguard their legitimation by fighting oppressive hierarchies, imperial hegemonies, exclusions. Integrations that become conquests can no longer be legitimate, even if they deploy the same nationalist narratives of liberation.

✤ ✤ ✤

Take East Central European nationally carried revolutions against the Soviet ethnic cleansing, homogenizing internationalism, imperial politics, and exploitative state economy. Not long after 1989, liberation carnivals imperceptibly flipped into resentful gasps of domination. Giroux notes: "We are now witnessing in the United States (and in Europe) the emergence of a new racism and politics of cultural difference expressed both in the reconfiguration of the relationship between Otherness and difference . . . and meaning and the politics of representation." "Old racism" used colonial language to justify slavery universally, "new racism" uses identity politics and multiculturalism to grow intolerant of multiracial and multigender polity—abroad and at home.[7]

A cultural intolerance of minority groups at home—Africans, gays, children, women, disabled, Jews, Moslems, Roma, Asians—collaborates with economic spoils extracted worldwide. Both distort the politics of emancipatory identity. They aid the conservative uses of diversity and multiculturalism to reconstruct the political correctness of White domination of the West. First, a victorious movement privileges its regional difference from others; later, it elevates this difference into a positive nationalist identity and a political principle of social integration. The nationalist principle of self-determination, by becoming a vehicle of social integration, imposes its own identity on difference. The hierarchies and homogeneity masked before by imperial universality are now exchanged for those of tribalized particular differences.

✤ ✤ ✤

I asked at the outset of this study whether or not a universalist opposition to exclusive particularisms delivers us from regional clashes of identity and difference? This is an appropriate question if it is noted that the political economy of liberal or even internationalist paradigms of universalism often becomes partial to dominant groups. The political and economic side-effects of this partiality *within* universalism are the global marginalization of minority groups. Historical versions of universalism hide cultural, ethnic, gender, class, and race biases. Universalism is hardly ever as universal as it claims to be. Even inter*nationalism*—Soviet or corporate—viewed by the oppressed within it, hides its partiality but from a gullible or smug onlooker. Regional movements of liberation strip down this not-so-noble (liberal?) lie.

Integrating Critical Race Theory within Critical Social Theory

In his contribution to the 1983 issue of *Praxis International* devoted to the critique of critical theory, Outlaw interrogates the Enlightenment universalism. He proposes to radicalize liberal democratic theory through the racial and ethnic identity politics of difference. Key are his two serious doubts: (1) "that nationalist (and, by extension, racial/ethnic, cultural) individualities are destroyed by the universality of capitalism"; (2) that they "will disappear with the achievement of socialism-communism." In both, he inveighs against the colonial and "paternalistic condescension" of a "master *discourse* of liberation" held by mainstream critical theory. He expands class analysis to comprise other related but nonreducible dimensions of liberation, such as racial and gender struggles.[8]

Note that Marković contributed an essay to the same volume. The sad irony is that while confirming Outlaw's two doubts, Marković has been one of the key intellectual ideologues of the Serbian nationalism of conquest under Beograd's government of Slobodan Milošević. Movements of liberation (e.g., in the antiracist, nationalist struggle of American or South African Blacks) and movements of conquest (e.g., in the ethnic cleansing of Bosnian Moslems by Bosnian Serbs) make strange bedfellows in the remakings of the NWO. Unholy alliances of liberation and conquest within nationalism occasion crises at the heart of social theory and its 'praxis international'. West and hooks grope for new paths in a postnational breaking of bread: "Cornel, it seems to me that one of the issues that keeps coming up in our critique of Black neonationalism and renewed Black liberation struggle is the evocation of icons without a sense of what kind of struggle must take place in order to carry out the mission of those icons."[9]

From the foregoing, I identify a dual problem in critical social theory. One cannot ignore the multiple faces of racial, ethnic, national, sexual, or gender liberation struggles. Yet one cannot ignore the multiple faces of oppression by racist nationalism, ethnocentrism, patriarchy, sexism, heterosexism of dominant cultures. Is this aporia an effect of some double bind, an undecidability in the very human or multicultural civilizational identity formation itself?

An excursus on deconstructive and existential or social undecidability. Leitch nicely defines deconstructive practices: "the purpose of the deconstructor is to produce . . . *undecidables* and to track their insistent operations through the text." This strategy is to invert hierarchies and oppositions. It "functions as a disorganizing structural force that invisibly inhabits and *transgresses* the opposition." The literary production of undecidables renders the responsibility of the critic "diminished, if not destroyed." Deconstructive undecidability cohabitates with ir/responsibility. "Without enduring human selves and intentions, without self-determination and reasonable motives, and without awareness of consequences and self-conscious deliberation, there can be no responsibility." Deconstruction is an ir/responsible site which opens "carnivalesque" possibilities; insisting on decidable norms would be ideological.[10]

Following Ebert, McLaren distinguishes between "ludic" and "resistance" postmodernism. 'Ludic' postmodernism produces undecidabilities in texts in which one intervenes aesthetically. 'Resistance' interventions expand textual productions into a critical social theory and practice. Read Leitch's helpful descriptions with the aid of McLaren's intervention: "Ludic postmodernism generally focuses on the fabulous combinatory potential of signs in the production of meaning and occupies itself with a reality that is constituted by the continual playfulness of the signifier and the heterogeneity of differences." *Resistance postmodernism* joins a critical social theory. "Resistance postmodernism brings to ludic critique a form of materialist intervention since it is not solely based on a textual theory of difference but rather on one that is social and historical. . . . [D]ifference is politicized by being situated *in* real social and historical conflicts rather than simply textual or semiotic contradictions." Just as Martin's material transformation of deconstruction proffers new possibilities for postmodern social theory, McLaren sets off *two sorts of undecidabilities*:

Resistance postmodernism does not abandon the undecidability or contingency of the social altogether; rather, the undecidability of history is understood as related to class struggle, the institutional-ization of asymmetrical relations of power and privilege, and the way historical accounts are contested by different groups.

Finally, McLaren appeals to difference not as a mere rhetorical space, a time lag: "Resistance postmodernism takes into account both the macropolitical level of structural organization [macroscopic evidence generated from innumerable singular sites of suffering in the NWO] and the micropolitical level of different and contradictory manifestations of oppression [e.g., body-politics or power in Foucault] as a means of analyzing global relations of oppression."[11]

Textual plays can empower a critical theory as resistance and politics of signification:

differences are produced according to the ideological production and reception of cultural signs. . . . "Signs are neither eternally predetermined nor pan-historically undecidable: they are rather 'decided' or rendered as 'undecidable' in the moment of social conflicts."[12]

From this brief detour, I may draw a 'no' to my query whether or not double binds as undecidable movements of liberation/conquest reside in identity formation itself. Resistance pedagogy roots cultural studies in existentially material struggles, thereby intervening in the political economy of textual and public-policy productions. Unmasking the White U.S. academic and foreign-policy plays on diversity need not debunk new coalitions among *critical post/modern social theorists and activists* in postcolonial literature and liberation struggles. It requires, however, grasping a Jamesonian insight that post/modern clashes of civilizations are produced by economic and social forms of life of late state socialism and capitalism, not by an inevitable core in human evolution. Insisting on an omnipresence of intertextual/global social undecidabilities implicates theorists and politicians who actively earn money by producing them in a *locus classicus* where Marx located German ideology and the political economy of his age.[13]

Singular universals as democratically shared multicultural and existential projects. Outlaw's two doubts are expressed in a critique of "the false universality of European and European-descendant world views." He, like West, situates critical theory and praxis in their historical contexts. Yet more emphatically than West and hooks, he suggests that the liberation movements of African Americans might require adopting "the struggle from the level of a group, i.e. ethnic (or nationalistic . . .) position." Outlaw, thus, considers the "group-centered politics" as strategically necessary, given the American, if not worldwide, macroscopic evidence of anti-Black racism. A strategically oppositional identity politics provides "the only viable position" for emancipatory group solidarity. Such a claim problematizes any liberal talk of "a social democracy based on pluralistic integration" of Black people. Significantly, Outlaw concedes that the realization of human needs requires political coalitions, even solidary bonds with others involved in global economic and political struggles. A regionally or civilizationally centered identity politics and "invidious ethnocentrism" must open up to a global liberation.[14]

Outlaw's insights become even more timely after the revolutionary changes of 1989 when many a critical theorist more resembles "confused liberal, bourgeois assimilationists" than radical democrats: "Too many leftists, like so very many liberals, have become entrapped by an extreme reaction to racism that views the correction to racism as involving *no* reference to national character." I wish to affirm two key implications of this analysis. First, "*a full appropriation of particularities*" and national self-interest historically empower concrete human beings and specific liberation struggles of groups marginalized as groups. Together with economic sources of oppression, "[t]heory must reflect the reality of the (relative) independence of race and ethnicity as positive determinants of historical human existence, along with other factors."[15]

Second, these "*social-natural kinds*" of racial, not racist, ethnic, not "invidiously ethnocentric," identity formations are deployed as a "third path" to empower an oppositional politics of difference as well as historically meaningful communities of meaning. Yet in themselves, these kinds disclose necessary, not sufficient, sociopolitical and economic alternatives. Global, anti-imperial concerns refigure the politics of the singular universal—democratically shared, multicultural and multigendered, existential projects of identity-in-difference. This politics, in order not to become a vapidly liberal multicultural diversity merely for market exports or strategic foreign policy, must join all oppressed and immiserated humanity. Globally flexible radical multicultural democracies could foster coalitions, invite solidarities, and collaborate across racial, ethnic, national, sexual, and gender lines of every otherwise legitimate difference or even strategic separation.[16]

I can sum up this concrete dialectic of the particular and the universal within social movements as follows: the plural character of social struggles curbs any identity politics from becoming one world-order driving for conquest. The emancipatory character of identity politics transforms the strategically employed transgressive politics of difference into democratic dissent, political coalitions, and even solidary bonds on behalf of social change.[17]

✦✦✦

The U.S. and European debate on multiculturalism is hijacked by the conservative and liberal as well as ludic agendas of economically dominant societies. It is difficult to apply 'multiculturalism' with some consistent and critical distance from these often dubious uses. McLaren indicates useful and invidious senses of its use. "A focus on the material and global relations of oppression can help us to avoid reducing the 'problem' of multiculturalism to simply one of attitudes and temperament or, in the case of the academy, to a case of textual disagreement and discourse wars." White hegemonic ubiquity can continue well under the veneer of diversity. Companies put up a public multicultural face, support the World Championship in soccer, and we even find their ads in the most distant parts of the world. There is, however, no real care for economically destitute people. Corporate executives and academic administrators introduce the jargon of diversity into their programs without having any genuine presence of marginalized groups and cultures in their ranks, classrooms, and curricula. They institutionalize, through liberal committees on diversity, romantic desires for the exotic; at the same time, they worry about Blacks and women taking over corporations. Both this desire and fear are all in the skewed imaginary; but anti-immigrant hysteria and minority bashing (e.g., anti-gay legislation in many U.S. states) operate in real life. Meanwhile the mainstream remains distant from marginalized cultures in the same way as do the vacation industry and tourists in their winter escapes to the Caribbean. McLaren unmasks this as a humanist anti-humanism of "conservative and liberal multiculturalism." The love of diversity "is really about the politics of assimilation because both assume that we really do live in a common egalitarian culture." Vapid exoticism emerges when we do not live with difference in our midst.[18]

✣ ✣ ✣

From Outlaw's critical race challenge to critical social theorists and from healthy suspicions of nationalisms of conquest, I may learn that whether one wholly separates or assimilates the questions of race, gender, and class, the result is a historically inadequate social analysis and short-circuited liberation. Outlaw nuances anthropological and class categories of free productive praxis to encompass "real, historical, *concrete* persons" in a multidimensionality of their emancipatory struggles. Critical theorists cannot relegate the social-existential categories that matter in the life-world, the body-matters of race and gender, to pseudoanalytic dustbins reserved for nonphilosophers in our departments. Outlaw's conclusion is unequivocal: "critical theory will have to be significantly revised if it is to face, for example, racial or ethnic identity in a fashion more adequate than an afterthought or as an *ad hoc* or strategic concession."[19]

What is a critical *we*? McLaren intimates a multicultural and existential democracy:

Attempting to abandon all vestiges of the dominant culture in the struggle for identity can lead to a futile search for premodern roots that, in turn, leads to a narrow nationalism. . . . [R]efusing to decolonize one's identity in the midst of the prevailing ideological and cultural hegemony can serve as a capitulation to assimilation and the loss of forms of critical historical agency.[20]

Is identity without identification—without assimilating all difference—possible? If yes, can one learn to resist (from within and without and across) intact communitarian borders and imperial fortresses? (I have serious doubts that these can prevent cycles of civilizational declines or their clashes.) Is democratic and economic justice possible in coalitions if not in solidarity with the politically significant differences of race, sex, and gender? The questions of political compatibility between difference and identity must be posed if *we*, as critical theorists and activists, are to empower genuinely multidimensional democracy in local and global human affairs. Postnational multiculture cannot possibly mean erasing from our lifeworlds all national, ethnic, racial, sexual, gender differences. Postnational identity cannot identify with the prevalent, mostly western, White, heterosexual, male notions of universality. Multicultural enlightenment requires anticolonial coalitions to craft its concrete singular universals. Further, one may not form democratic justice without safeguarding the material—cultural, existential, economic—conditions of its attendant postcolonial solidarity. Minimally, anticolonial praxis of liberation learns to resist new conquests.

2. Coalition and Solidarity

The categories of multicultural differences and concrete identity are incompatible insofar as we insist on preserving the sovereignty of nation-states as the most optimal political units of anticolonial struggle and postcolonial integration. They are incompatible insofar as we set difference and identity undialectically—within the homogenizing universalized or homogenizing particularized understanding of the *we*. They are incompatible if we mean by the multicultural and the democratic an innocuous diversity rather than an existentially concrete polity.

We can form a coalitional and solidary 'we' critically. Individual and group identities then become historical agents of democratic change. Identities foster differences without fragmenting or disempowering agency, differences empower specific identities without homogenizing them. Multivalent dissent tries to hold broad anticolonial coalitions. Aiming at radical multicultural and existential democracy, relational agency promotes postcolonial global solidarity.

A Dialectic of the Universal and the
Particular in Critical Social Theory

Balibar problematizes the received universalisms and particularisms. Consider the nation-state: it invokes universalisms and particularisms, often one over against the other, and mostly with contradictory and destructive outcomes. Balibar disputes a commonly held view that racism, nationalism, or patriarchy represent "an *extreme* form of particularisms" in opposition to universal ideals. He thinks that exclusionary categories can variously underpin universalisms. They "divide the universality of the human species into exclusive transhistorical groups which are supposed to be separated by *essential* differences." The differences are "understood and institutionalized as hierarchical differences."[21]

While modern nation-states invent and maintain particular identities over against other groups, "nationalism as an ideology is *also universalistic*." Nation-states play out variations on the messianic dogma—their world-historical specialness. An idea of "the elect" nation incarnates a dubious version of anything *we* should envision in singular universals. The elect is

immediately universal in its singularity: in fact it has to *empty* this singularity of any particularistic feature or mode of being and *fill* it with universalistic elements, usually a secularized version of the great universalistic religions, with their messianic notion of human brotherhood.[22]

❖ ❖ ❖

*It is easy to discern the two-faced character of modern elect nation-states, e.g., the superpowers. The U.S. vital national interests become embedded in a special policing mission for the world (preserving democracy by building up the Guatemala military, mining the Nicaragua Harbors, starving out Cuba, invading Panama, Iraq, Haiti). The manifest destiny of the defunct Soviet Empire lives and dies with saving acts of inter*nationalist *interventions (in Poland, Hungary, Czechoslovakia, Afghanistan, or an internal colonization of non-Russians). This two-faced character of nation-states is coterminous with the five-hundred-year conquest of the New World. La Conquista proceeded along the Comtean indigenist imaginary (echoed by Latin American leaders, reflected in attempts to pacify the Chiapas rebellion by the outgoing Mexican president Salinas, and even among some liberal intellectuals, like Carlos Fuentes in the group San Angel) of mainstreaming the 'backward' traditions into a modern nation. Established nation-states retain this Janus-face in spite of emancipatory nationalisms which foster constitutional democratic polities. Note a Fukuyama-like claim by Hans Magnus Enzensberger:*

I do not believe for a moment in this alleged explosion of national-ism. Nineteenth-century nationalism arose from the need to con-struct modern nations, and alongside all the unpleasant chauvinist qualities it had a constructive aspect. That was the age to which we owe our democratic systems and constitutions. Contemporary neo-nationalism, on the other hand, has no constructive aspect what-ever. . . . To my mind this has more to do with bad folklore tradi-tions, than with matters of substance.[23]

One grasps even better what is at issue by studying the relation between nation-states and colonized first peoples. For example, 'Indian', ethnicity, and nation-state are emerging concepts. They become transformed in an indigenist or assimilationist continuum from uncontacted or "just-contacted" 'Indian' cul-tures (e.g., Uru-eu-wau-wau) to self-organized ethnicities responding differently to colonizing national identity formations (e.g., Nicaraguan Miskitu, the Pana-manian Kuna, or Ecuadorian Shuar federation), to ladino-run and White-domi-nated nation-states. Both assimilationist and differentiating models of multicul-tural life emerge from these contacts. Liberal or conservative multiculturalism relies on a version of assimilation. This ideal may lead to a total disappearance of a culture, or it can admit "folklorization" and "exoticization" of 'diversity' by the colonizing nation-state (a Guatemalan tourist promotion of 'native' Mayan dresses was imposed on the indigenous by the colonists). The same cultural ele-ments may, however, support critical traditionalism and even resistance multi-culturalism. Resisting cultures grow both through a hermeneutics of recovery and a critical invention of traditions. Resistance may appeal to post/modern ele-ments of global life. Oppressed traditions form coalitions, intervene in tyranni-cal nation-states, enter global public spaces of solidarity (as seen in the role of Witnesses for Peace or international accompaniments in Central America); since 1789 they struggle for human and civil rights and, in the twentieth century with help of the U.N. charter, for national self-determination.[24]

What if one employed what McLaren, Giroux, or hooks (pace Freire) call transgressive, border, critical pedagogies—resisting the fake multicultural world order of buttressed fundamentalist civilizations incapable of comprehending the sense of existing 'multiculturally'? McLaren wants these to facilitate "nomadic forms of individual and collective agency that open up new assemblages of desire and modes of being-in-the-world." Transgressive agency recovers a second level of immediacy of uncontacted cultures. In a mediated multicultural immediacy, one resists enclosed fortresses of empty diversity. I call this a second or mediated immediacy since in it cultures have passed through an undoing of the colonial nation-state. To this end, McLaren adopts a pedagogical practice of giving "white students a sense of their own identity as an emergent ethnicity." The pedagogi-cal task is to denaturalize Whiteness, its "Euroimperial aesthetics." Whiteness is ironized as an "epidermically challenged" state of cultural and political exis-

*tence. It has never been some mainstream horizon of the indigenist imaginary.²⁵
Nation-states have in their modern origins signed a Faustian (or Jacobin,
Stalinist, National Socialist, NWO?) pact among markets, culture, and conquest. Along with problematizing Whiteness (following Sandoval, Anzaldúa,
Freire, or Minh-ha), McLaren advocates a border pedagogy of tactical subjectivities and resistance cultures. A tactical agency provides affirmative consciousness for those who are excluded, live between borders or with mestizaje identity.
McLaren sums up very well with a statement on the multiculturally and existentially democratic coalitions between pedagogies of critical traditionalism and
critical post/modern social theory.*

The sites of our identity within postmodernity are various; as seekers of liberation, we recognize the heterogeneous character of our
inscription into colonial texts of history and cultural discourses of
empire: New sites of agency are erupting at the borderlines of cultural instability, in the transgressive act of re-membering, and
through the disavowal and refashioning of consciousness in the in-
between spaces of cultural negotiation and translation.²⁶

✣ ✣ ✣

The nation-state incarnates in history a concrete aporia. The singularity of elect nations takes on an unmediated, immediately universal
character. National agency homogenizes and closets the concrete singularity of differences in its restricted quarters. Balibar identifies this
enforced space as racist supplements to nationalism. Racism meets the
need for recognition with unfair hierarchies, socioeconomic inequities, or
scapegoating within its borders. The "status groups" emerge on bent
backs of new pariahs. By anchoring an elected nation in the immediacy
of a cultural trait or event, there haunts our justice "*the ideal nation* inside
the nation." An abstractly singular universal contravenes an existentially
material singular universal.²⁷

It gets worse! Balibar indicts racism not as one of the particularized
aberrations of nationalism. Racism *is* a universalism, and vice versa; it is
"a symptom of the contradiction between particularism and universalism
which *primordially* affects nationalism" (emphasis added). Racism
inscribes a "double-bind" into nationalist (individual or group) identity
claims. One cannot easily draw "a clear-cut *line of demarcation* between
universalism and racism," or, as Outlaw wishes, between liberationist-
nationalist-racialist or "anti-invidious ethnocentrism" and conquering-
racist or "invidious ethnocentrism." Left to their enjoyments of particularity or universality, uncritical identity-formations tend to internally
codetermine each other.²⁸

If this is so, then it should be silly to try to overcome racist or sexist universalism by celebrating particular differences over against identity politics. The issue is not opting for either universalism or particularism—indeed, racism takes the form of the immediate, homogenizing, hence false singular universal. Racism is inscribed into new nationalist and fundamentalist wars of Fukuyama's end of history. The existentially material issue of liberation today is the 'how' of both universalism and particularism. Is either possible without immiseration, patriarchy, and racism? "Perhaps such a transformation would have to start with a different way of handling such categories as, precisely, the 'universal', 'difference', the 'singular'."[29]

The margin of error for socially integrating a noninvidious nationalism, ethnocentrism, or racialism within the NWO is thin. Once people get marching to icons incited by passions alone, while excluding this or that name on the living quilt against oppression, and without broadly democratic coalitional and solidary means and ends, who can stop the runaway train? Why not evoke that hope of which a human heart filled with rage against injustice, hatred of misery, scorn of stupid power, and love for a concrete face is capable? This calls for a multiple emergent 'we' on the other side of those marginalizing identity bonds which are built on exclusionary differences. Must we resign to a world order with identity politics shaped by the clashes among dominant fundamentalist civilizations—multiculturalism for global export and liberal foreign policy, and conservative assimilative cultures for home rule?[30]

If *we* are to invoke at all the notion of community with regionally global solidary bonds, or at least preserve existential competencies for coalitional politics, then *we* need to learn from those who hunger for justice together across differences. They have already refused, from within, particular historical universals of immediate racist or chauvinist communities, solidarities, coalitions. In groping for concrete democracy, *we* cannot, therefore, rely on the intimacy of nationalist or village or neighborhood or pub bonding alone to know how not to become closed fortresses. *We* need others than *us* to stop us from that folly. And *we* must not be blind to the post-1989 pan-European or North American imperial-racist nationalism. If distorted social identities enliven particular states and universally determine the NWO, it is hard to distinguish nationalisms of liberation (patriotism rallied against oppression) from nationalisms of conquest (nationalism of victors defining social integration). Balibar doubts as much:

I have never found any means to draw the line of demarcation between 'patriotism' and 'nationalism', or if you prefer between clean, moderate, defensive nationalism which only aims at preserving an identity, and dirty, excessive and aggressive nationalism which leads to imperialist policies or to internal oppression of ethnic minorities.[31]

If there have never been modern nations without nationalism, if Balibar is right that today there are but nation-states, then forming a critical 'we' necessitates giving up the very idea that ethnie-, race, national, or gender difference alone could ever integrate itself *qua* anticolonial coalition and postcolonial solidarity. Identity and difference are emerging concepts. They are at times modern fictions by which institutions—such as the military, prisons, churches, schools—discipline individuals within their frontiers. The success of the modern nation-state can be measured by the degree of creating what Balibar calls "a fictitious ethnicity." This is never an accomplished deed. For that one may thank the interplay between race and class, or gender and class, or race and gender. Nationalism has never created what it promises by its messianism—social equality for all national citizens. Nationalism presupposes some economic surplus of inferior groups within its borders. One can never be sufficiently patriotic to overcome tensions between the needs for intimate community and the need for a fresh supply of unpatriotic scapegoats. Balibar names racism, in Derridean terms, a supplement or excess of "nationalism *within* nationalism itself." The racist *"supernationalism"* constitutes a particular *limpieza de sangre* and a universal manifest destiny. "There is no intrinsic end to this process: the excess does not suppress the contradiction, it merely displaces it."[32]

A Dialectic of Coalition and Solidarity

I return to Outlaw's argument for integrating race and class analyses of oppression into a "multinational movement." He speculates about the achieved goal under three possible options for this integration: (1) "an open, democratic, pluralistic society"; (2) "a federation of semiautonomous republics of nationalities"; and (3) "separate sovereign states of nationalities."[33]

Outlaw's qualified 'yes' to the Black solidarities of liberation presupposes a critique of the Euro-American anti-Black solidarities of conquest. It is important to note that precisely as a critical social theorist, he attacks the "liberal-democratic, socialist, or communist principles of universality and equality in the midst of the domination of political, economic, and cultural life by a particular race and/or ethnie(s)." He invigorates the political significance of Du Bois's claim for "The Conservation of Races" and ethnie-based communal bonds: they are pace setters of struggles against racially based economic oppression. "'Difference', rather than similarity, has become a significant basis of political mobilization." Outlaw's social integration of race and class analyses admits to adopting resistance postmodernism and multiculturalism and requires rejection of ludic postmodernism, abstract liberalism, and uncritical traditionalism.[34]

Outlaw defends a strategic use of the politics of difference. This move really deploys a multicultural transgressive agency and a strategic politics of identity. We meet here a dialectic which joins the politics of identity and difference against homogenizing universalisms of the liberal nation-state and against any type of imperial internationalism.

> Individuals are necessary, but they are neither sufficient nor self-sufficing. . . . Whether or not an individual can enjoy a relatively unrestricted and flourishing life is tied to the well-being of the group; the well-being of the group requires concerted action predicated on self-valorization within the context of a shared identity without succumbing to chauvinism.[35]

Outlaw's integration of race and class meets Balibar's concerns halfway. Outlaw argues for the "democratically 'multi-cultural'" goal of this strategy. He is mindful of the dubiousness of some of his earlier intellectual sources in Yugoslavia and the Soviet Union. There emerge today unholy red-black alliances between the left and right nationalists of conquest. It is understandable that he wants to nurture racial and ethnic differences, "while preserving and enhancing social and intellectual life without sacrificing political unity in the process." This dual requirement for "a revised notion of democracy" is to preserve existentially communicative modern individuals in multicultural ethnic and racial "group-based cultures" which integrate the individual.[36]

Beyond strategic resistances to oppression, ethnie- or race-based communal bonds play for Outlaw positive social roles in democracy-to-come. Treated as "*social-natural kinds*," they steer the culturally integrative dynamism of human evolution. The proposal I raise is not to opt for individuals or communal bonds at the expense of one or the other: each category must be rendered as critical and existentially material. A question for liberation is, which or whose *social-natural kind* shall we adopt and which or whose shall we jettison? My query does not arise from insipid social constructivism, which rightly bothers Outlaw (he views racial bonds as just as real as anyone's fears of stepping in front of a runaway bus, and buses are socially constructed). Answering what or who shall I or *we* be/come, one may not rely on individualization through socialization *as such*. Social-natural performatives of liberation are existential matters for critical social theorists and activists.[37]

One can grasp now more eagerly the import of West's call for existential democracy. Both multicultural coalitions and solidarities (local and global) are compromised by one-dimensional universalist orders. Balibar warns forcefully against racist universalism within particularism. One cannot abandon universalizing either. Social struggle must be (and, indeed, they are) waged from both sides at once. Outlaw helps us to reiterate this dual requirement. Liberationists fail if they reproduce in "a nationalist 'heaven'" new "class divisions." Existential democracy, if it is to be just multiculturally and materially, ought to build from a certain politics of difference and identity but without posing the following false either-or: either race or gender or class. Overcoming gender apartheid or racist nation-states cannot legitimate other cleansing of sexual or "racial or ethnic distinctions." Straight and lesbian women's strategic separation from patriarchy is halfhearted when ignoring within its ranks the specific struggles by women of color. Gay men's liberation is half-baked if replicating the identity structures of a patriarchal or racist "right to fuck" in relation to vulnerable gays. Antiracist Black nationalists gain Pyrrhic in-house victories if they admit any identity structures of White hypermasculinity into their communities.[38]

✤ ✤ ✤

The North American workers' solidarity, if separated from Mexican or East European workers' solidarity, and when severed from coalitions with antiracist and antipatriarchal solidarities in the U.S. and worldwide, supplements incomplete unities with exclusionary undertones. Local trade unions offer a shortlived victory in opposing the immiserating effects of global trade agreements. "NAFTA is a death sentence for the indigenous people."[39] Nationalisms of liberation can flip into conquest, and local social movements may fail to break down other apartheids. Such local movements can become ineffective and self-destructive, and play into the hands of the planetary corporate conquest. The artificial scarcity of full-time jobs with health and pension benefits becomes the means for the global economic recovery. The jobless economic recovery and the growth of profitable, cheap-labor prison industries provide cover-ups for the new slavery in existing democracies. This is not to criticize the local movements as such, on the contrary. The problem lies with certain academic theories, which limit social analysis to local narratives alone, and with unliberated social forms of life, which such theories may justify. The indigenous, e.g., in Chiapas, express a global solidarity and form coalitions with other movements across multiple lines of struggle. They see it as urgent to oppose the key false universal of the NWO: the monetary internationalism and multiculturalism of the corporate raids. One learns here to refuse false particulars of racist and sexist difference. They supplement individual and group identities and feed new false universals. One learns from those in struggle, rather than from academic discourses on identity and differ-

ence, how to project concrete imaginary universals. Interactive universals are projected from local sites of dissent yet globally. Only thus they break the boundaries which prevent solidary agencies of struggling social groups from joining in broader coalitions across all borders.

✦✦✦

When analyses of political economy are joined with other multiple faces of oppression, there arises Outlaw's possibility of "a multinational movement" for a democracy across the lines of difference and identity.[40] Blurring such lines turns liberation into the conquests of marginalized difference or marginalized identity by dominant identity. Fragmentation into formal diversity or ludic local and civilizational multiculturalism poses dangers to marginalized identity and difference. The critical theory and praxis of democracy require dissenting individuals and resisting groups capable of anticolonial coalition and postcolonial solidarity. This competence is formed by refusing all injustice. Oppressions split apart have a poorer chance to undo dominating identity than if interlocked in coalitional or solidary bonds. By interlocking them, *our* struggles already inhabit the loci of radically democratic singular universals to come.

3. Dissent and Democracy

It would be helpful to get still more down to earth about the liberation project of radical multicultural and existential democracy. I enlist help from Marcuse and Fanon. Both care in ways not lost on dissenting individuals and communities in resistance. This care kindles existential interventions in critical post/modern social theory by a new generation of thinkers who translate concrete philosophy into coalitions and solidarity with the immiserated.

The young Marcuse recorded such pathos in an existential variant of Critical Theory:

> At the end of his life journey Kierkegaard recognized and seized the public sphere . . . as the essential sphere of effective action. . . . [H]e went, in the Socratic sense of this activity, into the street: wrote article after article in a daily newspaper, gave out pamphlets, pressed his entire struggle in the decisiveness of the historical moment. This struggle in the public sphere . . . was much more directed in all acuteness at a concrete movement of contemporary human beings, aimed at a "genuine" change of human existence, and his attacks and demands were directed steadily at concrete ways and tasks of this

existence, holding the possibilities of achievement of the moment in full view. Only when one grasps how much Kierkegaard, in the fulfillment of his concrete philosophizing, came upon the urgent moment of a real decision, upon a true movement and transformation of contemporary existence, only then can one understand the sharpness of his attack, the agitational violence of his public performance, the sought out clash with the representative personalities of the public, the revolutionary concretion of his demands (such as quitting the State Church).[41]

Read Marcuse's existentially material critical social theory along with Fanon:

The colonized . . . who [write] for . . . [colonized] people ought to use the past with the intention of opening the future, as an invitation to action and a basis for hope. But to ensure that hope and to give it form, . . . [one] must take part in action and throw . . . [one]self body and soul into the national struggle. You may speak about everything under the sun; but when you decide to speak of that unique thing in . . . [human] life that is represented by the fact of opening up new horizons, by bringing light to your own country, and by raising yourself and your people to their feet, then you must collaborate on the physical plane.[42]

Is not there an internal link between the agitational violence of a public existential performance and decolonization? "[D]ecolonization is always a violent phenomenon." Concrete democracy *qua* anticolonial and postcolonial attitude incarnates, then, a concrete material phenomenon of "the replacing of a certain 'species' of men by another 'species' of men."[43]

An Excursus, Or: A Letter On Antihumanism

I agree with Bhabha's rejection of "the natural(ized), unifying discourse of 'nation', 'peoples', or authentic 'folk' tradition." I share the view that cultures and traditions are the "transnational and translational" strategies necessary for survival. Yet I make my rejoinder with the following nuance: an existentially multicultural humanism partakes in/arises from resistances by the oppressed; it parts from ludic textual plays of abstractly antihumanist postcoloniality.[44]

Marcuse and Fanon grasp that decolonization means the death of Man. Insurgent literature portrays 'Man' as a patriarchal and epidermically challenged colonial desire of masters. One may distinguish from *their* deaths other antihumanist celebrations—the death of the last man and the end of the subject. To wit, those who celebrate an empty set may still live in a bad faith of anti-Black racism or Man's hypermasculinity. Gordon harkens to Kierkegaard, Sartre, and Dostoyevsky to unmask the latter carnival as that of the living dead. One could fare worse than to let the dead bury the dead! Fanon cannot console *us* even with Habermas's good (?) faith in Europe's second chance! "Leave this Europe where they are never done talking of Man, yet murder men everywhere they find them, at the corner of every one of their own streets, in all the corners of the globe." From a post-Husserlian Prague, Gordon conjures up a new Fanonian "Crisis of European Man."[45]

As an existential activist and revolutionary, Fanon does not throw out the human baby with the dirty water of Europe's inhuman humanism. European antihumanism has a racist underside. Why else would the 'Europe' after the death of European Man prescind from *all* humanism? Since when does historical Europe—an antihuman humanist monster of Columbus, Auschwitz, Gulag, Hiroshima—define humanity? After the colonial conquests by western moderns, who gains from relegating the human face to antihumanist postmodern textuality?

Decolonization never takes place unnoticed, for it influences individuals and modifies them fundamentally. It transforms spectators crushed with their inessentiality into privileged actors. . . . It brings a natural rhythm into existence, introduced by new men, and with it *a new language and a new humanity. Decolonization is the veritable creation of new men.*[46]

As if co-writing Fanon's text, Marcuse sounds rare hope for "a human universe without exploitation and toil." The rarity of such hope makes it ring hollow in the oligopolies of the West. It echoes the exhausted, at best liberal, imagination of some postmodern and critical social theorists. Yet it empowers those imaginative escapists and democratic *refuseniki* who speak today, e.g., from the Lacandón jungle. Mentioning hope threatens a rupture, "the historical break in the continuum of domination—as expressive of the needs of a new type of man." A postracist, postpatriarchal, postcolonial solidarity—it would sustain democracy as an imagined, invented, embodied new *social-natural kind*—requires dissent from a "conservative continuum of needs," from the very socialized "biological foundation" of exclusionary and commodity relations. A Marcusean performative *body politics* dissents from socialized racist, sexist, commodified sensitivity; "but such rupture can be envisaged only in a revolution . . . which, by virtue of this 'biological' foundation, would have the chance of turning quantitative technical progress into qualitatively different ways of life."[47] Marcuse's transgressive agency raises a specter of a type of man with a different sensitivity as well as consciousness: men who would speak a different language, have different gestures, follow different impulses; men who have developed an instinctual barrier against cruelty, brutality, ugliness.[48]

Following Derrida, Bhabha raises an important question: "How does the deconstruction of the 'sign', the emphasis on indeterminism in cultural and political judgment, transform our sense of the 'subject' of culture and the historical agent of change?" Derrida in writings on Marx *de facto* emerges as a resistance postmodernist; Bhabha tilts towards the ludic pole of the U.S. postmodern scene. While not supporting S. Huntington's strategic global multiculturalism, he echoes the Fukuyamaesque neoliberalism of Lyotard's grand end of "grand narratives":

If we contest the "grand narratives," then what alternative temporalities do we create to articulate the differential (Jameson), contrapuntal (Said), interruptive (Spivak) historicities of race, gender, class, nation within a growing transnational culture? Do we need to rethink the terms in which we conceive of community, citizenship, nationality, and the ethics of social affiliation?[49]

I cannot agree more that critical thinkers should refigure the terms in which they conceive of community, citizenship, nationality, and the ethics of social affiliation. Bhabha sharpens the key question I very much want to have discussed: "How does agency come to be specified and individuated, outside the discourses of individualism?" He specifies a new individuation as "the interrogative agency" or "as a position that is an effect of the 'intersubjective': contiguous with the social and yet contingent." Subject-positions (they are questions on the outside of discourses of individualism, holism, teleology) "produce a subversive strategy of subaltern agency that negotiates its own authority through a process of iterative 'unpicking' and incommensurable, insurgent relinking." Refusing the Cartesian quest for certainty, Bhabha opts for a "genealogy of postcolonial agency"—"the individuation of the agent occurs in a moment of displacement."[50]

Many converge today with Bhabha on the famous insight into "subaltern agency," or with what McLaren names a hybrid "third space." Some invoke this discovery while struggling with Hegel, others have sought agency as a 'third way' or 'path'. Note Kierkegaard's complex definition of self as a post-Cartesian performative third or a posited relation that relates itself to itself: cultural as well as religious identity is conceived in existentially social and humanist terms as situated yet constructed or invented, never transparently given. Even Habermas shows that critical theory and praxis cannot rely on the philosophy of subject conceived of as unencumbered atom existing prior to linguistic-social grammars. One begins existentially and theoretically in intersubjective practices of communicative action. Bhabha spends precious time deconstructing a straw "libertarian or freefloating" agency, a notion which since Descartes no critical post/modernist but some die-hard rationalists would seriously defend.[51]

I do not grasp why a genealogy of agency is a postcolonial phenomenon, why the latter would be a "threat to agency." The phenomenon Bhabha describes is not by definition postmodern—as if nobody at least since the nineteenth century had thought of a situated and historical agency. Further, this "threat" is not in itself postcolonial. There exist pernicious colonial threats to agents; First World transgressions and specters do not always empower critical and postcolonial struggles to boot. Finally, the genealogy described by Bhabha precludes a Cartesian or Robinson Crusoe-like agency, but not situated, responsible, and liberation praxis.[52]

I resonate with Bhabha's, Lyotard's, or even S. Huntington's desires to decenter western hegemony. I have serious doubts that literary allusions to an agency (i) "outside the sentence"; (ii) realized as "the time-lag"; (iii) "without a cause"; and (iv) "'outside' the author," proffer that (v) "transgressive agency" or "antagonistic agency" or (vi) "postcolonial agency" which empowers or even interests the wretched of the earth. I doubt this in spite of McLaren's recourse to Bhabha for critical border pedagogies and transgressive agency. I doubt it despite finding Bhabha's position open to Derrida's *Specters* and despite his gesturing toward Fanon.[53]

Let me sum up my reasons. Derrida parts with the U.S. postmodern academy when he intimates that deconstruction was always already in an alliance with the needs of the wretched of the earth. Whether his allusions are genuine or not does not interest me in this conversation; quite the contrary, by opting to take Derrida earnestly, I prohibit myself from placing him antagonistically to Sartre's or Marcuse's alliances with Fanon. The needs of the wretched are not always those of the academy, however transgressive, hybrid, or subaltern the languages it employs. The wretched of the earth must speak with a face in our sentences, not be celebrated as an outside margin. They must invade our time, not remain a gap in it. They do struggle for a cause, even if the First World academy might have lost the sense of its cause. And they author a more just life, even if western civilization has tired of authoring itself responsibly. Bhabha's metaphoric nicely grafts the language of transgressivity onto a postcolonial agenda. Will this agenda do more than decenter itself from an intact center (it is S. Huntington's foreign-policy advice for the post–Cold War 'multicultural' world)? Does not it exoticize perpetual margins, their time-lags, their subaltern lives? Does not it spare its own positionality from specters of deconstruction, from the wrath of a post-colonial genealogy to come? Gordon leaves us with no such hesitation when he links this evasion in the Sartrean-Fanonian parlance (his Fanon being ostensibly different from Bhabha's Fanon) to bad faith.[54]

Forgetting and Remembering—
Great Refusals of the Cycles of Decline

I wish to employ the Marcusean dialectic to think through trans-gressive agency and democratic dissent. How can *we* differentiate the liberating specters of the new languages and new humans of existential democracy from the ghostly specters of the drunks of purges, fascist aesthetics, mass lobotomy, ethnic cleansing, etc.?

✦✦✦

At least two styles of renaming resurfaced in a post-1989 Europe. Somebody played a great joke on Czech and Slovak people—or only to infuriate them more—and designed shortly before November 1989 a new hundred-koruna banknote with the image of Klement Gottwald, the hated first Communist premier. This banknote is now a rare item. When these notes were in circulation, people wrote all kinds of names under Gottwald's stare. Often his eyes had two holes gaping out. This green hundred-koruna bill became a public space of popular creativity. Stores refused to honor the currency, as if to proclaim the politics and the economy of the regime dead. And I recall how useless was my 1988 map of Prague already in December 1989. The name of Gottwald vanished from the subway station on the C line of Prague Metro and from many other streets and squares. Even the city named after him was renamed with the speed of light.

After the November events, popular competitions—spontaneous 'truth commissions' on one's robbed past—to replace hated old symbols took place. Overnight names sprang up like late winter flowers on the street corners, bridges, public houses, squares. For weeks suggestions were pasted over those from previous days only to stabilize with the most heartfelt choice. In a carnival atmosphere and at a public performance, Havel later institutionalized hundreds of these new names which won contests. For Havel names and stories shape memory and identities. Words descending from tyrannies become dead slogans, mere ciphers, not-so-noble lies of state guardians, an imposed rewriting of living stories. Giving places and history back their genius loci and solidarity is, then, both a dramatic and existential act, both an ethical and political danger posed by past memory. Renaming enacts the future by dangerous remembering, by a publicly performed choice of the present, by joyous forgetting of a tortured past, so that we *may begin.*[55]

Not all and everywhere is well with forgetting or memory. We are familiar with the clips on the evening TV news, showing the removal of the super-man, godlike sculptures of Lenin. Kundera tells us in his Book *that these Lenins were the flowers of forgetting planted in cement all over the Soviet empire. But do we know the new gods with clay human feet who took Lenin's place? That anyone should become a human divinity is a problem elucidated well in Sartre's description of the human desire to be God, in Camus's desire that none of us, rebels in solidarity, shall become one, as well as in Marx's critique of money as a visible pimp-god. Ignoring these leftists (Kierkegaard decried that Christ was smuggled out from Christendom, and this is obviously true of Marx in Marxdom), the State Party nominated itself to be the new priesthood presiding over Lenin's revolution and its* ens causa sui. *The Party promoted secular myths and rituals for socialist baby-citizens, for socialist marriages, for socialist afterlife, for internationalist military conquests, for the growing of crops . . . you name it. The State employed secular clergy who invented new sacred aesthetics, architecture, sculptures, symbols, names, and who performed the rituals and imparted blessings. So what do we make of the desire that today something or someone should take the place of this secular sacral?*

One day the Square of the National Uprising against the Nazis became in one city a Hlinka square and in another a street adorned with Rev. Tiso's bust and in still another a square with Bandera's sculpture. Hlinka, Tiso, Bandera— these are the old nationalist gods of clerofascism, they are worshipped by today's 'Paper Heads'. I witnessed the flags of the Third Reich on the streets of Frankfurt for the first time when West Germans, still not unified in a new nation-state, won the World Championship in soccer. We know now that in the footsteps of these symbols march skinheads attacking Turks in Germany and Roma throughout the East. What follows are the demands that the few Jews who resettled in Ukraine and Russia or Slovakia and Poland pack up or face a new pogrom. What follows are pillage, rape, and cruel genocide justified by that insecure Greater Serbia or Mother Russia. In 1492 this type of conquest was carried out in the name of the Cross—on the backs of the Jews expelled from Spain along with Moslems and later on the backs of enslaved Native Americans and Africans. Creative renaming, that we need; the issue is which are the new *languages that deliver us to genuine democracy? Which are the specters of liberation, which are the specters of living hell?*

✦✦✦

Marcuse describes the high points of 1968 in Paris and Berkeley and those of civil rights marches in the North American South. One of his 1969 sketches captures futuristically a dangerous memory of Prague's Velvet Revolution on November 17, 1989. The text provides a caption for the Prague photo by Pavel Štecha. Although the photo records a protest twenty years later than Marcuse's caption, and a protest against that other state capitalism misnamed socialism to boot, it marks a genuine, so often betrayed, groping for a new life in each situation:

> The ingression of the aesthetic into the political also appears at the other pole of the rebellion against society of affluent capitalism, among the nonconformist youth. Here, too, the reversal of meaning, driven to the point of open contradiction: giving flowers to the police, "flower power"—the redefinition and very negation of the sense of "power"; the erotic belligerency in the songs of protest; the sensuousness of long hair, of the body unsoiled by plastic cleanliness.[56]

Like Fanon, Marcuse gropes for a new sensibility, "a new *language* to define and communicate the 'values' (language in the wider sense which includes words, images, gestures, tones)." There is no guarantee now for the future career of uttered and written words, even those written on this page. No symbol of achieved liberation (e.g., red flag or institutionalized languages of inclusion or pierced body) succeeds to carry liberation to others on its own without renewed alliances with the wretched of the earth, still among us, who communicate their pain today. Remembering and repeating one's beginnings forward (i.e., futuristically with dangerous memory) might allow hope to live now, might resist the historical, reactive cycles of decline.[57]

To shake up the conformity of western affluence, an alliance must be global and across identity interests in order to stay alert during active forgetting and remembering. New languages that resist the cleansing and the sacralization of the *status quo* prod "the rupture with the continuum of domination." One recognizes new masters of domination by their old-new rhetoric because they have not effected "a rupture with the vocabulary of domination." Marcuse identifies core "semantic elements of the revolution" for these times. The core cannot be an abstract textual revolution in a poetic language alone. An untimely revolution (a Nietzschean specter transfigures into that of Marx) invokes our material and cultural memory. A new language "is not, cannot be, an instrumentalist language." Liberating languages refuse the nostalgic forgetting of the past victims of history as well as fanatic utopian dreams.[58]

In the "refusal of the actual," a demoting of the clay gods, whether secular nationalism or sacral fundamentalism, takes place. Imaginative universals are reined in by an interaction among plural struggles to prevent both myths and enlightenments from plunging into a disastrous spirit of seriousness. Otherwise a fatal decline of poetry and revolution becomes the outcome of renaming—in memory and forgetting. If Adorno found it hard to philosophize and poetize after Auschwitz, then Marcuse does not want to abandon us to cynical reason or one-dimensional politics. In this both are forever right. Marcuse proposes "the rupture with the linguistic universe of the Establishment," and he draws inspiration in a *parallel polis* of "subcultural groups." They employ "obscenities" (found in the mainstream media advertising) to undo "the false and hypocritical name[s]." Unlike Adorno's curious distaste for jazz, Marcuse locates "a systematic linguistic rebellion" among the Hippies. We begin to meet increasingly disillusioned adolescent children of the NWO baby-boomers. Marcuse is already aware that refusals draw strength not only from the language of civil rights but also from blues, soul, jazz; nowadays from punk, funk, rap, and other forms of mythmaking, downshifting, culture jamming, media subverting, and downright philosophizing on existence at the margins.[59]

✤✤✤

Some will say that the wretched of the earth have become tired, coopted. Perhaps some will point out how the oppressed partake in their own oppression. (Some young women in my class told me that marriage and love are worth it all: they are first battered by their lovers, then by husbands; and they stay in bad marriages.) From the TV images of angry Blacks, beaten or killed by angry cops, to undocumented foreign and prison slave labor, the poor are taught these days 'family values' in the U.S. style—they are evangelized to put up or shut up, etc. Yet there are numerous groups that voice a wake-up call. Enough already! It is for their sake that dangerous memory, joyous hope, and an active forgetting of the impossible are given today.

✤✤✤

"Introducing Invention into Existence"

When Fanon remarks that "intellectual alienation is a creation of middle-class society," he unmasks failures to theorize the colonized time and space of the oppressed. Leaps without transformed institutions cannot affect the margins of the mainstream political economy. And Fanon's singular leaps already dissemble Kierkegaard's hero of resignation. Resigned, one hardly becomes—unlike Kierkegaard's faithful knight, Marcuse's concrete philosopher, or Marx's revolutionary—responsible for new singular universals of radical multicultural and existential democracy. Fanon is a concrete philosopher and a revolutionary. He demonstrates how Marx's historical revolution and existentially material leaps should be viewed dialectically. The concrete philosopher and the concrete revolutionary, each, must be singularly and sociopolitically responsible. As *dissenting democratic agents*, each affects life within the ethical-universal.[60]

Envision Fanon's radical positionality: "the real *leap* consists in introducing invention into existence." Marcuse's category of the 'great refusal' bespeaks a kinship with this sociopolitical reading of leap. (It is a reading recorded in Sartre's singular universal and Fanon's invention of a postracist lifeworld.) When Marcuse invokes the wretched of the earth, this allies him with Fanon's at once existential and Marxian senses of leap. One need not privilege one category—race, gender, sex, class—over the rest. Marcuse engages regional and political liberation struggles. He begins to thematize racism and patriarchy as distinct forms of oppression, and like Sartre he envisions democracy beyond formal liberal terms as radically political, multicultural, and economic. With Fanon, his refusals engender the personal and social aspects of liberation within the entire existence of the marginalized. The entirety of human existence in need of transformation joins the personal with the institutional.[61]

If one refigures Marcuse's refusals through Fanon's existential inventions, leaps can serve to link transgressive singularities with personal and global agencies of liberation. Existentially material leaps proffer historical inventions. Such leaps live without historical teleologies or determined essences. Leapers learn to refuse, they dance, in a body politics, that is, performatively. Performatives that matter raise "the specter of a world which could be free." This world portends "the real spectre of liberation." The specter that matters is the "Enemy . . . of all doing and undoing." Hope's refusals raise the "specter which haunts not only bourgeoisie but all exploitative bureaucracies."[62]

A concrete critical theory of liberation today gathers refusing voices from multiple margins. This thought can deliver on earlier promissory notes that democracy-to-come must become morally and sociopolitically anticolonial and ethically postcolonial.

4. Democracy as Anticolonial Coalition and Postcolonial Solidarity

Says Fanon: "History teaches us clearly that the battle against colonialism does not run straight away along the lines of nationalism." Perhaps nobody matches his "Pitfalls of National Consciousness," a devastating critique of the backward role played by victorious yet narrow social integrations in anticolonial struggles and postcolonial transitions. I know of few more timely texts for analyzing the NWO than this chapter from *The Wretched of the Earth*.[63]

Can identity politics empower the liberation struggles of oppressed minorities—Black nationalists or other separatist groups? There is a hard lesson to be learned from Fanon's exposure of the ascending middle class. This grouping comes into being at the moment it begins to collaborate with the neocolonial situation. Nationalists first mobilize the oppressed around anticolonial group identity to overthrow the masters. Second, they steal the keys to the postcolonial heavens. And, third, they do not enter but prevent others from entering liberation. Fanon heartily despises impostor liberationists or conservative revolutionaries although they, too, are only exploited by the old-new masters of the neocolonial order. Precisely as servile appendages of the masters, such ascending minorities become a lumpen or pseudo bourgeoisie.

☩ ☩ ☩

In the U.S. some have become tokens of the reactionary game on diversity in the corporations, the Supreme Court and other institutions, and in the academy in particular. The tokens of diversity are just that—chips to be tossed around by the business gamble. They are a concession and a 'politically correct' cover-up by administrators who could not care less about a postcolonial way of running their institutions (e.g., in hiring, equity in surplus distribution, basic program changes). As one African American peer said during a tense moment, Blacks have to demonstrate Herculean capacities and performance to be hired and kept, while a mediocre fellow from the dominant majority has all rules of the game in his favor. Even 'other' minorities are preferred to Blacks, especially when they can pass as 'White' in the anti-Black world. One more African American hire—and they are taking over the Department, the Corporation, etc. Oh, poor White male me! Look at the pink-faced new conservative revolutionary who worries down the hallway that more than 1–2% Blacks in our midst is one percent too many! The worry is that another Black hire will drop the price of our business neighborhoods. Becoming a token in this dirty, at best merely liberal, play on diversity makes little difference; it forces the 1% token into Fanon's lumpen or pseudo middle class.

In East Central Europe some have exchanged the status of the Party nomen-klatura for the dogmas of free-trade agreements peppered with an admixture of xenophobic nationalism. This trade is free for those who have resources; and resourceful new kingpins guard their birth rights with nationalist and naturalist myths of origins. The state-capital-logic was shaped by a totalitarian security lie that it embodied socialism on the way to Communism. The private-capital-logic is being shaped by laws of the jungle and a nationalist or even a new national socialist lie about equal starting points. In spite of the internationalist rhetoric, the Party-run nation-states deployed internal nationalism, racism, and sexism to supplement exploitative surplus labor policies. Minority groups fared badly in massive internal prison-slave populations (one strike and you were out!). The rich uranium mines in Czechoslovak Jáchymov were cleaned empty by the Soviet arms production; many forced laborers lost years of free life and many their very lives. There were captive nations of East Europe and Asia colonized by the Soviet and Chinese empires. Such internationalist 'help' is lived out nowadays unhindered in the imperial backyards of U.S. corporate raids and during foreign missions—'uphold democracy' or else! Both past and present situations, despite the sham changes in rhetoric, offer cheap surplus labor—children, women, slaves—and raw materials.

An ignoble lie about socialism on the way to Communism explains why the breakdown of its slave system is interpreted through a neoliberal discourse as the failure of socialism. This undermining of memory has been more successful than even Senator McCarthy's and President Reagan's lies. East Europeans are allergic to any mention of gender or racial gaps: 'one has had it with that talk about gender equity in socialism'. Many are unable to recognize how a new capital logic provides masks behind which former Communist bosses run a new dirty business: 'western capitalism began also with the robber barons and here it took a bit longer to prepare for this private phase on the way to democracy'. Nationalist and neoliberal rhetoric produces bizarre cover-ups for a Communist-cum-bourgeois multicultural neocolonialism.

Look at East German territories before unification: they called this a DM-Nationalism! And today? The lands east of East Germany—traditionally eyed by Napoleon and Hitler, those two precocious single-currency, EC-Market, pan-European nationalists—are up for grabs.[64] *West European and global multinationals, former Party bosses and the mafias, all operate in the light of day as beasts of prey. New antimigrant laws in the U.S., France, or Germany, and the outright rise of neo-Nazi movements in Slovakia, Ukraine, or the Russian Federation, hide behind the rhetoric of making the world safer for culturally diverse markets. This freedom does not extend, nor can it extend when delivered by the West, either to the indigenous in Mexico and Latin America, or to blockaded Cubans (Miami expats have already conspired with the U.S. corporations to economically partition Cuba), or to Blacks in North America, Africa, the Caribbean, or to Roma and Moslems in Europe. I would ask, could the U.S. foreign interventions, keeping so often in power the ruling oligarchy, live with genuine postcolonial democracy in Guatemala, Haiti, Kuwait, Timor, Cuba, at home?*

✦✦✦

Fanon shows how the struggle for national self-determination (pan-African or pan-Arab) confuses postcolonial democracy with "neo-liberal universalism." The latter's veneer of national interests hides an antidemocratic core. The ascending "national middle class" abandons the poor. It joins the path of "a bourgeoisie which is stupidly, contemptibly, cynically bourgeois" by providing an alibi and doing the dirty work for neo-colonial masters.[65]

✦✦✦

Dudinska, a Jew from Slovakia and a student activist during the November 1989 events in Prague, decries in a 1993 New York Times *interview, "From Prague a Student of Lost Ideals," the betrayal of her hope for democracy with a human face. She voices the complaint of many a student who inaugurated the Velvet Revolution only to find radical dreams being stolen (just as at China's Tiananmen Square) by political and economic realities. On November 17, 1989 students marched through Prague, commemorating the death of Jan Opletal, the Czech student killed by the Nazis. Their march was crushed by the special red beret units of state police. Students were forced into a narrow alley, then for hours cruelly beaten, and in numerous cases physically damaged. The national militias were secretly mobilized by the Party boss Jakeš, ready for the international job that the Soviets did in August 1968. The blood of idealist students gave an impetus to the general strike by theater actors. Stages became the first open political and civic discussion clubs from where emerged the Czech Civic Forum and the Slovak Public Against Violence. Students and actors were joined by labor. A week of growing popular protest followed. Events of days ushered in the collapse of the forty-year rule. History was made in short cycles of leaps; a new cycle of decline made a stage entrance. Later in December Havel's first government took over. In the transitional period from totalitarianism to active civil society other groups exploited anxiety and ethnic conflicts. In Dudinska's words: "They just, you know, put away the Communist newspeak and began to speak in the national language." Nationalism aids in the overthrow of the hated rule; "later on it falls into the wrong hands," thereby fueling a "new-found evil."*

While former dissidents and the first leaders of the Civic Forum and the Public Against Violence were caricatured as irrelevant intellectual dreamers, the new middle class got itself politically and professionally organized. Those that risked their skin in 1989 became stagehands. Havel, by trying to remain above political parties, made himself weak. He could not calm the nationally divided Parliament and stop the subsequent cabinet divorce of Czecho-Slovakia, nor even bring about a national referendum that would have reversed the dirty political game. The forces leading up to the split have been unleashed by the Catholic Slovak nationalist, Ján Čarnogurský. During the past regime this man took part in a secret spiritual summer camp organized in Šumava, Southern Bohemia by a well known Prague Catholic dissident family. When Čarnogurský was released from prison and became the first premier of the post-Communist Slovakia, he suddenly lost his memory of prodemocracy Czechs. Slovakia über alles—even Catholicism. He deployed nationalist Christianity (one hears echoes from Nazi times in the Slovak state) to frustrate constitutional reforms and Havel's efforts to resolve national disputes without dividing the Federation. Čarnogurský promised that Slovakia would gain in nine to ten years a nation-state status, thereby becoming a small star in the European Community and the U.N. The federal divorce was completed, however, by a less compromising, more ruthless, utmost vulgar, and cynically lying ex-Communist populist, the new Slovak pre-

mier, Vladimír Mečiar. Unwilling to wait ten years for a Slovak independence or his own free reign of power, Mečiar exploited Čarnogurský's still rather procedural give-and-take approach. At this time the new Czech premier, Václav Klaus, called Mečiar's bluff. Klaus exploited the Slovak situation to accelerate privatization in Bohemia without having to carry the financial burden of higher Slovak unemployment and a weaker economy. Why not sacrifice the country for free markets and political glory!? The cabinet divorce was dead done. These two premiers have been lording over a divided country: using some version of the nationalist line, they pursue strictly economic and power interests. In Slovakia, these are the squandering of state property along nepotistic lines. In the Czech Republic, Klaus privatizes everything while keeping tight political control and centralization—a long tradition of absolutist monarchies in the region. Even with powers divided since 1996 between Klaus's minority government and Miloš Zeman's social democratic opposition in the upper house of the Parliament, genuine democracy is still to come.

For Dudinska, "the Prague revolutionaries dreamt of a democracy where, in her words, 'each of us is born with a certain role to play, and if you are free, you will find your role'." Havel dreams such dreams in Summer Meditations *and from a postsurgery bed. This democracy exists neither in the West nor in former colonies. In Serbia students and labor are only now, after Slobodan Milosević's nationalist decline of several years, writing its other chapter.*

✛ ✛ ✛

Fanon unmasks the intermediary, historically failing role of the nationalist middle class:

> Seen through its eyes, its mission has nothing to do with transforming the nation; it consists, prosaically, of being the transmission line between the nation and a capitalism, rampant though camouflaged, which today puts on the mask of neo-colonialism. The national bourgeoisie will be quite content with the role of the Western bourgeoisie's business agent.[66]

Nationalism, to become an effective MBA program and agent for the new colonial masters, must find cheap surplus labor. I discussed that Balibar discovers an inherent contradiction between the emancipatory story of nationalism, preached to the believing masses, and its role as the pimp of the colonial masters. Fanon gets at this issue when he explains how nationalism passes "to ultra-nationalism, to chauvinism, and finally to racism." Whether in the former colonies on the African Ivory Coast, or East Germany and Ukraine, or Governor Peter Wilson's California— racism and patriarchy provide an internal surplus by ideologically supplementing nationalism. Chauvinism serves as a business program and an agent-intermediary. In promises of pan-African and pan-Arab liberation, Fanon unmasks how the tokenized groups are used to replace the ruling ranks of current masters. Ascending tokens become "a permanent seesaw between African unity, which fades quicker and quicker into the mist of oblivion, and a heartbreaking return to chauvinism in its most bitter and detestable form."[67]

Fanon charges that the nationalist middle class, failing to promote postcolonial solidarity, contributes to tribal violence. His insight is as much true of the anti-Dahoman and anti-Voltaic racial riots on the Ivory Coast at the time of his writing, as of the anti-Bosnian, anti-Macedonian, anti-Roma, anti-gay, or other cleansing today. Fanon corrects the shortsightedness of any liberation movement which separates its solidarity from global coalitions.

> African unity, that vague formula, yet to which the men and women of Africa were passionately attached, and whose operative value served to bring immense pressure to bear on colonialism, African unity takes off the mask, and crumbles into regionalism inside the hollow shell of nationality itself.[68]

Fanon admits that "the national front" can be effective against colonialism. He doubts, however, that nationalism, insofar as it tries to take over the role of colonial masters or become their tokenized business agent, can sustain broad coalitions and solidarity against paternalism, tribalism, or religious wars. The nationalism of liberation becomes conquest; it now "promotes the ingrafting and stiffening of racism which was characteristic of the colonial era."[69]

Western racism feeds on contempt. It hides disdain behind notions of human equality with western liberal terms for what counts as 'human'. The racism of the neocolonial middle class feeds on self-defense and fear. Out of fear, then, the new agents of western racists "hasten to make their own fortunes and to set up a national system of exploitation." The problem with becoming a token is not that job opportunities improve one's economic situation. They should. But affirming 1% at the expense of 99%, allowing oneself to be used "to put obstacles in the path of this 'Utopia'"—that is a scandal. To unmask the nationalist "dictatorship of the bourgeoisie," Fanon adopts a radical democratic standpoint:

> The national bourgeoisie . . . have decided to bar the way to . . . [postcolonial] unity, to that coordinated effort on the part of two hundred and fifty million men to triumph over stupidity, hunger, and inhumanity at one and the same time. This is why we must

understand that African unity can be achieved through the upward thrust of the people, and under the leadership of the people, that is to say, in defiance of the interest of the bourgeoisie.[70]

The desire for strong populist leaders in eastern Europe and the Russian Federation has replaced the dictatorship of the Party. It was and still is a bad idea to invite any dictatorship, instead of a popular post-colonial sovereignty, to occupy transitional periods to democracy. People might have to wait for democracy a whole eternity under either state-party rule or new bosses. Whether the Party or a nationalist vanguard, it "does not share its profits with the people." Milosević, Kravčuk, Mečiar, Zhirinovsky, and others—to them in the post-1989 East falls what Fanon exposes as "the dual role of stabilizing the regime and of perpetuating the domination of the bourgeoisie." Sadly, Fanon is right that even honest leaders can be used and then relegated to oblivion. Do Fanon's warnings strike home as far as Havel's second presidency?[71]

[The aporia of an honest leader:] to become the general president of that company of profiteers impatient for their returns which constitutes the national bourgeoisie. In spite of his frequently honest conduct and his sincere declarations, the leader as seen objectively is the fierce defender of these interests, today combined, of the national bourgeoisie and the ex-colonial companies. His honesty, which is his soul's true bent, crumbles away little by little.[72]

The bottom line of a nationalist mythmaking is economic neocolonialism. The myths are sutured by loans (foreign debt) and gifts (attached strings). Hacking into the World Bank or the International Monetary Fund could be number one in the *Top Ten* locally global, prodemocracy refusals of this gift (poison) today. "At one and the same time the poverty of the people, the immoderate money-making of the bourgeois caste, and its widespread scorn for the rest of the nation will harden thought and action." Neocolonialism is supplemented, in accord with strategy planning, by racist paternalism, chauvinism, or tribalism. Instead of genuine democracy, one is invited "to become drunk on the remembrance of the epoch which led up to independence."[73]

Fanon likens the middle-class nationalists to a "dictatorship of the national-socialist type," or to "fascism . . . which has triumphed for half a century in Latin America." His insight only warns with recent memories of Sarajevo and Srebrenica. Fascism "is the dialectic result of states which were semi-colonial during the period of independence." Here and within the U.S. sphere of influence, "the greatest wealth is surrounded by the greatest poverty." In this situation "the army and the police constitute the pillars of the regime." The new free markets are ruled by mafias and the army. The foreign advisors—business and military—are never too far away.[74]

On the ashes of the deposed colonial empires grow "ethnic" or "tribal" dictatorships. I do not witness a glorious multicultural Phoenix rising up from them. Fanon calls these the "regimes of the family sort" or simply "stupidity," "imposture," and "intellectual and spiritual poverty." That they are! He might be describing the dead Ceaucescu's Rumania or the drives for that Greater Serbia, Russia, or Slovakia: "The ministers, the members of the cabinet, the ambassadors and local commissioners are chosen from the same ethnological group as the leader, sometimes directly from his own family." Fanon thinks that separatism is only strategically provisional at best, it cannot provide an antidote to tyranny. The separatists can emerge suddenly "with five tribes, who also want to have their own ambassadors and ministers."[75]

I take it Fanon suggests that against conquests, national liberation movements must form an anticolonial sovereignty and postcolonial, indeed, postnational solidarity. Nationalist profiteers, those turncoats and drones who sit on thrones of the deposed ruling *nomenklatura*, do not have an economic and political strength, or care little, to checkmate neo-colonial masters. People must organize cooperatives and enter democratic public life. As an existential thinker and a revolutionary, Fanon's radical democratic sentiments raise the hope that people have no need of a dictatorship—whether by a national bourgeoisie, or by a populist, or by national-socialists, or by civil servants, or by ethnic and tribal groups, or by a vanguard Party.[76]

That famous dictatorship, whose supporters believe that it is called for by the historical process and consider it an indispensable prelude to the dawn of independence, in fact symbolizes the decision of the bourgeois caste to govern the underdeveloped country first with the help of the people, but soon against them. The progressive transformation of the party into an information service is the indication that the government holds itself more and more on the defensive.[77]

I reiterate a hunch that what died in the Communist East was a dictatorship of state capitalism. Like its western wealthier brother, it was fortified by security and information apparatus, ornamented by welfare state policies, fraught with legitimation crises. *That dictatorship* of the proletariat has been a myth. Revolution did not happen for or by the people. They were "held in check either by mystification or by the fear inspired by the police force."[78]

Fanon, taking the Algerian revolution as an example, critiques herd mentality and the reliance on strong-hand leaders or elitist parties. "[W]e must above all rid ourselves of the very Western, very bourgeois and therefore contemptuous attitude that the masses are incapable of governing themselves. In fact, experience proves that the masses understand perfectly the most complicated problems."[79] This contempt for the masses is shared by Nietzsche and vanguardist philosophies alike. (These include those revolutionaries—from Russia to Cuba to China—whose International discriminates against other 'social-natural kinds'. These same kinds, plus the Communists, were targeted by the Holocaust.) The contempt is reinforced when leaders are the admired tokens who do not join people in liberating their entire existence. This contempt has been inherited in the West by many a revolutionary, nationalist, or separatist movement.

Fanon takes a clue from a certain reading of western existential tradition. He applies this clue beyond middle-class existential revolts. Marcuse and Fanon join in this common insight. Both grasp that existential*ist* brooding, or mere talk of youth nihilism, do not yet inspire political responsibility. This responsibility must become the bread and butter, or *tortillas y frijol*, of what Cornel West invokes under existential democracy. Otherwise West's programmatic project inspires but a private brooding, and lives become mere tokens. Says Fanon:

Nobody, neither leader nor rank-and-filer, can hold back the truth. The search for truth in local attitudes is a collective affair. . . . The collective struggle presupposes collective responsibility at the base and collegiate responsibility at the top. Yes, everybody will have to be compromised in the fight for the common good. No one has clean hands; there are no innocents and no onlookers. We all have dirty hands; we all are soiling them in the swamps of our country and in the terrifying emptiness of our brains. Every onlooker is either a coward or a traitor.[80]

This Sartrean notion of dirty hands need not legitimate an existential and social undecidability. In a Fanonian purview, the notion raises an either/or choice for every citizen. Existential democracy requires, as Havel would put it, an existentially responsible self-choice of democratic citizens. Fanon anticipates Havel's admonition: "To educate the masses politically is to make the totality of the nation a reality to each citizen." Fanon agrees that the personal is social, and vice versa. "Individual experience, because it is national and because it is a link in the chain of national existence, ceases to be individual, limited, and shrunken and is enabled to open out into the truth of the nation and of the world." This relation gives us "the continuous dialectical truth of the nation" as opposed to conquests that rob citizens of all political responsibility. Existential democracy as anticolonial politics and postcolonial community requires a detribalized identity.[81]

If identity must not mean a death of viable traditions or a birth of vapid liberal diversity, then let it develop into a democratic equivalent of multicultural existential identity-in-difference—regionally and globally. I derived this equivalent theoretically from 'singular universals'. Radical multicultural and existential democracy defines personal and social identities as lived performatives. As if Fanon worried that we might not get the point:

We have seen in the preceding pages that nationalism, that magnificent song that made the people rise against oppressors, stops short, falters, and dies away on the day that independence is proclaimed. Nationalism is not a political doctrine, nor a program. If you really wish your country to avoid regression, or at best halts and uncertainties [i.e., long and short cycles of decline], a rapid step must be taken from national consciousness to political and social consciousness.[82]

Can West's most recent encouragement to keep faith in existential democracy, with which I opened my concluding reflections on great refusals today, raise credible specters of liberation? I judge that Fanon would consent if this included the following: (1) "an economic program" about the "division of wealth and social relations"; (2) anticolonial political coalitions, "that is to say that no demagogic formula and no collusion with the former occupying power can take place of a program"; and (3) new humanist forms of ethical life rooted in postcolonial solidarity.[83]

The national government, if it wants to be national, ought to govern by the people and for the people, for the outcasts and by the outcasts. . . . the national government . . . ought first to give back their dignity to all citizens, fill their minds and feast their eyes with human things, and create a prospect that is human because conscious and sovereign men dwell therein.[84]

Conclusions

My confidence comes not because I hold a privileged standpoint theory or a special access to any particular liberation struggle. Rather, I find Fanon, like Havel, speaking profoundly to dimensions of my East Central European experience of dissent against Soviet colonialism. Fanon addresses the migrant life

between borders and cultures, brought home by critical race and gender theorists.
He does not confound the academic language of multiculturalism, or the conser-
vatively strategic neoliberal policy planning for a civilizationally complex world,
with specters of liberation. Mindful that my own thinking and writing draws on
a limited and fallible experience, Fanon's insights ring to me with a definitive
urgency.

Fanon's passion for the outcast, Marcuse's hope for an existentially mate-
rial critical social theory of great refusals, and West and hook's breaking bread
with others for a viable form of life, all sound invidiously untimely merely for
tired or reactive ears. Are not the latter's antihuman music but the offspring of
Eurocentric world-travel? Do we need any of this progeny when imagining,
inventing, and introducing globally regional democracies? Are critical
post/modern social theorists open to an other of Eurocentric headings? There are
urgent conditions at the margins. The ranks of the wretched among us have been
swelling since Fanon wrote for them. Those living and working in the world cen-
ters of power could do worse than form political coalitions and solidarity with
their plight. Humans do not enjoy their marginality among other humans. They
teach the tired, cynical, coopted intellectuals about radical hope. "First World,
Ha Ha Ha!" might be the chant for one of the most significant, yes even tragi-
cally humorous, rallying clashes today.[85]

Today's chances for radical multicultural and existential democracy, if
such hope is given to us at all, may not arrive for the sake of a 'European' White-
Man, though the struggling Euro-American peoples already raise liberating
specters from cultural and social margins. We know that there has always been
more than one Europe or America. A good rallying question is not about
Europe's chance; rather, for the sake of which or whose 'Europe' shall chances be
given?

Habermas recognizes in pragmatism "the third productive reply to Hegel,
after Marx and Kierkegaard": pragmatism offers that "radical-democratic
humanism" which complements Marx and Kierkegaard with procedural democ-
ratic theory and institutional justice. West's existential democratic project,
inspired by the same three replies to Hegel, suggests how to radicalize Haber-
mas's radical democratic pragmatism. Pushing this inquiry in a promising direc-
tion, West and others excavate suppressed dimensions of pragmatism, cognizant
of race and gender matters in ways proceduralists are not. This marginalized
pragmatism draws on multicultural modernities, and some of these come from
critical traditions not born on European shores. Why not join a concretely mate-
rial critical social theory with a praxis for the sake of radical multicultural and
existential democracy? This venture need not shut eyes to complex global civi-
lizations. Instead, it seeks more nuanced refusals of domination. The many faces
that oppression takes appear due to racism and patriarchy, or economic immiser-
ation supplemented by either of the other forms.[86]

Europe-lovers, especially those like me born there, might prefer the old

winding cobblestone streets and narrow quarters of that African, Arab, Christ-
ian, Jewish, Romany, Slavic, Turkish . . . , old, at one time 'barbarian', world to
the asphalted deserts and the visual or cultural chaos of a NWO shopping mall.
And many might prefer the less naïvely religious or sentimental, yet more
socially responsible consciousness: despite the death-of-god syndrome (can only
a God save us now?), the fortress mentality, and ongoing genocidal anti-multi-
cultural wars within Europe's borders (or perhaps thanks to them), most Euro-
pean countries care more equally for citizens and even immigrants in the basic
areas of health, housing, and education than the U.S. can dream of achieving in
the next decade. That the U.S. mainstream tends to identify at large all such
arrangements with 'Communism' (read: un-American, i.e., undemocratic, life)
indicates social consciousness at the level of a crustacean, in spite of greater
strides in multiracial and multicultural coexistence in the Americas than in
Europe. Europe practices coalitional and solidary bonding (European busing),
even as for centuries it has fought misery, tyrants, genocides, Gulags, and gas
ovens. Even so, immiserated 'foreigners' among us the last Europeans (Kristeva
finds strangers always already living within) remain "unloved and unwanted."
But 'barbarians' keep coming even though Augustine wanted to save 'Europe' in
his ideal polis; *we have learned that today's barbarians at the fortress gates are*
tomorrow's civilizations. One hopes that cycles of decline may become shorter,
that they intensify and reverse within a single generation, that their memory
spreads across borders. One may hope that none of this must require a major
social collapse or wars to effect a self-corrective process of learning, whereby
humans come to prefer existential siblinghood and self-development to hatred. A
1996 episode of Star Trek *suggests that a civilizational evolution in social con-*
sciousness might require the First Contact *with a wholly other (extraterrestrial)*
civilization to redirect human imagination and energies. Maybe that's what the
invocations of a saving god or a more secular ideal communication community
likewise indicate. However, the best in existential and post/modern Euro-Amer-
ican traditions have come to suspect that waiting at the twilight of ghostly idols
might resemble Samuel Beckett's Waiting for Godot. *We may still tell one*
another—while in messianic waiting, while creatively working for liberation—
that longing after the exoticized goddess Europa *is a useless passion.*[87]

    Even if no new Manifesto has been issued, I dare to speak of a renaissance
in existential philosophy within critical post/modern social theory. This
renascence addresses the heart of the crisis of 'Europe' as an imperial Head, of
'European Man' as a patriarchal idea, and of 'European WhiteMan' as a hege-
monic racist construction. If the Euro-American, lyrically sentimental, and glob-
ally flexible rhetoric of becoming the new world's 'Number One' is not already
found preposterously arrogant, it will eventually be laughed out of its spirit of
seriousness and in the end passed over as a strangely absurd relic of bygone
times. A thought of its welcome death might be considered heretical. Yet such
heresies may edify one to love more wholesomely the historical places and times

of one's birth and existence, especially if such love is informed by hopeful irony and is kept sober by the tragic humor of shared history. One could love one's own Europe (wherever it might be) worse than that. With the aid of irony and humor, a new social consciousness may be crafted out of radical dissent and waged for the sake of inclusive democracy. Dissent and democracy are minimally the two major existential and multicultural axes of great refusals today. Their specters are raised by the oppressed across and at the same time within civilizational fault lines. The oppressed in critically lived-out traditions are variously shaping a new multicultural enlightenment, refusing in individual and communal existence the global imaginary and the material reach of the NWO. Our chances and hope in the present age rise or fall with their liberation.

NOTES

Key to References

For several different citations occurring in a single paragraph of the main text, usually one summary note for all references is given either at the end of that paragraph, or before or after a long indented citation. Each note indicates clearly all cited sources. References follow this form: author, abbreviated or shortened title, and page numbers. (Arabic or small Roman numerals after the title indicate pages of the previously cited title unless noted otherwise.) When the original language edition and the published English translation of a work are both cited, the first page reference is to the original, the second reference after the "/" is to the corresponding pages in the English translation. For full titles and bibliography, see *Works Cited* following the notes.

Abbreviations

Adorno:	ND	Negative Dialectics
Benhabib:	SS	Situating the Self
——— and Cornell:	FC	Feminist Contentions
	FaC	Feminism as Critique
Butler:	BM	Bodies that Matter
	EE	"Endangered/Endangering"
	FCR	"For a Careful Reading"
	GT	Gender Trouble
Derrida:	OH	The Other Heading
	SM	Specters of Marx
Fanon:	BSWM	Black Skin, White Masks
	WoE	The Wretched of the Earth
Foucault:	DP	Discipline and Punish
	DIE	"Dream, Imagination, and Existence"
	FR	The Foucault Reader
	HS	The History of Sexuality
	LCP	Language, Counter-Memory, Practice
	PK	Power/Knowledge
	PPC	Politics, Philosophy, Culture
	UP	The Use of Pleasure
Fraser:	JI	Justice Interruptus
	UP	Unruly Practices
Gordon:	BF	Bad Faith and Antiblack Racism
	F	Fanon
Habermas:	AG	Das Absolute und die Geschichte

AS	Autonomy and Solidarity
DE	"Diskursethik"
EAS	Eine Art Schadensabwicklung
EzD	Erläuterungen zur Diskursethik
FuG	Faktizität und Geltung
GpI	"Geschichtsbewußtsein"
GuS	"Gerechtigkeit und Solidarität"
GW	"Die grosse Wirkung"
ICI	"An Intersubjectivist Concept"
HB	"Herbert Marcuse über Kunst und Revolution"
HRPS	"Human Rights and Popular Sovereignty"
ILH	"Im Lichte Heideggers"
JA	Justification and Application
KFnT	"Kommunikative Freiheit"
KHI	Knowledge and Human Interests
KuK	Kultur und Kritik
LC	Legitimation Crisis
LJPS	"Jürgen Habermas On The Legacy of Jean-Paul Sartre"
MHgH	"Mit Heidegger gegen Heidegger denken"
MkH	Moralbewußtsein
MS	"Moralität und Sittlichkeit"
NC	The New Conservatism
ND	Nachmetaphysisches Denken
NR	Die nachholende Revolution
PDM	Der Philosophische Diskurs
PFG	"Postscript to Faktizität und Geltung"
PpP	Philosophisch-politische Profile
PT	"Psychic Termidor . . ."
SiK	"Die Scheinsrevolution und ihre Kinder"
SnI	"Staatsburgerschaft"
SR	"Struggles for Recognition"
TCA	The Theory of Communicative Action, vols. 1 and 2
TiTD	"Transzendenz von innen"
TP	"Theorie und Politic"
TuK	Texte und Kontexte
ÜMS	"Über Moralität und Sittlichkeit"
V	Vorwort zur Neuaflage
VaZ	Vergangenheit als Zukunft
Vpem	"Vom pragmatischen, ethischen . . ."
VV	"Volkssouverentität als Verfahren"
WaW	"Work and Weltanschauung"
WhS	"Nachholende Revolution . . . Was heißt Sozialismus heute?"
ZG	"Zum Geleit"

	ZRHM	Zur Rekonstruktion des Historischen
		Materialismus
Havel:	PP	"The Power of the Powerless"
Hegel:	PR	Hegel's Philosophy of Right
Horkheimer and		
Adorno:	DoE	Dialectic of Enlightenment
Ingram:	RHP	Reason, History, and Politics
Kierkegaard:	A	Attack upon Christendom
	CA	The Concept of Anxiety
	CI	The Concept of Irony
	CUP	Concluding Unscientific Postscript
	E/O	Either/Or, vols. 1 and 2
	FT	Fear and Trembling
	JP	Journals and Papers
	PC	Practice in Christianity
	PF	Philosophical Fragments
	PV	The Point of View
	SuD	The Sickness unto Death
	TA	Two Ages
Marcuse:	AD	The Aesthetic Dimension
	EC	Eros and Civilization
	EoL	An Essay On Liberation
	N	Negations
	ODM	One-Dimensional Man
	RR	Reason and Revolution
Marsh:	CAL	Critique, Action, and Liberation
Matuštík:	PI	Postnational Identity
—— and		
Westphal:	KPM	Kierkegaard in Post/Modernity
Sartre:	C	Critique of Dialectical Reason
	K	"Kierkegaard"
Taylor:	EA	The Ethics of Authenticity
	PR	"Politics of Recognition," in Taylor,
		Multiculturalism
	SS	Sources of the Self
West:	KF	Keeping Faith
	RM	Race Matters
Young:	C	"Comments on Seyla Benhabib, Situating
		the Self"
	JPD	Justice and the Politics of Difference

1. The Need for Recognition

1. Matuštík, PI, xx and n. 11; 3–28. For a critique of Heidegger's version of existential philosophy, see Habermas, GW, MHgH (ZG and AS with reference to

Marcuse's critique of Heidegger), and WaW. On self-realization, see Habermas, TCA, vol. 2, chap. 5 on Mead, ND/ICI and GpI (both with reference to Kierkegaard; cf. MHgH). For the persistence of "existential" categories in Habermas, consult his AG, DE, EzD/JA, FuG, GpI, GuS, KFnT, MkH, MS, ND, NR, SR, TuK, TiTD, ÜMS, Vpem, and again ZG and AS (with reference to his sympathy with the Marcusean existential variant of critical theory), and LJSP and AS (with reference to his ongoing sympathy to Sartre's category of freedom). He noted his new interest in these topics in our conversation at the World Congress of Philosophy in Brighton, August 1988 (Matuštík, PI, 259–64). For a summary essay on these developments, see Matuštík, "Existence." On works that now pursue this aim, see chronologically, Cooke, "Habermas," "Realizing the Post-Conventional Self," and "Authenticity and Autonomy"; Ferrara, "Postmodern Eudaimonia," "Justice and the Good," *Modernity and Authenticity*, "Authenticity and the Project of Modernity," and "Authenticity and Intersubjectivity"; Pamerleau, "Existentialism"; Thiruvengadam, "Democracy"; Anderson, "The Persistence" and "Recognizing Autonomy"; Rehg, "Existentialism"; Honneth, *Kampf* (cf. Anderson's intro. to the Eng. trans.); Weir, *Sacrificial Logics*, on existential self-identity, 13, 124–26, 130; and Kögler, "Self-Empowered Subject," whose "hermeneutic reflexivity" supports my sense of existential correctives to Habermas. Cf. concluding para. to chap. 9 below.

2. Matuštík, PI, part 1, on all three contributions.

3. Habermas, SR. I began to address this issue in PI, parts 2 and 3, and in Matuštík and Westphal, KPM. In my present considerations, I am guided by Rehg's questions ("Existentialism"), the growing interest in existential issues among Habermasian theorists (see n. 1 above), and the groundbreaking study of recognition in Willett's *Maternal Ethics*.

4. Walzer, "Comment," in Taylor, *Multiculturalism*, 99–103; Habermas, SR, 109.

5. Taylor, PR, 32.

6. Taylor, PR, 32. The internal citation is by Mead, *Mind*. For other Habermasian formulations, see Taylor, EA, 32–35; cf. with an earlier more elaborate account by Habermas, TCA, vol. 2, chap. 5; ND/ICI (chap. on Mead); and SR, 109.

7. Cf. Taylor's SS with MacIntyre's *After Virtue*.

8. Habermas, TCA, vol. 2, chap. 5, sec. 3; ND; Gordon's critical ontology, BF, 130–37.

9. See Habermas, MS and MkH; and Taylor, SS.

10. Cf. Young, JPD and C; Benhabib, "In Defense of Universalism" and "The Generalized and the Concrete Other"; Benhabib and Cornell, *Feminism*, 77–95.

11. Habermas, SR, 119; cf. on feminism in SR, 109, 113–17; on the Persian Gulf, VaZ; and chaps. 3, 4, 6, and 9 below on Habermas's idea of Europe's second chance.

12. Habermas, SR, 109; Taylor, EA, 110f.

13. Taylor, EA, 22, 39f., 52f., 66f., 110f., 118. Cf. Taylor's EA with critical traditionality (Blaney and Inayatullah, Dallmayr, Gandhi, Kothari, Nandy), critical gender and race theory (chaps. 5, 6, 9 below), and the complex positions of M. L. King, Jr. (see Moses, *Politics*), Sub. Marcos, and Havel (on latter two, chap. 8 below).

14. Habermas, SR, 109. Cf. Fanon's WoE and Nandy's *Illegitimacy of Nationalism.*

15. On postconventional ethics, see Benhabib, SS; Honneth, *Kampf* 274–87; and Matuštík, PI, 259–64; on existential, multicultural, ethical, coalitional and solidary, and radically democratic forms of life, see chaps. 2–3, 5–7, and 9 below.

16. Honneth (*Kampf* 148–225, and the summary chart 211) expands (via Marx, Sartre, and Sorel) Habermas's reading of Hegel's early Jena writings and Kant through Mead. On "tactile sociality," see Willett, *Maternal Ethics*, chap. 2; cf. Taylor, EA, 16ff., 21ff., 25–29, 32–41, 43, 57–60, 63–69, 71ff., 79f., 90–93; J. Anderson, "The Persistence," 101ff.; and Ferrara, "Authenticity and the Project of Modernity," 244f., 260–78.

17. See Willett and Matuštík, "Internet Conversations." Willett (*Maternal Ethics* 24–29) employs Daniel Stern's work on "cross-modal correspondence" to rethink Hegel's struggle for recognition (part 2) and to interpret African American narratives of recognition (part 3). See on intentionality and sympathy, Matuštík's essays on "Merleau-Ponty"; on phenomenological and formal symmetry, and ethical asymmetry, chaps. 5–6 below.

18. Taylor, EA, chap. 6 on subjectivism; 35–41 on the second point, 43–53 on the first.

19. Taylor, EA, 38–41. Ferrara holds that in modernity only *phronesis* can reconcile the normative demands of autonomy with the extranormative ones of authenticity ("Authenticity and the Project of Modernity," 243, 253, 260–78; cf. J. Anderson, "The Persistence," 104).

20. Taylor, EA, 43–53, 58, 69, 91; PR; Habermas speaks of transcendence on "this side" of communicatively structured forms of life, cf. TiTD; KFnT; Matuštík, PI, 12–17, 97–99.

21. See Marsh, *Post-Cartesian Meditations*; and CAL; and chap. 4 below.

22. Taylor, EA, 44 and 45—citations above; cf. 50, and chaps. 6–7 and 9 below.

23. Taylor, EA, 51 and 52—citations above.

24. Habermas, SR, 109 (the words in brackets appear on this page in other sentences).

25. On these critiques, see Nagl, "Zeight die Habermassche . . ." I defend Habermas on this very point, Matuštík, PI, chap. 2. Honneth develops this further in *Kampf*.

26. I agree with Ferrara: authenticity justifies neither subjectless formalism nor a centerless subject of postmodernism. Another authentication of validity and normative conditions is needed ("Authenticity and the Project of Modernity," 266ff.). I disagree with a *phronetic* approach (243, 247, 250, 253, 260). If the issue between authenticity and autonomy is not about normativity or about which of the two terms presupposes the other, but about forms of concretion, then one must redefine communicative competence in order to comprise in equal manner authenticity and autonomy (cf. J. Anderson, "The Persistence," 104f.).

27. Cf. Taylor's work in progress (Ernest Gellner's Institute on Nationalism, Prague, The Central European University, Feb. 8, 1995). Du Bois, "The Conservation of Races" and *The Souls*; Outlaw, *On Race and Philosophy*, 135–57; West, KF; cf. my discussion of the singular individual and universal, chaps. 2, 6, and 9 below.

28. Habermas, SR, 116.

29. Habermas, SR, 122; cf. Honneth's *Kampf* and Willett's *Maternal Ethics*.

30. Habermas, SR, 122–28. The sharp-knife metaphor is used by Habermas to separate ethical and moral domains. Cf. Horkheimer, "Traditional and Critical Theory." I am sympathetic to Laclau and Mouffe's *(Hegemony)* Gramscian radical democracy; I doubt that they want to integrate this politics into a critical theory. Theoretical reasons for my doubt become apparent in my dialogues with Derrida and Habermas (chaps. 2–4), Foucault, Butler, Cornell, and Marcuse (chaps. 5, 7), and I. Young, West, Outlaw, and Fanon (chaps. 6, 9).

31. Young commented on my presentation, "you have nicely reconciled Taylor and Habermas, but this shows only how both miss the same difficulty: the political economy of the politics of recognition." Cf. her "Unruly Categories"; Fraser's JI and "Rejoinder" for discussion of redistribution and recognition; Blum, "Recognition"; Greider's and S. Huntington's approaches to the NWO; and Ingram, RHP, 287: "the political struggle for recognition and identity is also an economic struggle for justice." On critical traditionalism, see above n. 13, cf. below chaps. 6, 9 (hooks, Fanon, Outlaw, West); on critical post/modern social theory, chaps. 3–5.

32. Outlaw, *On Race and Philosophy*, 181. Cf. Habermas, SR, 122–28; and Cooke, "Authenticity and Autonomy."

33. Taylor, PR, 52–56, 58–61, 64.

34. Habermas, SR, 131f., 139; cf. Nandy's *Illegitimacy of Nationalism* and *Traditions*.

35. (On Chiapas, see chap. 4, sec. 3, and chap. 8 below; on the arrogance of the idea of 'Europe', see chaps. 3, 6, and 9 below, and the conclusion to the book.)

36. I replace both dual- and unified-systems theorizing with a more complex and yet more flexible *existentially material key*; and I develop it in forms of refusal below: dissent (chap. 2); deconstructive and critical social theory (chaps. 3–4); genealogy, aesthetics of existence, performativity, transgressive agency (chaps. 5 and 7); ethical communities (chap. 6); two case studies of self-limiting democratic revolutions (chap. 8); and multicultural and existential democracy (chap. 9).

37. I take seriously Wolin's worries (*The Terms of Cultural Criticism*; "Left Fascism"), yet I affirm critical links between discourse-theoretical and existential approaches.

38. "Television Man" is the appropriate title of a song by Talking Heads. The idea of the greengrocer's protest (in Havel) becoming an antitelevision protest comes from my friend, Ramsey Eric Ramsey (cf. "Politics of Dissatisfaction"); see epigraphs to chaps. 8–9 below.

39. I learned from my student, N. Mićunović, whose "Critique of Nationalism" records a literary irony of East Europeans without misogyny. Sartre affirms fraternity in *Hope Now* but is skeptical in *Critique*, vol. 1, 405–44 where the hell is still found in others (fraternity-terror); cf. with Rorty's "Fraternity Reigns." On irony, humor, tragedy, forgetting, memory, see Matuštík, PI; chaps. 7–9 below; cf. Dallmayr, "Global Development?" 273.

40. Willett explained in our private conversation that infants on day one both demand recognition (to be held) and exercise resistance to bodily violation (desire to be put down).

41. On the last series of questions, cf. Rehg, "Existentialism," 140.

42. Žižek, "Eastern Europe's Republic of Gilead," 200. On radical democracy, see chap. 4, and on this critique of nationalism, chaps. 6 and 9 below. Greider's, not S. Huntington's, argument can credibly address this aporia within the NWO (see Works Cited).

43. See Young, JPD; and chap. 6 below.

44. Žižek, "Eastern Europe's Republic of Gilead," 194 and 205, on the purported theft of my enjoyment that has never been my very own, 196–200; cf. Nandy's *Illegitimacy of Nationalism*; and the Kristevian strangers to ourselves alluded to in chaps. 3, 5, and 6 below.

45. See Balibar, "Racism and Nationalism," Balibar and Wallerstein, *Race*. For a certain priority of class in relation to gender and race struggles, see Marsh, CAL, 282–89, 344–47; and my discussion of this in chaps. 4 (sec. 3) and 9 below.

46. Cf. Habermas, TCA, vol. 2; Greider, *One World*; and Nandy, "Cultural Frames."

47. On existential-performative identity, see Matuštík, PI, chap. 5; Sartre, *Anti-Semite* 55–58 (cf. Michnik, "Bojím sa antikomunistov"); Fanon, BSWM,

109–40; Marcuse, ODM; Young, C, JPD; Bartky, *Femininity*; Cruikshank, *The Gay and Lesbian Liberation*; and P. Huntington, "Towards a Dialectical Concept of Autonomy." Gordon defines authenticity "as a form of taking hold of existence from a choice of bad faith" (BF, 61; see 51, on good faith; 67–71, on racism in abstract universalism; and 151f., on the politics of difference in Fanon or I. Young rather than Taylor or Honneth). Nandy's critical traditionality ("Cultural Frames"; cf. Blaney and Inayatullah, "Prelude") offers a more existentially concrete conversation than the received liberal-communitarian debate, and it complements the new western multicultural enlightenment—chaps. 3, 5—and existential democracy—chap. 9 below.

48. Cf. Du Bois, "The Conservation of Races"; *The Souls*; and Kierkegaard, R; SuD. On Sartre, see n. 47 above.

49. On the last point, see Laclau and Mouffe, *Hegemony*, 105–14; see Gordon: "rationality may have dimensions that some of us may consider to be quite nonrational" (BF, 71). "To *remain* in good faith requires realizing the possibility of being in bad faith" (56). See below chaps. 5 (on Butler's case study of the Rodney King beating), and 9 (on Fanon and Outlaw). Cf. Kögler's ("Self-Empowered Subject") "hermeneutic reflexivity" with "existential dissent" (Matuštík, PI, vi, ix–xi, xvi, and chaps. 2 and 5 below).

50. Cf. epigraphs above, and in chaps. 6 and 9 below. On material limits of (neo)liberal democracies, see chaps. 3, 4, 8, and 9 below. On imaginative universals, see P. Huntington, "Fragmentation, Race, and Gender" and *Ecstatic Subjects*; and chap. 6 below.

2. Dissenting Individuals

1. Hall, *Word and Spirit*; Westphal, *Kierkegaard's Critique*; Macpherson, *The Political Theory*; Adorno, *The Jargon.*; cf. on Kierkegaard and modernism, Adorno, Apel, Habermas, Horkheimer, Kellner, Lukács, Marcuse, Marsh, Perkins, and Wolin; on postmodernism, Brown, Caputo, Derrida, Lorraine, and M. Taylor; and on communitarianism, MacIntyre and C. Taylor.

2. Kierkegaard, TA, 106—first two citations; PV, 128—last citation; cf. chaps. 4, 6, 9 below.

3. Westphal, *Kierkegaard's Critique*, 31ff.; Hegel's PR; and chap. 6 below.

4. Kierkegaard, TA, 62f.; McBride, "Sartre's Debt to Kierkegaard: A Partial Reckoning"; P. Huntington, "Heidegger's Reading of Kierkegaard Revisited: From Ontological Abstraction to Ethical Concretion," in Matuštík and Westphal, KPM, 18–42 and 43–65; and Fraser, "Multiculturalism, Antiessentialism, and Radical Democracy: A Genealogy of the Current Impasses in Feminist Theory"; and "From Redistribution to Recognition? Dilemmas of Justice in a 'Post-Socialist' Age," JI, 173–88; and 11–39; and n. 1 to chap. 1 above.

5. Kierkegaard, FT, 54–57, 60, 70, 82; cf. Brown, "Hegelian Silences and the Politics of Communication: A Feminist Appropriation," in Mills, *Feminist Interpretations*, 299–319.

6. Kierkegaard, FT, 55, 59, 74, 79; PC, 88 on Anti-Climacus; cf. S. Huntington, *Clash*.

7. Kierkegaard SuD; cf. Butler, GT, BM, and chaps. 5 and 7 below.

8. Kierkegaard, E/O, vol. 2:204. For the same point viewed via Foucault, see Kögler, "Self-Empowered Subject." I reread Foucault and Butler existentially (chaps. 5, 7 below).

9. Kierkegaard, E/O, vol. 2:157–77—citation above; cf. 219–24; CUP 251–300; 420–31; Fraser shows how radical democracy overcomes a split of antiessentialism and multiculturalism by linking both to social egalitarianism (see n. 4 above); cf. S. Huntington, *Clash*, 318–21.

10. Kierkegaard, CUP, 202ff., 323; MacIntyre, *After Virtue*, 5, 39–49, 73, 203, 242; Taylor, SS; Caputo, *Radical Hermeneutics*; *Against Ethics*; "Hermeneutics"; and M. Taylor, *Altarity*.

11. Kierkegaard, CUP, 423—citation; cf. 189–250. See Emmanuel, "Reading Kierkegaard"; on decisionism, see Matuštík, PI, index and chap. 5; and Habermas's DE.

12. Kierkegaard, CUP, 529, 534, 537. Cf. chap. 6 below on 'singular universal'.

13. Marcuse, "Über konkrete Philosophie"; works from 1928–33; ODM, EoL, and EC; Kellner, *Herbert Marcuse*, 66; Habermas, AS, 150, 159; Kosík, *Dialectics*; Sartre, "Kierkegaard." On a recent renaissance in existential social theory, see references in nn. 1–3 to chap. 1 above, and chap. 9 below; Gordon, BF, F, and essays in *Existence*; P. Huntington, *Ecstatic Subjects*; Marsh, "The *Corsair*," CAL, and "Marx and Kierkegaard"; Matuštík, "Existence," "Kierkegaard," "Kierkegaard's Existential Philosophy," PI, and essays in Matuštík and Westphal, KPM; and Westphal, *Kierkegaard's Critique*. Cf. the above with Adorno, *Kierkegaard*; Apel, *Diskurs*, 24, 26–29, 32f., 34–41, 56, 103–216; Best and Kellner, "Modernity"; Brown, "Grave Voices"; Buber, "The Question"; Caputo, *Against Ethics*; Lévinas, *Collected Philosophical Papers*, 133, 143f., 150; Lorraine, *Gender*, 115f., 118f.; Lukács, *Die Zerstörung*, 219–69; and Wolin, *The Terms of Cultural Criticism*, 89, 128.

14. Habermas, ND, 209/170; on the latter point, GpI; cf. S. Huntington, *Clash*; Butler, BM and *Excitable Speech*.

15. Habermas, ND, 202–9/164–70—all citations above.

16. Habermas, GpI; cf. EzD, 176–85, 188, 203f./JA, 69–76, 78f., 91f., on Taylor's communitarian ethics; 185–99/76–88, on Apel's ultimate transcendental grounds of morality. Habermas cites Taylor and Apel as convex mirrors of neo-

existential decisionism. Climacus's existential pathos teaches the difficulty of beginnings; de Silentio, Vigilius Haufniensis, and Anti-Climacus show how one passes through the facticity of anxiety, despair, and fear and trembling; and Kierkegaard's critique of the age and rereading of his authorship throw individuals-in-communities into ongoing objective uncertainties of existential faith (CUP, 525–55, 203; FT; CA; PC, 85–94; TA; PV). Cf. Fraser, JI, 186f.; on Nandy see n. 47 to chap. 1 above.

17. Kierkegaard, TA, 60–112; Tolić, "Im ersten postmodernen Krieg"; Kirmmse, *Kierkegaard*, 245–47, 264–78, 400–404, 408–22, 449–81; and S. Huntington, *Clash*, 301–21.

18. On this see Habermas, GpI; and Matuštík, PI. Cf. subtitle of S. Huntington's *Clash*.

19. Havel, "The Post-Communist Nightmare"; n. 10 to chap. 8 below; Michnik, "Bojím sa" and "An Embarrassing Anniversary"; and on 'postsocialist', see Fraser, JI.

20. Habermas (PFG, 148) praises law for taking "advantage of a permanent risk of dissensus to spur on legally institutionalized public discourses" and "reducing the conflict potential of unleashed individual liberties through norms that can coerce only so long as they are recognized as legitimate on the fragile basis of unleashed communicative liberties." Cf. FuG, 55f.

21. I object to S. Huntington's (*Clash*, 28, 57) restriction of Havel's multiculturalism to superficial global policy-making, excluding it for any intracivilizational social evolution; cf. Matuštík, PI; Havel, PP; and chaps. 1 (sec. 3) above, and 3 and 8 below.

22. Taylor, SS, 27ff., 34ff., 495, 524 n. 12, 508–13; cf. EA.

23. Taylor, SS, 462, 465, 480, and 481; cf. 456, 459, 461.

24. Taylor, SS, 449f., 453; cf. works by MacIntyre with S. Huntington's view in *Clash*.

25. Taylor, SS, 490–93.

26. Taylor, SS, 508–21.

27. Habermas, EzD, 176–85/JA, 69–76. Turning 180 degrees from Taylor, Habermas rejects Apel's grounding the moral point of view by transcendental warrants (*Letztbegründung*).

28. Habermas, EzD, 176–84/JA, 69–76.

29. On "ethical-existential," see Habermas, NR, 118–26, 141, and 144 (invoking Kierkegaard); Vpem, 103ff., 109, 111/4ff., 9, 11; and 112/12 (referring to Kierkegaard's SuD); cf. Habermas, MS, 221, 225f.; TkH, 2:167f./109f.; TiTD, 149f./242f. (Fiorenza's ed. intro. 10f.); FuG, 125f.; and Matuštík, PI, chap. 5, "The Performative Mode of Identity."

30. See nn. 1–3 to chap. 1 above. Ferrara argues both for the posttraditional ethics of the good and exemplary universalism (justice is conceived along *eudaimonistic* lines as the largest and most comprehensive context of the good, i.e., humankind). With these two moves, he wants to sidestep the split between procedural legitimacy (e.g., Habermas) and authenticity (e.g., Kierkegaard). While this approach may reconcile the Kantian and the Hegelian-Aristotelian perspectives in moral theory, it does little to clarify existential self-choice. I argue that dissent is about the mode of choosing which qualifies both *eudaimonistic* or clinical questions of the good and the moral procedures of legitimation. I think likewise that Cooke's insightful attempt to improve on Habermas's proceduralism is too dependent on the debate about the priority of the right and the good and on Habermas's characterization of authenticity in the communitarian categories of ethical self-realization. On postconventional *Sittlichkeit*, see Benhabib, SS, 11f., 68–88, 146; and Honneth's *Kampf*, 274–87.

31. Young holds that substantive goods of community cannot be the pluralistic basis for democratic politics and economy (JPD, chap. 8); Fraser defends a radical democracy that joins antiessentialist identity and multicultural differences in a 'postsocialist' project of equality (JI, 173–88). Existential dialectic is not harmed by disagreements between Fraser's (11–39, 189–205) bifocal articulations of recognition (culture) and redistribution (economy), and Young's pluralist material-cultural theorizing of the politics of identity and difference, and economy ("Unruly Categories," sec. 3). Cf. Tong, *Feminist Thought*, chaps. 6–8 on socialist, existentialist, and postmodern feminism; and chaps. 3–6 below.

32. Habermas, EzD, 183f./JA, 74; Adorno, ND; Marcuse, EC, EoL, and AD.

33. Derrida, OH, 11f./5f.—citations above.

34. Derrida discussed with me an interest in Kierkegaard's FT while at Prague's Central European University (Feb. 28–Mar. 9, 1992); cf. his *Gift*; Caputo, "Hyperbolic Justice," *Against Ethics*; and "Instants, Secrets, and Singularities: Dealing Death in Kierkegaard and Derrida," in Matuštík and Westphal, KPM, 216–38; S. Huntington's *Clash* counsels an anti-post/modern multiculturalism for foreign affairs and a monocultural traditionalism for the home order.

35. Derrida, OH, 75–78/77–80. I said ("Kierkegaard," 224 n. 18) and hold below in chaps. 3–4 that Derrida's reading of Kierkegaard (*Gift*) is implied in his reading of Marx (SM), and vice versa. This is brought out by fear and trembling which are inscribed into hope for bonds among the oppressed (OH). In his text on Marx (SM), such coalitional and solidary bonds take on an affinity of a new International. As I. Young, I do not find Fraser's dual-systems analytical split of recognition (lifeworld) and redistribution (system) advantageous; I do not affirm a unified-system (race-gender-sex-class) but an existentially material, critical post/modern social theory.

36. Caputo, "Hyperbolic Justice," 16; on Derrida's Kierkegaard, cf. 10f., 15, 19 n. 11.

37. S. Huntington, *Clash*, 318–21. Bhabha ("Interrogating Identity") depicts Fanon as "the purveyor of the transgressive and transitional truth" (183); he does not transgress without agency: "his Hegelianism restores hope to history; his existentialist evocation of the 'I' restores the presence of the marginalized; his psychoanalytic framework illuminates the madness of racism" (184); on ludic postmodernism/invidious ethnocentrism, cf. chap. 9, sec. 1 below.

38. Kierkegaard, FT, 82ff.; PC, 85–94, xv–xvii; and JP, vol. 6: entries 6690, 6699; PV; A. Cf. Wolin's "Carl Schmitt." See Martin, *Matrix and Line*, 142 (MacIntyre's or Derrida's Paris), chap. 5. (the unnameable community), 193f. (transgressive politics), 162 (Jameson's critique of "postmodern pastiche"); cf. Jameson, *Postmodernism*, 16–19, 21, 25, 34.

39. Cf. Lyotard, *Postmodern Condition*.

40. See Havel, *Dopisy Olze*, letters nos. 122–44; and Matuštík, PI, part 3.

41. Dobbs, "'Information Guerillas'"; I. Young, "Government"; S. Huntington, *Clash*.

42. ✦✦✦ Postscriptum: *An objection has been raised that my reading of the concept of 'undecidability' in Derrida is a serious misreading if not just a street version of deconstruction, viz., conflating undecidability with existential and social irresponsibility. My point is not about the scholarship concerning the undecidability of Derrida's or Kierkegaard's authorships. I raise an existential issue about certain practices in deconstruction and authoring. During my earlier presentation of portions from chap. 4 below (see acknowledgments), I employed two senses of undecidability in order to further elucidate my reading of 'Derrida 1 and 2'. 'Undecidability 1' refers to the impossibility of deciding the meaning of an authorship (textual undecidability), whereas 'undecidability 2' designates the impossibility of deciding how to be existentially and socially responsible for one's authoring and acting (practical undecidability). Any worry about misreading Derrida becomes serious insofar as this distinction is leveled down. The counterfactual condition of a valid defense on Derrida's behalf presupposes some affirmation that 1 could not legitimate 2. If 1 is to function as an enabling occasion for individual responsibility or social praxis, it can never come to mean also 2. And if this distinction holds, then it must be true that while the ethical significance of 1 is clear enough from reading Derrida and other deconstructive analyses of texts, this ethic remains insufficient to provide us with a mature social theory. To equate the ethical significance of deconstruction with a developed critical social theory and praxis equals leveling 1 into 2, opting solely for 'Derrida 1', and watering down the urgency of 'Derrida 2'. With Derrida's SM, there now emerges a new urgency that a certain street version of deconstruction and critical theory might make both more concrete. Going to the street corner might be after all what Kierkegaard and Marcuse did and what the present age could require of us existentially and politically.* ✦✦✦ Kierkegaard, A; and Marcuse, "Über konkrete Philosophie." Multiculturally enlightened singular universals go beyond Sartre's *Anti-Semite* (part 4, and Walzer's preface); cf. Charmé, "Authenticity"; and chaps. 6, 9 below.

3. Multicultural Enlightenment

1. S. Huntington, *Clash*, 305ff.; cf. 19–35, 125–54, 183–206, 266–321.

2. Derrida, OH (conference, "The Cultural Identity of Europe," May 20, 1990), 11, 61f./5, 61f.—first citation; and 6/12—second citation; Habermas, SnI (conference, "Identity and Difference in Democratic Europe," European Commission, Brussels, May 23–25, 1991), 635/493—last two citations above; cf. NR; and I. Young, "Government."

3. Habermas, GpI; on Kierkegaard, HRPS; Matuštík, PI, part 1; and chaps. 1–2 above.

4. On recognition and redistribution, see Fraser, JI.

5. Habermas, FuG, 124–35; Matuštík, PI, 259–64; preceding n. 4, and chaps. 1–2 above.

6. Habermas, GpI; Hobsbawm, *Nations*, 9f.; and on performatives, chaps. 5 and 7 below.

7. Derrida, OH, 17f./10ff.; S. Huntington, *Clash*, 56–78; cf. excursus in chap. 1 above.

8. Derrida, 19f./13f.—first citation; 23f./19—all other citations above; cf. 28/24.

9. Derrida, OH, 30–35/26–32.

10. Derrida, OH, 34–38/31–35; cf. Fukuyama, *The End of History*; S. Huntington, *Clash*, 31f. (like Derrida rejecting Fukuyama's view), 125–54 (for anti-Derridean reasons).

11. Derrida, OH, 41ff./39ff.—all citations above; on Havel, see Matuštík, PI, chaps. 8–9, and chap. 8 below; cf. S. Huntington, *Clash*, 19–35, 290f., 305ff., 318–21.

12. Derrida, OH, 48f./47f.—all citations above; cf. 46f./44f.

13. Derrida, OH, 55/54f.—citation above. Unlike my argument, Martin's *Matrix and Line* (chap. 3) follows the differences in the views of language among Habermas, Davidson, and Derrida; cf. the review of Martin's book, co-authored by Matuštík and P. Huntington.

14. Derrida, OH, 56f./56f.; his lectures at Prague's Central European University (Feb. 28–Mar. 8, 1992) focused on capital as a cultural and a money center. Cf. Dubiel, "Beyond Mourning"; Matuštík, PI, chap. 8; on non-Communist leftism, see Habermas, NR 188–203.

15. Derrida, OH, 57f./57—all citations above.

16. Habermas, TCA, vol. 2 (on lifeworld and system); Fraser, JI (on recognition and redistribution); Sartre, *Critique*, vol. 1 (on scarcity); Tong, *Feminist*

Thought, chap. 6 (on dual- and unified-systems); I. Young, "Unruly Categories" (critiques Fraser's dual method in JI); and Fraser's "Rejoinder."

17. Derrida, OH, 58/58; cf. this approach with Laclau and Mouffe, *Hegemony*.

18. Kierkegaard, FT. Tucker ("Identity Crisis") criticizes appeals to radical self-choice. He argues that its radicality fits with the individualism of modern fundamentalism (289f.). Yet this view cannot stand because of its disregard of the political axis of Kierkegaard's pseudonymous authorship, wherein de Silentio's FT must be read along with Kierkegaard's (PC; A) critical theory of and activism against the established religious and political orders. Tucker's critique (290, n. 5, and Wolin, "Carl Schmitt") is more true of post-Heideggerian and postmodern ab/uses of Kierkegaard, than of the communicative-ethical praxis required by dramatic authorship. The latter is pursued by early Marcuse and Sartre; and I develop this via Habermas's discourse model of popular sovereignty (see chap. 2 above).

19. On critique of the new right-wing dogmatism, see Havel, *Letní přemítání*, 44–60, 95.

20. Derrida, OH, 78/80—first citation, and 75f./77—all other citations.

21. Derrida, OH, 75–78/76–80—all citations above.

22. Cf. Habermas's reading of Derrida in PDM; Derrida's reply to Habermas in *Limited Inc*, 156–58; and "L'Affair Derrida," debating the translation and inclusion of Derrida's interview about Heidegger's politics (Wolin's *Heidegger Controversy*). Derrida's interview, "Philosopher's Hell," was published in 1987 by the French *Le Nouvel Observateur* that granted these rights for the translation of the interview to Wolin and Columbia University Press in October 1991. Because of Derrida's great displeasure and at his legally supported insistence, Columbia University Press scrapped the first issue of Wolin's book which included Derrida's essay. The translation of Derrida's essay was no longer allowed to appear in the MIT 1992 reissue of Wolin's book. "L'Affair Derrida" implies bad faith on the part of both critics and defenders of Derrida. Neither *Le Nouvel Observateur* nor Wolin requested Derrida's own permission (as a matter of courtesy to the author) to publish Wolin's translation of Derrida's piece in Wolin's Columbia University Press volume on Heidegger. Furthermore, Derrida lambasts *The New York Review of Books* for dubbing the entire incident tendentiously as "L'Affair Derrida." This heading abridges Derrida's right to respond and exploits Wolin's and Sheehan's critical essays for the journal's own tabloid-marketing purposes (see Derrida, *Points*, 422–54, and 482–87). ✤✤✤ *I do not find it philosophically necessary to take sides in this academic debate between certain modernists and postmodernists. I argue instead that for Derrida, or for any of the signatories of the supporting letter on his behalf ("L'Affair Derrida," April 22, 69), to defend one's First Amendment authorial rights against the presumed uncharitable manner in which Wolin's book came to include and critique Derrida's piece, the Derrideans must, for better or worse, appeal to critical modern rationality and to the political ideas of 1789. No amount of textual undecidabil-*

ity can help Derrida to decide the case existentially and politically. At this juncture, would Derrida want to make a virtue out of 'the death of the author' thesis when it comes to defending his own authorial position? On what grounds may he justify his question to Wolin, "did he think I was dead?" (March 25, p. 65) It is the unwillingness of 'Derrida 1' to acknowledge explicitly the normative presuppositions of the performance of 'Derrida 2' and, at the same time, the latter's reliance on modernity in making a case against Wolin, rather than what he thinks or does not think about Habermas, Heidegger, or Wolin's command of French, that I find crippling for any thorough sociopolitical critique. Derrida cannot have it both ways: he cannot vindicate himself against a perceived uncourteous editor without admitting protonormative grounds to deconstructive theory. Sheehan says that Derrida has won, "he killed off Wolin's book" (April 25, p. 69). Fair enough judgment! Yet I am not shaken by this authorcide or the cynical consequences of its true disclosure. Opposing the killing in Yugoslavia, unmaking the philosophical defense of ethnic cleansing by such normal academics as Mihaijlo Marković, who has become a political 'Heidegger' of the left, are among examples of that for which it is imminent to spill ink and sign a signature. Still an edification issues from 'victory' and 'death' in this exchange: one learns of the need to theorize institutional and normative contexts for deconstructive interventions. By recognizing the sociopolitical service rendered by deconstructive practice, we may launch coalitions among critical post/modern social theorists for our times. ✛✛✛ [Cf. Sheehan's "A Normal Nazi"; Doder, "Belgrade Professor."]

23. Cf. Butler, GT, BM; Honneth, "Decentered Autonomy"; Laclau and Mouffe, *Hegemony*; and Mouffe, *Dimensions*. Unlike the latter two, I do not restrict Gramscian radical democracy to an emphatically antinormative politics of difference or cultural pluralism. I agree with Fraser, JI: *"cultural differences can be freely elaborated and democratically mediated only on the basis of social equality"* (186).

4. Specters of Deconstruction and Critical Theory

1. "Now, if there is a spirit of Marxism which I will never be prepared to renounce, it is not merely the critical idea or the questioning posture (a consistent deconstruction must insist on them even as it likewise learns that this is not the last or first word). . . . To break with the 'party form' or with some form of the State or the International does not mean to jettison every form of practical or effective organization. It is exactly the contrary that matters to us here" (Derrida, SM, 146f./89). *Postsocialist* (instead of Lyotard's postmodern) subtitles Fraser's JI.

2. Marx, Letter to Ruge (Sept. 1843), *Early Writings*, 207 and 209—two citations above.

3. Derrida, SM, 72, 100, 105, 164, 168, 171/40, 57, 61, 99f., 103ff. "[A] radicalization is always indebted to the very thing which it radicalizes. That is why I spoke of the Marxist memory and tradition of deconstruction, of its Marxist 'spirit'" (152f./92f.).

4. L. Gordon raised this question during my presentation: "Is Marx a deconstructionist's daddy or is Derrida's 'reading' Marx a ruse, a smoke screen?"

This questioning polemicizes *with* or *about* Derrida, but how is its concern existentially and politically urgent for *us*?

5. Derrida's Marx-lectures were given in Moscow, Prague, at New York University, and at University of California at Irvine. The course on The Philosophy of Social Science, originated in Korčula summer school by Habermas, moved in 1993 from Dubrovnik to Prague. The Midwest Critical Theory Roundtable was founded in 1993 in St. Louis and met there again in 1994 and 1997; in 1995 it met at Northwestern University in conjunction with Habermas's fall lectureship, and in 1996 at University of Illinois in Urbana-Champaign.

6. Derrida, SM, 142, 152/86, 92.

7. Mathias Kettner questioned my Prague reading (May 1995) of Derrida's book: "why should critical theorists find in Derrida's Marx anything they do not know already?"

8. Derrida, SM, 14/xviii, and 17/xx. Cf. Kierkegaard, FT, 9–14.

9. I gave a misleading impression ("Kierkegaard," 224 n. 18) that Caputo made an exegetical error by not reading "Kierkegaard along with Marx" in Derrida's SM and *Gift*. See n. 35 to chap. 2 above; cf. Caputo, "Instants, Secrets, and Singularities: Dealing Death in Kierkegaard and Derrida," in Matuštík and Westphal, KPM, 216–38.

10. On 'messianic promise' vs. 'messianic dogma', see Derrida, SM, 56, 88, 109, 111f., 124, 126, 147, 265–68/28, 50, 64, 65f., 73, 75, 89, 167–69; on the doctrine of ends, 37f., 70, 97–126, 142, 164, 195/14f., 38, 56–75, 86, 100, 120. Cf. Derrida, "The Ends of Man," and Kierkegaard's claim that Christianity is not a doctrine but existence-communication (CUP); and "Rotation of Crops," E/O, vol. 1. In Kierkegaard, aesthetics is dialectically linked to ethics. This link carries existential implications rather than Platonic suspicions of art and poetry or Habermasian suspicions of deconstruction. I can consistently criticize meretricious aestheticizing practices in deconstruction and affirm self-transformative and socially revolutionary deconstructive art. Marcuse's unmasking of one-dimensionality and Adorno's of the culture industry echo this Kierkegaardian ironization of aesthetic existence. Affirmations of an aesthetic dimension in refusals resembles Kierkegaard's *either/or usage* of 'aesthetic'. Kierkegaard's authorship is aesthetic production; yet each book, like Derrida's SM, can be a subversive act.

11. Derrida, SM, 35f., 145f., 149, 151ff./13f., 88f., 90f., 92ff.

12. On authorship and authoring, see Matuštík, PI, chap. 9. (On the two senses of 'undecidability', see last n. to chap. 2 above and excursus in chap. 9, sec. 1 below.)

13. Eribon, "Marx, penseur du XXIe siècle," 50f.

14. Derrida, SM, 69, 73, 130–55/37, 40, 78–94.

15. Derrida, SM, 60–62, 68, 148, 266f./31–32, 36, 90, 167.

16. Derrida, SM, 35, 268f./13, 169.

17. On 'specter' in Derrida, see SM, 34f., 69, 80, 116f., 163–66, 168, 175, 190f./12f., 37f., 45, 68, 99–102, 103, 107, 117.

18. Derrida, SM, 141, 164, 195/85, 100, 120.

19. Derrida, SM, 141/85.

20. Derrida, SM, 37f., 97–127/14f., 55–75.

21. Derrida, SM, 70/38.

22. On Kierkegaard's TA, see also Matuštík, PI, chap. 10.

23. Derrida, SM, 36, 91, 115, 141/14, 52, 67, 85. I translate "évidence" literally rather than as "obvious fact" to render Derrida's experiential sense of phenomenological evidence.

24. Derrida, SM, 141/85—both above citations, cf. "Deconstruction," 37.

25. See Derrida, SM, 142, 145, 148f., 152/86, 88, 89f., 92; cf. chap. 3 above.

26. Derrida, SM, 93f., 109, 116, 140, 166–68, 170, 180f., 266–69/ 53f., 63f., 67f., 84f., 101–3, 104, 109f., 167–69; cf. OH; on Foucault, see chaps. 5 and 7 below.

27. Derrida, SM, 62, 148, 190f./33, 90, 116f.; cf. Matuštík, PI, chap. 10.

28. Derrida, SM, 88, 139–68; cf. 39, 58/50, 84–103; cf. 16, 39.

29. Kierkegaard, JP, year 1848: entry no. 4131. Matuštík, PI, 107–9, and part 3.

30. Derrida, SM, 134–39/81–84—all above citations; cf. 69, 73, 130ff./37, 40, 78ff.

31. Derrida, SM, 141/85 vs. complementary views of Fukuyama and S. Huntington.

32. On "singularity," see Derrida, SM, 56, 58, 60, 87, 111, 124, 141, 149, 166ff., 170, 177, 268/28, 29, 31, 49, 65, 73, 85, 91, 101ff., 104, 109, 169.

33. Eribon, "Marx," 53.

34. Derrida, SM, 141/85; Sartre, "Kierkegaard." Derrida echoes this Kierkegaardian-Sartrean term (discussed in chap. 6 below) in his "absolutely universal attention to the singular" (Derrida's response to Caputo, in "A Conversation with Jacques Derrida").

35. Kierkegaard, TA, 106—all citations above. Derrida's reply to Eribon evokes Sartre.

36. Derrida, SM, 19, 39, 42, 87, 110, 129, 137, 141f., 255/1, 16, 18, 49, 64, 77, 83, 85, 161. In an introduction to a representative anthology on the 1960s debate

between existential philosophy and Marxism, Novack identifies "the core of Existentialism"; he paraphrases Merleau-Ponty who anticipates the Shakespearean refrain from Derrida's book: "The times have been thrown so far out of joint that to many it appears almost hopeless to attempt to set them right" (Novack, ed., *Existentialism versus Marxism*, 5).

37. Derrida, SM, 39/16—first citation, and 141f./85—second (indented) citation above.

38. Derrida, SM, 141/85; 142/86; 147/89—three citations above.

39. Derrida, SM, 142/86—first citation (emphasis added), and 146f./89—last citation above.

40. Derrida, SM, 147/89—first citation, and 142/86—last two citations; cf. chap. 9, sec. 3 below.

41. Derrida, SM, 146f./89, OH, 12/6—citations above; cf. Popkin's "Comments" 58–65 (Marcuse, EoL, and Derrida, "Ends of Man," affected by 1968); P. Huntington, "Heidegger's Reading of Kierkegaard Revisited: From Ontological Abstraction to Ethical Concretion," in Matuštík and Westphal, KPM, 43–65; Habermas, PT; and Anderson, "On Hegel," 262–65.

42. Cf. Habermas, PT, 70–72; and Kellner, *Herbert Marcuse*, 32–68.

43. Derrida, SM, 147/89.

44. Derrida, "A Conversation with Jacques Derrida" (citations are Derrida's responses to Caputo). "New humanism" is discussed by Schrag and Martin; cf. chaps. 5 and 9 below.

45. Derrida, SM, 58/29 and 142/86.

46. Matuštík, PI, 8–20; 46ff.

47. See "Proceedings"; cf. Chomsky, *Year 501* with S. Huntington's *Clash*.

48. Derrida, SM, 145–49/88–90—citations above, cf. "Deconstruction," 34.

49. Žižek, *Tarrying With The Negative*, chap. 6: "Enjoy Your Nation as Yourself!"

50. Douglass, *Narrative*, 21–26, 48–51, 52–58, 68, 84–92, 120–26; cf. Willett, *Maternal Ethics*, part 3, on intersubjectivity derivative neither from Hegelian, Kojèvian, and Lacanian master-and-slave struggles for recognition nor a postmodern demise of liberation narratives.

51. See Derrida, SM, 15f., 147f./xix, 90; cf. "Force of Law, 'The Mystical Foundation of Authority'," *Deconstruction*; and Habermas, FuG.

52. Derrida, "A Conversation with Jacques Derrida" (Derrida's response to Caputo and Walter Brogan). In this conversation, Derrida made an emphatic declaration of love for the Great Books, "the dead White males," and the western Canon. I could not resist finding Derrida's remarks—given the limited context of

his conversation with White male academics and while speaking on the soil of a major Catholic university—playing into conservative reactions to multicultural demands in education. Cf. Caputo's excellent text, *Deconstruction*.

53. Derrida, "The Ends of Man," 32f.—all citations above, cf. "Of the Humanities."

54. See below chap. 8, sec. 2, on 'Laughters and Grins'; cf. Harris, "Believe It or Not"; Kohák, *Patočka*; and McCumber, "Time in the Ditch."

55. "Comunicados," Dec. 31, 1993 and Jan. 6, 1994; and the speech by Marcos to the National Democratic Convention (New Aguascalientes, Mexico, Aug. 8, 1994).

56. Habermas, VaZ, 32f./22—citations by Habermas and Haller above; cf. 10–44/5–32.

57. Derrida, SM, 138f./83f. Cf. Kellner, *The Persian Gulf TV War*.

58. Habermas, VaZ, 18/11—first and last citation, and 32f./22—all other citations above. "After Hitler and Auschwitz, the Germans have every reason for being particularly sensitive to universalism; that is, for the indivisibility of internationally recognized human rights and for a civilized mode of human interaction" (VaZ, 40/28). Cf. Jewish critics, Chomsky, "Nefarious Aggression," "Aftermath," "What They Say Goes"; and Derrida, SM, 138f./83f., and "Deconstruction," 29.

59. Ingram, RHP, 236–46, 394f.; Marsh, CAL, 145, 161–76, 233; Fraser, JI; Laclau and Mouffe, *Hegemony*; S. Huntington, *Clash*; and Neaman, "Mutiny."

60. Ingram, RHP, 136f.; Marsh, CAL, 168; Walzer, *Spheres*, 295–303; Habermas, FuG.

61. Marsh, CAL, chap. 12; Ingram, RHP, chap. 5.

62. On Marx, see Habermas, TCA, vol. 2; and Postone, *Time*, chap. 6; cf. Cohen, "It's not a transition"; Hoffman, "Russian Mogul" on post-Communist baron, Boris Berezovsky.

63. Marsh, CAL, 239 and 271—citations above; cf. 252ff.

64. Marsh, CAL, 240–47.

65. Marsh, CAL, 254, 261.

66. Ingram, RHP, 203 and 237; citing Habermas, AS, 183.

67. Marsh, CAL, 263; cf. Habermas, NR, 199; and Laclau and Mouffe, *Hegemony*.

68. See Ingram, RHP, 236–42.

69. Habermas, AS, 148f., 188f.

70. Cf. Marsh, CAL, 186, 210ff., 213; Marcuse, *Soviet Marxism*; Resnick and Wolff, "Between State and Private Capitalism." Cf. chaps. 8 and 9 (sec. 4) below.

71. Ingram, RHP, 237–41, 246, 258, 272, 394f.; Marsh, CAL, 272, 275, 288, 306ff., 314, 323; Schweickart, *Against Capitalism*, 96; Gould, *Rethinking Democracy*; and Postone, *Time* 40f., 274ff., 324, 393f., and chap. 6 analyzing deficits in Habermas's reading of Marx.

72. Marsh, CAL, 283.

73. Balibar, *Masses*; Balibar and Wallerstein, *Race*; and Fraser, JI.

74. Firestone, *The Dialectic of Sex*, 20 and 15—citations above. Cf. Hartmann, "The Unhappy Marriage"; Young, JPD and "Comments."

75. See chaps. 1 above, and 6 and 9 below.

76. Firestone, *The Dialectic of Sex*, 12.

77. Marsh, CAL, 218, 247, 282–89, 341–47.

78. Yeatman, *Postmodern Revisionings*, 1–10—all citations above. Cf. Marsh, CAL, 59–64, 73f., 213–15, 222, 225f., 291–94, 308–12, 354f.; Jameson, *Postmodernism*; Beverley and Oviedo, *The Postmodernism Debate*; Dirlik, "The Postcolonial Aura"; Prakash, "Postcolonial Criticism"; Williams and Chrisman, *Colonial Discourse*; and n. 4 above.

79. Cf. Heidegger, "Only A God"; Sartre, *Being and Nothingness*, *Critique*, vol. 1, "Kierkegaard," *Hope Now*; Rorty, "Fraternity"; and Kierkegaard, CUP.

80. See Kierkegaard, CUP, on monasticism, and inwardness; Matuštík, PI, 164ff.; 140–49; on degenerate political regimes and psyches, Plato's *Republic*, bks. 8–9; cf. chap. 8 below.

81. See n. 12 to chap. 2 above, an excursus and conclusion to chap. 8, and sec. 3 in chap. 9 below. Cf. Matuštík, "Democratic Multicultures"; and Lonergan, *Insight*, 225–44.

82. Cf. Sartre's *Anti-Semite* with Rorty's *Contingency*; and chap. 2 above.

83. Epigraphs to each chap. and chap. 8 below in particular push the outer bounds of this imaginative—at once theoretical and practical—hope and project.

84. Cf. Kundera, *The Book*, part 7, "The Border."

85. Marcuse, N, 3–42; 134–58; Martin, *Politics*, 48, 197–230, 269f. nn. 4 and 6; and *Humanism*, 125f.

5. Hope and Refusal

1. ✦✦✦ *Claims that Marcuse's hope offers a bad social theory were raised during my presentations both by some postmodern critics (Society for Phenomenology and Existential Philosophy, Seattle 1994 and Chicago 1995) and some critical social theorists*

(annual Prague meeting, May 1994 and May 1995). Against the politically liberal/libertarian and economically neoliberal horizon of present markets and power, such claims conjure up ghosts of complicity. Should not one be solidary with those for whom hope is given yet part company with this horizon and figures cast on its ground? The veterans of Prague Spring (1968) and students who lived through the Velvet Revolution (1989) were more receptive in considering, critically, the need for this hope (lectures in Prague 1994–95) than were the two above groupings. ✦✦✦

2. On disciplines, see Foucault, DP; and on the "aesthetics of existence," UP, 12, 89–93; and PPC, 47–53; on "the new sensibility," see Marcuse, EoL, chap. 2. I draw on the body-performativity in Butler, BM, 1–23, 187–91, 219f., 223–42; her speech-acts theory and deconstruction, "For a Careful Reading," 133–37, and *Excitable Speech*; and performativity in critical race theory, EE. On a critically performative ethics of 'asymmetrical reciprocity', see below my discussion of D. Cornell and I. Young; on critical theory of political economy and culture, Fraser, JI.

3. Foucault, HS, vol.1:95f.; and Marcuse, ODM, 52—for the respective citations above. I am inspired by Paul Breines's "Revisiting Marcuse with Foucault: *An Essay on Liberation* Meets *The History of Sexuality*," and Kellner, "A Marcuse Renaissance?" both in Bokina and Lukes, *Marcuse*, 41–56 and 245–67. Cf. chaps. 3–4 above, and 7 and 9 below.

4. Poster, "Foucault and the Problem of Self-Constitution," in Caputo and Yount, *Foucault*, 64f. See Foucault, DIE (1953, written during Ph.D. studies).

5. Cf. Foucault's lead quote with Marcuse's *ethos* of liberation (EoL, 24–26, 48, 49, 88).

6. The key essays for reading this double movement of transgression and agency are Foucault's homage to Georges Bataille, "A Preface to Transgression" (1963), LCP, 29–52; Foucault's three readings of Kant: "Qu'est-ce-que" ("What is Critique" [1978]); "The Art of Telling the Truth" (1983), in Kelly, *Critique and Power* 139–48; and "What Is Enlightenment?" (1983), in Foucault, FR, 32–50. Cf. Hoy and McCarthy, *Critical Theory*; and James Schmidt and Thomas E. Wartenberg, "Foucault's Enlightenment: Critique, Revolution, and the Fashioning of the Self," in Kelly, *Critique and Power*, 283–314.

7. Foucault, HS, vol. 1:93; for a shift from his earlier positions, see "Two Lectures" (1976), P/K, 92. I rely on Butler's BM where she modifies her position from her earlier GT. Cf. Sawicki, *Disciplining Foucault* and "Foucault and Feminism"; and Young, JPD.

8. Foucault, "Two Lectures," P/K, 96 and 98—citations above; on "nonpositive affirmation," see "A Preface to Transgression," LCP, 35f.

9. Foucault, DIE. Cf. Poster, in Caputo and Yount, *Foucault*, 63–80.

10. Habermas claims to have done away with the subject-centered reason better than the poststructuralists discussed in his PDM. He might have implicated himself in abstracting from existential concretion. Marcuse is critical of existen-

tia*list* decisionism; yet he reverses any formalism by retaining, even in his later works, the early existential project of concrete philosophy. Cornell, "What is Ethical Feminism?" foregrounds this move via Adornian-Derridean correctives to the politics of recognition.

11. Foucault, "Two Lectures," P/K, 99; cf. 97, 101.

12. Cf. essays in Novack, *Existentialism*; and works by Wolin.

13. Foucault, "A Preface to Transgression," LCP, 34f.—all citations above (emphasis added).

14. Foucault, "A Preface to Transgression," LCP, 36—citations above.

15. On Marcuse's early Heideggerian years, see Kellner's *Marcuse*, chaps. 1–3; Marcuse's writings from the 1920–30s; and an essay, "Sartre's Existentialism"; cf. Sartre, *Critique*, vol. 1. I argue against Alfred Schmidt ("Existential Ontology and Historical Materialism in the Work of Herbert Marcuse," in Pippin, *Marcuse*, 47–67) that Marcuse's attempt to join critical social theory with existential phenomenology represents his strength. He helps to overcome the material deficits in formal methodologies, such as Habermas's, and the normative deficits in restricted interventionist strategies, such as Foucault's.

16. Foucault, HS, vol. 1:94–95—citations above.

17. Foucault, HS, vol. 1:95.

18. Fraser, "Foucault on Modern Power: Empirical Insights and Normative Confusions," UP, 17–34. 'Otherwise than being' is Lévinas's ethical rejoinder to Heidegger's uncritical ontology; and the last question is really Lenin's. Given the failed Soviet answer as well as the NWO today, the rejoinder and the question carry even more weight now.

19. Foucault, P/K, 62 and 126; cf. 63–77.

20. Foucault, P/K, 127f.

21. Foucault, P/K, 130–33.

22. Marcuse, "Über konkrete Philosophie"; Sartre, "Kierkegaard"; and chap. 2 above.

23. Foucault, P/K, 133.

24. Foucault, P/K, 56—first citation; 76—second citation; and 81—rest of citations above.

25. Foucault, P/K, 82f.—all citations above. The return of the repressed, one-dimensionality, and specters of liberation are Marcuse's terms used by me to read Foucault.

26. Foucault, P/K, 83—first four citations, and 145—last citation above; cf. 85, 97; and Marcuse, "Philosophy and Critical Theory," N, 141–43.

27. Marcuse, N, 143. On the 'fact' of Blackness, Fanon, BSWM, chap. 5.

28. Foucault, "On the Genealogy of Ethics," FR, 351; cf. 76–97.

29. On Sartre, cf. Poster, in Caputo and Yount, *Foucault*, 66; on critical ontology that does not presuppose a fixed authenticity, Gordon, BF; on existential-performatives, Matuštík, PI, chap. 5. On Derrida's new enlightenment, see chaps. 3–4 above.

30. Foucault, "On The Genealogy of Ethics," FR, 343; cf. Poster, in Caputo and Yount, *Foucault*, 73f.

31. Foucault, DP, 28ff.—citations above; and 25 on the "'political economy' of the body."

32. Foucault, DP, 25f.—citations above; cf. HS, vol. 1:95f.; P/K, 82f.; and Marcuse, EoL.

33. Foucault, DP, 23f.; cf. "The Political Technology of Individuals," *Technologies of the Self*, 145–62 and ed. intro., 4.

34. Foucault, DP, 26—citations above.

35. Horkheimer, *Kritische Theorie*. Gordon, BF. On a forgetfulness of body in critical theory, see Matuštík, PI, 100–103.

36. Foucault, "Politics and Ethics," FR, 380—first citation, and 379—last two citations above.

37. Foucault, "Two Lectures," P/K, 108. Cf. Adorno, ND.

38. Foucault, "On The Genealogy," FR, 372. Cf. Kierkegaard, SuD, part 1, A, a. While agreeing in general with Fraser's critique of Foucault (UP, 17–66), I find promising the new reading of the Foucault/Habermas debate in Kelly's *Critique and Power*.

39. Foucault, "On The Genealogy," FR, 344ff.

40. Foucault, "On The Genealogy," FR, 343, cf. 348.

41. Foucault, "Politics and Ethics," FR, 377—citations above; see "On The Genealogy," FR, 350 for separating ethics from politics; on this in Havel, cf. Matuštík, PI, part 3.

42. I side with Foucault, Sartre, Marcuse, and Habermas against the emphatic communitarianism of C. Taylor's EA and PR (see chaps. 1–2 above).

43. On Foucault's three readings of Kant, see n. 6 above.

44. Butler, FCR, 134, cites Derrida's discussion ("Signature, Event, Context," *Limited Inc*) of Austin (*How to Do Things with Words*); cf. her BM, 1–23, 219–42; *Excitable Speech*; and EE on Foucault.

45. Butler, FCR, 133—first citation, and 134—last two citations above; cf. GT, 142.

46. Butler, FCR, 134. On the 'what' and the 'how', see Kierkegaard's CUP.

47. Butler, FCR, 135, cf. GT, 140f.

48. Cf. Butler's early work on feminist existentialists, "Variation on Sex and Gender"; cf. GT, 111–28, 140–49.

49. Butler, BM, 125; 121–40; cf. Matuštík, PI 107–26. (On borders, see chap. 6 below.)

50. Butler, EE, 15f.—all citations above.

51. Butler, EE, 17.

52. Butler, EE, 19; Fanon, BSWM, 109–40; Du Bois, *The Souls*, 43–53; Gordon, BF.

53. Butler, EE, 20.

54. Butler, BM, 2—citation above; 5–12; cf. 218f.

55. Butler, "Variation," 128f.—citations above; Beauvoir, *The Second Sex*, 301; and Kierkegaard, E/O, vol. 1, and R. Cf. n. 48 above.

56. Derrida, *Limited*, 18. Butler, BM, 15—citation above; cf. 13, 22, 219f.

57. Butler, BM, 15, 187, 225, 230—on citationality; and 191—her suggestion on the last point. Cf. Kierkegaard's SuD, part 1, A, a. (On existential democracy, see chap. 9 below.) Butler insists that her category of performativity "is not a return to an existential theory of the self as constituted through its acts, for the existential theory maintains a prediscursive structure for both the self and its acts. It is precisely the discursively variable construction of each in and through the other that has interested me here" (GT, 142). In developing my existential communications theory, inspired by Kierkegaard's communication model and by the Czech phenomenological and dramatic traditions (see Matuštík, PI, and chaps. 2 above and 8 below), I *agree* with Butler's interest. For that reason I *disagree* with her truncated existential theory. And I argue that notions of repetition, iterability, or citationality need a critical theory of existential performatives.

58. Butler, "Variation," 139—first citation, and 137—last citation above; cf. her *Subjects*, 217–38; and Marcuse, ODM, 257.

59. Butler, "Variation," 140ff. Despite her disillusionment with Marcuse's EC (part 2), Butler will not hurt her position by distinguishing Freud's reality principle from Marcuse's performance principle (the latter is a historically contingent, criticizable form of the former). Cf. Butler, *Subjects*, 217–38 with C. Fred Alford, "Marx, Marcuse, and Psychoanalysis: Do They Still Fit after All These Years?" in Bokina and Lukes, *Marcuse*, 131–46.

60. Cf. Martin, *Humanism*, 47–57, 59, 62, 70, 128–33; cf. an excursus on anti-humanism in chap. 9, sec. 3, below.

61. Foucault, DIE, 49; 51; Merleau-Ponty, *The Primacy of Perception*, 96–155, 150f. Cf. Marsh, *Post-Cartesian Meditations*.

62. Foucault, DIE, 53.

63. Foucault, DIE, 55 and 57—two short citations, and 59—the last long citation above.

64. Foucault, DIE, 67f.—citations above. Lévinas speaks of the ethical as otherwise than being because the ethical originates in the call of the other within a face-to-face encounter.

65. Sawicki, "Foucault and Feminism," 30–33—all citations above. Fraser ("Pragmatism") integrates "Benhabib's quasi-Habermasian approach" (160f.), "Butler's quasi-Foucauldian framework" (161–64), and Cornell's "ethical and utopian thinking" and the "project of denaturalizing critique" (164ff.) into a neo-pragmatist synthesis of the Habermasian and Foucauldian ethical and political feminism (167f.).

66. Fraser, "Pragmatism," 161—first two, and 162—last two citations above.

67. Cornell, "What is Ethical Feminism?" 78—all citations above; cf. "Two Lectures," "The Poststructuralist Challenge," and *The Philosophy of the Limit*, 14–38, 56–61.

68. Cornell, "What is Ethical Feminism?" 79—all citations above.

69. Benhabib, SS; Honneth, *Kampf*; Taylor, EA; PR; and chaps. 1 above and 6 below.

70. They share a corrective to Taylor (Habermas) despite differences: on recognition and redistribution, see Fraser's JI, Young's critique "Unruly Categories," and Fraser's "Rejoinder."

71. Young, C, 167, and "Asymmetrical Reciprocity," secs. 2, 4–5, 7; Cornell, *The Philosophy of the Limit*, 13–38; Benhabib, SS, 54; Honneth, *Kampf*; and chap. 6 below.

72. Young, C, 167–72 and "Asymmetrical Reciprocity," sec. 3; cf. Benhabib, "In Defense of Universalism."

73. Cornell, *The Philosophy of the Limit*, 85f.; 55—citations above; cf. 60f.; on 'correspondences', see my discussion of Willett in chap. 1 above.

74. On translatability, see Davidson, *Inquiries*; and Gadamer, *Truth and Method*; further Fanon, BSWM; Merleau-Ponty, *Phenomenology*; Matuštík, two essays on "Merleau-Ponty"; Beauvoir, *The Ethics* and *The Second Sex*; Sartre, *Anti-Semite*; and *Critique*, vol. 1:256–69, 322, 350, 355, 408f., 506, 509, 531; and chaps. 1–4 above, and 6 below.

75. Benhabib, "The Generalized and the Concrete Other," in Benhabib and Cornell, *Feminism*, 77–95; Honneth, "The Other of Justice," in White, *The Cambridge Companion*, 316; Critchley, "Habermas und Derrida"; Young, JPD and C; Kristeva, *Strangers*; and next chap.

6. Communities in Resistance

1. I draw on Willett and Matuštík, "Internet Conversations"; on ethical vulnerability, see Matuštík, PI, chap. 2; "Merleau-Ponty's Phenomenology"; and chap. 1 above; on reciprocal phenomenological symmetry and asymmetrical ethical reciprocity see chap. 5 above.

2. Kierkegaard, JP, 1854, vol. 4, no. 4238.

3. On critiques of identity logic, see Adorno, ND; on political existentialism, Marcuse, "The Struggle Against Liberalism in the Totalitarian View of the State," N, 31f.; cf. 78.

4. I place among neoliberals, Fukuyama and Nozick; proceduralists, center-liberal Rawls and left-liberal Habermas; communitarians, nostalgic MacIntyre, S. Huntington, Sandel, to some extent C. Taylor, progressive Walzer, and a spectrum of multicultural, race, and gender views; cf. comments on Taylor in PR; and chaps. 1 above and 9 below.

5. On 'hybridity', see Anzaldúa, *Borderlands* and "Bridge"; Lugones, "Hispaniendo y Lesbiando," "On *Borderlands*," and "Playfulness"; Lugones and Spelman, "Have We Got a Theory for You!" Giroux and McLaren, *Between Borders*, 218f.; Giroux, *Disturbing Pleasures*, 60ff.; Bhabha, "The Postcolonial and the Postmodern: the Question of Agency," *The Location*, 171–97; Schwarz and Dienst, *Reading*, 10f., 137f., 187, 192; Néstor García Canclini, "The Hybrid: A Conversation with Margarita Zires, Raymundo Mier, and Mabel Piccini," in Beverley and Oviedo, *The Postmodernism Debate*, 77–92; Shohat and Stam, *Unthinking Eurocentrism*, 37–49; and R. Young (*Colonial Desire*, 4–28, 231) on hybridity in a nineteenth-century imaginary of race and the colonial desire of interracial sex from which postcolonial desire is not yet free. Existentially harnessed critical traditionalism (Du Bois, Gandhi, Kothari, Nandy) can empower communities in resistance.

6. Avineri, "Hegel and Nationalism," 463. Hegel would reject the anti-Black racism of the U.S. supremacists as well as the German sources cited by Hernnstein and Murray (*The Bell Curve*); cf. Lane, "The Tainted Sources of 'The Bell Curve'."

7. Avineri, "Hegel and Nationalism," 476—citation (he agrees with the reading of Hegel by Marcuse, RR, 237); cf. 464f., 467–74. I differ from Gallagher ("Some Particular Limitations," sec. 3): it is descriptively and hermeneutically true that particularity limits universality. Concrete expressions for the relation of particularity and universality give us a more critical angle on how the limit constrains

universal aspirations than would the communitarian privileging of particularistic traditions defended by Gallagher. Can one take nations as particulars to build constitutional democratic states? I do not find problems with a critical adaptation of Greek *phronesis* to root democracy in cultural particularity—this I think marks the critical traditionality of Nandy (*Illegitimacy of Nationalism*; and n. 5 above), as well as the existential democratic models of Havel (PP), Masaryk (*Ideály*), or West (KF), and Fanon (BSWM, WoE). I seek singular universals not on uncritically communitarian but on existentially material grounds (chaps. 1 above and 8–9 below).

8. Avineri, "Hegel and Nationalism," 482f.; Hegel, PR, add. to para. 339.

9. Avineri, "Hegel and Nationalism," 483f.—citations above.

10. Avineri, "Hegel and Nationalism," 484; Hobsbawm, *Nations*, 9f.; and B. Anderson, "Exodus," 316—citations above. Cf. Anderson, on maps and imagined homes (319) and hybridity (333 and n. 6, citing Prakash, "Postcolonial Criticism," 8, who in turn names Bhabha as the source for the "vocabulary of hybridity" in postcolonial discourse). Concepts of hybridity and transgression get attention in poststructuralism; they inform practices of coalitional politics pursued pretheoretically also before postmodern *ethos* became prevalent. Cf. Du Bois, *The Souls*, chap. 14; Beverley and Oviedo, introduction to *The Postmodernism Debate*, 4f., and essays therein; Williams and Chrisman, *Colonial Discourse*; Anderson, *Imagined Communities*; on social identities as emergent concepts, Urban and Sherzer, *Nation-States and Indians*, 12–16; Giroux and McLaren, *Between Borders*, 214; Blaut, *The Colonizer's Model*; on critical traditionalist alternatives to ethnocentric-nationalist communitarianism and disencumbered liberalism, see Blaney and Inayatullah, "Prelude"; Nandy "Cultural Frames"; Kothari, *Transformation and Survival* and *Growing Amnesia*; Dallmayr, "Global Development?"; and nn. 5, 7 above, and 75–76 below.

11. Derrida, SM, 90/51; cf. 105–27/61–75; chap. 4 above; Kojève, *Introduction*; Norris, *Uncritical Theory*, 126–58; and subtitle of Greider, *One World*.

12. See Walsh, "VW," A-16, for the 1936 photo of Hitler's infantile smile at the moment when Volkswagen's founder, Ferdinand Porsche, explains the future car design.

13. Westphal, *Hegel*, ix–xi, and chaps. 5–7; cf. 84–89.

14. Hegel, PR, para. 321–40. Hegel's failure of nerve is echoed in the global policy thesis of S. Huntington's *Clash* (see the opening to chap. 3 above).

15. Westphal, *Hegel*, 87 and 89; cf. 116–17, 130f.

16. See Habermas, VaZ, 17–19, 29–44, 136, 138, 152/10–12, 19–31, 103, 105, 115; and chap. called "Europe's Second Chance," 97–129/73–98. On Habermas's reading of Hegel via Kant in moral theory, see Matuštík, PI, chap. 2. On contemporary interpretations of the Hegelian theme of the end of history, see Westphal, *Hegel*, xi, 129ff.; Kojève, *Introduction*, 71–74, 75–99, 112, 154–68. Cf. Norris, *Uncritical Theory*, 126–58.

17. Hegel, PR, para. 321–22.

18. Hegel, PR, para. 325–26; cf. Kant "Perpetual Peace," 345f./87f.

19. Hegel, PR, para. 324.

20. Hegel, PR, para. 331–34—citations above; cf. 336; and Kant "Perpetual Peace," 343f./85f.

21. Habermas, GpI, 169/257. Hegel, PR, para. 340; cf. Gallagher, "Some Particular Limitations," sec. 3.

22. See Habermas, SnI; GpI; SR; VaZ; VV; and PDM (on the concept of a higher-level intersubjectivity, chaps. 1–3, 11–12). Cf. Taylor, PR, 25–74.

23. Hegel, PR, para. 333.

24. I find no substantive disagreements on this between Habermas, and the Gramscian position of Laclau and Mouffe. Cf. Mouffe's claim in *Dimensions of Radical Democracy*, 13f.

25. Habermas, SR, 107; cf. 128–35; on emergent concepts, Urban and Sherzer, *Nation-States and Indians*, 5–16. Just as with critical modernists (e.g., Habermas), Nandy's crititical traditionality does not "museumize" traditions ("Cultural Frames," 117; cf. 114–16).

26. Habermas, SnI, 660/515—first citation, and VaZ, 32/22—last citation.

27. Habermas, SnI, 636/494f. He fulfills Foucault's request but not exactly on his terms: "What we need, however, is a political philosophy that isn't erected around the problem of sovereignty, nor therefore around the problems of law and prohibition. We need to cut off the King's head: in political theory that has still to be done" (Foucault, P/K, 121; cf. 78–108).

28. Habermas, SnI, 638/496, and 642/499—two citations above. On permanent revolution, see Matuštík, PI, 192, 197, 216, 253–57, 263f.; and Habermas, VV.

29. Habermas, VaZ, 100/75; cf. SnI, 651/507; and chaps. 4 above and 9 below.

30. Habermas, SnI, 643/500—first two citations, and 649/505—last two citations above; see VV, part 2. Cf. Young's "idea of a heterogeneous public" (JPD, 158, 183–91).

31. Habermas, SnI, 651/507—all citations above; cf. SR, 116–22; chaps. 1 and 3 above.

32. Habermas, SnI, 654/510.

33. Habermas, SnI, 656–59/512f.; in last citation above, Rehg mistranslates *ethnisch* as *ethical*.

34. Habermas, SR, 140ff.—all citations above.

35. Habermas, SR, 142—citations above; cf. S. Huntington, *Clash*, and chap. 3 above.

36. Habermas (SR, 143–48) debates asylum in Germany without pursuing global socioeconomic aims. On the unfinished job of the Freedmen's Bureau, see Du Bois, *Souls*, 54–78.

37. Habermas, SnI, 659/514—citations above; cf. WhS; Nancy S. Love, "What's Left of Marx?" in White, *The Cambridge Companion to Habermas*, 46–66; and chaps. 1, 4 above.

38. Habermas, SnI, 659f./514—citations above.

39. Habermas, SnI, 659f./514f.—first two citations, VaZ, 33/22—last citation above; Dienst, *Still Life*; Kellner, *The Persian Gulf*; and on TV-protest, chap. 1 above.

40. For critiques of communitarian and organicist ideals of communities, see Friedman, "Feminism"; Young, JPD, chap. 8; and Caraway, *Segregated Sisterhood*, chap. 6.

41. Honneth, "Diskursethik," 186–89, 191, 193.

42. Habermas, SR, 122, 137; cf. 134f.; Taylor, PR; Fraser, JI, 11–39, 173–223; "A Rejoinder"; and Young, "Unruly Categories." For my argument, Fraser's and Young's disagreements (on adopting a dual set of symbolic-material categories or a complex polyvalent set) are less crucial than an agreement that the liberal-communitarian debate (e.g., Habermas-Taylor, Benhabib) as well as radical democratic projects (e.g., Laclau and Mouffe) may misrecognize the materially normative dimensions of justice. My existentially material key builds from this agreement, even though I find Young's position theoretically more nuanced than Fraser implies.

43. Benhabib, SS, 11; "The Generalized and the Concrete Other," in Benhabib and Cornell, *Feminism*, 77–95; on postconventional ethics, also Honneth, *Kampf*, 274–87 (J. Anderson's intro. to Eng. trans.); Matuštík, PI, 259–64; and chap. 1 above. Nancy S. Love, "What's Left of Marx," in White, *The Cambridge Companion to Habermas*, 58f.: "from each according to his [or her] ability, to each according to his [or her] needs," cites Marx, "Critique of the Gotha Program," in Tucker, *Marx-Engels Reader*, 531; cf. Young, "Asymmetrical Reciprocity."

44. Benhabib, SS, 11; 165. P. Huntington ("Fragmentation, Race, and Gender") expands imaginative universalism; cf. Outlaw, epigraph to chap. 9 below. On limits of formal democracy, see Sartre, *Anti-Semite*; *Hope Now*; and Marcuse, "Repressive Tolerance."

45. Ricoeur, *Oneself*, 256; cf. 250–62, 290f.; and Havel, PP.

46. Cf. Young, JPD; Cornell, *Beyond Accommodation*; Martin, *Matrix and Line*; Nancy, *The Inoperative Community*; Derrida, OH and SM; Laclau and Mouffe, *Hegemony*.

47. Young, JPD, 236—citation above; on critique of community, see 98f., 142–48, 152f., and her chap. 8; on individuals, 232; and on dialogue with Gordon and Lawson, consult "Racism." Young takes over Kristeva's subjects-in-process, linking them to Adorno's logic/ Derrida's language of nonidentity: groups contain individuals who are strangers to themselves and others (Kristeva, *Strangers;* and *Nations*). Young does not elaborate how Kristeva's psychoanalytic theory of drives fits with the politics of difference. On compensating for a weakness in Kristeva's view of subjectivity, see Meyers's pragmatic approach (*Self* and "Personal Autonomy"); and P. Huntington's feminist dialectic of agency (*Ecstatic Subjects*).

48. On global democracy, cf. Dahbour, "Globalization"; Young, "Government"; Mićunović, "Critique of Nationalism"; Matuštík, PI; on communities of meaning, see Outlaw; on urban-rural debate, Martin, "Marxism and the Countryside"; Waller, "The Urban Blindspot of the Left"; and on Young's last point, "What is Critical about Critical Theory?"

49. Green, "The Diverse Community." Martin, *Matrix and Line*, chap. 5. Laclau and Mouffe, *Hegemony*, 48–51, 66–71, 85–88, 93–97, 105–14, 121f., 134–38, 144f., 166–71, 176–93. On Willett, see chap. 1 above. Does S. Huntington's *Clash* reproduce the urban-rural split?

50. Anzaldúa, *Borderlands* and "Bridge." Anzaldúa and Lugones theorize the hispano-lesbian border crossings; essays in Anzaldúa, *Making Face*, part 6, expand coalitional politics to Blacks (see there Audre Lorde's "I Am Your Sister: Black Women Organizing Across Sexualities," 321–25; cf. Anzaldúa's body politics of "making faces," xv–xxvi and Fanon's BSWM); cf. Lugones, "On Borderlands," "Playfulness," Lecture, and her questions after the Plenary discussion (see "Racism"); Lugones and Spelman, "Have We Got a Theory for You!"; Giroux and McLaren, *Between Borders*, 218f.; Giroux, *Disturbing Pleasures*, 60ff.; Godway and Finn, *Who is this 'We'?*; and Young, JPD, on five faces of oppression. Fraser's depiction ("Rejoinder," 128) of Young as "'brazenly' pentagonist, an ominously militarist stance," is gratuitous.

51. See Giroux's *Disturbing Pleasures*, part 1, and chap. 8: "Paulo Freire and the Rise of the Border Intellectual." Cf. the positions of critical traditionalists (n. 5 above).

52. Young, JPD, 226—first citation, and 231—other citations above; cf. "Asymmetrical Reciprocity."

53. Lugones, "On *Borderland*," 35; cf. B. Anderson, *Imagined Communities.*

54. Gardner, "Global Regionalism," 58f.; cf. Dirlik, "The Postcolonial Aura," 342–48; Lugones, Lecture; Prakash, "Postcolonial Criticism," 15ff.; B. Anderson, "Exodus," 326f.; Jameson, *Postmodernism;* Shohat and Stam, *Unthinking Eurocentrism*, 46–49, 100–31, 337–59.

55. Hegel, PR; Habermas, SR; Taylor, PR. This question marks a groundbreaking theorizing begun with Beauvoir and Fanon. On a renaissance in existential feminism, see works by Alcoff, Bartky, hooks, P. Huntington, Weir, Willett;

cf. my reading of Butler, Cornell, Young, and chaps. 1 (nn. 1–3 there) and 5 above, and 7 below; on existential race theory, Gordon, Outlaw, West, essays in Gordon's anthology, *Existence*, and chap. 9 below.

56. Young, JDP, chap. 8; Havel, PP; Martin, *Matrix and Line*, chap. 5; Kristeva, *Strangers* and *Nations*; Derrida, OH; and P. Huntington, *Ecstatic Subjects*.

57. Sartre, "Kierkegaard," 166f.—citations above; cf. 153, 157f., 163, 167.

58. Friedman, "Feminism," 276—first citation, and 290—last two citations above.

59. Benhabib, SS, 164; Young, C, 167, and "Asymmetrical Reciprocity"; Cornell, *The Philosophy of the Limit*, 13–38; Caraway, *Segregated Sisterhood*, 171; Friedman, "Feminism," 285, 289f.; Outlaw, *On Race and Philosophy*, 182; Sartre, *Anti-Semite*, 57; chap. 5, sec. 2, above; on need for recognition in Irigaray and Kristeva, see P. Huntington, "Fragmentation, Race, and Gender" and *Ecstatic Subjects*; on a post-Sartrean existential-multicultural democracy, see Charmé, "Authenticity." Sartre's "concrete liberalism" differs from classical "Liberalism 1" and communitarian "Liberalism 2" (chap. 1 above); but his social ontology falls short of existentially multicultural democracy. Beauvoir's existentialist-feminist subject is seen as embedded in his masculinist categories (Nye, *Feminist Theory*, 73–114).

60. Sartre, *Anti-Semite*, 146—two citations below; cf. epigraphs to chaps. 4 and 6 by King; Ernest Allen, Jr., "On the Reading of Riddles: Rethinking Du Boisian 'Double Consciousness'," in Gordon, *Existence*, 49–68; n. 59 above; works by Outlaw; Du Bois; chaps. 3 above, 9 below.

61. Nancy, *Inoperative Community*, xxxviii.

62. Nancy, *Inoperative Community*, xl; cf. on communitarianism, 2f., 9, 15, 17, 20, 22f.; singularity, 6f., 27; "an ideal distance," Kierkegaard, TA, 62f.; and Matuštík, PI, 234–38.

63. Nancy, *Inoperative Community*, 15, and 35—the last citation above.

64. Cf. Bhabha, "The Postcolonial and the Postmodern: the Question of Agency," *The Location*, 171–97; Derrida, SM, 58/29, 142/86, 146f./89; Beverley and Oviedo, *The Postmodernism Debate*; Giroux and McLaren, *Between Borders*; hooks, *Teaching to Transgress*; Laclau and Mouffe, *Hegemony*; Zavarzadeh and Morton, *Theory as Resistance*; Prakash, "Postcolonial Criticism"; Williams and Chrisman, *Colonial Discourse*; and Young, JPD, 33–38, chaps. 2 and 6, and 248–60.

65. Sartre, "Kierkegaard," 167.

66. Sartre, "Kierkegaard," 168f.—all citations above.

67. Kierkegaard, PV, 128; and chaps. 1, 4–5 above and 9 below.

68. On existential and material limits of certain approaches, cf. P. Huntington, "Fragmentation, Race, and Gender." Bartky's critical social phenomenology,

Femininity, complements proceduralism (e.g., in Benhabib, SS, 3–6, 8, 11, 163–65, 190, 227f.). For integrating Kristeva with Irigaray to envision the symbolic orders on the other side of patriarchy, see Cornell, *Beyond Accommodation,* chap. 1, 166–96, 205. For a critique of Kristeva and Lacan's symbolic, see Fraser, "Uses and Abuses of French Discourse Theories for Feminist Politics," in Fraser and Bartky, *Revaluing French Feminism,* 177–94. For a rejoinder to formalist-procedural theories (as in Benhabib) and to a poststructuralist evasion of critical social approach (as in Butler), see Fraser, "False Antitheses." On performatives, see Butler, BM; Matuštík, PI, chap. 5; and chap. 5 above.

69. Cf. Gordon, BF and F; Husserl's *Crisis;* and chap. 9 below.

70. Friedman, "Feminism," 276f.—citations above; cf. 281.

71. Friedman, "Feminism," 284.

72. Friedman, "Feminism," 285—both citations above. She objects that Sandel's communitarian response to Rawls's *Theory of Justice* (add *Political Liberalism*) conflates communities of place with those of choice. This parallels Mead's distinction between the given and self-directed dimensions of self. Habermas uses Mead to differentiate conventional and postconventional identity; cf. Ricoeur's given *idem-* and narrative *ipse-*identity (*Oneself,* see his index for terms); on Habermas, Kierkegaard, and Mead, cf. Matuštík, PI, chap. 4.

73. Friedman, "Feminism," 286–90. Cf. works by P. Huntington and Meyers.

74. Caraway, *Segregated Sisterhood,* 172f., and 174—last citation above.

75. Caraway, *Segregated Sisterhood,* 180ff.; cf. 189ff.; on Lugones, 198f. Nelly Richard, "Cultural Peripheries: Latin America and Postmodern De-centering," in Beverley and Oviedo, *The Postmodernism Debate,* 157; "Latin American Subaltern Studies Group: Founding Statement" (in Beverley and Oviedo, 110–21); and Guha and Spivak, *Selected Subaltern Studies.*

76. Caraway, *Segregated Sisterhood,* 199f. (cites Arendt's *Human Condition,* 47f., 303); on Marcuse, 186; and 192–95 on Laclau and Mouffe's "chain of democratic equivalences"; cf. her conclusion on Havel as an example of existential sobriety (see Ricoeur, n. 45 above). Allen (n. 60 above) searches with Du Bois for a path between assimilation and nationalism. Cf. Nandy's Gandhian-Tagorean critical traditionalism, *Illegitimacy of Nationalism.*

77. Kristeva, *Strangers,* 1.

78. Kristeva, *Strangers,* 2f. "The modification in the status of foreigners that is imperative today leads one to reflect on our ability to accept new modalities of otherness. No 'Nationality Code' would be practicable without having that question slowly mature within each of us and for each of us" (2). See, on border crossers, Giroux, *Disturbing Pleasures,* 61f.; on Freire as border intellectual, 141–52; on traveling pedagogies, 153–71.

79. Habermas's system/lifeworld analysis and his reading of the commentaries on Marx (TCA, vol. 2, last chap., never works through any of Marx's texts) amounts to endorsing a capitalist mode of production with a human face—or simply a 'good' capitalism.

80. Halleck, "Zapatistas On-Line"; Norris, *Uncritical Theory*, 126; n. 39 to chap. 9 below; cf. Rabinbach, "German Intellectuals"; Arato and Benhabib, "The Yugoslav Tragedy," 331; and epigraphs to chap. 4 above.

81. Kant, *Perpetual Peace*, 343f./85f.—citations below; cf. Lummis, "Globocop."

82. Kant, *Perpetual Peace*, 345f./88—citations below; cf. Greider, *One World*.

83. Kant, *Perpetual Peace*, 356ff./100ff.—citations above; cf. Nandy, "Cultural Frames"; Blaney and Inayatullah, "Prelude"; Young, "Government"; vs. S. Huntington, *Clash*.

84. Kant, *Perpetual Peace*, 358/103—emphasis added; cf. 360/105.

7. Clowning and Refusal

1. See n. 1 to chap. 5 above. Cf. Laclau and Mouffe, *Hegemony*.

2. See West, RM and KP, and chap. 9 below.

3. See. n. 59 to chap. 5 above.

4. Derrida, SM, 141/85; cf. Mouffe's intro., *Dimensions*; and S. Huntington's *Clash*.

5. Derrida, SM, 141/85. See chaps. 2–4 and 6 above.

6. See Kierkegaard, TA, part 3, on liberal and conservative apathy, short-lived enthusiasms, and leveling; FT, on *knights of resignation and knights of faith*; Habermas, TiTD and NR, on his last two messianic allusions; and sec. 2 below, on the 'third way'.

7. Derrida, SM, 141/85.

8. Cf. Derrida, "Ends of Man" (May 12, 1968) and SM with Marcuse, EoL.

9. E.g., Kojève, Sartre, Merleau-Ponty, Fanon, Beauvoir, Kosík, Patočka, Havel, Michnik, Bartky, Outlaw, Schrag, West, recently Martin's Derridean-Marxist humanist posthumanism, Gordon's existential critique of anti-Black racism, or Kothari's and Nandy's critical traditionalist projects. Cf. chaps. 1 and 6 above and 9 below.

10. Derrida and Foucault claim affinities with the early Frankfurt School, but their links to Habermas are complex and to Marcuse not quite fair. On affini-

ties between the early Frankfurt School and the Delhi crititical traditionalists, Kothari and Nandy, see Dallmayr, "Global Development?" 261, 263, 276; as radical democratic humanists (262), I find them closer to Marcuse, Sartre, or Fanon than to western exports of uncritical postmodernism.

11. See Sartre, *Critique*, vol. 1, last three chaps.

12. On Sartre and Fanon in this regard, consult works by Gordon.

13. This contrast between Derrida and Marcuse is brought out by Popkin's "Comment" (on Derrida's "Ends of Man"); on this see K. Anderson, "On Hegel," 262–65.

14. K. Anderson, "On Hegel," 264. In the panel, "What is Critical . . . ," I. Young harkens to Marcuse's imaginative critical theory while retaining a postmodern difference.

15. See Marcuse's epigraph to preface above.

16. Horkheimer and Adorno, DoE, xiv, xvi, 8–12, 26–29.

17. Horkheimer and Adorno, DoE, 4, 10–13, 15–33, 54, 64–167.

18. See Horkheimer and Adorno, DoE, 3f., 24, 38f., 43, 46, 121, 164–67.

19. Horkheimer and Adorno, DoE, 32–39, 124f., 144–47, 158.

20. West, KF, 265–70—first citation, and Horkheimer and Adorno, DoE, 41—second citation above; cf. 40, xi–xv; Zavarzadeh and Morton, *Theory*; and chap. 9 below.

21. Horkheimer and Adorno, DoE, 164; cf. 144, 155, 167; and Marcuse, N, 153.

22. This argument continues my discussion from chap. 5 above.

23. Cf. Jameson, *Postmodernism*; S. Huntington, *Clash*; and Greider, *One World*.

24. Marcuse, EC, 17—citations above.

25. Marcuse, EC, 17—citation above; on Nietzsche, see Marcuse, EoL, 6, 22, 31, 45.

26. Cf. Marcuse, EC, 34–54 with Sartre's *Critique*, vol. 1, and *Hope Now*.

27. See Marcuse, EC, 78–92.

28. Marcuse, ODM, 52; cf. EC, 93; EoL, ix.

29. Marcuse, ODM, 100.

30. Marcuse, ODM, 68.

31. Marcuse, ODM, 68.

32. Kellner, *Marcuse*, 159, cf. 170. On inner/outer, see index entries in Matuštík, PI.

33. Marcuse, ODM, 8—first two citations, and 6—last citation above.

34. See Matuštík, PI: on inner and outer in Hegel, Marx, Habermas, and Kierkegaard, 16, 153–84; and on leveling, 75, 149, 234–43, 247f.

35. Marcuse, ODM, 209ff.

36. See Shierry Weber Nicholsen, "The Persistence of Passionate Subjectivity: Eros and Other in Marcuse, by Way of Adorno," in Bokina and Lukes, *Marcuse*, 159f.

37. Marcuse, ODM, 8f.—citations above; cf. "Repressive Tolerance," 99, 104f., 117f.; Sartre's *Anti-Semite* and *Hope Now*, 83f.

38. Marcuse, ODM, 10 (original emphasis); on instinctual and existential sources of protest, see 6 and 9f. Cf. "Repressive Tolerance," 95, 116f.

39. See Matuštík, PI, 10.

40. Marcuse, ODM, 8f., 64; cf. Matuštík, PI, 234–43; and Kierkegaard, TA, 63f.

41. See such films as "The Atomic Café" and Slovak "Papierové hlavy" [Paper Heads].

42. Marcuse, ODM, 107, 108 n. 26, and 110—citations above; cf. 108, 113, and N, 143, 153.

43. Marcuse, ODM, 117–20, 123.

44. Marcuse, ODM, 52; cf. 1–3, 113–20.

45. On this Derrida, see the beginning of sec. 1 in this chap.

46. Talking Heads, "Road to Nowhere." Cf. Matuštík, PI, viii–ix.

47. Marcuse, ODM, 111—first citation, and 118f.—second citation above.

48. Marcuse, ODM, 167.

49. Marcuse, ODM, 123; cf. 132, 140, 167–69, 193, 195.

50. Marcuse, ODM, 63f., 69, 70, 90.

51. Marcuse, ODM, 134; cf. 2, 10, 16, 18, 23, 41, 44, 134, 165.

52. Marcuse, ODM, 14; cf. subtitle of Jameson, *Postmodernism*; S. Huntington, *Clash*.

53. On the role of the corrective, see Matuštík, PI, 153–56.

54. Cf. Sartre's preface to Fanon, WoE with Marcuse's "Repressive Tolerance," 103f., 110, 116f.; and EoL, 6. On Fanon, see chap. 9 below and epigraph to 2 above.

55. Marcuse, EoL, 6, 35, 46f., 56, 66; cf. S. Huntigton's *Clash*; Greider, *One World*.

56. Gordon, BF, 166; I. Young, "Asymmetrical Reciprocity," and chap. 4, sec. 3 above.

57. Marcuse, EoL, 6f.; "Repressive Tolerance" 110, 116; cf. Fanon, WoE.

58. Cf. Habermas, "Europe's Second Chance" (VaZ); Derrida, OH; and chap. 9 below.

59. Marcuse, EoL, 7; cf. Fanon, BSWM, 92, 224 and Gordon, F.; Havel's "How Europe Could Fail" defends a "supranational community" set in Euro-concerns for the future of "the idea of Europe." His advocacy of democratic rights is tied to Central European anxieties and its projected intellectual or spiritual mission. While Havel takes a global perspective on such issues as the environment and technology development, he does not link directly his dissident struggle for human rights with the plight of the wretched of the earth. ("Europe today lacks an ethos; it lacks imagination, it lacks generosity. . . . Europe does not appear to have achieved a genuine and profound sense of responsibility for itself as a whole, and thus for the future of all those who live in it" [3]). Cf. Hobsbawm, "The New Threat to History."

60. Gordon, BF, F, *Existence*; West, RM; and Marcuse, EoL, ix–x, 6f., 35 n. 8, 47, 61.

61. Marcuse, RR, x–xi; dissertation, *Schriften*, vol.1:13; and Kellner, *Marcuse*, 20f., 279.

62. See Fanon's epigraph to chap. 2 above (BSWM, 229); cf. Adorno, *Kierkegaard* and ND; on Marcuse's radical action, see Kellner, *Marcuse*, 40–44.

63. Marcuse, ODM, 242–45; 255–57; see Kellner's *Marcuse*, 279.

64. See Kellner, *Marcuse*, 279–81.

65. I concur on this with the basic thesis of Wolin's "Left Fascism."

66. On this I concur with Marcuse; cf. "Repressive Tolerance" and "The Struggle Against Liberalism in the Totalitarian View of the State," in N. Cf. Sartre, *Anti-Semite*. See "Comunicados": "Llama el EZLN a un encuentro intercontinental antiliberalismo" (Jan. 1996), "Caminos contra el neoliberalismo, so sólo lamentos" (Apr. 4, 1996), and "Invitación al Encuentro Intercontinental por la Humanidad y Contra el Neoliberalismo" (May 1996).

67. While Tucker (*Phenomenology and Politics*) differentiates Havel's democratic aims from Heidegger's aversion to deliberative democracy, he does not set

apart the former's concrete humanism with a human face from the latter's abstract antihumanism.

68. Marcuse, EoL, 88, and *Soviet Marxism*; Kellner's *Marcuse*, 457 n. 8. In implicating *all* philosophy of existence in Heidegger's fascist politics, Wolin is consistent throughout his Prague presentations on this topic (Blue Monday, Charles University, May 1995 and 1996, and The Center for Theoretical Study, May 1996); cf. his "Carl Schmitt" (in *The Terms of Cultural Criticism*), *Labyrinths* 109, 112, 120, 137, 165, 169, 179, and "Left Fascism."

69. Cf. Mills's *Racial Contract*; and chap. 4, sec. 3 above.

70. Marcuse, ODM, 52—citation above; cf. 68f, 123, 132, 134, 140–43, 167, and 225–46.

71. Marcuse, N, 143; cf. ODM, 203–15.

72. See Marcuse, ODM, 214–18; EC, 139, 143, 146, 152, 167f.

73. Marcuse, ODM, 45–55; EC, ix–xi, and chap. 1, sec. 3 above.

74. Steigerwald (*Herbert Marcuses dritter Weg*, 9f., 42, 344f.) mocks Marcuse from the standpoint of orthodox Marxism. From the angle of North American left-liberalism, Wolin categorizes Marcuse (referring to Lukács) as a "romantic anticapitalist," and links Marcuse's new sensibility (along with Adorno, Benjamin, Bloch, and Bataille) to "a widely shared anticivilizational ethos . . . of the fascist sensibility, both left and right" ("Left Fascism," 422 and 428 n. 85; cf. n. 81). In the end, Wolin identifies a 'third way' *as such* with the German young conservatives as a fascist path beyond socialism and liberalism (421). Habermas offers a more sympathetic insight into Marcuse (see AS, 147–50, 189f., 207, 231–35; *Antworten* 11f.; Borgosz, *Herbert Marcuse*, 9); cf. Lukács, *Existentialisme* (critique of Sartre), and Sartre, *Search* (response to Lukács). See Marcuse, "Sartre's Existentialism" (review of Sartre's *Being and Nothingness*), and "The Struggle Against Liberalism," N (critique of possessive individualism leading to the Nazi decisionist political existentialism). On Lukács's exchange with Sartre and Merleau-Ponty, see Kadarkay, *Georg Lukács*, 392–401. Cf. Novack, *Existentialism*; Whiteside, *Merleau-Ponty*, 224–79; and Matuštík, PI, chap. 10. On popular uses of 'third way', see Simons, "Dutch."

75. Tucker's *Phenomenology and Politics*, part 2, misreads broad democratic ideals in existential revolution and nonpolitical politics. Howard (*Political Judgments*, see "Antipolitics") pits nonpolitical politics against democracy. Could not the former undo the "two hundred years of error" (3, 10, 44) which closed flexible democratic political spheres into totalitarian politics or economism? I support my view not only with Havel's PP, sec. 3, but also with Nandy's "Cultural Frames" (opens with Amilcar Cabral's African dissidence [113], continues with Frankfurt School's and Gandhi's critiques of the West [114ff.], ends with Gandhian-Tagorean-Fanonian options [117f., 120–23; Dallmayr, "Global Development? 272–75]), and Moses's *Revolution* on M. L. King, Jr.'s philosophy of nonviolence (epigraphs to chaps. 4, 6 above).

76. Havel, "Kdo oželí volby."

77. These lyrics are from the album and film, *The Wall*, by Pink Floyd.

78. Marcuse, ODM, 254—citation; cf., 68, 223. Habermas admits transcendence on *this* side of the world of discourse in TCA, vol. 2:51–53/82–86; cf. Matuštík, PI, 16f., 99; n. 6 above.

79. Marcuse, ODM, 120; and 123, citing Ernst Bloch.

80. Marcuse, N, 143.

81. Marcuse, ODM, 14.

82. Marcuse, ODM, 199.

83. Marcuse, ODM, 18; cf. 52.

84. Marcuse, ODM, 2, 18—citations above; cf. 41, 44, 134, 165, 182, 215; N, 135, 141, 144, 153.

8. Ski Masks and Velvet Faces

1. Havel, *Letní přemítání*, 45 and 95.

2. E.g. the Swiss publisher, Ringier ČR, produces a dozen Czech publications, such as *Mladá fronta Dnes*, *Blesk*, and *Lidové noviny*.

3. Brodsky and Havel, "An Exchange," 28 and 30; cf. Ash, "Prague."

4. Brodsky and Havel, "An Exchange," 28, 30 (Havel cites Brodsky).

5. Brodsky and Havel, "An Exchange," 29. See Havel, *Letní přemítání*, 89.

6. Brodsky and Havel, "An Exchange," 28; Havel, *Dopisy*; Salzburg speech (July 27, 1990), *Vážení občané*, 9–13.

7. Brodsky and Havel, "An Exchange," 30.

8. See Kundera, *Life Is Elsewhere*.

9. Brodsky and Havel, "An Exchange," 29. Cf. Moses, *Revolution*: "I think that [M. L.] King establishes grounds for a new age of social and political philosophy, superseding both tired schools of thought that sought to legitimate cold war antagonisms, namely Marxist-Leninism and what I dub 'cowboy-capitalism'" (2).

10. Cf. Matuštík, PI, 226–27; 304f. n. 62. See Berman, "The Philosopher-King," 56, 47–48, on the public-family dispute over who should be allowed to buy Václav Havel's 50 percent share of Prague's landmark, Lucerna, restituted after 1989 to the two Havel brothers, Václav and Ivan. Should it be Chemapol, a major

Czech company with shady ex-Communist and mafia links, with Havel donating all sale profit to charity; should it be his sister-in-law, Ivan Havel's wife, Dáša, who would keep and run 100 percent of Lucerna? While the Czech court is deciding the property issue between Václav and Dáša, the more exemplary question of the incompatibility between democracy and capitalism comes home to roost. Berman reports Havel's ambivalent response in a recent interview: "People want capitalism, but when somebody [e.g. Chemapol] builds it, they object. 'I hate the hypocrisy,' he [Havel] said" (56). Where lies the hypocrisy? If it lies in the mask of robber-capitalism with a human face, should not the poet of democracy have the courage to disclose it? Perhaps these questions and the recent economic and political crisis of Klaus's government reintroduce a demand to 'live in truth'. See n. 19 to chap. 2 above.

11. Michnik, "Bojím sa antikomunistov," and "More Humility."

12. Brodsky and Havel, "An Exchange," 29f.—citations above; cf. Havel, Jerusalem speech (Apr. 26, 1990), *Projevy*, 100–103 (for the appeals to Kafka); and Copenhagen speech (May 28, 1991), *Vážení občané*, 81–85 (with reference to Kierkegaard).

13. Havel, speeches: Salzburg (July 27, 1990) and Oslo conference about hatred (Aug. 28, 1990), *Vážení občané*, 9–13, 19–26.

14. West, KF, xiv; chap. 9 below; on postsecular, see Martin, *Matrix and Line*.

15. "Comunicados: Contra el Neoliberalismo y por la Humanidad," Jan. 1996.

16. "Comunicados: Libertad, demoracia y justicia, delirio del EZLN," Aug. 30, 1996.

17. St. Augustine, *The City of God*, bk. 4, chap. 4.

18. Cited in Ross, *Rebellion*, 8.

19. Marcos, *Processo*, Aug. 8, 1994, cited in Ross, *Rebellion*, 4.

20. On irony and humor, cf. Kierkegaard, CUP, CI; and Matuštík's "Review."

21. Cf. Havel, PP, sec. 3; and "Comunicados: Primera Declaration de la Selva Lacandóna," Jan. 1994.

22. Nietzsche, *Gay Science*, in *The Portable Nietzsche*, 95f.

23. Cited in Ross, *Rebellion*, 61.

24. Cited in Ross, *Rebellion*, 296f. and 18—two citations above.

25. Ross, *Rebellion*, 300f.; cf. Katzenberger, "Interview with Marcos," *First World*, 70.

26. "Comunicados," Jan. 9, 1994.

27. See "Comunicados," Aug. 30, 1996.

28. Russakoff, "A Clash," 1.

29. "Comunicados," May 31, 1994.

30. Ross, *Rebellion*, 54.

31. See the full text of the Law of Women in Katzenberger, *First World*, 109f.

32. "Comunicados: Contra el Neoliberalismo y por la Humanidad," Jan. 1996.

33. From *The Daily Telegraph*, reprinted in *USA Today*, Feb. 26, 1996, 7B.

34. Cf. Fanon, BSWM.

35. "Comunicados: Contra el Neoliberalismo y por la Humanidad," Jan. 1996.

36. Rifkin, "Civil Society."

37. "Comunicados: A la sociedad civil nacional e internacional," Feb., 1996; "Comunicados: Cuarta Declaration de la Selva Lacandona," Jan. 1996; and "Comunicados: Libertad, democracia y justicia, delirio del EZLN," Aug. 30, 1996.

38. Ash, "Prague," 41 and 34. Cf. Netočný, "Klaus." See the book cover above for Turnley's photo, "The Dismantling of the Berlin Wall": it marks the complexity of the liberation specters. The punk who hammers passionately at the Wall, sometime on November 9, 1989, displays a Nazi war cross on his leather jacket. Cf. n. 56 to chap. 9 below.

39. Ash, "Prague," 38f.

40. See Matuštík, PI, part 3.

41. Cf. Shohat and Stam, "Aesthetics of Resistance," *Unthinking Eurocentrism*, 292–333; cf. my discussion of Foucault's aesthetics of existence in chaps. 5 and 7 above. See on M. L. King, Jr., Moses's *Revolution*.

42. See excursus in chap. 4 above.

43. "Comunicados: Cuarta Declaración de la Selva Lacandóna," Jan. 1996.

44. See n. 56 to chap. 9 below.

9. Radical Multicultural and Existential Democracy

• 1. Marcuse, EoL, 71—first citation, and Habermas, AS, 150—second citation; cf. S. Huntington's *Clash*, 183–321. On Europe, cf. Husserl, *Crisis*; Patočka, *Kacířské eseje*; Derrida, OH, and *The Gift*, 1–34; Fanon, WoE; Gordon, F.; and n. 45 below.

2. West, KF, xi (emphasis added); cf. xii, xiv, xvi–xvii; cf. on Havel's "existential revolution," Matuštík, PI, part 3; and Havel, PP.

3. West, KF, xi; cf. 21 on Heidegger and Marcuse. Du Bois (cf. Kenan's new intro. to *Souls*), West, hooks, and numerous others (see authors in Gordon, *Existence*) are radical existential humanists, not antihumanists. The category of 'new humanism' occurs in Schrag's *Communicative Praxis*, 197–214 and Martin's *Humanism*. Cf. my view of concrete democracy and Sartre's *Anti-Semite* (see Walzer's new intro., and last n. to chap. 2 above).

4. West, KF, xii; hooks, *Teaching to Transgress*, 7; Lugones, "On *Borderlands*," 34 (Anzaldúa, *Borderlands*); Peter McLaren, "Multiculturalism and the Postmodern Critique: Toward a Pedagogy of Resistance and Transformation," in Giroux and McLaren, *Between Borders*, 192–222; Zavarzedeh and Morton, *Theory as Resistance*; cf. West's (Outlaw below) *two modernities* and critical traditionalism and critical modernism in Nandy, "Cultural Frames"; and Blaney and Inayatullah, "Prelude"; vs. S. Huntington, *Clash*, 56–78, 91–95.

5. Lugones, "On *Borderlands*," 35; cf. the Plenary "Racism"; Dirlik, "The Postcolonial Aura," 331 (cf. 333 n. 6, citing Prakash, "Postcolonial Criticism," 8, and criticizing Bhabha for reducing socioeconomic issues to psychological and poststructuralist linguistic analyses). On a material view of postcoloniality, see Young, JPD; McLaren in Giroux and McLaren, *Between Borders*, 192–222; cf. the foreign liberal politics of difference and a reactionary civilizational defense of identity politics, S. Huntington, *Clash*, 125–245.

6. Balibar and Wallerstein, *Race, Nation, Class*, 45f.; and excursus in chap. 1 above.

7. Giroux, "Living Dangerously: Identity Politics and the New Cultural Racism," in Giroux and McLaren, *Between Borders*, 36f.; cf. the main argument by S. Huntington, *Clash*, 312–21.

8. Outlaw, "Critical Theory," 139, 143f.—citations above; cf. "Race and Class," 125; and panel called "What is Critical About Critical Theory?"

9. hooks and West, *Breaking Bread*, 95; cf. Outlaw, "Author" and his epigraph; S. Huntington, *Clash*, 19–35, 246–98.

10. Leitch, *Deconstructive Criticism*, 180—first two citations (second emphasis added), and 266f.—all other citations above.

11. McLaren in Giroux and McLaren, *Between Borders*, 198ff.—all citations above; see Ebert, "Political Semiosis," 115–18, 129; Martin, *Matrix and Line*; and chaps. 4–5, 7 above.

12. McLaren in Giroux and McLaren, *Between Borders*, 205 (internal citation by Zavarzedeh and Morton, "Signs," 156).

13. Mouffe's radical democracy "postulates the very impossibility of a final realization of democracy. It affirms that the unresolvable tension between the

principle of equality and liberty is the very *condition for the preservation of the indeterminacy and undecidability* which is constitutive of modern democracy. Moreover, it constitutes the principal guarantee against any attempt to realize a final closure that would result in the elimination of the political and the negation of democracy" (Mouffe, *Dimensions of Radical Democracy*, 13, emphasis added; cf. Laclau and Mouffe, *Hegemony*, 111ff., 140–43, 169, 179, 191ff.; S. Huntington, *Clash*, 301–21; and Jameson, *Postmodernism*). In chaps. 2–5, 7 above, I contest existential-social undecidability as a consequence of performative social categories (with their descriptive or textual undecidability).

14. Outlaw, "Philosophy," 61f., 84—first citations, and *On Race and Philosophy*, 12f.—last citation above; cf. this position with S. Huntington's "groping for groupings" (*Clash* 125–35); on two modernities, see West, KF, xii, and n. 4 above.

15. Outlaw, "Race and Class," 126—all citations above.

16. Outlaw, *On Race and Philosophy*, 7f., 12f., 21.—cited terms above; on second point, see Outlaw, "Philosophy," 84, and "Race and Class," 126; cf. S. Huntington, *Clash*, 318–21.

17. Gomberg ("How Racial Identities Contribute to Racism") reduces "antiracist activism" to antiracist class struggle. He argues "that racial identities contribute to racial subordination of black people." To destroy racial inequality and develop a society free from racism, he strengthens "class identity at the expense of racial identity." His position rests on the fact that racialized identifications that were shaped by enslaving Africans continue to subordinate and economically exploit Black people long after the Civil War reversed this practice. Just as thinking that one is White "contributes to racism," so "internalizing a black identity," despite of its "more favorable reputation," "tends to undermine the broadest struggles against racism." He frowns even at tactical uses of oppositional Black identity and argues for personal identity shaped by class-based antiracism. "Racial identities would be understood as an invention of the capitalists (and their predecessors). . . . [T]hey would be perceived as imposed identities and would not be internalized. In their place would arise antiracist working class identities and new uses of 'we'." He envisions this "we" in revolutionary terms of "antiracist communism." One can agree with Gomberg that a certain liberal universalism and a Marxist "tactical marriage between nationalism and internationalism" failed to find viable alternatives to "the racist organization of poverty and unemployment." But must *we* follow him or Sartre's lopsided social ontology in *Anti-Semite* that in democracy-to-come no 'we' is to affirm African American or Jewish identity? Must we accept an assimilationist polity as a consequence of this brand of liberal leftism or concrete liberalism? Like Sartre, Gomberg finds it uninteresting to ask about the "compatibility of universalism with racial or ethnic identities." Is not this the question (can we have democracy without ethnic cleansing?) which *we* must raise in any critical social theory and praxis of just recognition (cf. his "Patriotism"; "Against Racism")?

18. McLaren in Giroux and McLaren, *Between Borders*, 195 and 204; cf. S. Huntington's *Clash*; Spencer, "Trends"; the *Black Scholar's* Reader's Forum called "Multiculturalism."

19. Outlaw, "Critical Theory," 143. Cf. my discussion of this in chap. 4, sec. 3 above.

20. McLaren in Giroux and McLaren, *Between Borders*, 206.

21. Balibar, *Masses*, 192.

22. Balibar, *Masses*, 193—all citations above. Sartre, "Kierkegaard." On a messianic promise vs. the dogma of messianism, see Derrida, SM; B. Anderson, *Imagined Communities*.

23. "Back to the Future," 46; cf. references in nn. 4 and 14 above.

24. Urban and Sherzer, *Nation-States and Indians*, 1–16 (eds. intro.)—all citations above.

25. McLaren in Giroux and McLaren, *Between Borders*, 214 (sources cited by McLaren: Anzaldúa, *Borderlands*, 105; Minh-ha, *When the Moon Waxes Red*, 228f.; Sandoval, "U.S. Third World Feminism," 15). I adopt from the stand-up comedian, George Lopez, the social construct of Whiteness as an "epidermically challenged" trait. Cf. Giroux, *Disturbing Pleasures*; hooks, *Teaching to Transgress*; and Freire, *The Politics of Education*.

26. McLaren in Giroux and McLaren, *Between Borders*, 218.

27. Balibar, *Masses*, 194—citations above; on the singular universal, see chaps. 2, 6 above.

28. Balibar, *Masses*, 195, 198—citations above; cf. Outlaw, *On Race and Philosophy*, 13.

29. Balibar, *Masses*, 199.

30. See S. Huntington, *Clash*, 301–21.

31. Balibar, *Masses*, 201f.

32. Balibar, *Masses*, 202–4; cf. Foucault, DP.

33. Outlaw, "Race and Class," 126–28.

34. Outlaw, "Against the Grain of Modernity: The Politics of Difference and the Conservation of 'Race'" (135–57), *On Race and Philosophy*, 141 and 140; cf. 136, 151–57.

35. Outlaw, *On Race and Philosophy*, 157; cf. 148.

36. Outlaw, *On Race and Philosophy*, 143—first citation, and 150—all other citations above. It would be beneficial to facilitate a conversation between the panelists in "Nationalism," who scrutinized and ironized various communities of meaning, and Outlaw, "Author," who adopted an emphatic nationalist claim against uncritical social constructivists.

37. Outlaw, *On Race and Philosophy*, 7, 12, 17. The example of a socially constructed bus and a rhetorical invitation to step in front of one are Outlaw's (see "Author"). Cf. Marcuse, "A Biological Foundation for Socialism?" EoL, and EC.

38. Balibar, *Masses*, 204—first citation, Outlaw, "Race and Class," 128, 126—last two citations above. Cf. Valenzuela and Garner, "The Right to Fuck" with Forman, "The People"; Cruikshank, *The Gay and Lesbian Liberation*; Champagne, *The Ethics*; and Foucault, UP.

39. "Interview with Subcomandante Marcos" by Medea Benjamin, cited from Katzenberger, *First World*, 67, and "Comunicados," Jan. 1, 1994. See chap. 6, sec. 1 above.

40. Outlaw, "Race and Class," 126. Cf. Young's plural-systems analysis in JPD.

41. Marcuse, "Über konkrete Philosophie," *Schriften*, vol. 1:401f.; cf. Habermas, AS, 150.

42. Fanon, WoE, 232.

43. Fanon, WoE, 35—citations above.

44. Bhabha, "The Postcolonial and the Postmodern: The Question of Agency" (171–97), *The Location*, 172; cf. Hobsbawm, *Nations*; Appiah, *In My Father's House*; and n. 4 above.

45. Fanon, WoE, 311—citation. Gordon, BF, 182ff.; his F (see subtitle and preface) was introduced in Prague echoing Husserl's *Crisis*; see Habermas, VaZ, 97–129/73–97.

46. Fanon, WoE, 36 (emphasis added).

47. Marcuse, EoL, 18f.—all citations above.

48. Marcuse, EoL, 21; cf. 10f., 32–36.

49. Bhabha, *The Location*, 174—all citations above; see 192 for a critique of Rorty's liberal irony; cf. Derrida, SM; and Shohat and Stam, *Unthinking Eurocentrism*.

50. Bhabha, *The Location*, 184f.

51. Bhabha, *The Location*, 185—both citations above; McLaren in Giroux and McLaren, *Between Borders*, 203 and x; Kierkegaard, SuD, part 1, A, a; Habermas, PDM; cf. Spivak, "Subaltern Studies"; Meyers, "Personal Autonomy"; P. Huntington, *Ecstatic Subjects*; and criticisms of Bhabha by Dirlik, "The Postcolonial Aura," 333 and n. 6. See. chap. 5 above.

52. Bhabha, *The Location*, 173. Butler (BM) corrected an earlier impression (GT) that gender performativity might be a kind of privileged postmodern voluntarism. See chaps. 5 and 7 above. Dirlik ("The Postcolonial Aura") exemplifies my second point.

53. Bhabha, *The Location*, 180, 184, 185, 189, 193, 196—for six items above; and on Fanon, Bhabha's "Interrogating Identity," in Goldberg, *Anatomy*; cf. McLaren in Giroux and McLaren, *Between Borders*, 203f.; Lyotard, *Postmodern Condition*; and S. Huntington, *Clash*, 301–12.

54. Gordon, BF, F; and Kenneth Mostern, "Decolonization as Learning: Practice and Pedagogy in Frantz Fanon's Revolutionary Narrative," in Giroux and McLaren, *Between Borders*, 253–71. Lugones exposes folkloristic inventions of 'Mexican-American'; yet how can the lingo of 'hybridization' itself resolve problems in the political economy of postcoloniality and attendant racism? Cf. Lugones, "On *Borderlands*," 35; Dirlik, "The Postcolonial Aura"; Prakash, "Postcolonial Criticism"; and chaps. 4 and 6 above. S. Huntington, *Clash*, chap. 12.

55. Cf. Kundera, *The Book* and *Testaments*; Dallmayr, "Global Development," 272–76 (on Nandy, "Cultural Frames," 114ff.; Kothari, *Growing Amnesia*; and the Tagorean-Gandhian critical traditionality); Moses, *Revolution* (on M. L. King, Jr.); on Havel, chap. 8 above.

56. Marcuse, EoL, 36; see the front cover photo by Pavel Štecha on paperback of Matuštík, PI; cf. n. 38 to chap. 8 above.

57. Marcuse, EoL, 33; on beginnings, see Kierkegaard, R, CUP; Matuštík, PI (index); cf. n. 16 to chap. 2, n. 81 to chap. 4, and chap. 8 above.

58. Marcuse, EoL, 33—all citations above.

59. Marcuse, EoL, 34ff.—citations above; cf. 44f. (on Adorno, ND); on cultural-media refusals—mythmaking, downshifting, culture jamming, media subvertising—see *Adbusters* (winter 1996), 63. *Parallel polis* is Václav Benda's term, used by me here analogically to Marcuse's (EoL, 65f.) extraparliamentary dissent, invented by the Czech cultural and political dissent, "Charta 77," against totalitarianism; cf. Moses, *Revolution*, 51ff., 92, 144ff., 202f.

60. Fanon, BSWM, 224; cf. on Kierkegaard, nn. 6, 78 to chap. 7, and chaps. 2–4 above.

61. Fanon, BSWM, 229—citation (in epigraph to chap. 2 above); Marcuse, "Repressive Tolerance," 110, 116; EoL, 6f.; Sartre's *Hope Now*, and preface to Fanon's WoE; my present discussion of Fanon is anticipated in chaps. 1 (sec. 3), 2 (sec. 2), and 7 (sec. 2) above.

62. Marcuse, EC, 93—first citation, ODM, 52—second two citations, and EoL, ix—last citation above; on performatives, cf. chap. 5 above.

63. Fanon, WoE, 148—citation above.

64. "DM" = German Mark, the currency of unified Germany. Cf. Walsh, "VW"; and Singer, "The Real Eurobattle."

65. Fanon, WoE, 148ff.—citations above.

66. Fanon, WoE, 152f.

67. Fanon, WoE, 156f.—citations above.

68. Fanon, WoE, 159.

69. Fanon, WoE, 159, 162—two citations above.

70. Fanon, WoE, 164—both short and indented citations above.

71. Fanon, WoE, 165—all citations above. Allusions to East European contexts are mine.

72. Fanon, WoE, 166.

73. Fanon, WoE, 167, 169—two citations above. Cf. conclusions to chap. 6 above.

74. Fanon, WoE, 172—citations above.

75. Fanon, WoE, 183f. See the first epigraph to chap. 8 above.

76. Fanon, WoE, 165, 172, 174f., 180–83.

77. Fanon, WoE, 182.

78. Fanon, WoE, 182. Cf. n. 70 to chap. 4 above.

79. Fanon, WoE, 188.

80. Fanon, WoE, 199.

81. Fanon, WoE, 200. On Havel, see Matuštík, PI, chap. 8; cf. Moses, *Revolution*.

82. Fanon, WoE, 203.

83. Fanon, WoE, 203f.—citations above.

84. Fanon, WoE, 205.

85. Shout from a 100,000 strong march in Mexico City (1994), Katzenberger, *First World*, ii (emphasis added); cf. hooks and West, *Breaking Bread*; and S. Huntington, *Clash*.

86. Habermas, AS, 148, 189—citations above; cf. Habermas's "special affinity with the existentialist, i.e., the Marcusean, variant of Critical Theory" (150); Butler, BM; Clarence Sholé Johnson, "Cornel West as Pragmatist and Existentialist," in Gordon, *Existence*, 243–61; Seigfried, *Pragmatism and Feminism*; on Du Bois's African American existential approach, see Kenan's intro. to Du Bois, *Souls*; cf. Moses, *Revolution*; and Young, JPD.

87. See Larsen, "Foreigners"—citation; Heidegger, "Only a God"; Kristeva *Strangers*; St. Augustine, *The City of God*; Sartre, *Being and Nothingness*; and Camus, *The Rebel* (last para.). Kundera (*Testaments*, part 1) defends self-irony and humor at the heart of the modern 'European novel' as well as in the critical traditionality of Salman Rushdie's *Satanic Verses*.

WORKS CITED

Adbusters: Journal of the Mental Environment. The Media Foundation, Vancouver, Canada. Internet address: http://www.adbusters.org/adbusters

Adorno, Theodor W. *The Jargon of Authenticity.* Trans. Knut Tarnowski and Frederic Will. Evanston, Ill.: Northwestern University Press, 1973.

——. *Kierkegaard: Construction of the Aesthetic.* Trans. Robert Hullot-Kentor. Minneapolis: University of Minnesota Press, 1989.

——. *Minima Moralia.* Trans. E. F. Jephcott. London: New Left, 1974.

——. *Negative Dialectics.* New York: Seabury, 1973.

"L'Affair Derrida." *The New York Review of Books* 40, nos. 1–2, January 14, 1993, 30–35; 40, no. 4, February 11, 1993, 44–45; 40, no. 6, March 25, 1993, 65–67; 40, no. 7, April 8, 1993, 49–50 (Emil Nolte and Thomas Sheehan exchange); and 40, no. 8, April 22, 1993, 68–69. (See also Sheehan, "A Normal Nazi.")

Alcoff, Linda. "Cultural Feminism versus Postructuralism: The Identity Crisis in Feminist Theory." *Signs* 13, no. 3 (1988): 405–36.

——. "Philosophy and Racial Identity." *Radical Philosophy* 75 (January/February 1995): 5–14.

Anderson, Benedict. *Imagined Communities: Reflections on the Origin and Spread of Nationalism.* London: Verso, 1983.

——. "Exodus." *Critical Inquiry* 20 (winter 1994): 314–27.

Anderson, Joel. "The Persistence of Authenticity." *Philosophy and Social Criticism* 21, no. 1 (1995): 101–9.

——. "Recognizing Autonomy in Oneself and in Others" (Prague: Conference on the Philosophy of Social Sciences, May 1995), ms.

——. Translator's introduction to Honneth, *Kampf um Anerkennung* (q.v. English text), x–xxi.

Anderson, Kevin. "On Hegel and the Rise of Social Theory: A Critical Appreciation of Herbert Marcuse's *Reason and Revolution*, Fifty Years Later," *Sociological Theory* 11, no. 3 (November 1993): 243–67.

Anzaldúa, Gloria. *Borderlands/La Frontera: The New Mestiza.* San Francisco: Spinsters/Aunt Lute, 1987.

————. "Bridge, Drawbridge, Sandbar, or Island: Lesbians-of-Color *Hacienda Alianzas.*" In Lisa Albrecht and Rose M. Brewer, eds., *Bridges of Power: Women's Multicultural Alliances*, 216–31. Philadelphia: New Society Publishers, 1990.

Anzaldúa, Gloria, ed. *Making Face, Making Soul/Haciendo caras: Creative and Critical Perspectives by Feminists-of-Color*. San Francisco: Spinster/Aunt Lute, 1990.

Apel, Karl-Otto. *Diskurs und Verantwortung: Das Problem des Übergangs zur postkonventionellen Moral*. Frankfurt a/M: Suhrkamp, 1988.

Appiah, Kwame Anthony. *In My Father's House: Africa in the Philosophy of Culture*. Oxford: Oxford University Press, 1992.

Arato, Andrew and Seyla Benhabib. "The Yugoslav Tragedy." *Praxis International* 13, no. 4 (January 1994): 325–31.

Arendt, Hannah. *The Human Condition*. Chicago: The University of Chicago Press, 1958.

Aronson, Ronald. *After Marxism*. New York: Guilford Press, 1995.

Ash, Timothy Garton. "Prague: Intellectuals and Politicians." *The New York Review of Books* 42, no. 1, January 12, 1995, 34–41.

Augustine. *The City of God*. Trans. Henry Bettenson, ed. David Knowles. New York: Penguin, 1981.

Austin, J. L. *How to Do Things with Words* (1962). Cambridge, Mass.: Harvard University Press, 1977.

Avineri, Shlomo. "Hegel and Nationalism." *The Review of Politics* 24 (1962): 461–84.

"Back to the Future." A Warsaw Conversation between Hans Magnus Enzensberger, Ryszard Kapuściński, and Adam Krzemiński. Trans. from the German by Rodney Livingstone. *The New York Review of Books* 41, no. 19, November 17, 1994, 41–47.

Balibar, Etienne. *Masses, Classes, Ideas: Studies on Politics and Philosophy Before and After Marx*. Trans. James Swenson. London: Routledge, 1994.

Balibar, Etienne and Immanuel Wallerstein. *Race, Nation, Class: Ambiguous Identities* (1988). Trans. Chris Turner. London: Verso, 1991.

Bartky, Sandra Lee. *Femininity and Domination: Studies in the Phenomenology of Oppression*. London: Routledge, 1990.

Beauvoir, Simone de. *The Ethics of Ambiguity*. Trans. Bernard Fretchman. New York: Citadel Press, 1948, 1991.

————. *The Second Sex*. Trans. H. M. Parshley. New York: Vintage Books, 1974.

Beckett, Samuel. *Waiting for Godot*. A tragicomedy in two acts. New York: Grove Press, 1954.

Benhabib, Seyla. "In Defense of Universalism—Yet Again! A Response to Critics of *Situating the Self*." *New German Critique*, 62 (spring–summer 1994): 173–89.

———. *Situating the Self: Gender, Community, and Postmodernism in Contemporary Ethics*. London: Routledge, 1992.

Benhabib, Seyla, ed. *Democracy and Difference: Contesting the Boundaries of the Political*. Princeton: Princeton University Press, 1996.

Benhabib, Seyla and Drucilla Cornell, eds. *Feminism as Critique*. Minneapolis: University of Minnesota Press, 1987.

Benhabib, Seyla, Judith Butler, Drucilla Cornell, and Nancy Fraser. *Feminist Contentions: A Philosophical Exchange*. Intro. by Linda Nicholson. London: Routledge, 1995.

Berman, Paul. "The Philosopher-King is Mortal." *The New York Times Magazine*, May 11, 1997, 32–37, 47–48, 56, 59.

Bernstein, Richard J., ed. *Habermas and Modernity*. Cambridge, Mass.: MIT Press, 1985.

Best, Steven and Douglas Kellner. "Modernity, Mass Society, and the Media: Reflections on the *Corsair* Affair." In Perkins, ed., *International Kierkegaard Commentary: The Corsair Affair* (q.v.), 23–61.

Beverley, John and José Oviedo, eds. *The Postmodernism Debate in Latin America*. Trans. Michael Aronna. A special issue of *Boundary 2: an international journal of literature and culture* 20, no. 3 (Durham, N.C.: Duke University Press, fall 1993).

Bhabha, Homi K. "Interrogating Identity: The Postcolonial Prerogative." In Goldberg, ed., *Anatomy of Racism* (q.v.), 183–209.

———. *The Location of Culture*. London: Routledge, 1994.

Blaney, David and Naeem Inayatullah. "Prelude to a Conversation of Cultures in International Society? Todorov and Nandy on the Possibility of Dialogue." *Alternatives* 19 (1994): 23–51.

Blaut, J. M. *The Colonizer's Model of the World: Geographical Diffusionism and Eurocentric History*. New York: Guilford Press, 1993.

Blum, Lawrence. "Recognition, Value, and Equality: A Critique of Charles Taylor and Nancy Fraser's Account of Multiculturalism." In Willett, ed., *Theorizing Multiculturalism* (g.v.).

Bokina, John and Steve Lukes, eds. *Marcuse: From the New Left to the Next Left*. Lawrence, Kans.: University Press of Kansas, 1994.

Borgosz, Józef. *Herbert Marcuse i filozofia trzeciej siły (Herbert Marcuse and the Philosophy of the Third Way)*. Warszawa: Pánstwowe Wydawnictwo Naukove, 1972.

Brodsky, Joseph and Václav Havel. "'The Post-Communist Nightmare': An Exchange." Havel's text trans. by Paul Wilson. *The New York Review of Books* 41, no. 4, February 17, 1994, 28–30.

Brown, Alison L. "Grave Voices: A Discussion about Praxis." *Man and World* 25 (1992): 5–19.

Buber, Martin. "The Question to the Single One." In *Between Man and Man*, 40–82. New York: MacMillan, 1965.

Butler, Judith. *Bodies that Matter: On the Discursive Limits of "Sex."* London: Routledge, 1993.

——— . "Endangered/Endangering: Schematic Racism and White Paranoia." In Gooding-Williams, ed., *Reading Rodney King* (q.v.), 15–22.

——— . *Excitable Speech: A Politics of the Performative*. London: Routledge, 1997.

——— . "For a Careful Reading." In Benhabib, et al., *Feminist Contentions* (q.v.), 127–43.

——— . *Gender Trouble: Feminism and the Subversion of Identity*. London: Routledge, 1990.

——— . *Subjects of Desire: Hegelian Reflections in Twentieth Century France*. New York: Columbia University Press, 1987.

——— . "Variation on Sex and Gender: Beauvoir, Wittig, and Foucault." In Benhabib and Cornell, eds., *Feminism as Critique* (q.v.), 128–42.

Camus, Albert. *The Myth of Sisyphus and Other Essays*. Trans. Justin O'Brien. New York: Alfred A. Knopf, 1960.

——— . *The Rebel: An Essay on Man in Revolt*. Trans. Anthony Bower. New York: Alfred A. Knopf and Random House, 1956.

Caputo, John D. *Against Ethics: Contributions to a Poetics of Obligation with Constant Reference to Deconstruction*. Bloomington, Ind.: Indiana University Press, 1993.

——— . "Beyond Aestheticism: Derrida's Responsible Anarchy." *Research in Phenomenology* 18 (1988): 59–73.

——— , ed. with a Commentary. *Deconstruction in a Nutshell: A Conversation with Jacques Derrida*. New York: Fordham University Press, 1997. (See also Derrida, "A Conversation with Jacques Derrida.")

——— . "Hermeneutics as the Recovery of Man." In Brice R. Wachtarhauser, ed., *Hermeneutics and Modern Philosophy*, 416–45. Albany, N.Y.: SUNY Press, 1986.

———. "Hyperbolic Justice: Deconstruction, Myth, and Politics." *Research in Phenomenology* 21 (1991): 3–20.

———. *Radical Hermeneutics: Repetition, Deconstruction, and the Hermeneutic Project.* Bloomington, Ind.: Indiana University Press, 1987.

Caputo, John and Mark Yount, eds. *Foucault and the Critique of Institutions.* University Park, Pa.: Penn State University Press, 1993.

Caraway, Nancy. *Segregated Sisterhood: Racism and the Politics of American Feminism.* Knoxville: University of Tennessee Press, 1991.

Champagne, John. *The Ethics of Marginality: A New Approach to Gay Studies.* Foreword by Donald E. Pease. Minneapolis: University of Minnesota Press, 1995.

Charmé, Stuart Zane. "Authenticity, Multiculturalism, and the Jewish Question." *Journal of the British Society for Phenomenology* 25, no. 2 (May 1994): 183–88.

Chomsky, Noam. "Aftermath: Voices from Below." *Z Magazine* (October 1991): 19–28.

———. "Nefarious Aggression." *Zeta Magazine* (October 1990): 18–29.

———. "What They Say Goes: The Middle East in the New World Order." In Peters, *Collateral Damage* (q.v.), 49–92.

———. *Year 501: The Conquest Continues.* Boston: South End Press, 1993.

Cohen, Stephen. "It's not a transition in Russia—it's a full-blown disaster." *Pittsburgh Post-Gazette,* December 22, 1996, E-1, 4.

"Comunicados del EZLN" (Spanish). Communiqués of the Zapatista National Liberation Army, signed by Marcos (public pseudonym). All references taken and translated from the EZLN Web Page on the internet at http://www.peak.org/~justin/ezln (January 1994–).

"Contesting the New World Order." Special Issue of *Polygraph,* 5 (Duke University, 1992).

Cooke, Maeve. "Authenticity and Autonomy: Taylor, Habermas, and the Politics of Recognition" (Prague: Conference on the Philosophy of Social Sciences, May 1995), ms.

———. "Habermas, Autonomy, and the Identity of the Self." *Philosophy and Social Criticism* 18, nos. 3–4 (1992): 269–91.

———. "Realizing the Post-Conventional Self." *Philosophy and Social Criticism* 20, nos. 1–2 (1994): 87–101.

Cornell, Drucilla. *Beyond Accommodation: Ethical Feminism, Deconstruction, and the Law.* London: Routledge, 1991.

———. *The Philosophy of the Limit.* London: Routledge, 1992.

————. "The Poststructuralist Challenge to the Ideal of Community." *Cardozo Law Review* 8 (April 1987): 989–1022.

————. "Two Lectures on the Normative Dimensions of Community in the Law." *Tennessee Law Review* 54 (winter 1987): 327–43.

————. "What is Ethical Feminism?" In Benhabib et al., *Feminist Contentions* (q.v.), 75–106.

Critchley, Simon. "Habermas und Derrida werden verheiratet." *Deutsche Zeitschrift zur Philosophie* 42, no. 6 (1994): 1025–36.

Cruikshank, Margaret. *The Gay and Lesbian Liberation Movement.* London: Routledge, 1992.

Dahbour, Omar. "Globalization and the Contradictions of Liberal Nationalism." A Plenary Presentation. Second National Radical Philosophy Conference, "Globalization From Below." Purdue University, November 14–17, 1996.

Dallmayr, Fred. "Global Development? Alternative Voices from Delhi." *Alternatives* 21, no. 2 (April–June 1996): 259–82.

Davidson, Donald. *Inquiries into Truth and Interpretation.* Oxford: Oxford University Press, 1985.

De Lauretis, Teresa. *Alice Doesn't: Feminism, Semiotics, Cinema.* Bloomington, Ind.: Indiana University Press, 1984.

Derrida, Jacques. "A Conversation with Jacques Derrida." A Roundtable Discussion with Walter Brogan, Thomas Busch, John D. Caputo, and Dennis Schmidt. Villanova University, October 3, 1994. (See also Caputo, *Deconstruction*.)

————. *Deconstruction and the Possibility of Justice.* Trans. M. Quaintance, ed. D. Cornell, M. Rosenfeld, D. G. Carlson. London: Routledge, 1992.

————. "The Deconstruction of Actuality." Interview by Brigite Sohm, Cristina de Peretti, Stéphane Douailler, Patrice Vermeren and Emile Malet. Trans. Jonathan Rée. *Radical Philosophy,* 68 (autumn 1994): 28–41.

————. "The Ends of Man." *Philosophy and Phenomenological Research* 30, no. 1 (1969): 31–57. (Reprinted in *Margins of Philosophy,* 109–36. Trans. Alan Bass. Chicago: University of Chicago Press.)

————. *The Gift of Death* (1992). Trans. David Wills. Chicago: University of Chicago Press, 1995.

————. *L'autre cap: Suivi de la démocratie ajournée.* Paris: Les Éditions de Minuit, 1991. (*The Other Heading: Reflections on Today's Europe.* Trans. Pascale-Anne Brault and Michael B. Naas. Bloomington, Ind.: Indiana University Press, 1992.)

————. *Limited Inc.* Ed. Gerald Graff, trans. Samuel Weber and Jeffrey Mehlman. Evanston, Ill.: Northwestern University Press, 1988.

————. "Of the Humanities and the Philosophical Disciplines. The Right to Philosophy from the Cosmopolitical Point of View (the Example of an International Institution)." Trans. Thomas Dutoit. *Surfaces* 4, no. 310, Folio 1 (1994): 1–10.

————. *Points . . . Interviews, 1974–1994.* Ed. Elisabeth Weber, trans. Peggy Kamuf and others. Stanford, CA: Stanford University Press, 1995.

————. *Spectres de Marx: L'État de la dette, le travail du deuil et la nouvelle Internationale.* Paris: Éditions Galilée, 1993. (*Specters of Marx: The State of Debt, the Work of Mourning, and the New International.* Trans. Peggy Kamuf. London: Routledge, 1994.)

Dewey, John. *Liberalism and Social Action. Later Works.* Vol. 11. Ed. Jo Ann Boydston. Carbondale: Southern Illinois University Press, 1991.

Dienst, Richard. *Still Life in Real Time: Theory after Television.* Durham, N.C.: Duke Univertsity Press, 1994.

Dirlik, Arif. "The Postcolonial Aura: Third World Criticism in the Age of Global Capitalism." *Critical Inquiry* 20 (winter 1994): 328–56.

Dobbs, Michael. "'Information Guerillas' Score Against Milosevic." *The Washington Post,* January 2, 1997, A-13.

Doder, Dusko. "Belgrade Professor Who Fought Tito Now Scorned as Serb Leader." *The Chronicle of Higher Education* 39, no. 31 (April 7, 1993), 37–38.

Douglass, Frederick. *Narrative of the Life of Frederick Douglass an American Slave, Written by Himself* (1845), ed. David W. Blight. New York: St. Martin's Press, 1993.

————. "What to the Slave Is the Fourth of July?" (July 5, 1852). In *Narrative* (q.v.), 141–45.

Dubiel, Helmut. "Beyond Mourning and Melancholia on the Left." *Praxis International,* 10, nos. 3–4 (October 1990–January 1991): 241–49.

Du Bois, Burghardt W. E. "The Conservation of Races." In Howard Brotz, ed., *African-American Social and Political Thought, 1850–1920,* 483–92. New Brunswick, N.J.: Transaction Publishers, 1992.

————. *The Souls of Black Folk.* A new intro. by Randall Kenan. New York: Penguin Books, 1995.

Dudinska, Natasha. "From Prague, a Student of Lost Ideals and New-Found Evils." *The New York Times,* June 13, 1993, E-7.

Dussell, Enrique. *Philosophy of Liberation.* Trans. Aquilina Martinez and Chistine Morowsky. Maryknoll, N.Y.: Orbis Books, 1980.

Ebert, Teresa. *Ludic Feminism and After: Postmodernism, Desire, and Labor in Late Capitalism.* Ann Arbor: University of Michigan Press, 1996.

———. "Political Semiosis in/of American Cultural Studies." *American Journal of Semiotics* 8, no. 1/2 (1991): 113–35.

Emmanuel, Steven M. "Reading Kierkegaard." *Philosophy Today* 36, nos. 3–4 (fall 1992): 240–55.

Eribon, Didier. "Marx, penseur du XXIe siècle," *Le Nouvel Observateur* (October 21–27, 1993): 50–53.

Fanon, Frantz. *Black Skin, White Masks.* Trans. Charles Lam Markmann. New York: Grove Press, 1967.

———. *The Wretched of the Earth.* Trans. Constance Farrington. New York: Grove Press, 1963.

Ferrara, Alessandro. "Authenticity and Intersubjectivity" (Prague: Conference on the Philosophy of Social Sciences, May 1995), ms.

———. "Authenticity and the Project of Modernity." *European Journal of Philosophy* 2, no. 3 (1994): 241–72.

———. "Justice and the Good from a *Eudaimonistic* Standpoint." *Philosophy and Social Criticism* 18, nos. 3–4 (1992): 333–54.

———. *Modernity and Authenticity: A Study in the Social and Ethical Thought of Jean-Jacques Rousseau.* Albany, N.Y.: SUNY Press, 1993.

———. "Postmodern Eudaimonia." *Praxis International* 11, no. 4 (January 1992): 387–411.

Firestone, Shulamith. *The Dialectic of Sex: The Case for Feminist Revolution.* Intro. by Rosalind Delmar. London: The Women's Press, 1979.

Forman, Miloš. Film director. "The People vs. Larry Flynt." Columbia Pictures, 1996.

Foucault, Michel. *Discipline and Punish: The Birth of the Prison* (1975). Trans. Alan Sheridan. New York: Random House, 1977.

———. "Dream, Imagination, and Existence." (An introduction to Ludwig Binswanger's "Dream and Existence.") Trans. Forrest Williams. *Review of Existential Psychology and Psychiatry* 19, no. 1 (1984–85): 29–78.

———. *The Foucault Reader.* Ed. Paul Rabinow. New York: Pantheon Books, 1984.

———. *The History of Sexuality. Vol 1: An Introduction.* (1976). Trans. Robert Hurley. New York: Random House, Vintage Books, 1980.

———. *Language, Counter-Memory, Practice: Selected Essays and Interviews.* Ed. Donald F. Bouchard, trans. Donald F. Bouchard and Sherry Simon. New York: Cornell University Press, 1977.

————. *Politics, Philosophy, Culture: Interviews and Other Writings 1977–1984*. Ed. Lawrence D. Kritzman, trans. Alan Sheridan and others. London: Routledge, 1988.

————. *Power/Knowledge: Selected Interview and Other Writings 1972–1977*. Ed. Colin Gordon, trans. Colin Gordon, Leo Marshall, John Mepham, Kate Soper. New York: Pantheon, 1980.

————. "Qu'est-ce-que la critique [Critique at *Aufklärgung*]." Compte rendu de la séance du 27 mai 1978. *Bulletin de la Société francaise de Philosophie* 84 (1990): 35–63.

————. *Technologies of the Self: A Seminar with Michel Foucault*. Ed. Luther M. Martin, Huck Gutman, and Patrick H. Hutton. Amherst, Mass.: University of Massachusetts Press, 1988.

————. *The Use of Pleasure: The History of Sexuality. Vol. 2*. (1984). Trans. Robert Hurley. New York: Random House, Vintage Books, 1985.

Franken, Al. *Rush Limbaugh Is a Big Fat Idiot*. New York: Delacorte, 1996.

Fraser, Nancy. "False Anthitheses: A Response to Seyla Benhabib and Judith Butler." In Benhabib et al., *Feminist Contentions* (q.v.), 59–74.

————. *Justice Interruptus: Critical Reflections on the "Postsocialist" Condition*. London: Routledge, 1997.

————. "Pragmatism, Feminism, and the Linguistic Turn." In Benhabib et al., *Feminist Contentions* (q.v.), 157–71.

————. "A Rejoinder to Iris Young." *New Left Review*, no. 223 (May/June 1997): 126–29.

————. *Unruly Practices: Power, Discourse, and Gender in Contemporary Social Theory*. Minneapolis: University of Minnesota Press, 1989.

Fraser, Nancy and Sandra Lee Bartky, eds. *Revaluing French Feminism: Critical Essays on Difference, Agency, and Culture*. Bloomington, Ind.: Indiana University Press, 1992.

Freire, Paulo. *Pedagogy of the Oppressed*. New York: Continuum, 1982.

————. *The Politics of Education: Culture, Power, and Liberation*. Trans. Donaldo Macado. Boston: Bergin and Garvey, 1985.

Friedman, Marilyn. "Feminism and Modern Friendship: Dislocating the Community." *Ethics* 99 (January 1989): 275–90.

Fukuyama, Francis. *The End of History and the Last Man*. New York: Free Press, 1992.

Gadamer, Hans-Georg. *Truth and Method*. Trans. G. Barden and J. Cumming. New York: Seabury Press, 1975.

Gallagher, Shaun. "Some Particular Limitations of Postconventional Universality." In Lenore Langsdorf and Stephen H. Watson with E. Marya Bower, eds., *Phenomenology, Interpretation, and Community*, 115–26. Albany, N.Y.: SUNY Press, 1996.

Gandhi, M. K. *Non-Violent Resistance (Satyagraha)*. New York: Schocken Books, 1961.

Gardner, James. "Global Regionalism." *New Perspectives Quarterly* 25 (winter 1992): 58–59.

Giddens, Anthony. "Reason without Revolution? Habermas' *Theorie des kommunikativen Handelns*." *Praxis International* 2, no. 3 (1982): 318–28.

Gilroy, Paul. *The Black Atlantic: Modernity and Double Consciousness*. London: Verso, and Cambridge, Mass.: Harvard University Press, 1993.

Giroux, Henry A. *Disturbing Pleasures: Learning Popular Culture*. London: Routledge, 1994.

Giroux, Henry A. and Peter McLaren, eds. *Between Borders: Pedagogy and the Politics of Cultural Studies*. London: Routledge, 1994.

Glenny, Misha. "Is Macedonia Next?" *The New York Times*, July 30, 1993, A-15.

Godway, Eleanor M. and Geraldine Finn, eds. *Who Is This 'We'? Absence of Community*. Montreal: Black Rose Books, 1994.

Goldberg, David Theo, ed. *Anatomy of Racism*. Minneapolis: University of Minnesota Press, 1990.

Gomberg, Paul. "Against Racism, Against Patriotism." *American Philosophical Association Newsletter on Philosophy and the Black Experience* 92, no. 1 (spring 1993): 18–19.

———. "How Racial Identities Contribute to Racism." Delivered at the American Philosophical Association, Central Division meeting, Kansas City, Mo., May 7, 1994.

———. "Patriotism is Like Racism." *Ethics* 101 (1990): 144–50.

Gooding-Williams, Robert, ed. *Reading Rodney King. Reading Urban Uprising*. London: Routledge, 1993.

Gordon, Lewis R. *Bad Faith and Antiblack Racism*. Atlantic Highlands, N.J.: Humanities Press, 1994.

———. *Fanon and the Crisis of European Man: An Essay on Philosophy and the Human Sciences*. London: Routledge, 1995.

Gordon, Lewis R., ed. *Existence in Black: An Anthology of Black Existential Philosophy*. London: Routledge, 1996.

Gordon, Lewis R., T. Denean Sharpley-Whiting, and Renee T. White, eds., *Fanon: A Critical Reader*. Cambridge, Mass.: Blackwell, 1996.

Gould, Carol. *Rethinking Democracy: Freedom and Social Cooperation in Politics, Economy, and Society*. Cambridge: Cambridge University Press, 1988.

Gramsci, Antonio. *Prison Notebooks*. Vol. 1. Ed. Joseph A. Buttigieg, trans. Joseph A. Buttigieg and Antonio Callari. New York: Columbia University Press, 1992.

Green, Judith. "The Diverse Community or the Unoppressive City: Which Ideal for a Transformative Politics of Difference?" *The Journal of Social Philosophy* 26, no. 1 (spring 1995): 86–102.

Greider, William. "Global Warning: Curbing the Free-Trade Freefall." *Nation* 264, no. 2 (January 13–20, 1997): 11–12, 14, 16–17.

————. *One World, Ready or Not: The Manic Logic of Global Capitalism*. New York: Simon and Schuster, 1997.

Guha, Ranajit and Gayatri Chakravorty Spivak, eds. *Selected Subaltern Studies*. Foreword by Edward Said. New York: Oxford University Press, 1988.

Gutmann, Amy. "Communitarian Critics of Liberalism." *Philosophy and Public Affairs* 14 (1985): 308–22.

Gutting, Gary, ed. *The Cambridge Companion to Foucault*. Cambridge: Cambridge University Press, 1994.

Habermas, Jürgen. *Autonomy and Solidarity: Interviews with Jürgen Habermas*. Ed. Peter Dews. London: Verso, revised and enlarged ed., 1992.

————. *Das Absolute und die Geschichte: Von der Zwiespältigkeit in Schellings Denken*. Ph.D. Dissertation, Universität Bonn, February 24, 1954.

————. "Die grosse Wirkung: Eine chronistische Anmerkung zu Martin Heideggers 70 Geburtstag." *Frankfurter Allgemenine Zeitung*, September 26, 1959. Cited from *Philosophisch-politische Profile* (q.v.), 76–85. ("Martin Heidegger: The Great Influence." In *Philosophical-Political Profiles* [q.v.], 53–60.)

————. *Die nachholende Revolution: Kleine politische Schriften VII*. Frankfurt a/M: Suhrkamp, 1990.

————. "Diskursethik—Notizen zu einem Begründungsprogramm." In Habermas, *Moralbewußtsein und kommunikatives Handeln* (q.v.), 53–126. ("Discourse Ethics: Notes on a Program of Philosophical Justification." In Habermas, *Moral Consciousness and Communicative Action* [q.v.], 43–115.)

————. *Eine Art Schadensabwicklung: Kleine Politische Schriften VI*. Frankfurt a/M: Suhrkamp, 1987. (Partially trans. in Habermas, *New Conservatism* [q.v.]).

————. *Erläuterungen zur Diskursethik*. Frankfurt a/M: Suhrkamp, 1991. (Partially trans. in: Habermas, *Justification and Application* [q.v.].)

———. *Faktizität und Geltung: Beiträge zur Diskurstheorie des Rechts und des demokratischen Rechtstaats.* Frankfurt a/M: Suhrkamp, 1992. (*Between Facts and Norms: Contributions to a Discourse Theory of Law and Democracy.* Trans. William Rehg. Cambridge, Mass: MIT, 1996.)

———. "Gerechtigkeit und Solidarität: Eine Stellungnahme zur Diskussion über 'Stufe 6'." In Wolfgang Edelstein and Gertrud Nunner-Winkler, eds., *Zur Bestimmung der Moral: Philosophische und sozialwissenschaftliche Beiträge zur Moralforschung,* 291–318. Frankfurt a/M: Suhrkamp, 1986. ("Justice and Solidarity: On the Discussion Concerning 'Stage 6'." In Michael Kelly, ed., *Hermeneutics and Critical Theory in Ethics and Politics,* 32–52. Cambridge, Mass.: MIT, 1990.)

———. "Geschichtsbewußtsein und posttraditionale Identität: Die Westorientierung der Budesrepublik." In Habermas, *Eine Art Schadensabwicklung* (q.v.), 161–79. ("Historical Consciousness and Post-Traditional Identity: The Federal Republic's Orientation to the West." In Habermas, *The New Conservatism* [q.v.], 249–67.)

———. "Herbert Marcuse über Kunst und Revolution." In *Kultur und Kritik* (q.v.), 345–51. ("Herbert Marcuse: On Art and Revolution (1973)." In *Philosophical-Political Profiles* [q.v.], 165–70.)

———. "Human Rights and Popular Sovereignty." Northwestern University, September 23, 1992. Public lecture.

———. "Im Lichte Heideggers." *Frankfurter Allgemenine Zeitung,* July 12, 1952, section "Bilder und Zeiten," no. 158.

———. "An Intersubjectivist Concept of Individuality." Paper presented at Brighton: World Congress of Philosophy, August 24, 1988. (This is a partial draft from Habermas, *Nachmetaphysisches Denken* [q.v.], 187–241 which does not include the Kierkegaard discussion.)

———. "Jürgen Habermas on the Legacy of Jean-Paul Sartre." Interview conducted by Richard Wolin. *Political Theory* 20, no. 3 (August 1992): 496–501.

———. *Justification and Application: Remarks on Discourse Ethics.* Trans. Ciaran P. Cronin. Cambridge, Mass.: MIT, 1993.

———. *Knowledge and Human Interests.* Trans. Jeremy J. Shapiro. Boston: Beacon Press, 1971. (*Erkenntnis und Interesse.* Frankfurt a/M: Suhrkamp, 1968.)

———. "Kommunikative Freiheit und negative Theologie." In Emil Angehrn, Hinrich Fink Eitel, Christian Iber, and Georg Lohmann, eds., *Dialektischer Negativismus: Michel Theunissen zum 60. Geburtstag,* 15–34. Frankfurt a/M: Suhrkamp, 1992. ("Communicative Freedom and Negative Theology." Trans. Martin J. Matuštík and Patricia J. Huntington. In Matuštík and Westphal, eds., *Kierkegaard in Post/Modernity* [q.v.], 182–98.)

———. *Kultur und Kritik: Verstreute Aufsätze.* Frankfurt a/M: Suhrkamp, 1973.

————. *Legitimation Crisis*. Trans. Thomas McCarthy. Boston: Beacon Press, 1975. (*Legitimationsprobleme im Spätkapitalismus*. Frankfurt a/M: Suhrkamp, 1973.)

————. "Mit Heidegger gegen Heidegger denken: Zur Veröffentlichung von Vorlesungen aus dem Jahre 1935." *Frankfurter Allgemenine Zeitung*, no. 170, July 25, 1953. Cited from *Philosophisch-politische Profile* (q.v.), 67–75. ("Martin Heidegger: On the Publication of Lectures from the Year 1935." Trans. Dale Ponikvar. *Graduate Faculty Philosophy Journal* 6, no. 2 [fall 1977]: 155–64.)

————. *Moralbewußtsein und kommunikatives Handeln*. Frankfurt a/M: Suhrkamp, 1983. (*Moral Consciousness and Communicative Action*. Trans. Christian Lenhardt and Shierry Weber Nicholsen. Cambridge, Mass.: MIT, 1990.)

————. "Moralität und Sittlichkeit: Treffen Hegels Einwände gegen Kant auch die Diskursethik zu?" In Wolfgang Kuhlmann, ed., *Moralität und Sittlichkeit: Das Problem Hegels und die Diskursethik*, 16–37. Frankfurt a/M: Suhrkamp, 1986. ("Morality and Ethical Life: Does Hegel's Critique of Kant Apply to Discourse Ethics?" In Habermas, *Moral Consciousness and Communicative Action* [q.v.], 195–215.)

————. "Nachholende Revolution und linker Revisionsbedarf: Was heißt Sozialismus heute?" In *Die nachholende Revolution* (q.v.), 179–204. ("What Does Socialism Mean Today?" *New Left Review*, 183 [1990]: 3–21.)

————. *Nachmetaphysisches Denken: Philosophische Aufsätze*. Frankfurt a/M: Suhrkamp, 1988. (*Postmetaphysical Thinking: Philosophical Essays*. Trans. William Mark Hohengarten. Cambridge, Mass.: MIT, 1992.)

————. *The New Conservatism: Cultural Criticism and the Historians' Debate*. Ed. and trans. Shierry Weber Nicholsen, intro. by Richard Wolin. Cambridge, Mass.: MIT, 1989. (This is a partial trans. of Habermas, *Eine Art Schadensabwicklung* [q.v.], with additional essays from other volumes.)

————. *Philosophisch-politische Profile*. Frankfurt a/M: Suhrkamp, 1971. (*Philosophical-Political Profiles*. Trans. Frederick G. Lawrence. Cambridge, Mass.: MIT, 1983. Incomplete edition.)

————. *Der Philosophische Diskurs der Moderne: Zwölf Vorlesungen*. Frankfurt a/M: Suhrkamp, 1985. (*The Philosophical Discourse of Modernity: Twelve Lectures*. Trans. Frederick Lawrence. Cambridge, Mass.: MIT, 1987.)

————. "Postscript to *Faktizität und Geltung*." *Philosophy and Social Criticism* 20, no. 4 (1994): 135–50.

————. "Psychic Thermidor and the Rebirth of Rebellious Subjectivity" (1980). In Bernstein, ed., *Habermas and Modernity* (q.v.), 67–77, 218 n.

————. "Die Scheinsrevolution und ihre Kinder: Sechs Thesen über Taktik, Ziele, und Situationsanalysen der oppositionellen Jugend." In *Die Linke Antwortet Jürgen Habermas*. Frankfurt a/M: Europäische Verlaganstalt, 1968.

———. "Staatsburgerschaft und nationale Identität. Überlegungen zur Europäischen Zukunft" (1990). ("Citizenship and National Identity: Some Reflections on the Future of Europe." *Praxis International* 12, no. 1 [April 1992]: 1–19.) Cited from Habermas, *Faktizität und Geltung* (q.v.), 632–60/491–515.

———. "Struggles for Recognition in the Democratic Constitutional State." Trans. Shierry Weber Nicholsen. In Taylor, C. et al., *Multiculturalism* (q.v.), 107–48.

———. *Texte und Kontexte*. Frankfurt a/M: Suhrkamp, 1991.

———. *Theorie des kommunikativen Handelns*. Frankfurt a/M: Suhrkamp. Band 1: *Handlungsrationalität und gesellschaftliche Rationalisierung*, 1981; Band 2: *Zur Kritik der funktionalistichen Vernunft*, 1985. (*The Theory of Communicative Action*. 2 vols. Trans. Thomas McCarthy. Boston: Beacon Press. Vol. 1: *Reason and the Rationalization of Society*, 1984; vol. 2: *Lifeworld and System: A Critique of Functionalist Reason*, 1987.)

———. "Theorie und Politik." In *Gespräche mit Herbert Marcuse* (q.v.), 9–63.

———. "Transzendenz von innen, Transzendenz ins Diesseits." In Habermas, *Texte und Kontexte* (q.v.), 127–56. ("Transcendence from Within, Transcendence in this World." Trans. Eric Crump and Peter P. Kenny. In Don S. Browning and Francis Schüssler Fiorenza, eds., *Habermas, Modernity, and Public Theology*, 226–50. New York: Crossroad, 1992.)

———. "Über Moralität und Sittlichkeit—Was macht eine Lebensform rational?" In Herbert Schnädelbach, ed., *Rationalität: Philosophische Beiträge*, 218–35. Frankfurt a/M: Suhrkamp, 1984.

———. *Vergangenheit als Zukunft*. Zürich: Pendo Verlag, 1990. (*The Past As Future: Interviewed by Michael Haller*. Trans. and ed. Max Pensky. Lincoln, Neb.: University of Nebraska Press, 1994.)

———. "Volkssouverentität als Verfahren" (1988). In Habermas, *Faktizität und Geltung* (q.v.), 600–31/463–90.

———. "Vom pragmatischen, ethischen, und moralischen Gebrauch der praktischen Vernunft." In Habermas, *Erläuterungen zur Diskursethik* (q.v.), 100–18. ("On the Pragmatic, the Ethical, and the Moral Employment of Practical Reason." In Habermas, *Justification and Application* [q.v.], 1–17.)

———. Vorwort zur Neuaflage (1990), *Strukturwandel der Öffentlichkeit*. Frankfurt a/M: Suhrkamp, 1990.

———. "Work and Weltanschaung: The Heidegger Controversy from a German Perspective." Trans. John McCumber. In *The New Conservatism* (q.v.), 140–72.

———. "Zum Geleit." In *Antworten auf Herbert Marcuse*, ed. Habermas, 9–16. Frankfurt: Suhrkamp, 1968.

———. *Zur Rekonstruktion des Historischen Materialismus*. Frankfurt a/M: Suhrkamp, 1982.

Hall, Ronald L. *Word and Spirit: A Kierkegaardian Critique of the Modern Age.* Bloomington, Ind.: Indiana University Press, 1993.

Halleck, Deedee. "Zapatistas On-Line." *NACLA: Report on the Americas* 28, no. 2 (Sept/Oct. 1994): 30–32.

Harbury, Jennifer. *Bridge of Courage: Life Stories of the Guatemalan Compañeros and Compañeras.* Intro. Noam Chomsky (2–29). Monroe, Mass.: Common Courage Press, 1994.

Harris, Leonard. "'Believe It or Not' or the Ku Klux Klan and American Philosophy Exposed." *Proceedings of the American Philosophical Association* 68, no. 5 (May 1995): 133–37.

Harris, Leonard, ed. *Philosophy Born of Struggle: Anthology of Afro-American Philosophy from 1917.* Dubuque, Iowa: Kendall/Hunt, 1983.

Hartmann, Heidi I. "The Unhappy Marriage of Marxism and Feminism: Towards a More Progressive Union." In Lydia Sargent, ed., *Women and Revolution.* Boston: South End Press, 1979.

Havel, Václav. *Dopisy Olze* (Letters To Olga). Praha: Atlantis, 1990.

———. "How Europe Could Fail." Trans. Paul Wilson. *The New York Review of Books* 40, no. 19, November 18, 1993, 3.

———. "Kdo oželí volby, ten je sám proti sobě" ("The One Who Gives Up on Voting Is Against Oneself"). *Mladá Fronta Dnes*, Prague, May 22, 1996, 4.

———. *Letní přemítání* (Summer Meditations). Praha: Odeon, 1991.

———. "The Post-Communist Nightmare." Trans. Paul Wilson. *The New York Review of Books* 40, no. 10, May 27, 1993, 8, 10.

———. "The Power of the Powerless." Trans. Paul Wilson. In *Living in Truth: Twenty-Two Essays Published on the Occasion of the Award of the Erasmus Prize to Václav Havel*, ed. Jan Ladislav. London: Faber and Faber, 1990.

———. *Projevy, leden–červen 1990 (Speeches, January–June 1990)*, ed. Vilém Přečan. Praha: Vyšehrad, 1990.

———. *Vážení občané, Projevy červenec 1990–červenec 1992 (Dear Citizens, Speeches, July 1990–July 1992).* Praha: Lidové noviny, 1992.

Hegel's Phenomenology of Spirit. Trans. A.V. Miller. London: Oxford University Press, 1977.

Hegel's Philosophy of Right. Trans. T. M. Knox. London: Oxford University Press, 1967.

Heidegger, Martin. "Only A God Can Save Us Now: An Interview with Martin Heidegger" (1976). Trans. David Schendler. *Graduate Faculty Philosophy Journal* 6, no. 1 (winter 1977): 5–27.

——. *The Question Concerning Technology and Other Essays.* Trans. William Lovitt. New York: Harper and Row, 1977.

Hernnstein, Richard J. and Charles Murray. *The Bell Curve.* New York: Free Press, 1994.

Hobsbawm, Eric J. *Nations and Nationalism since 1780: Programme, Myth, Reality.* Cambridge: Cambridge University Press, 1990.

——. "The New Threat to History." *The New York Review of Books* 40, no. 21, December 16, 1993, 62–64.

Höffer, Bruni, Heinz Dieterich, and Klaus Meyer, eds. *Das Fünfhundert-jährige Reich.* Médico International, 1990.

Hoffman, David. "Russian Mogul Epitomizes New Power of Capitalism." *The Washington Post,* January 10, 1997, A1, 26.

Honneth, Axel. *Critique of Power: Reflective Stages in Critical Social Theory.* Trans. Kenneth Baynes. Cambridge, Mass.: MIT, 1991.

——. "Decentered Autonomy: The Subject after the Fall." Paper presented at the meeting of the Society for Phenomenology and Existential Philosophy. Boston, October 9, 1992.

——. "Diskursethik und implizites Gerechtigkeitskonzept: Eine Diskussionsbemerkung." In Wolfgang Kuhlmann, ed., *Moralität und Sittlichkeit: Das Problem Hegels und die Diskursethik,* 183–93. Frankfurt a/M: Suhrkamp, 1986.

——. *Kampf um Anerkennung: Zur moralischen Grammatik sozialer Konflikte.* Frankfurt a/M: Suhrkamp, 1992. (*The Struggle for Recognition: The Moral Grammar of Social Conflicts.* Trans. Joel Anderson. New York: Polity Press, 1995, and Cambridge, Mass.: MIT, 1996.)

——. "The Other of Justice: Habermas and the Ethical Challenge of Postmodernism." In White, ed., *The Cambridge Companion to Habermas* (q.v.), 289–323.

hooks, bell. *Teaching to Transgress: Education as the Practice of Freedom.* London: Routledge, 1994.

——. *Yearning: Race, Gender, and Cultural Politics.* Boston: South End Press, 1991.

hooks, bell and Cornel West, *Breaking Bread: Insurgent Black Intellectual Life.* Boston: South End Press, 1991.

Horkheimer, Max. *Kritische Theorie* (1968), ed. Alfred Schmidt. Vols. 1 and 2. Frankfurt a/M: Fischer, 1977.

——. "Traditional and Critical Theory." Trans. Matthew J. O'Connell. In Horkheimer. *Critical Theory,* 188–243. New York: Herder and Herder, 1972.

Horkheimer, Max and Theodor W. Adorno. *Dialectic of Enlightenment* (1944). Trans. John Cumming. New York: Continuum, 1987.

Howard, Dick. *Political Judgments*. Lanham: Rowman and Littlefield, 1996.

Hoy, David Couzens and Thomas McCarthy. *Critical Theory*. Cambridge, Mass.: Blackwell, 1994.

Huntington, Patricia J. *Ecstatic Subjects, Utopia, and Recognition: Kristeva, Heidegger, Irigaray*. Albany, N.Y.: SUNY Press, 1998.

———. "Fragmentation, Race, and Gender: Building Solidarity in the Postmodern Era." In Gordon, ed., *Existence in Black* (q.v.), 185–202.

———. "Towards a Dialectical Concept of Autonomy: Revisiting the Feminist Alliance with Poststructuralism." *Philosophy and Social Criticism* 21, no. 1 (1995): 37–55.

Huntington, Samuel P. *The Clash of Civilizations and the Remaking of World Order*. New York: Simon and Schuster, 1996.

Husserl, Edmund. *The Crisis of European Sciences and Transcendental Phenomenology*. Trans. David Carr. Evanston, Ill.: Northwestern University Press, 1970.

Ignatieff, Michael. *Blood and Belonging: Journeys into the New Nationalism*. London: BBC Books, 1993.

Ingram, David. *Reason, History, and Politics: The Communitarian Grounds of Legitimation in the Modern Age*. Albany, N.Y.: SUNY Press, 1995.

Jameson, Fredric. *Postmodernism, or The Cultural Logic of Late Capitalism*. Durham, N.C.: Duke University Press, 1991.

Kadarkay, Arpad. *Georg Lukács: Life, Thought, and Politics*. Cambridge, Mass.: Basil Blackwell, 1991.

Kant, Immanuel. *On History*. Trans. Lewis White Beck, Robert E. Anchor, and Emil L. Fackenheim. Indianapolis: Bobbs-Merrill, 1963. (*Königliche Preussische Akademie der Wissenschften*. Vols. 7 and 8. Berlin, 1902–38.)

———. "Perpetual Peace." In Kant, *Königliche Preussische Akadamie* (q.v.), 343–86/*On History* (q.v.), 85–135. Trans. Lewis White Beck. Bobbs-Merrill, 1957.

Katzenberger, Elaine, ed. *First World, Ha Ha Ha! The Zapatista Challenge*. San Francisco: City Lights, 1995.

Kellner, Doug. *Herbert Marcuse and the Crisis of Marxism*. Berkeley: University of California Press, 1984.

———. *The Persian Gulf TV War*. Boulder: Westview Press, 1992.

Kelly, Michael, ed. *Critique and Power: Recasting the Foucault/Habermas Debate*. Cambridge, Mass.: MIT, 1994.

Kierkegaard, Søren. *The Concept of Irony: With Continual Reference to Socrates*. Ed. and trans. Howard V. Hong and Edna H. Hong. Princeton: Princeton University Press, 1989.

———. *Concluding Unscientific Postscript to "Philosophical Fragments."* 2 Vols. Ed. and trans. Howard V. Hong and Edna H. Hong. Princeton: Princeton University Press, 1992.

———. *Fear and Trembling*. Ed. and trans. Howard V. Hong and Edna H. Hong. Princeton: Princeton University Press, 1983.

———. *Journals and Papers*. 7 Vols. Ed. and trans. Howard V. Hong and Edna H. Hong, assisted by Gregor Malantschuk. Index by Nathaniel Hong and Charles Baker. Bloomington, Ind.: Indiana University Press, 1967–1978.

———. *The Point of View for My Work as an Author*. Includes, "'The Individual': Two 'Notes' Concerning My Work as an Author," and *My Activity as a Writer*. Trans. Walter Lowrie. New York: Harper, 1962.

———. *Practice in Christianity*. Ed. and trans. Howard V. Hong and Edna H. Hong. Princeton: Princeton University Press, 1991.

———. *The Sickness unto Death*. Ed. and trans. Howard V. Hong and Edna H. Hong. Princeton: Princeton University Press, 1980.

———. *Søren Kierkegaard's Samlede Voerker*. Vols. 1–14. Eds. A. B. Drachman, J. L. Heiberg, and H. O. Lange. Copenhagen: Gylendal, 1901–1906.

———. *Two Ages: The Age of Revolution and the Present Age*. Ed. and trans. Howard V. Hong and Edna H. Hong. Princeton: Princeton University Press, 1978.

King, Martin Luther, Jr. *Where Do We Go from Here: Chaos or Community?* Boston: Beacon Press, 1967.

Kirmmse, Bruce H. *Kierkegaard in Golden Age Denmark*. Bloomington, Ind.: Indiana University Press, 1990.

Kögler, Hans Herbert. "The Self-Empowered Subject: Habermas, Foucault and Hermeneutic Reflexivity." *Philosophy and Social Criticism* 22, no. 4 (1996): 13–44.

Kohák, Erazim. *Jan Patočka: Philosophy and Selected Writings*. Chicago: University of Chicago Press, 1989.

Kojève, Alexandre. *Introduction to the Reading of Hegel: Lectures on the Phenomenology of Spirit*. Assembled by Raymond Queneau, ed. Allan Bloom, trans. James H. Nichols, Jr. Ithaca, N.Y.: Cornell University Press, 1980.

Kosík, Karel. *Dialectics of the Concrete: A Study on Problems of Man and World*. Trans. Karel Kovanda with James Schmidt. Dordrecht: D. Reidel Publishing Co., 1976.

Kothari, Rajni. *Growing Amnesia: An Essay on Poverty and the Human Consciousness.* Delhi: Viking, 1993.

———. *Transformation and Survival: In Search of a Humane World Order.* Delhi: Ajanta, 1988.

Kristeva, Julia. *Nations Without Nationalism.* Trans. Leon S. Roudiez. New York: Columbia University Press, 1993.

———. *Revolution in Poetic Language.* Trans. Margaret Waller. New York: Columbia University Press, 1984.

———. *Strangers to Ourselves.* Trans. Leon S. Roudiez. New York: Columbia University Press, 1991.

Kroker, Arthur and Marilouise Kroker, eds. *The Last Sex: Feminism and Outlaw Bodies.* New York: St. Martin's Press, 1993.

Kundera, Milan. *The Book of Laughter and Forgetting* (1978). Trans. Michael Henry Heim. New York: Penguin, 1980.

———. "The Czech Wager." *The New York Review of Books,* 27, nos. 21–22, January 22, 1981, 21–22.

———. *Life Is Elsewhere* (1973). Trans. Petr Kussi. New York: Penguin, 1974.

———. *Testaments Betrayed: An Essay in Nine Parts.* Trans. from the French by Linda Asher. New York: HarperCollins, 1993.

———. "The Tragedy of Central Europe." Trans. from the French by Edmund White. *The New York Review of Books,* 31, no. 7, April 26, 1984, 33–38.

Kymlicka, Will. "Liberalism and Communitarianism." *Canadian Journal of Philosophy* 18 (1988): 181–204.

———. *Multicultural Citizenship: A Liberal Theory of Minority Rights.* Oxford: Oxford University Press, 1995.

Laclau, Ernesto and Chantal Mouffe. *Hegemony and Socialist Strategy: Towards a Radical Democratic Politics.* London: Verso, 1985.

Lane, Charles. "The Tainted Sources of 'The Bell Curve'." *The New York Review of Books,* 40, no. 20, December 1, 1994, 14–19.

Larsen, Ross. "Foreigners: Unloved and Unwanted." *The Prague Post,* December 11–17, 1996, A-1, 4.

Leitch, Vincent B. *Deconstructive Criticism: An Advanced Introduction.* New York: Columbia University Press, 1983.

Lévinas, Emmanuel. *Collected Philosophical Papers.* Trans. Alphonso Lingis. Dordrecht: Martinus Nijhoff, 1987.

Lonergan, Bernard. *Insight: A Study of Human Understanding.* New York: Long-mans, Green, 1957.

Lorraine, Tamsin E. *Gender, Identity, and the Production of Meaning.* Boulder, Colo.: Westview Press, 1990.

Lugones, María. "Hispaniendo y Lesbiando: On Sarah Hoagland's *Lesbian Ethics.*" *Hypatia* 5, no. 3 (fall 1990): 138–46.

———. Lecture at the meeting of the Society for Women in Philosophy (SWIP). Cincinnati, Ohio, October 2, 1993.

———. "On *Borderlands/La Frontera*: An Interpretive Essay." *Hypatia* 7, no. 4 (fall 1992): 31–37.

———. "Playfulness, 'World'-Travelling, and Loving Perception." *Hypatia* 2, no. 2 (summer 1987): 3–19.

Lugones, María and Elizabeth V. Spelman. "Have We Got a Theory for You! Feminist Theory, Cultural Imperialism, and the Demand for 'The Woman's Voice'." *Women's Studies International Forum* 6, no. 6 (1983): 573–81. Reprinted in Anzaldúa, ed., *Making Face* (q.v.).

Lukács, György. *Die Zerstörung der Vernunft, Werke 9.* Darmstadt: Luchterhand, 1974.

———. *Existentialisme ou marxisme?* Paris: Nagel, 1948.

Lummis, C. Douglas. "Globocop? Time to Watch the Watchers." *The Nation* 259, no. 9 (September 26, 1994): 302–4, 306.

Lyotard, Jean-Francois. *The Postmodern Condition: A Report on Knowledge.* Trans. G. Bennington and B. Massumi. Minneapolis: University of Minnesota Press, 1984.

MacIntyre, Alasdair. *After Virtue: A Study of Moral Theory,* 2d ed. London: Duckworth, 1985, 1987.

———. *Whose Justice? Which Rationality?* Notre Dame, Ind.: University of Notre Dame Press, 1988.

Macpherson, C. B. *The Political Theory of Possesssive Individualism.* Oxford: Clarendon Press, 1962.

Malcolm X. "Any Means Necessary to Bring about Freedom." In Steve Clark, ed., *Malcolm X Talks to Young People,* 184–88. New York: Pathfinder Press, 1991.

Marcuse, Herbert. *The Aesthetic Dimension: Towards a Critique of Marxist Aesthetics.* Boston: Beacon Press, 1978.

———. *An Essay On Liberation.* Boston: Beacon Press, 1969.

———. "Beiträge zu einer Phänomenologie des Historischen Materialismus." *Philosophische Hefte* 1, no. 1 (Berlin, 1928): 45–68.

——. "The Concept of Negation in the Dialectic." (Prague Hegel Conference, 1966.) *Telos*, 8 (1971): 130–32.

——. *Eros and Civilization: A Philosophical Inquiry into Freud*. Boston: Beacon Press, 1974.

——. *Gespräche mit Herbert Marcuse*. Frankfurt a/M: Suhrkamp, 1978.

——. *Hegels Ontologie und die Grundlegung einer Theorie der Geschichtlichkeit*. Frankfurt a/M: V. Klosterman, 1932.

——. *Negations: Essays in Critical Theory*. Trans. Jeremy J. Shapiro. London: Free Association Books, 1988.

——. "Neue Quellen zur Grundlegung des Historischen Materialismus." *Die Gesellschaft*, 9 (part 2), 8 (Berlin, 1932): 136–74.

——. *One-Dimensional Man: Studies in the Ideology of Advanced Industrial Society* (1964), with a new introduction by Douglas Kellner. Boston: Beacon Press, 1991.

——. *Reason and Revolution: Hegel and the Rise of Social Theory*. With a new preface, "A Note on Dialectic" (1960). Boston: Beacon Press, 1960.

——. "Repressive Tolerance." In Herbert Marcuse, Robert Paul Wolff, and Barrington Moore, Jr., *A Critique of Pure Tolerance*, 81–117. Boston: Beacon Press, 1965, with a new postscript by Marcuse, 1968, 117–23.

——. "Sartre's Existentialism" (1948). In *From Luther to Popper*, 157–90. Trans. Joris de Bres. London: Verso, 1988.

——. *Schriften*. Vols. 1–5. Frankfurt a/M: Suhrkamp, 1978–1992.

——. *Soviet Marxism: A Critical Analysis*. New York: Columbia University Press, 1958, 1969.

——. "Theory and Politics: A Discussion." (First published in *Gespräche* [q.v.]), *Telos*, 38 (1978–79): 124–53.

——. "Transzendentaler Marxismus?" *Die Gesellschaft*, 7 (part 2), no. 10 (Berlin, 1930): 304–26.

——. "Über konkrete Philosophie." *Archiv für Sozialwissenschaft und Sozialpolitik* 62 (Tübingen, 1929): 111–28. Cited from *Schriften* (q.v.), vol. 1, 385–406.

——. "Zum Problem der Dialektik." *Die Gesellschaft*, 7 (part 1), 1 (Berlin, 1930): 15–30 and *Die Gesellschaft*, 8 (part 2), no. 12 (Berlin, 1931): 541–57.

Marković, Mihailo. "The Idea of Critique in Social Theory." *Praxis International* 3, no. 2 (July 1983): 108–20.

Marsh, James L. "The *Corsair* Affair and Critical Social Theory." In Perkins, ed., *International Kierkegaard Commentary: The Corsair Affair* (q.v.), 63–83.

———. *Critique, Action, and Liberation*. Albany, N.Y.: SUNY Press, 1995.

———. "Marx and Kierkegaard on Alienation." In Perkins, ed., *International Kierkegaard Commentary: The Present Age* (q.v.), 155–74.

———. *Post-Cartesian Meditations: An Essay in Dialectical Phenomenology*. New York: Fordham University Press, 1988.

Martin, Bill. *Humanism and Its Aftermath: The Shared Fate of Deconstruction and Politics*. Atlantic Highlands, N.J.: Humanities Press, 1995.

———. "Marxism and the Countryside." A Presentation. Second National Radical Philosophy Conference, "Globalization From Below." Purdue University, November 14–17, 1996.

———. *Matrix and Line: Derrida and the Possibilities of Postmodern Social Theory*. Albany, N.Y.: SUNY Press, 1992.

———. *Politics in the Impasse: Explorations in Postsecular Social Theory*. Albany, N.Y.: SUNY Press, 1996.

Marx, Karl. *Early Writings*. Trans. Rodney Livinstone and Gregor Benton. New York: Vintage Books, 1975.

Marx, Karl and Friedrich Engels. *The Communist Manifesto* (1848). Trans. Samuel Moore. New York: Washington Square Press, 1964.

Masaryk, Tomáš Garrigue. *Ideály Humanitní*. Praha: Melantrich, 1990. Contains: "Ideály Humanitní" (Humanist Ideals) (1901); "Problém malého národa" (Problem of a Small Nation) (1905); and "Demokratism v politice" (Democratism in Politics) (1912).

Matuštík, Martin J. "Democratic Multicultures and Cosmopolis: Beyond the Aporias of the Politics of Identity and Difference." *Method* 12 (1994): 63–89.

———. "Existence and the Communicatively Competent Self." In Lewis E. Hahn, ed. (founded by Paul Arthur Schilpp), *The Library of Living Philosophers: Jürgen Habermas*. Open Court Press, forthcoming.

———. "Kierkegaard as Socio-Political Thinker and Activist." *Man and World* 27, no. 2 (April 1994): 211–24.

———. "Kierkegaard's Existential Philosophy and Praxis as the Revolt Against Systems." *The Edinburgh Encyclopedia of Continental Philosophy*. Ed. Simon Glendinning. The Edinburgh University Press, 1998.

———. "Merleau-Ponty on Taking the Attitude of the Other." *Journal of the British Society for Phenomenology* 22, no. 1 (January 1991): 44–52.

———. "Merleau-Ponty's Phenomenology of Sympathy." *Auslegung* 17, no. 1 (January 1991): 41–65.

————. *Postnational Identity: Critical Theory and Existential Philosophy in Habermas, Kierkegaard, and Havel*. New York: Guilford Press, 1993.

————. Review of Perkins, ed., *International Kierkegaard Commentary: The Corsair Affair* (q.v.). *Man and World* 26 (1993): 93–97.

————. "Transcendental-Phenomenological Retrieval and Critical Theory." *Method* 8, no. 1 (March 1990) 94–104.

Matuštík, Martin and Patricia J. Huntington. Review of Martin, *Matrix and Line* (q.v.), *Radical Philosophy Review of Books*, no. 8 (December 1993): 4–12.

Matuštík, Martin and Merold Westphal, eds. *Kierkegaard in Post/Modernity*. Bloomington, Ind.: Indiana University Press, 1995.

McBride, William L. *Sartre's Political Theory*. Bloomington, Ind.: Indiana University Press, 1991.

McCumber, John. "Time in the Ditch: American Philosophy and the McCarthy Era." *Diacritics* 26, no. 1 (Spring 1996): 33–49.

Mead, George Herbert. *Mind, Self, and Society: From the Standpoint of a Social Behaviorist*. Chicago: University of Chicago Press, 1934.

Merleau-Ponty, Maurice. *The Primacy of Perception*. Evanston, Ill.: Northwestern University Press, 1964.

Meyers, Diana T. "Personal Autonomy or the Deconstructed Subject. A Reply to Heckman." *Hypatia* 7, no. 1 (winter 1992): 124–32.

————. *Self, Society, and Personal Choice*. New York: Columbia University Press, 1989.

Michnik, Adam. "An Embarrassing Anniversary." *The New York Review of Books* 40, no. 11, June 10, 1993, 19–21.

————. "Bojím sa antikomunistov s tvárami boľševikov" (I am Afraid of the Anti-communists with the Faces of Bolsheviks) (Interview). *Kultúrny život* (Bratislava), June 11, 1992, 3.

Mićunović, Natalija. "Critique of Nationalism." Ph.D. dissertation, Purdue, 1996.

Mills, Charles. *The Racial Contract*. Ms.

Mills, Patricia Jagenowicz, ed. *Feminist Interpretations of G.W.F. Hegel*. University Park, Pa.: The Pennsylvania State University Press, 1996.

Minh-ha, Trinh T. *When the Moon Waxes Red: Representation, Gender, and Cultural Politics*. London: Routledge, 1991.

"More Humility, Fewer Illusions—A Talk between Adam Michnik and Jürgen Habermas." Trans. Rodney Livingstone. *The New York Review of Books* 41, no. 6, March 24, 1994, 24–29.

Moses, Greg. *Revolution of Conscience: Martin Luther King, Jr, and Philosophy of Non-violence.* New York: Guilford Press, 1997.

Mouffe, Chantal, ed. *Dimensions of Radical Democracy: Pluralism, Citizenship, Community.* London: Verso, 1992.

"Multiculturalism, Postmodernism, and Racial Consciousness." The Black Scholar Reader's Forum. *The Black Scholar* 23, nos. 3–4 (summer/fall 1993): 47–80 and 24, no. 1 (winter 1994): 15–22.

Nagl, Ludwig. "Zeight die Habermassche Kommunikationstheorie einen 'Ausweg aus der Subjektphilosophie'? Erwägungen zur Studie *Der Philosophische Diskurs der Moderne.*" In Manfred Frank, Gérald Raulet, and Willem van Reijen, eds., *Die Frage nach dem Subjekt,* 364–72. Frankfurt a/M: Suhrkamp, 1988.

Nancy, Jean-Luc. *The Inoperative Community.* Trans. Peter Connor, et al. Minneapolis: University of Minnesota Press, 1991.

Nandy, Ashis. "Cultural Frames for Social Transformation: A Credo." *Alternatives* 12, no. 1 (January 1987): 113–23.

———. *The Illegitimacy of Nationalism: Rabindranath Tagore and the Politics of Self.* Delhi: Oxford University Press, 1994.

———. *Traditions, Tyranny, and Utopias: Essays in Politics of Awareness.* Delhi: Oxford University Press, 1987.

"Nationalism and Multiculturalism." Plenary forum with Omar Dahbour, Natalija Mićunović, Jeff Paris, and Hans Seigfried. The Second National Radical Philosophy Conference, "Globalization From Below." Purdue University, November 14–17, 1996.

Neaman, Elliot. "Mutiny on Board Modernity: Heidegger, Sorel, and Other Fascist Intellectuals." *Critical Review* 9, no. 3 (summer 1995): 371–401.

Netočný, Tomáš. "Klaus označil skleníkový efekt za nesmysl." ("Klaus Referred to the Greenhouse Effect as Nonsense.") *Mladá Fronta Dnes,* June 14, 1997, 4.

Nietzsche, Friedrich. *The Portable Nietzsche.* Ed. Walter Kaufmann. New York: Viking, 1968.

Norris, Christopher. *Uncritical Theory: Postmodernism, Intellectuals, and the Gulf War.* Amherst, Mass.: University of Massachusetts Press, 1992.

Novack, George, ed. *Existentialism versus Marxism: Conflicting Views on Humanism.* New York: Dell Publishing Co., 1966.

Nye, Andrea. *Feminist Theory and the Philosophies of Man.* London: Routledge, 1988.

"Out of the Shadows: The Communities of Population in Resistance in Guatemala, a Struggle for Survival." Washington: Epica/CHRLA Report, 1993.

Outlaw, Lucius T., Jr. "Author Meets Critics." Discussion of Outlaw's *On Race and Philosophy* (q.v.) by Leonard Harris and Daphne Thompson. Panel at The Second National Radical Philosophy Conference, "Globalization From Below." Purdue University, November 14–17, 1996.

———. "Critical Theory in a Period of Radical Transformation," *Praxis International* 3, no. 2 (July 1983): 138–46.

———. *On Race and Philosophy*. London: Routledge, 1996.

———. "Philosophy, Hermeneutics, Social-Political Theory: Critical Thought in the Interest of African-Americans." In Harris, ed., *Philosophy Born of Struggle* (q.v.), 60–87.

———. "Race and Class in the Theory and Practice of Emancipatory Social Transformation." In Harris, ed., *Philosophy Born of Struggle* (q.v.), 117–29.

———. "Towards a Critical Theory of 'Race'." In Goldberg, ed., *Anatomy of Racism* (q.v.), 58–82.

Paci, Enzo. *The Function of the Sciences and the Meaning of Man*. Trans. Paul Piccone and James Hanson. Evanston, Ill.: Northwestern University Press, 1972.

Pamerleau, William. "Existentialism and Discourse Ethics." Ph.D. Dissertation, Purdue University, 1994.

Patočka, Jan. *Kacířské eseje o filosofii dějin* (Heretical Essays about the Philosophy of History). Intro. Ivan Dubský. Praha: Academia, 1990.

———. *Tři studie o Masarykovi* (*Three Studies about Masaryk*). Praha: Mladá fronta, 1991.

Perkins. Robert L., ed. *International Kierkegaard Commentary: The Corsair Affair*, vol. 13. Macon: Mercer University Press, 1990.

———. *International Kierkegaard Commentary: The Present Age and the Age of Revolution*, vol. 14. Macon: Mercer University Press, 1984.

Peters, Cynthia. *Collateral Damage. The New World Order at Home and Abroad*. Boston: South End Press, 1992.

Piercy, Marge. *Woman On The Edge Of Time*. New York: Fawcett Press, 1976.

Pink Floyd. *The Wall*. Music album and feature film. Pink Floyd Music Limited/Columbia Records, 1979.

Plato. *The Great Dialogues of Plato*. Trans. W. H. D. Rouse. New York: Dutton Signet, 1984.

Popkin, Richard. "Comment on Professor Derrida's Paper." *Philosophy and Phenomenological Research* 30, no. 1 (1969): 58–65.

Postone, Moshe. *Time, Labor, and Social Domination: A Reinterpretation of Marx's Critical Theory*. Cambridge, England: Cambridge University Press, 1993.

Prakash, Gyan. "Postcolonial Criticism and Indian Historiography," *Social Text*, nos. 31–32 (1992): 8–19.

Presbey, Gail, Karsten J. Struhl, and Richard E. Olsen, eds. *The Philosophical Quest: A Cross-Cultural Reader.* New York: McGraw-Hill, Inc. 1995.

"Proceedings of the II Encuentro Continental: Campaña 500 Años de Resistencia Indígena, Negra y Popular." Quetzaltenango, Guatemala, October 7–12, 1991.

Rabinbach, Anson. "German Intellectuals and the Gulf War." *Dissent* (fall 1991): 459–63.

"Racism." A Plenary Panel with Lewis Gordon, Bill Lawson, and Iris Marion Young. First National Radical Philosophy Conference. Des Moines, Iowa: Drake University, November 5, 1994.

Ramsey, Ramsey Eric. "Politics of Dissatisfaction: The Heretical Marxisms of Reich and Bloch." *Rethinking Marxism* 8, no. 2 (summer 1995): 24–38.

Rawls, John. *A Theory of Justice.* Cambridge, Mass.: Harvard University Press, 1971.

———. *Political Liberalism.* New York: Columbia University Press, 1993.

Rehg, William. "Existentialism and Formal Pragmatics." *Philosophy and Social Criticism* 21, no. 2 (1995): 135–40.

———. *Insight and Solidarity: A Study in the Discourse Ethics of Jürgen Habermas.* Berkeley: University of California Press, 1994.

Resnick, Stephen and Richard Wolff. "Between State and Private Capitalism: What Was Soviet 'Socialism'?" *Rethinking Marxism* 7, no. 1 (spring 1994): 9–30.

Ricoeur, Paul. *Oneself as Another.* Trans. Kathleen Blamey. Chicago: University of Chicago Press, 1992.

Riefenstahl, Leni. Film director. "Triumph of the Will." Commissioned by Adolph Hitler (1934). Vidcrest, 1984.

Rifkin, Jeremy. "Civil Society in the Information Age: Workerless Factories and Virtual Companies." *The Nation* (February 26, 1996): 11–12, 14–16.

Rorty, Richard. *Contingency, Irony, and Solidarity.* Cambridge: Cambridge University Press, 1989.

———. "Fraternity Reign: The Case for a Society Based not on Rights but on Unselfishness." *The New York Times Magazine*, September 29, 1996, 155–58.

Ross, John. *Rebellion from the Roots: Indian Uprising in Chiapas.* Monroe, Maine: Common Courage Press, 1995.

Ross, Stephen David. *Injustice and Restitution: The Ordinance of Time*. Albany, N.Y.: SUNY Press, 1993.

Russakoff, Dale. "A Clash of Values over a School Ban." *The Washington Post*, February 24, 1995, A 1, 8.

Sandoval, Chela. "U.S. Third World Feminism: The Theory and Method of Oppositional Consciousness in the Postmodern World." *Genders* 10 (1991): 1–24.

Sartre, Jean-Paul. *Anti-Semite and Jew* (1946). Trans. George J. Becker. Preface by Michael Walzer, v–xxvi. New York: Schocken Books, 1995.

———. *Critique of Dialectical Reason*. Vol. 1. Trans. Alan Sheridan-Smith. London: New Left Books, 1976.

———. *Critique of Dialectical Reason*. Vol. 2. Ed. Arlette Elkaim-Sartre, trans. Quintin Huare. New York: Verso, 1991.

———. "Kierkegaard: The Singular Universal" (1972). In *Between Existentialism and Marxism*, 152–90. New York: New Left Books, 1974.

———. *Search for a Method*. Trans. H. Barnes. New York: Alfred A. Knopf, 1963.

Sartre, Jean-Paul and Benny Lévy. *Hope Now: 1980 Interviews*. Trans. Adrian van den Hoven, intro. by Ronald Aronson. Chicago: University of Chicago Press, 1996.

Sawicki, Jana. *Disciplining Foucault: Feminism, Power, and the Body*. London: Routledge, 1991.

———. "Foucault and Feminism: Toward a Politics of Difference." *Hypatia* 1, no. 2 (fall 1986): 23–36.

Schrag, Calvin O. *Communicative Praxis and the Space of Subjectivity*. Bloomington, Ind.: Indiana University Press, 1989.

———. *The Resources of Rationality: A Response to the Postmodern Challenge*. Bloomington, Ind.: Indiana University Press, 1992.

Seigfried, Charlene Haddock. *Pragmatism and Feminism: Reweaving the Social Fabric*. Chicago: University of Chicago Press, 1996.

Sheehan, Thomas. "A Normal Nazi." *The New York Review of Books* 40, nos. 1–2, January 14, 1993, 30–35. (See also "L'Affair Derrida.")

Shohat, Ella and Robert Stam. *Unthinking Eurocentrism: Multiculturalism and the Media*. London: Routledge, 1994.

Schwarz, Henry and Richard Dienst, eds. *Reading the Shape of the World: Towards an International Cultural Studies*. Boulder, Colo.: Westview Press, 1996.

Schweickart, David. *Against Capitalism*. Cambridge: Cambridge University Press, 1993.

Simons, Jon. *Foucault and the Political.* London: Routledge, 1995.

Simons, Marlise. "Dutch Take 'Third Way' to Prosperity." *The New York Times,* June 16, 1997, A-6.

Singer, Daniel. "The Real Eurobattle: The Move to a Common Currency Masks a Struggle over the Social Shape of Europe." *The Nation* (December 22, 1996): 20–23.

Soros, George with Byron Wien and Krisztina Koenen, *Soros on Soros: Staying Ahead of the Curve.* New York: John Wiley and Sons, 1995.

Spencer, Jon Michael. "Trends of Opposition to Multiculturalism." *The Black Scholar* 23, no. 2 (winter/spring 1993): 2–5.

Spivak, Gayatri Chakravorty. "Subaltern Studies: Deconstructing Historiography." In Ranahjit Guha and Spivak, eds., *Selected Subaltern Studies,* 3–32. New York, 1988.

Star Trek: First Contact. Paramount Pictures film, a Rick Berman production, 1996.

Steigerwald, Robert. *Herbert Marcuses dritter Weg.* Cologne: Pahl-Rugenstein, 1958.

Talking Heads. "Television Man" and "Road to Nowhere." Songs in *Little Creatures.* Music album. Sire Records Co. and Talking Heads Tours, Inc., 1985.

Taylor, Charles. *The Ethics of Authenticity.* Cambridge, Mass.: Harvard University Press, 1991.

———. "The Liberal-Communitarian Debate." In Nancy Rosenblum, ed., *Liberalism and the Moral Life.* Cambridge, Mass.: Harvard University Press, 1989.

———. *Sources of the Self: The Making of the Modern Identity.* Cambridge, Mass.: Cambridge University Press, 1989.

Taylor, Charles, K. Anthony Appiah, Jürgen Habermas, Steven C. Rockefeller, Michael Walzer, and Susan Wolf. *Multiculturalism: Examining the Politics of Recognition.* Ed. Amy Gutmann. Princeton: Princeton University Press, 1994.

Taylor, Marc C. *Altarity.* Chicago: University of Chicago Press, 1987.

Theunissen, Michael. *Negative Theologie der Zeit.* Frankfurt a/M: Suhrkamp, 1991.

Thiruvengadam, Raj. "Democracy as Mass Communicative Action." Ph.D. Dissertation, Purdue University, 1994.

Tolić, Dubravka Oraić. "Im ersten postmodernen Krieg befindet sich Europa jenseits von Gut und Böse." Trans. Ulrich Dronske, PEN-Congress, Dubrovnik, 1993. *Frankfurter Allgemeine Zeitung,* no. 113, May 17, 1993, 13.

Tong, Rosemarie. *Feminist Thought: A Comprehensive Introduction.* Boulder and San Francisco: Westview Press, 1989.

Tucker, Aviezer. "Identity Crisis." Review essay on Matuštík, *Postnational Identity* (q.v.). *Telos*, nos. 98–99 (winter 1993–spring 1994): 287–93.

———. "The New Jews." *Telos*, nos. 98–99 (winter 1993–spring 1994): 209–15.

———. *Phenomenology and Politics: Philosophy of the Signatories of Charter 77. From Patočka to Havel*. Ms.

———. "Reflections on a Fairy Godfather." Review essay on Soros, *Soros on Soros* (q.v.). *Telos*, no. 106 (winter 1996): 195–202.

Tucker, Robert C., ed. *The Marx-Engels Reader*. New York: Norton, 1978.

Turnley, David. "The Dismantling of the Berlin Wall" (November 9, 1989). Photograph. Detroit Free Press, Blackstar.

Urban, Greg and Joel Sherzer, eds. *Nation-States and Indians in Latin America*. Austin, Texas: University of Texas Press, 1991.

Valenzuela, Tony and Alex Garner. "The Right to Fuck." *Gay and Lesbian Times*, October 19, 1995, 39.

Waller, Signe. "The Urban Blindspot of the Left." A Presentation. Second National Radical Philosophy Conference, "Globalization From Below." Purdue University, November 14–17, 1996.

Walsh, Mary Williams. "VW Falls into a Publicity Pothole." *Los Angeles Times*, December 1, 1996, A-1, A-16.

Walzer, Michael. *Spheres of Justice: A Defense of Pluralism and Equality*. New York: Basic Books, 1983.

Weir, Allison: *Sacrificial Logics: Feminist Theory and the Critique of Identity*. London: Routledge, 1996.

West, Cornel. *Keeping Faith: Philosophy and Race in America*. London: Routledge, 1993.

———. *Race Matters*. Boston: Beacon Press, 1993.

Westphal, Merold. *Hegel, Freedom, and Modernity*. Albany, N.Y.: SUNY Press, 1992.

———. *Kierkegaard's Critique of Reason and Society*. Macon, Ga.: Mercer University Press, 1987, reprinted by Penn State University Press, 1991.

"What is Critical about Critical Theory?" A Roundtable with David Ingram, Alison Jaggar, James L. Marsh, Martin J. Matuštík, and Iris M. Young. Second National Radical Philosophy Conference, "Globalization From Below." Purdue University, November 15, 1996.

White, Stephen K., ed. *The Cambridge Companion to Habermas*. Cambridge: Cambridge University Press, 1995.

Whiteside, Kerry H. *Merleau-Ponty and the Foundation of an Existential Politics*. Princeton: Princeton University Press, 1988.

Willett, Cynthia. *Maternal Ethics and Other Slave Moralities*. London: Routledge, 1996.

————, ed. *Theorizing Multiculturalism: A Guide to the Current Debate*. Cambridge, Mass.: Blackwell, forthcoming.

Willett, Cynthia and Martin J. B. Matuštík. "Internet Conversations." Internet, October 24–29, 1996.

Williams, Patrick and Laura Chrisman, eds. *Colonial Discourse and Post-Colonial Theory: A Reader*. New York: Columbia University Press, 1994.

Wittgenstein, Ludwig. *On Certainty* (1969). Ed. G. E. M. Anscombe and G. H. von Wright, trans. Denis Paul and G. E. M. Anscombe. Oxford: Blackwell, 1974.

Wolin, Richard. "Carl Schmitt, Political Existentialism, and the Total State." *Theory and Society* 19 (1990): 389–416.

————. *Labyrinths: Explorations in the Critical History of Ideas*. Amherst, Mass.: University of Massachusets Press, 1995.

————. "Left Fascism: Georges Bataille and the German Ideology." *Constellations: An International Journal of Critical and Democratic Theory* 2, no. 3 (January 1996): 397–428.

————. *The Terms of Cultural Criticism: The Frankfurt School, Existentialism, Poststructuralism*. New York: Columbia University Press, 1992.

Wolin, Richard, ed. *The Heidegger Controversy: A Critical Reader*. First published by Columbia University Press, 1991; now only by Cambridge, Mass.: MIT, 1992.

Yeatman, Anna. *Postmodern Revisionings of the Political*. London: Routledge, 1994.

Young, Iris Marion. "Asymmetrical Reciprocity: On Moral Respect, Wonder, and Enlarged Thought." *Constellations: An International Journal of Critical and Democratic Theory* 3, no. 3 (1997): 340–63.

————. "Comments on Seyla Benhabib, *Situating the Self*." *New German Critique*, no. 62 (spring–summer 1994): 165–72.

————. "Government Without States." A Plenary Presentation. Second National Radical Philosophy Conference, "Globalization From Below." Purdue University, November 14–17, 1996.

————. *Justice and the Politics of Difference*. Princeton: Princeton University Press, 1990.

————. "Unruly Categories: A Critique of Nancy Fraser's Dual Systems Theory." *New Left Review*, no. 222 (1997): 147–60.

Young, Robert J. C. *Colonial Desire: Hybridity in Theory, Culture, and Race*. London: Routledge, 1995.

Zavarzadeh, Mas'ud and Donald Morton. "Signs of Knowledge in the Contemporary Academy." *American Journal of Semiotics* 7, no. 4 (1990): 149–60.

——. *Theory as Resistance: Politics and Culture after (Post)Structuralism*. New York: Guilford Press, 1994.

Žižek, Slavoj. "Eastern Europe's Republics of Gilead." In Mouffe, ed., *Dimensions of Radical Democracy* (q.v.), 193–207.

——. *For They Know Not What They Do: Enjoyment as a Political Factor*. London: Verso, 1991.

——. *Tarrying with The Negative: Kant, Hegel, and the Critique of Ideology*. Durham, N.C.: Duke University Press, 1993.

INDEX